The
Great Controversy
&
The Bible
Made Plain

TEACH Services, Inc.
Brushton, New York

Copyright © 1997 TEACH Services, Inc.

ISBN 1-57258-095-X
Library of Congress Catalog Card No. 97-80349

Published by

TEACH Services, Inc.
RR 1, Box 182
Brushton, New York 12916

The Great Controversy Between Christ and Satan

From The Destruction of Jerusalem to the End of the Controversy

By Mrs. E. G. White

Preface

It is with much pleasure that we send forth this book, volume IV. of the series on "The Great Controversy Between Christ and Satan." Volume I., beginning with the fall of Satan, embraces old-testament history. Volume II. contains the life of Christ; Volume III., the lives of the apostles; and this volume, giving first a sketch of our Lord's great prophecy (which, in brief, covers the whole dispensation), contains a history of the church in her warfare to her final redemption, and vividly describes the triumph of the people of God, the destruction of Satan and all his followers, and the renewing of the earth, which ends the awful controversy between the Son of God and the powers of darkness.

Apart from the Bible, this series presents the most wonderful and intensely interesting history of the world, from the entering of sin to the complete restitution of all things, that has ever been published. And as the closing events of the dispensation are the most momentous,— the destruction of Satan and all that pertains to his work, and the revealing of the coming glory, being unparalleled by all events that precede them,— so the contents of this book are, in many respects, more deeply interesting than those of the volumes which preceded it. The closing chapters are most thrilling. They will be best appreciated, however, by those who read all the four volumes in connection.

We would say to those who have felt disappointed because this volume was not issued sooner, that we believe the delay was providential, as the book contains matter of great interest and importance which it would not have contained had it been published sooner. And still this volume does not give all that the writer has to present on the closing scenes of this dispensation. Some matters which could not possibly be inserted in this work (space being limited), will be published separately. As it is, this book is larger than was intended.

We have faith that the merciful father is in kindness bestowing upon his waiting people the light and instruction which they specially need in the perils of the last days. God is willing to give his spirit to those who ask him, to those who call upon him in truth. We believe that the writer has received the illumination of the holy spirit in preparing these pages,— in laying before us the nature of The Great Controversy between Christ and Satan, that we may be warned against the snares of the enemy, and prepared for an inheritance with the saints in light.

While many subjects here presented are of wondrous depth,— relating to "the deep things of god,"— they are presented in language easy to be understood. And we are happy in knowing that the reading of these works leads to greater love for the Holy Scriptures, and to reverence for the God of grace, in Whom are all the treasures of wisdom and knowledge.

That this volume may prove a blessing to all who read it, and redound to the glory of the most high, is the earnest prayer of the publishers.

Contents

THE GREAT CONTROVERSY
BETWEEN CHRIST & SATAN

Chapter 28
The Tempter in Eden— A Plan for Man's Overthrow— God's
Warning Disbelieved— Death the Penalty of Transgression—
Immortality the Gift of God— Satan's Deception— Life in
Disobedience— Doctrine of Eternal Torment Introduced—
God's Character Misrepresented— Cruelty is Satanic— God
Takes no Delight in Torture— Theory of Eternal Torment
Revolting— A Cause of Infidelity— Universalism the Opposite
Error— A Universalist Sermon— The Fate of Amnon—
Wresting of the Scriptures— Salvation is Conditional— The
Wicked could not Enjoy Heaven— God's Mercy in their
Destruction— Consciousness of the Dead a Fallacy— What the
Bible Teaches— The Judgment and the Resurrection.

Chapter 29
Natural Immortality its Foundation— Materialization a
Counterfeit— Heresies Taught by Spirits— Spiritual
Manifestations not the Result of Trickery— A Revival of
Ancient Witchcraft— Adapted to Deceive all Classes— Refined
and Intellectual Aspects— Grosser Forms of Spiritualism— No
Distinction between Righteousness and Sin— The Bible
Rejected— The Hour of Temptation— The Refuge of Lies to
be Swept Away.

Chapter 30
Romanism Gaining Favor— Her Former Cruelty Excused—
The Claim of Infallibility— True Christians in Roman
Church— Catholicism Opposed to the Gospel— Her Power
Increasing in this Country—A Cause of Apprehension— Pomp
and Splendor of her Worship— The Roman and the Jewish
Church Compared— God's Character Misrepresented—
Contrast between Christ and the Pope— The Romish Church
Unchanged— Protestants Blinded by False Charity— The
Secret of Rome's Power— How an Age of Intellectual Light is
Favorable to her Success— Protestants Following in the Steps
of Papists— The Sunday Movement— How Sunday Came first
to be Observed— First Sunday Law a Heathen Statute— The
Term "Lord's Day"— Measures for Sunday Enforcement—
Lack of Scriptural Authority—The Roll from Heaven—A Daring
Forgery— Pretended Miracles— A Remarkable Confession—

The Church of Abyssinia— Rome's Enmity toward the True Sabbath— History of the Past to be Repeated— Popery Strengthening her Forces— Purpose of the Romanists.

God's Favor to this Country— His Blessings Repaid with Ingratitude— The Impending Conflict— Agencies to Combine against Righteousness and Truth— Prevalence of Skepticism— Growing Contempt for the Scriptures— Philosophical Idolatry— Results of Setting aside God's Law— Temperance Reform and the Sunday Movement— Spiritualism Changing its Form— Accepted by Papists and Protestants— Satan's Power to Control the Elements— Terrible Calamities— God's People Accused as Troubles of the Nation— Liberty of Conscience Disregarded— Romish Tyranny Revived— Our Land in Jeopardy.

Satan's Activity— The Last Great Delusion— The Bible the Detector of Error— An Understanding of the Prophecies Essential— Danger of Following Human Leaders— The Jews an Example— Ignorance of the Bible a Sin— How to Understand the Scriptures— A Humble and Teachable Spirit— Why Theologians so often Err— Necessity of Prayer— Modern Infidelity— Every Character to be Tested— Who will Endure the Trial?

The Mighty Angel— Application of his Message— Light for all who Seek It— Reformers in Past Ages— Preaching of the Third Message— Effect of the Warning— Opposition Extends the Knowledge of the Truth— Christ's Ambassadors not to Remain Silent— God's Providence in the National Councils— The Closing Work— Worldwide Extent— Power and Glory— Fruits of Missionary Efforts.

Christ's Ministration Closed— God's People in Affliction and Distress— Illustration from the Time of Jacob's Trouble— Jacob's Night of Wrestling— Faith and Penitence Prevail— God cannot Excuse Evil— His Mercy to the Penitent— Power of Importunate Prayer— The Prophetic Woe— Destructive Power of Evil Angels— False Christs— Satan personates the World's Redeemer— Religious and Secular Authorities Combine against God's People— Decree that they may be Put to Death— The Mountains a Hiding-place— Imprisonment and Bondage— God does not Forsake his Servants— The Day-and-night Cry— Angels Guard the Righteous— Their Appearance in Human Form— God's Promise to his People.

Satan and his Hosts Consumed— The Earth Renewed— The Home of the Saved— The Universal Anthem.

THE BIBLE MADE PLAIN

Chapter 1

Destruction of Jerusalem

"The days shall come upon thee, that thine enemies shall cast a trench about thee, and compass thee round, and keep thee in on every side, and shall lay thee even with the ground, and thy children within thee; and they shall not leave in thee one stone upon another; because thou knewest not the time of thy visitation." [LUKE 19:43, 44.]

From the crest of Olivet, Jesus looks upon Jerusalem. Fair and peaceful is the scene spread out before him. In the midst of gardens and vineyards and green slopes studded with pilgrims' tents, rise the terraced hills, the stately palaces, and massive bulwarks of Israel's capital. The daughter of Zion seems in her pride to say, "I sit a queen, and shall see no sorrow;" as lovely now, and deeming herself as secure in Heaven's favor, as when, ages before, the royal minstrel sung, "Beautiful for situation, the joy of the whole earth, is Mount Zion," "the city of the great King." [PS. 48:2.] In full view are the magnificent buildings of the temple. The rays of the setting sun light up the snowy whiteness of its marble walls, and gleam from golden gate and tower and pinnacle. "The perfection of beauty" it stands, the pride of the Jewish nation. What child of Israel could gaze upon the scene without a thrill of joy and admiration! But far other thoughts occupy the mind of Jesus. "When he was come near, he beheld the city, and wept over it." [LUKE 19:41.] Amid the universal rejoicing of the triumphal entry, while palm branches wave, while glad hosannas awake the echoes of the hills, and thousands of voices declare him king, the world's Redeemer is overwhelmed with a sudden and mysterious sorrow. He, the Son of God, the Promised One of Israel, whose power has conquered death, and called its captives from the grave, is in tears, not of ordinary grief, but of intense, irrepressible agony.

His tears were not for himself, though he well knew whither his feet were tending. Before him lay Gethsemane. Not far distant was the place of crucifixion. Upon the path which he was soon to tread must fall the horror of great darkness as he should make his soul an offering for sin. Yet it was not a contemplation of these scenes that cast the shadow upon him in this hour of gladness. No forebodings of his own superhuman anguish clouded that unselfish spirit. He wept for the doomed thousands of Jerusalem,— because of the blindness and impenitence of those whom he came to bless and save.

The history of a thousand years of privilege and blessing, granted to the Jewish people, was unfolded to the eye of Jesus. The Lord had made Zion his holy habitation. There prophets had unsealed their rolls and uttered their warnings. There priests had waved their censers, and daily offered the blood of slain lambs, pointing forward to the Lamb of God. There had Jehovah dwelt in visible glory, in the Shekinah above the mercy-seat. There rested the base of that mystic ladder connecting earth with Heaven,— that ladder upon which angels of God descended and ascended, and which opened to the world the way into the holiest of all. Had Israel as a nation preserved her allegiance to Heaven, Jerusalem would have stood forever, the elect metropolis of God. But the history of that favored people was a record of backsliding and rebellion. They had resisted Heaven's grace, abused their privileges, slighted their opportunities.

Amid forgetfulness and apostasy, God had dealt with Israel as a loving father deals with a rebellious son, admonishing, warning, correcting, still saying in the tender anguish of a parent's soul, How can I give thee up? When remonstrance, entreaty, and rebuke had failed, God sent to this people the best gift of Heaven; nay, he poured out to them all Heaven in that one gift.

For three years the Son of God knocked at the gate of the impenitent city. He came to his vineyard seeking fruit. Israel had been as a vine transplanted from Egypt into a genial soil. He dug about his vine; he pruned and cherished it. He was unwearied in his efforts to save this vine of his own planting. For three years the Lord of light and glory had gone in and out among his people. He healed the sick; he comforted the sorrowing; he raised the dead; he spoke pardon and peace to the repentant. He gathered about him the weak and the weary, the helpless and the desponding, and extended to all, without respect to age or character, the invitation of mercy: "Come unto me, all ye that labor and are heavy-laden, and I will give you rest." [MATT. 11:28.]

Regardless of indifference and contempt, he had steadfastly pursued his ministry of love. No frown upon his brow repelled the suppliant. Himself subjected to privation and reproach, he had lived to scatter blessings in his path, to plead with men to accept the gift of life. The waves of mercy, beaten back by the stubborn heart, returned in a tide of untiring love. But Israel had turned from her best friend and only helper. The pleadings of his love had been despised, his counsels spurned, his warnings ridiculed.

The hour of grace and reprieve was fast passing; the cup of God's long-deferred wrath was almost full. The cloud of wrath that had been gathering through ages of apostasy and rebellion, was about to burst upon a guilty people, and He who alone could save them from their impending fate had been slighted, abused, rejected, and was soon to be crucified. When Christ should hang on Calvary's cross, Israel's day as a nation favored and blessed of God would be ended. The loss of even one soul is a calamity in comparison with which the gain of a world sinks into insignificance; but as Christ looked upon Jerusalem, the doom of a whole city, a whole nation, was before him; that city, that nation which had once been the chosen of God,— his peculiar treasure.

Prophets had wept over the apostasy of Israel. Jeremiah wished that his eyes were a fountain of tears, that he might "weep day and night for the slain of the daughter of his people." What, then, was the grief of Him whose prophetic glance took in, not years, but ages? He beholds the destroying angel hovering over the ancient metropolis of patriarchs and prophets. From the ridge of Olivet, the very spot afterward occupied by Titus and his army, he looks across the valley upon the sacred courts and porticoes, and with tear-blinded eyes he sees, in awful perspective, the walls surrounded by alien armies. He hears the tread of the hosts mustering for battle. He hears the voice of mothers and children crying for bread in the besieged city. He sees her holy and beautiful house, her palaces and towers, given to the flames, and where once they stood, only a heap of smoldering ruins.

He looks down the ages, and sees the covenant people scattered in every land, like wrecks on a dessert shore. He sees in the temporal retribution about to fall upon her children, but the first draught from that cup of wrath which at the final Judgment she must drain to its dregs. Divine pity, yearning love, finds utterance in the mournful words: "O Jerusalem, Jerusalem, thou that killest the prophets, and stonest them which are sent unto thee, how often would I have gathered thy children together, even as a hen gathereth her chickens under her wings, and ye would not!" [MATT. 23:37.] Oh that thou, a nation favored above every other, hadst known the time of thy visitation, and the things that belong unto thy peace! I have stayed the angel of justice, I have called thee to repentance, but all in vain. It is not merely servants, delegates, and prophets, whom thou hast refused and rejected, but the Holy One of Israel, thy Redeemer. If thou art destroyed, thou art alone responsible. "Ye will not come to me that ye might have life."

Christ saw in Jerusalem a symbol of a world hardened in unbelief and rebellion, and rushing on to meet the retributive judgments of God. The woes of a fallen race, pressing upon his soul, forced from his lips that exceeding bitter cry. He saw the record of sin traced in human misery, in tears and blood; his heart was moved with infinite pity for the afflicted and suffering ones of earth; he yearned to relieve all. But he knew that even his hand might not turn back the incoming tide of human woe; few would seek their only source of help. He was willing to suffer and to die to bring salvation within their reach; but few would come to him that they might have life.

The Majesty of Heaven in tears! the Son of the infinite God troubled in spirit, bowed down with anguish! The scene filled all Heaven with wonder. That scene reveals to us the exceeding sinfulness of sin; it shows how hard a task it is, even for infinite power, to save the guilty from the consequences of transgressing the law of God. Jesus, looking down to the last generation, saw the world enclosed in a deception similar to that which caused the destruction of Jerusalem. The great sin of the Jews was their rejection of Christ; the great sin of the Christian world would be their rejection of the law of God, the foundation of his government in Heaven and earth. The precepts of Jehovah would be despised and set at naught. Millions in bondage to sin, slaves of Satan, doomed to suffer the second death, would refuse to listen to the words of truth in their day of visitation. Terrible blindness! strange infatuation!

Two days before the Passover, when Christ had for the last time departed from the temple, after denouncing the hypocrisy of the Jewish rulers, he again went out with his disciples to the Mount of Olives, and seated himself with them upon a grassy slope overlooking the city. Once more he gazed upon its walls, its towers and palaces. Once more he beheld the temple in its dazzling splendor, a diadem of beauty crowning the sacred mount.

A thousand years before had the psalmist magnified God's favor to Israel in making her holy house his dwelling-place: "In Salem is his tabernacle, and his dwelling-place in Zion." [PS. 76:2.] "He chose the tribe of Judah, the Mount Zion which he loved. And he built his sanctuary like high palaces." [PS. 78:68, 69.] The first temple had been erected during the most prosperous period of Israel's history. Vast stores of treasure for this purpose had been collected by King David, and the plans for its construction were made by divine inspiration. Solomon, the wisest of Israel's monarchs, had completed the work. This temple was the most magnificent building which the world ever saw. Yet the Lord had declared by the prophet Haggai, concerning the second temple, "The glory of this latter house shall be greater than of the former." "I will shake all nations, and the Desire of all nations shall come, and I will fill this house with glory, saith the Lord of hosts." [HAG. 2:9, 7.]

After the destruction of the temple by Nebuchadnezzar, it was rebuilt about five hundred years before the birth of Christ, by a people who from a lifelong captivity had returned to a wasted and almost deserted country. There were then among them aged men who had seen the glory of Solomon's temple, and who wept at the foundation of the new building, that it must be so inferior to the former. The feeling that prevailed is forcibly described by the prophet: "Who is left among you that saw this house in her first glory? and how do ye see it now? is it not in your eyes in comparison of it as nothing?" [HAG. 2:3.] Then was given the promise that the glory of this latter house should be greater than of the former.

But the second temple had not equaled the first in magnificence; nor was it hallowed by those visible tokens of the divine presence which pertained to the first temple. There was no manifestation of supernatural power to mark its dedication. No cloud of glory was seen to fill the newly erected sanctuary. No fire from Heaven descended to consume the sacrifice upon its altar. The Shekinah no longer abode between the cherubim in the most holy place; the ark, the mercy-seat, and the tables of the testimony were not to be found therein. No voice sounded from Heaven to make known to the inquiring priest the will of Jehovah.

For centuries the Jews had vainly endeavored to show wherein the promise of God, given by Haggai, had been fulfilled; yet pride and unbelief blinded their minds to the true meaning of the prophet's words. The second temple was not honored with the cloud of Jehovah's glory, but with the living presence of One in whom dwelt the fullness of the Godhead bodily,— who was God himself manifest in the flesh. The "Desire of all nations" had indeed come to his temple when the Man of Nazareth taught and healed in the sacred courts. In the presence of Christ, and in this only, did the second temple exceed the first in glory. But Israel had put from her the proffered gift of Heaven. With the humble Teacher who had that day passed out from its golden gate, the glory had forever departed from the temple. Already were fulfilled the Saviour's words, "Your house is left unto you desolate." [MATT. 23:38.]

The disciples had been filled with awe and wonder at Christ's prediction of the overthrow of the temple, and they desired to understand more fully the meaning of his words. Wealth, labor, and architectural skill had for more than forty years been freely expended to enhance its splendors. Herod the Great had lavished upon it both Roman wealth and Jewish treasure, and even the emperor of the world had enriched it with his gifts. Massive blocks of white marble, of almost fabulous size, forwarded from Rome for this purpose, formed a part of its structure; and to these the disciples had called the attention of their Master, saying, "See what manner of stones and what buildings are here!" [MARK 13:1.]

To these words, Jesus made the solemn and starting reply, "Verily I say unto you, There shall not be left here one stone upon another, that shall not be thrown down." [MATT. 24:2.]

With the overthrow of Jerusalem the disciples associated the events of Christ's personal coming in temporal glory to take the throne of universal empire, to punish the impenitent Jews, and to break from off the nation the Roman yoke. The Lord had told them that he would come the second time. Hence at the mention of judgments upon Jerusalem, their minds revert to that coming, and as they are gathered about the Saviour upon the Mount of Olives, they ask, "When shall these things be? and what shall be the sign of thy coming, and of the end of the world?" [MATT. 24:3.]

The future was mercifully veiled from the disciples. Had they at that time fully comprehended the two awful facts,— the Redeemer's sufferings and death and the destruction of their city and temple,— they would have been paralyzed with horror. Christ presented before them an outline of the prominent events to transpire before the close of time. His words were not then fully understood; but their meaning was to be unfolded as his people should need the instruction therein given. The prophecy which he uttered was twofold in its meaning: while foreshadowing the destruction of Jerusalem, it prefigured also the terrors of the last great day.

Jesus declared to the listening disciples the judgments that were to fall upon apostate Israel, and especially the retributive vengeance that would come upon them for their rejection and crucifixion of the Messiah. Unmistakable signs would precede the awful climax. The dreaded hour would come suddenly and swiftly. And the Saviour warned his followers: "When ye therefore shall see the abomination of desolation, spoken of by Daniel the prophet, stand in the holy place (whoso readeth let him understand), then let them which be in Judea flee into the mountains." [MATT. 24:15, 16.] When the idolatrous standards of the Romans should be set up in the holy ground, which extended some furlongs outside the city walls, then the followers of Christ were to find safety in flight. When the warning sign should be seen, judgment was to follow so quickly that those who would escape must make no delay. He who chanced to be upon the housetop must not go down through his house into the street; but he must speed his way from roof to roof until he reach the city wall, and be saved "so as by fire." Those who were working in the fields or vineyards must not take time to return for the outer garment laid aside while they should be toiling in the heat of the day. They must not hesitate a moment, lest they be involved in the general destruction.

In the reign of Herod, Jerusalem had not only been greatly beautified, but by the erection of towers, walls, and fortresses, added to the natural strength of its situation, it had been rendered apparently impregnable. He who would at this time have foretold publicly its destruction, would, like Noah in his day, have been called a crazed alarmist. But Christ had said, "Heaven and earth shall pass away, but my words shall not pass away." [MATT. 24:35.] Because of her sins, wrath had been denounced against Jerusalem, and her stubborn unbelief rendered her doom certain.

The Lord had declared by the prophet Micah: "Hear this, I pray you, ye heads of the house of Jacob, and princes of the house of Israel, that abhor judgment, and pervert all equity. They build up Zion with blood, and Jerusalem with iniquity. The heads thereof judge for reward, and the priests thereof teach for hire, and the prophets thereof divine for money; yet will they lean upon the Lord, and say, Is not the Lord among us? none evil can come upon us." [MICAH 3:9-11.]

How exactly did these words describe the corrupt and self-righteous inhabitants of Jerusalem! While claiming to rigidly observe the law of God, they were transgressing all its principles. They hated Christ because his purity and holiness revealed their iniquity; and they accused him of being the cause of all the troubles which had come upon them in consequence of their sins. Though they knew him to be sinless, they had declared that his death was necessary to their safety as a nation. "If we let him thus alone," said the Jewish leaders, "all men will believe on him; and the Romans shall come and take away both our place and nation." [JOHN 11:48.] If Christ were sacrificed, they might once more become a strong, united people. Thus they reasoned, and they concurred in the decision of their high priest, that it would be better for one man to die than for the whole nation to perish.

Thus had the Jewish leaders "built up Zion with blood, and Jerusalem with iniquity." And yet, while they slew their Saviour because he reproved their sins, such was their self-righteousness that they regarded themselves as God's favored people, and expected the Lord to deliver them from their enemies. "Therefore," continued the prophet, "shall Zion for your sake be plowed as a field, and Jerusalem shall become heaps, and the mountain of the house as the high places of the forest." [MICAH 3:12.]

For forty years after the doom of Jerusalem had been pronounced by Christ himself, the Lord delayed his judgments upon the city and the nation. Wonderful was the long-suffering of God toward the rejecters of his gospel and the murderers of his Son. The parable of the unfruitful tree represented God's dealings with the Jewish nation. The command had gone forth. "Cut it down; why cumbereth it the ground?" [LUKE 13:7.] but divine mercy had spared it yet a little longer. There were still many among the Jews who were ignorant of the character and the work of Christ. And the children had not enjoyed the opportunities or received the light which their parents had spurned. Through the preaching of the apostles and their associates, God would cause light to shine upon them; they could see how prophecy had been fulfilled, not only in the birth and life of Christ, but in his death and resurrection. The children were not condemned for the sins of the parents; but when, with a knowledge of all the light given to their parents, the children rejected the additional light granted to themselves, they became partakers of the parents' sins, and filled up the measure of their iniquity.

The long-suffering of God toward Jerusalem, only confirmed the Jews in their stubborn impenitence. In their hatred and cruelty toward the disciples of Jesus, they rejected the last offer of mercy. Then God withdrew his protection from them, and removed his restraining power from Satan and his angels, and the nation was left to the control of the leader she had chosen. Her children had spurned the grace of Christ, which would have enabled them to subdue their evil impulses, and now these became the conquerors. Satan aroused the fiercest and most debased passions of the soul. Men did not reason; they were beyond reason,— controlled by impulse and blind rage. They became Satanic in their cruelty. In the family and in the nation, alike among the highest and the lowest classes, there was suspicion, envy, hatred, strife, rebellion, murder. There was no safety anywhere. Friends and kindred betrayed one another. Parents slew their children, and children their parents. The rulers of the people had no power to rule themselves. Uncontrolled passions made them tyrants. The Jews had accepted false testimony to condemn the innocent Son of God. Now false accusations made their own lives uncertain. By their actions they had long been saying, "Cause the Holy One of Israel to cease from before us." [ISA. 30:11.] Now their desire was granted. The fear of God no longer disturbed them. Satan was at the head of the nation, and the highest civil and religious authorities were under his sway.

The leaders of the opposing factions at times united to plunder and torture their wretched victims, and again they fell upon each other's forces, and slaughtered without mercy. Even the sanctity of the temple could not restrain their horrible ferocity. The worshipers were stricken down before the altar, and the sanctuary was polluted with the bodies of the slain. Yet in their blind and blasphemous presumption the instigators of this hellish work publicly declared that they had no fear that Jerusalem would be destroyed, for it was God's own city. To establish their power more firmly, they bribed false prophets to proclaim, even when Roman legions were besieging the temple, that the people were to wait for deliverance from God. To the last, multitudes held fast to the belief that the Most High would interpose for the defeat of their adversaries. But Israel had spurned the divine protection, and now she had no defense. Unhappy Jerusalem! rent by internal dissensions, the blood of her children, slain by one another's hands, crimsoning her streets, while alien armies beat down her fortifications and slew her men of war!

All the predictions given by Christ concerning the destruction of Jerusalem were fulfilled to the letter. The Jews experienced the truth of his words of warning, "With what measure ye mete, it shall be measured to you again."

Signs and wonders appeared, foreboding disaster and doom. A comet, resembling a flaming sword, for a year hung over the city. An unnatural light was seen hovering over the temple. Upon the clouds were pictured chariots mustering for battle. Mysterious voices in the temple court uttered the warning words, "Let us depart hence." The eastern gate of the inner court, which was of brass, and so heavy that it was with difficulty shut by a score of men, and having bolts fastened deep into the firm pavement, was seen at midnight to be opened of its own accord.

For seven years a man continued to go up and down the streets of Jerusalem, declaring the woes that were to come upon the city. By day and by night he chanted the wild dirge, "A voice from the east; a voice from the west; a voice from the four winds; a voice against Jerusalem and the temple; a voice against the bridegroom and the bride; and a voice against all the people." This strange being was imprisoned and scourged; but no complaint escaped his lips. To insult and abuse he answered only, "Woe to Jerusalem! woe, woe to the inhabitants thereof!" His warning cry ceased not until he was slain in the siege he had foretold.

Not one Christian perished in the destruction of Jerusalem. Christ had given his disciples warning, and all who believed his words watched for the promised sign. After the Romans had surrounded the city, they unexpectedly withdrew their forces, at a time when every-thing seemed favorable for an immediate attack. In the providence of God the promised signal was thus given to the waiting Christians, and without a moment's delay they fled to a place of safety,— the refuge city Pella, in the land of Perea, beyond Jordan.

Terrible were the calamities which fell upon Jerusalem in the siege of the city by Titus. The last desperate assault was made at the time of the Passover, when millions of Jews had assembled within its walls to celebrate the national festival. Their stores of provision, which if carefully preserved would have been sufficient to supply the inhabi-tants for years, had previously been destroyed through the jealousy and revenge of the contending factions, and now all the horrors of starvation were experienced. A measure of wheat was sold for a talent. Great numbers of the people would steal out at night, to appease their hunger by devouring herbs and wild plants growing outside the city walls, though they were often detected, and punished with torture and death. Some would gnaw the leather on their shields and sandals. The most inhuman tortures were inflicted by those in power to force from the want-stricken people the last scanty supplies which they might have concealed. And these cruelties were not infrequently practiced by men who were themselves well fed, and who were merely desirous of laying up a store of provision for the future.

Thousands perished from famine and pestilence. Natural affection seemed to have been utterly destroyed. Children would be seen snatching the food from the mouths of their aged parents. The question of the prophet, "Can a woman forget her sucking child?" [ISA. 49:15.] received the answer within the walls of that doomed city, "The hands of the pitiful women have sodden their own children; they were their meat in the destruction of the daughter of my people." [LAM. 4:10.]

The Roman leaders endeavored to strike terror to the Jews, and thus cause them to surrender. Those prisoners who resisted when taken, were scourged, tortured, and crucified before the wall of the city. Hundreds were daily put to death in this manner, and the dreadful work continued until, along the valley of Jehoshaphat and at Calvary, crosses were erected in so great numbers that there was scarcely room to move among them. So terribly was fulfilled the profane prayer uttered forty years before, "His blood be on us, and on our children." [MATT. 27:25.]

Titus would willingly have put an end to the fearful scene, and thus have spared Jerusalem the full measure of her doom. He was filled with horror as he saw the bodies of the dead lying in heaps in the valleys. Like one entranced, he looked from the crest of Olivet upon the magnificent temple, and gave command that not one stone of it be touched. Before attempting to gain possession of this stronghold, he made an earnest appeal to the Jewish leaders not to force him to defile the sacred place with blood. If they would come forth and fight in any other place, no Roman should violate the sanctity of the temple. Josephus himself, in a most eloquent appeal, entreated them to surrender, to save themselves, their city, and their place of worship. But his words were answered with bitter curses. Darts were hurled at him, their last human mediator, as he stood pleading with them. The Jews had rejected the entreaties of the Son of God, and now expostulation and entreaty only made them more determined to resist to the last. In vain were the efforts of Titus to save the temple; One greater than he had declared that not one stone was to be left upon another.

The blind obstinacy of the Jewish leaders, and the detestable crimes perpetrated within the besieged city, excited the horror and indignation of the Romans, and Titus at last decided to take the temple by storm. He determined, however, that if possible it should be saved from destruction. But his commands were disregarded. After he had retired at night to his tent, the Jews, sallying from the temple, attacked the soldiers without. In the struggle, a firebrand was flung by a soldier through an opening in the porch, and immediately the chambers about the holy house were in a blaze. Titus rushed to the place, followed by his generals and legionaries, and commanded the soldiers to quench the flames. His words were unheeded. In their fury the soldiers hurled blazing brands into the chambers adjoining the temple, and then with their swords they slaughtered in great numbers those who had found shelter there. Blood flowed down the temple steps like water. Thousands upon thousands of Jews perished. Above the sound of battle were heard voices shouting, "Ichabod!"—the glory is departed.

The fire had not reached the holy house itself when Titus entered, and, beholding its unsurpassed splendor, he was impelled to a last effort for its preservation. But in his very presence, a soldier thrust a lighted torch between the hinges of the door, and in an instant the flames burst out within the sanctuary. As the red glare revealed the walls of the holy places, glittering with gold, a frenzy seized the soldiers. Goaded on by a desire for plunder, and filled with rage by the resistance of the Jews, they were beyond control.

The lofty and massive structures that had crowned Mount Moriah were in flames. The temple towers sent up columns of fire and smoke. As the lurid tide rolled on, devouring everything before it, the whole summit of the hill blazed like a volcano. Mingled with the roar of the fire, the shouts of the soldiers, and the crash of falling buildings, were heard the frantic, heart-rending cries of old and young, priests and rulers. The very mountains seemed to give back the echo. The awful glare of the conflagration lighted up the surrounding country, and the people gathered upon the hills, and gazed in terror upon the scene.

After the destruction of the temple, the whole city soon fell into the hands of the Romans. The leaders of the Jews forsook their impregnable towers, and Titus found them solitary. He gazed upon them with amazement, and declared that God had given them into his hands; for no engines, however powerful, could have prevailed against those stupendous battlements. Both the city and the temple were razed to their foundations, and the ground upon which the holy house had stood was "plowed as a field." More than a million of the people were slaughtered; the survivors were carried away as captives, sold as slaves, dragged to Rome to grace the conqueror's triumph, thrown to wild beasts in the amphitheaters, or scattered as homeless wanderers throughout the earth.

The Jews had forged their own fetters; they had loaded for themselves the cloud of vengeance. In the utter destruction that befell them as a nation, and in all the woes that followed them in their dispersion, they were but reaping the harvest which their own hands had sown. Their sufferings are often represented as a punishment visited upon them by the direct decree of God. This is a device by which the great deceiver seeks to conceal his own work. By stubborn rejection of divine love and mercy, the Jews had caused the protection of God to be withdrawn from them, and Satan was permitted to rule them according to his will. The horrible cruelties enacted in the destruction of Jerusalem are a demonstration of Satan's vindictive power over those who yield to his control.

We cannot know how much we owe to Christ for the peace and protection which we enjoy. It is the restraining power of God that prevents mankind from passing fully under the control of Satan. The disobedient and unthankful have great reason for gratitude for God's mercy and long-suffering in holding in check the cruel, malignant power of the evil one. But when men pass the limits of divine forbearance, that restraint is removed. God does not stand toward the sinner as an executioner of the sentence against transgression; but he leaves the rejecters of his mercy to themselves, to reap that which they have sown. Every ray of light rejected, every warning despised or unheeded, every passion indulged, every transgression of the law of God, is a seed sown, which yields its unfailing harvest. The Spirit of God, persistently resisted, is at last withdrawn from the sinner, and then there is left no power to control the evil passions of the soul, and no protection from the malice and enmity of Satan. The destruction of Jerusalem is a fearful and solemn warning to all who are trifling with the offers of divine grace, and turning away the pleadings of divine mercy. Never was given a more decisive testimony to God's hatred of sin, and to the certain punishment that will fall upon the guilty.

The Saviour's prophecy concerning the visitation of judgments upon Jerusalem is to have another fulfillment, of which that terrible scene was but a faint shadow. The second advent of the Son of God is foretold by lips which make no mistake: "Then shall all the tribes of the earth mourn, and they shall see the Son of man coming in the clouds of heaven, with power and great glory. And he shall send his angels with a great sound of a trumpet, and they shall gather together his elect from the four winds, from one end of heaven to the other." [MATT. 24:30, 31.] Then shall they that obey not the gospel be consumed with the spirit of his mouth, and destroyed with the brightness of his coming. [2 THESS. 2:8.]

Let men beware lest they neglect the lesson conveyed to them in the words of Christ. He has declared that he will come the second time, to gather his faithful ones to himself, and to take vengeance on them that reject his mercy. As he warned his disciples of Jerusalem's destruction, giving them a sign of the approaching ruin that they might make their escape, so he has warned his people of the day of final destruction, and given them signs of its approach, that all who will may flee from the wrath to come. Those who behold the promised signs are to "know that it is near, even at the door." "Watch ye therefore," are his words of admonition. "If thou shalt not watch, I will come on thee as a thief."

The world is no more ready now to credit the warning than were the Jews in the days of our Saviour. Come when it may, the end will come unawares to the ungodly. When life is going on in its unvarying round; when men are absorbed in pleasure, in business, in traffic, in money-making; when religious leaders are magnifying the world's progress and enlightenment, and the people are lulled in a false security,— then, as the midnight thief steals within the unguarded dwelling, so shall sudden destruction come upon the careless and ungodly, "and they shall not escape."

Chapter 2

Persecution in the First Centuries

When Jesus revealed to his disciples the fate of Jerusalem and the scenes of the second advent, he foretold also the experience of his people from the time when he should be taken from them, to his return in power and glory for their deliverance. From Olivet the Saviour beheld the storms about to fall upon the apostolic church, and, penetrating deeper into the future, his eye discerned the fierce, wasting tempests that were to beat upon his followers in the coming ages of darkness and persecution. In a few brief utterances, of awful significance, he foretold the portion which the rulers of this world would mete out to the church of God. The followers of Christ must tread the same path of humiliation, reproach, and suffering which their Master trod. The enmity that burst forth against the world's Redeemer, would be manifested against all who should believe on his name.

The history of the early church testified to the fulfillment of the Saviour's words. The powers of earth and hell arrayed themselves against Christ in the person of his followers. Paganism foresaw that should the gospel triumph, her temples and altars would be swept away; therefore she summoned her forces to destroy Christianity. The fires of persecution were kindled. Christians were stripped of their possessions, and driven from their homes. They "endured a great fight of afflictions." They "had trial of cruel mockings and scourgings, yea, moreover of bonds and imprisonment." [HEB. 11:36.] Great numbers sealed their testimony with their blood. Noble and slave, rich and poor, learned and ignorant, were alike slain without mercy.

Wherever they sought refuge, the followers of Christ were hunted like beasts of prey. They were forced to seek concealment in desolate and solitary places. "Destitute, afflicted, tormented, of whom the world was not worthy, they wandered in deserts, and in mountains, and in dens and caves of the earth." [HEB. 11:37, 38.] The subterranean excavations connected with the city of Rome afforded shelter for thousands. Long galleries had been tunneled through earth and rock to procure material for the vast structures of the capital, and the dark and intricate network of passages extended for miles beyond the walls. In these underground retreats, many of the followers of Christ, when suspected and proscribed, found a home; and here also they buried their dead. When the Lifegiver shall awaken those who have fought the good fight, many a martyr for Christ's sake will come forth from those gloomy caverns.

Under the fiercest persecution, these witnesses for Jesus kept their faith unsullied. Though deprived of every comfort, shut away from the light of the sun, making their home in the dark but friendly bosom of the earth, they uttered no complaint. With words of faith, patience, and hope, they encouraged one another to endure privation and distress. The loss of every earthly blessing could not force them to renounce their belief in Christ. Trials and persecutions were but steps bringing them nearer their rest and their reward.

They called to mind the words of their Master, that when persecuted for Christ's sake they were to be exceeding glad; for great would be their reward in Heaven; for so had the prophets been persecuted before them. Like God's servants of old, they were "tortured, not accepting deliverance, that they might obtain a better resurrection." [HEB. 11:35.] They rejoiced that they were accounted worthy to suffer for the truth, and songs of triumph ascended in the midst of crackling flames. Looking upward by faith, they saw Christ and angels leaning over the battlements of Heaven, gazing upon them with the deepest interest, and regarding their steadfastness with approval. A voice came down to them from the throne of God, "Be thou faithful unto death, and I will give thee a crown of life." [REV. 2:10.]

In vain were Satan's efforts to destroy the church of Christ by violence. The great controversy in which the disciples of Jesus yielded up their lives did not cease when these faithful standard-bearers fell at their post. By defeat they conquered. God's workmen were slain, but his work went steadily forward. The gospel continued to spread, and the number of its adherents to increase. It penetrated into regions that were inaccessible, even to the eagles of Rome. Said a Christian, expostulating with the heathen rulers who were urging forward the persecution: "You may torment, afflict, and vex us. Your wickedness puts our weakness to the test, but your cruelty is of no avail. It is but a stronger invitation to bring others to our persuasion. The more we are mowed down, the more we spring up again. The blood of the Christians is seed."

Thousands were imprisoned and slain; but others sprung up to fill their places. And those who were martyred for their faith were secured to Christ, and accounted of him as conquerors. They had fought the good fight, and they were to receive the crown of glory when Christ should come. The sufferings which they endured brought Christians nearer to one another and to their Redeemer. Their living example and dying testimony were a constant witness for the truth; and, where least expected, the subjects of Satan were leaving his service, and enlisting under the banner of Christ.

Satan therefore laid his plans to war more successfully against the government of God, by planting his banner in the Christian church. If the followers of Christ could be deceived, and led to displease God, then their strength, fortitude, and firmness would fail, and they would fall an easy prey.

The great adversary now endeavored to gain by artifice what he had failed to secure by force. Persecution ceased, and in its stead were substituted the dangerous allurements of temporal prosperity and worldly honor. Idolaters were led to receive a part of the Christian faith, while they rejected other essential truths. They professed to accept Jesus as the Son of God, and to believe in his death and resurrection; but they had no conviction of sin, and felt no need of repentance or of a change of heart. With some concessions on their part, they proposed that Christians should make concessions, that all might unite on the platform of belief in Christ.

Now was the church in fearful peril. Prison, torture, fire, and sword were blessings in comparison with this. Some of the Christians stood firm, declaring that they could make no compromise. Others reasoned that if they should yield or modify some features of their faith, and unite with those who had accepted a part of Christianity, it might be the means of their full conversion. That was a time of deep anguish to the faithful followers of Christ. Under a cloak of pretended Christianity, Satan was insinuating himself into the church, to corrupt their faith, and turn their minds from the word of truth.

At last the larger portion of the Christian company lowered their standard, and a union was formed between Christianity and paganism. Although the worshipers of idols professed to be converted, and united with the church, they still clung to their idolatry, only changing the objects of their worship to images of Jesus, and even of Mary and the saints. The foul leaven of idolatry, thus introduced into the church, continued its baleful work. Unsound doctrines, superstitious rites, and idolatrous ceremonies were incorporated into her faith and worship. As the followers of Christ united with idolaters, the Christian religion became corrupted, and the church lost her purity and power. There were some, however, who were not misled by these delusions. They still maintained their fidelity to the Author of truth, and worshiped God alone.

There have ever been two classes among those who profess to be followers of Christ. While one class study the Saviour's life, and earnestly seek to correct their defects and to conform to the Pattern, the other class shun the plain, practical truths which expose their errors. Even in her best estate, the church was not composed wholly of the true, pure, and sincere. Our Saviour taught that those who willfully indulge in sin are not to be received into the church; yet he connected with himself men who were faulty in character, and granted them the benefits of his teachings and example, that they might have an opportunity to see and correct their errors. Among the twelve apostles was a traitor. Judas was accepted, not because of his defects of character, but notwithstanding them. He was connected with the disciples, that, through the instructions and example of Christ, he might learn what constitutes Christian character, and thus be led to see his errors, to repent, and, by the aid of divine grace, to purity his soul "in obeying the truth." But Judas did not walk in the light so graciously permitted to shine upon him. By indulgence in sin, he invited the temptations of Satan. His evil traits of character became predominant. He yielded his mind to the control of the powers of darkness, he became angry when his faults were reproved, and thus he was led to commit the fearful crime of betraying his Master. In like manner do all who cherish evil under a profession of godliness hate those who disturb their peace by condemning their course of sin. When a favorable opportunity is presented, they will, like Judas, betray those who for their good have sought to reprove them.

The apostles encountered those in the church who professed godliness while they were secretly cherishing iniquity. Ananias and Sapphira acted the part of deceivers, pretending to make an entire sacrifice for God, when they were covetously withholding a portion for themselves. The Spirit of truth revealed to the apostles the real character of these pretenders, and the judgments of God forever rid the church of this foul blot upon its purity. This signal evidence of the discerning Spirit of Christ in the church was a terror to hypocrites and evil-doers. They could not long remain in connection with those who were, in habit and disposition, constant representatives of Christ; and as trials and persecution came upon his followers, those only who were willing to forsake all for the truth's sake desired to become his disciples. Thus, as long as persecution continued, the church remained comparatively pure. But as it ceased, converts were added who were less sincere and devoted, and the way was opened for Satan to obtain a foothold.

But there is no union between the Prince of light and the prince of darkness, and there can be no union between their followers. When Christians consented to unite with those who were but half converted from paganism, they entered upon a path which led farther and farther from the truth. Satan exulted that he had succeeded in deceiving so large a number of the followers of Christ. He then brought his power to bear more fully upon them, and inspired them to persecute those who remained true to God. None could so well understand how to oppose the true Christian faith as could those who had once been its defenders; and these apostate Christians, uniting with their half-pagan companions, directed their warfare against the most essential features of the doctrines of Christ.

It required a desperate struggle for those who would be faithful to stand firm against the deceptions and abominations which were disguised in sacerdotal garments and introduced into the church. The

Bible was not accepted as the standard of faith. The doctrine of religious freedom was termed heresy, and its upholders were hated and proscribed.

After a long and severe conflict, the faithful few decided to dissolve all union with the apostate church if she still refused to free herself from falsehood and idolatry. They saw that separation was an absolute necessity if they would obey the word of God. They dared not tolerate errors fatal to their own souls, and set an example which would imperil the faith of their children and children's children. To secure peace and unity they were ready to make any concession consistent with fidelity to God; but they felt that even peace would be too dearly purchased at the sacrifice of principle. If unity could be secured only by the compromise of truth and righteousness, then let there be difference, and even war.

Well would it be for the church and the world if the principles that actuated those steadfast souls were revived in the hearts of God's professed people. There is an alarming indifference in regard to the doctrines which are the pillars of the Christian faith. The opinion is gaining ground, that, after all, these are not of vital importance. This degeneracy is strengthening the hands of the agents of Satan, so that false theories and fatal delusions which the faithful in ages past imperiled their lives to resist and expose, are now regarded with favor by thousands who claim to be followers of Christ.

The early Christians were indeed a peculiar people. Their blameless deportment and unswerving faith were a continual reproof that disturbed the sinner's peace. Though few in numbers, without wealth, position, or honorary titles, they were a terror to evil-doers wherever their character and doctrines were known. Therefore they were hated by the wicked, even as Abel was hated by the ungodly Cain. For the same reason that Cain slew Abel did those who would throw off the restraint of the Holy Spirit, put to death God's people. It was for the same reason that the Jews rejected and crucified the Saviour,— because the purity and holiness of his character was a constant rebuke to their selfishness and corruption. From the days of Christ until now, his faithful disciples have excited the hatred and opposition of those who love and follow the ways of sin.

How, then, can the gospel be called a message of peace? When Isaiah foretold the birth of the Messiah, he ascribed to him the title, "Prince of peace." When angels announced to the shepherds that Christ was born, they sung above the plains of Bethlehem, "Glory to God in the highest, and on earth peace, good will toward men." [LUKE 2:14.] There is a seeming contradiction between these prophetic declarations and the words of Christ, "I came not to send peace, but a sword." [MATT. 10:34.] But rightly understood, the two are in perfect harmony. The gospel is a message of peace. Christianity is a system, which, received and obeyed, would spread peace, harmony, and happiness throughout the earth. The religion of Christ will unite in close brotherhood all who accept its teachings. It was the mission of Jesus to reconcile man to God, and thus to his fellow-man. But the world at large are under the control of Satan, Christ's bitterest foe. The gospel presents to them principles of life which are wholly at variance with their habits and desires, and they rise in rebellion against it. They hate the purity which reveals and condemns their sins, and they persecute and destroy those who would urge upon them its just and holy claims. It is in this sense— because the exalted truths it brings, occasion hatred and strife— that the gospel is called a sword.

The mysterious providence which permits the righteous to suffer persecution at the hand of the wicked, has been a cause of great perplexity to many who are weak in faith. Some are even ready to cast away their confidence in God because he suffers the basest of men to prosper, while the best and purest are afflicted and tormented by their cruel power. How, it is asked, can One who is just and merciful, and who is also infinite in power, tolerate such injustice and oppression? This is a question with which we have nothing to do. God has given us sufficient evidence of his love, and we are not to doubt his goodness because we cannot understand the workings of his providence. Said the Saviour to his disciples, foreseeing the doubts that would press upon their souls in days of trial and darkness, "Remember the word that I said unto you, The servant is not greater than his lord. If they have persecuted me, they will also persecute you." [JOHN 15:20.] Jesus suffered for us more than any of his followers can be made to suffer through the cruelty of wicked men. Those who are called to endure torture and martyrdom, are but following in the steps of God's dear Son.

"The Lord is not slack concerning his promise." [2 PET. 3:9.] He does not forget or neglect his children; but he permits the wicked to reveal their true character, that none who desire to do his will may be deceived concerning them. Again, the righteous are placed in the furnace of affliction, that they themselves may be purified; that their example may convince others of the reality of faith and godliness; and also that their consistent course may condemn the ungodly and unbelieving.

God permits the wicked to prosper, and to reveal their enmity against him, that when they shall have filled up the measure of their iniquity, all may see his justice and mercy in their utter destruction. The day of his vengeance hastens, when all the transgressors of his law and the oppressors of his people will meet the just recompense of their deeds; when every act of cruelty or oppression toward God's faithful ones will be punished as though done to Christ himself.

There is another and more important question that should engage the attention of the churches of today. The apostle Paul declares that "all that will live godly in Christ Jesus shall suffer persecution." [2 TIM. 3:12.] Why is it, then, that persecution seems in a great degree to slumber?— The only reason is, that the church has conformed to the world's standard, and therefore awakens no opposition. The religion current in our day is not of the pure and holy character which marked the Christian faith in the days of Christ and his apostles. It is only because of the spirit of compromise with sin, because the great truths of the word of God are so indifferently regarded, because there is so little vital godliness in the church, that Christianity is apparently so popular with the world. Let there be a revival of the faith and power of the early church, and the spirit of persecution will be revived, and the fires of persecution will be rekindled.

Chapter 3

The Roman Church

The apostle Paul, in his second letter to the Thessalonians, foretold the great apostasy which would result in the establishment of the papal power. He declared that the day of Christ should not come, "except there come a falling away first, and that man of sin be revealed, the son of perdition; who opposeth and exalteth himself above all that is called God, or that is worshiped; so that he as God sitteth in the temple of God, showing himself that he is God." And furthermore, the apostle warns his brethren that "the mystery of iniquity doth already work." [2 THESS. 2:3, 4, 7.] Even at that early date he saw, creeping into the church, errors that would prepare the way for the development of the papacy.

Little by little, at first in stealth and silence, and then more openly as it increased in strength and gained control of the minds of men, the mystery of iniquity carried forward its deceptive and blasphemous work. Almost imperceptibly the customs of heathenism found their way into the Christian church. The spirit of compromise and conformity was restrained for a time by the fierce persecutions which the church endured under paganism. But as persecution ceased, and Christianity entered the courts and palaces of kings, she laid aside the humble simplicity of Christ and his apostles for the pomp and pride of pagan priests and rulers; and in place of the requirements of God, she substituted human theories and traditions. The nominal conversion of Constantine, in the early part of the fourth century, caused great rejoicing; and the world, arrayed in robes of righteousness, walked into the church. Now the work of corruption rapidly progressed. Paganism, while appearing to be vanquished, became the conqueror. Her spirit controlled the church. Her doctrines, ceremonies, and superstitions were incorporated into the faith and worship of the professed followers of Christ.

This compromise between paganism and Christianity resulted in the development of the man of sin foretold in prophecy as opposing and exalting himself above God. That gigantic system of false religion is a masterpiece of Satan's power,— a monument of his efforts to seat himself upon the throne to rule the earth according to his will.

Satan once endeavored to form a compromise with Christ. He came to the Son of God in the wilderness of temptation, and, showing him all the kingdoms of the world and the glory of them, offered to give all into his hands if he would but acknowledge the supremacy of the prince of darkness. Christ rebuked the presumptuous tempter, and forced him to depart. But Satan meets with greater success in presenting the same temptations to man. To secure worldly gains and honors, the church was led to seek the favor and support of the great men of earth, and having thus rejected Christ, she was induced to yield allegiance to the representative of Satan,— the bishop of Rome.

It is one of the leading doctrines of Romanism that the pope is the visible head of the universal church of Christ, invested with supreme authority over bishops and pastors in all parts of the world. More than this, the pope has arrogated the very titles of Deity. He styles himself "Lord God the Pope," assumes infallibility, and demands that all men pay him homage. Thus the same claim urged by Satan in the wilderness of temptation is still urged by him through the church of Rome, and vast numbers are ready to yield him homage.

But those who fear and reverence God meet this Heaven-daring assumption as Christ met the solicitations of the wily foe: "Thou shalt worship the Lord thy God, and him only shalt thou serve." [LUKE 4:8.] God has never given a hint in his word that he has appointed any man to be the head of the church. The doctrine of papal supremacy is directly opposed to the teachings of the Scriptures. The pope can have no power over Christ's church except by usurpation.

Romanists have persisted in bringing against Protestants the charge of heresy, and willful separation from the true church. But these accusations apply rather to themselves. They are the ones who laid down the banner of Christ, and departed from the faith once delivered to the saints.

Satan well knew that the Holy Scriptures would enable men to discern his deceptions and withstand his power. It was by the word that even the Saviour of the world has resisted his attacks. At every assault, Christ presented the shield of eternal truth, saying, "It is written." To every suggestion of the adversary he opposed the wisdom and power of the word. In order for Satan to maintain his sway over men, and establish the authority of the papal usurper, he must keep them in ignorance of the Scriptures. The Bible would exalt God, and place finite men in their true position; therefore its sacred truths must be concealed and suppressed. This logic was adopted by the Roman Church. For hundreds of years the circulation of the Bible was prohibited. The people were forbidden to read it, or to have it in their houses, and unprincipled priests and prelates interpreted its teachings to sustain their pretensions. Thus the pope came to be almost universally acknowledged as the vicegerent of God on earth, endowed with supreme authority over Church and State.

The detector of error having been removed, Satan worked according to his will. Prophecy had declared that the papacy was to "think to change times and laws." [DANIEL 7:25.] This work it was not slow to attempt. To afford converts from heathenism a substitute for the worship of idols, and thus to promote their nominal acceptance of Christianity, the adoration of images and relics was gradually introduced into the Christian worship. The decree of a general council finally established this system of Popish idolatry. To complete the sacrilegious work, Rome presumed to expunge from the law of God the second commandment, forbidding image worship, and to divide the tenth commandment, in order to preserve the number.

The spirit of concession to paganism opened the way for a still further disregard of Heaven's authority. Satan tampered with the fourth commandment also, and essayed to set aside the ancient Sabbath, the day which God had blessed and sanctified, and in its stead to exalt the festival observed by the heathen as "the venerable day of the sun." This change was not at first attempted openly. In the first centuries the true Sabbath had been kept by all Christians. They were jealous for the honor of God, and, believing that his law is immutable, they zealously guarded the sacredness of its precepts. But with great subtlety, Satan worked through his agents to bring about his object. That the attention of the people might be called to the Sunday, it was made a festival in honor of the resurrection of Christ. Religious services were held upon it; yet it was regarded as a day of recreation, the Sabbath being still sacredly observed.

Constantine, while still a heathen, issued a decree enjoining the general observance of Sunday as a public festival throughout the Roman empire. After his conversion, he remained a staunch advocate of Sunday, and his pagan edict was then enforced by him in the interests of his new faith. But the honor shown this day was not as yet sufficient to prevent Christians from regarding the true Sabbath as the holy of the Lord. Another step must be taken; the false Sabbath must be exalted to an equality with the true. A few years after the issue of Constantine's decree, the bishop of Rome conferred on the Sunday the title of Lord's day. Thus the people were gradually led to regard it as possessing a degree of sacredness. Still the original Sabbath was kept.

The arch-deceiver had not completed his work. He was resolved to gather the Christian world under his banner, and to exercise his power through his vicegerent, the proud pontiff who claimed to be the representative of Christ. Through half-converted pagans, ambitious prelates, and world-loving churchmen, he accomplished his purpose. Vast councils were held, from time to time, in which the dignitaries of the church were convened from all the world. In nearly every council the Sabbath which God had instituted was pressed down a little lower, while the Sunday was correspondingly exalted. Thus the pagan festival came finally to be honored as a divine institution, while the Bible Sabbath was pronounced a relic of Judaism, and its observers were declared to be accursed.

The great apostate had succeeded in exalting himself "above all that is called God, or that is worshiped." [2 THESS. 2:4.] He had dared to change the only precept of the divine law that unmistakably points all mankind to the true and living God. In the fourth commandment, God is revealed as the Creator of the heavens and the earth, and is thereby distinguished from all false gods. It was as a memorial of the work of creation that the seventh day was sanctified as a rest-day for man. It was designed to keep the living God ever before the minds of men as the source of being and the object of reverence and worship. Satan strives to turn men from their allegiance to God, and from rendering obedience to his law; therefore he directs his efforts especially against that commandment which points to God as the Creator.

Protestants now urge that the resurrection of Christ on Sunday, made it the Christian Sabbath. But Scripture evidence is lacking. No such honor was given to the day by Christ or his apostles. The observance of Sunday as a Christian institution has its origin in that "mystery of lawlessness" which, even in Paul's day, had begun its work. Where and when did the Lord adopt this child of the papacy? What valid reason can be given for a change concerning which the Scriptures are silent?

In the sixth century the papacy had become firmly established. Its seat of power was fixed in the imperial city, and the bishop of Rome was declared to be the head over the entire church. Paganism had given place to the papacy. The dragon had given to the beast "his power, and his seat, and great authority." [REV. 13:2.] And now began the 1260 years of papal oppression foretold in the prophecies of Daniel and John. [DAN. 7:25; REV. 13:5-7.] Christians were forced to choose, either to yield their integrity and accept the papal ceremonies and worship, or to wear away their lives in dungeon cells, or suffer death by the rack, the fagot, or the headsman's ax. Now were fulfilled the words of Jesus, "Ye shall be betrayed both by parents, and brethren, and kinsfolks, and friends; and some of you shall they cause to be put to death. And ye shall be hated of all men for my name's sake." [LUKE 21:16, 17.] Persecution opened upon the faithful with greater fury than ever before, and the world became a vast battle-field. For hundreds of years the church of Christ found refuge in seclusion and obscurity. Thus says the prophet: "The woman fled into the wilderness, where she hath a place prepared of God, that they should feed her there a thousand two hundred and three-score days." [REV. 12:16.]

The accession of the Roman Church to power marked the beginning of the Dark Ages. As her power increased, the darkness deepened. Faith was transferred from Christ, the true foundation, to the pope of Rome. Instead of trusting in the Son of God for forgiveness of sins and for eternal salvation, the people looked to the pope, and to the priests and prelates to whom he delegated authority. They were taught that the pope was their mediator, and that none could approach God except through him, and, further, that he stood in the place of God to them, and was therefore to be implicitly obeyed. A deviation from his requirements was sufficient cause for the severest punishment to be visited upon the bodies and souls of the offenders. Thus the minds of the people were turned away from God to fallible, erring, and cruel men, nay more, to the prince of darkness himself, who exercised his power through them. Sin was disguised in a garb of sanctity. When the Scriptures are suppressed, and man comes to regard himself as supreme, we need look only for fraud, deception, and debasing iniquity. With the elevation of human laws and traditions was manifest the corruption that ever results from setting aside the law of God.

Those were days of peril for the church of Christ. The faithful standard-bearers were few indeed. Though the truth was not left without witnesses, yet at times it seemed that error and superstition would wholly prevail, and true religion would be banished from the earth. The gospel was lost sight of, but the forms of religion were multiplied, and the people were burdened with rigorous exactions.

They were taught not only to look to the pope as their mediator, but to trust to works of their own to atone for sin. Long pilgrimages, acts of penance, the worship of relics, the erection of churches, shrines, and altars, the payment of large sums to the church,— these and many similar acts were enjoined to appease the wrath of God or to secure his favor; as if God were like men, to be angered at trifles, or pacified by gifts or acts of penance!

Notwithstanding vice prevailed, even among the leaders of the Romish Church, her influence seemed steadily to increase. About the close of the eighth century, Papists put forth the claim that in the first ages of the church the bishops of Rome had possessed the same spiritual power which they now assumed. To establish this claim, some means must be employed to give it a show of authority; and this was readily suggested by the father of lies. Ancient writings were forged by monks. Decrees of councils before unheard of were discovered, establishing the universal supremacy of the pope from the earliest times. And a church that had rejected the truth greedily accepted these deceptions.

The few faithful builders upon the true foundation were perplexed and hindered as the rubbish of false doctrine obstructed the work. Like the builders upon the wall of Jerusalem in Nehemiah's day, some were ready to say, "The strength of the bearers of burdens is decayed, and there is much rubbish, so that we are not able to build." [NEH. 4:10.] Wearied with the constant struggle against persecution, fraud, iniquity, and every other obstacle that Satan could devise to hinder their progress, some who had been faithful builders became disheartened; and for the sake of peace and security for their property and their lives they turned away from the true foundation. Others, undaunted by the opposition of their enemies, fearlessly declared, "Be not ye afraid of them; remember the Lord, which is great and terrible;" [NEH. 4:14.] and they proceeded with the work, every one with his sword girded by his side.

The same spirit of hatred and opposition to the truth has inspired the enemies of God in every age, and the same vigilance and fidelity have been required in his servants. The words of Christ to the first disciples are applicable to his followers to the close of time: "What I say unto you, I say unto all, Watch." [MARK 13:37.]

The darkness seemed to grow more dense. Image worship became more general. Candles were burned before images, and prayers were offered to them. The most absurd and superstitious customs prevailed. The minds of men were so completely controlled by superstition that reason itself seemed to have lost her sway. While priests and bishops were themselves pleasure-loving, sensual, and corrupt, it could only be expected that the people who looked to them for guidance would be sunken in ignorance and vice.

Another step in papal assumption was taken, when, in the eleventh century, Pope Gregory VII. proclaimed the perfection of the Romish Church. Among the propositions which he put forth, was one declaring that the church had never erred, nor would it ever err, according to the Scriptures. But the Scripture proofs did not accompany the assertion. The proud pontiff next claimed the power to depose emperors, and declared that no sentence which he pronounced could be reversed by any one, but that it was his prerogative to reverse the decisions of all others.

A striking illustration of the tyrannical character of this advocate of infallibility was given in his treatment of the German king, Henry IV. For presuming to disregard the pope's authority, this monarch was declared to be excommunicated and dethroned. In order to make his peace with Rome, Henry crossed the Alps in midwinter that he might humble himself before the pope. Upon reaching the castle whither Gregory had withdrawn, he was conducted, without his guards, into an outer court, and there, in the severe cold of winter, with uncovered head and naked feet and in a miserable dress, he awaited the pope's permission to come into his presence. Not until he had continued three days fasting and making confession did the pontiff condescend to grant him pardon. Even then it was only upon condition that the emperor should await the sanction of the pope before resuming the insignia or exercising the power of royalty. And Gregory, elated with his triumph, boasted that it was his duty "to pull down the pride of kings."

How striking the contrast between the overbearing pride of this haughty pontiff and the meekness and gentleness of Christ, who represents himself as pleading at the door of the heart for admittance, that he may come in to bring pardon and peace, and who taught his disciples,

"Whosoever will be chief among you, let him be your servant." [MATT. 20:27.]

The advancing centuries witnessed a constant increase of error in the doctrines put forth from Rome. Even before the establishment of the papacy, the teachings of heathen philosophers had received attention and exerted an influence in the church. Many who professed conversion still clung to the tenets of their pagan philosophy, and not only continued its study themselves, but urged it upon others as a means of extending their influence among the heathen. Thus were serious errors introduced into the Christian faith. Prominent among these was the belief in man's natural immortality and his consciousness in death. This doctrine laid the foundation upon which Rome established the invocation of saints and the adoration of the virgin Mary. From this sprung also the heresy of eternal torment for the finally impenitent, which was early incorporated into the papal faith.

Then the way was prepared for the introduction of still another invention of paganism, which Rome named purgatory, and employed to terrify the credulous and superstitious multitudes. By this heresy is affirmed the existence of a place of torment, in which the souls of such as have not merited eternal damnation are to suffer punishment for their sins, and from which, when freed from impurity, they are admitted to Heaven.

Still another fabrication was needed to enable Rome to profit the fears and the vices of her adherents. This was supplied by the doctrine of indulgences. Full remission of sins, past, present, and future, and release from all the pains and penalties incurred, were promised to all who would enlist in the pontiff's wars to extend his temporal dominion, to punish his enemies, or to exterminate those who dared deny his spiritual supremacy. The people were also taught that by the payment of money to the church they might free them- selves from sin, and also release the souls of their deceased friends who were confined in the tormenting flames. By such means did Rome fill her coffers, and sustain the magnificence, luxury,and vice of the pretended representatives of Him who had not where to lay his head.

The scriptural ordinance of the Lord's supper had been supplanted by the idolatrous sacrifice of the mass. Papist priests pretended, by their senseless mummery, to convert the simple bread and wine into the actual body and blood of Christ. With blasphemous presumption, they openly claimed the power to "create their Creator." All Christians were required, on pain of death, to avow their faith in this horrible, Heaven-insulting heresy. Those who refused were given to the flames.

In the thirteenth century was established that most terrible of all the engines of the papacy,— the Inquisition. The prince of darkness wrought with the leaders of the papal hierarchy. In their secret councils, Satan and his angels presided, while unseen in the midst stood an angel of God, taking the fearful record of their iniquitous decrees, and writing the history of deeds too horrible to appear to human eyes. "Babylon the great" was "drunken with the blood of the saints." The mangled forms of millions of martyrs cried to God for vengeance upon that apostate power.

Popery had become the world's despot. Kings and emperors bowed to the decrees of the Roman pontiff. The destinies of men, both for time and for eternity, seemed under his control. For hundreds of years the doctrines of Rome had been extensively and implicitly received, its rites reverently performed, its festivals generally observed. Its clergy were honored and liberally sustained. Never since has the Roman Church attained to greater dignity, magnificence, and power.

The noontide of the papacy was the world's moral midnight. The Holy Scriptures were almost unknown, not only to the people, but to the priests. Like the Pharisees of old, the Papist leaders hated the light which would reveal their sins. God's law, the standard of righteousness, having been removed, they exercised power without limit, and practiced vice without restraint. Fraud, avarice, and profligacy prevailed. Men shrank from no crime by which they could gain wealth or position. The palaces of popes and prelates were scenes of the vilest debauchery. Some of the reigning pontiffs were guilty of crimes so revolting that secular rulers endeavored to depose these dignitaries of the church as monsters too vile to be tolerated upon the throne. For centuries there was no progress in learning, arts, or civilization. A moral and intellectual paralysis had fallen upon Christendom.

In the condition of the world under the Romish power was presented a fearful and striking fulfillment of the words of the prophet Hosea: "My people are destroyed for lack of knowledge. Because thou hast rejected knowledge, I will also reject thee." "Seeing thou hast forgotten the law of thy God, I will also forget thy children." "There is no truth, nor mercy, nor knowledge of God in the land. By swearing, and lying, and killing, and stealing, and committing adultery, they break out, and blood toucheth blood." [HOSEA 4:6, 1, 2.] Such were the results of banishing the word of God.

Chapter 4

The Waldenses

Amid the gloom that settled upon the earth during the long period of papal supremacy, the light of truth could not be wholly extinguished. In every age there were witnesses for God,— men who cherished faith in Christ as the only mediator between God and man, who led the Bible as the only rule of life, and who hallowed the true Sabbath. How much the world owes to these men, posterity will never know. They were branded as heretics, their motives impugned, their characters maligned, their writings suppressed, misrepresented, or mutilated. Yet they stood firm, and from age to age maintained their faith in its purity, as a sacred heritage for the generations to come.

The history of God's faithful people for hundreds of years after Rome attained to power, is known alone to heaven. They cannot be traced in human records, except as hints of their existence are found in the censures and accusations of their persecutors. It was the policy of Rome to obliterate every trace of dissent from her doctrines or decrees. Everything heretical, whether persons or writings, was destroyed. A single expression of doubt, a question as to the authority of papal dogmas, was enough to cost the life of rich or poor, high or low. Rome endeavored also to destroy every record of her cruelty toward dissenters. Papal councils decreed that books and writings containing such records should be committed to the flames. Before the invention of printing, books were few in number, and in a form not favorable for preservation; therefore there was little to prevent the Romanists from carrying out their purpose.

No church within the limits of Romish jurisdiction was long left undisturbed in the enjoyment of freedom of conscience. No sooner had the papacy obtained power than she stretched out her arms to crush all that refused to acknowledge her sway, and one after another, the churches submitted to her dominion.

In Great Britain a primitive Christianity had very early taken root. Faithful men had preached the gospel in that country with great zeal and success. Among the leading evangelists was an observer of the Bible Sabbath, and thus this truth found its way among the people for whom he labored. Toward the close of the sixth century, missionaries were sent from Rome to England to convert the barbarian Saxons. They induced many thousands to profess the Romish faith, and as the work progressed, the papal leaders and their converts encountered the primitive Christians. A striking contrast was presented. The latter were simple, humble, and scriptural in character, doctrine, and manners, while the former manifested the superstition, pomp, and arrogance of Popery. The emissary of Rome demanded that these Christian churches acknowledge the supremacy of the sovereign pontiff. The Britons meekly replied that they desired to love all men, but that the pope was not entitled to supremacy in the church, and they could render to him only that submission which was due to every follower of Christ. Repeated attempts were made to secure their allegiance to Rome; but these humble Christians, amazed at the pride displayed by her apostles, steadfastly replied that they knew no other master than Christ. Now the true spirit of the papacy was revealed. Said the Romish leader, "If you will not receive brethren who bring you peace, you shall receive enemies who will bring you war. If you will not unite with us in showing the Saxons the way of life, you shall receive from them the stroke of death." These were no idle threats. War, intrigue, and deception were employed against these witnesses for a Bible faith, until the churches of Britain were destroyed, or forced to submit to the authority of the pope.

In lands beyond the jurisdiction of Rome, there existed for many centuries bodies of Christians who remained almost wholly free from papal corruption. They were surrounded by heathenism, and in the lapse of ages were affected by its errors; but they continued to regard the Bible as the only rule of faith, and adhered to many of its truths. These Christians believed in the perpetuity of the law of God, and observed the Sabbath of the fourth commandment. Churches that held to this faith and practice, existed in Central Africa and among the Armenians of Asia.

But of those who resisted the encroachments of the papal power, the Waldenses stood foremost. For centuries the churches of Piedmont maintained their independence; but the time came at last when Rome demanded their submission. After ineffectual struggles against her tyranny, the leaders of these churches reluctantly acknowledged the supremacy of the power to which the whole world seemed bowing down. A considerable number, however, refused to yield to the authority of pope or prelate. They were determined to maintain their allegiance to God, and to preserve the purity and simplicity of their faith. A separation took place. Some of the protesters crossed the Alps, and raised the standard of truth in foreign lands. Others retired into the more secluded valleys among the mountains, and there maintained their freedom to worship God.

The religious belief of the Waldenses was founded upon the written word of God, the true system of Christianity, and was in marked contrast to the errors of Rome. But those herdsmen and vine-dressers, in their obscure retreats, shut away from the world, had not themselves arrived at the truth in opposition to the dogmas and heresies of the apostate church. Theirs was not a faith newly received. Their religious belief was their inheritance from their fathers. They contended for the faith of the apostolic church, — "the faith once delivered to the saints."

Among the leading causes that had led to the separation of the true church from Rome, was the inveterate hatred of the latter toward the Bible Sabbath. As foretold by prophecy, the papal power cast down the truth to the ground. The law of God was trampled in the dust, while the traditions and customs of men were exalted. The churches that were under the rule of the papacy were early compelled to honor the Sunday as a holy day. Amid the prevailing error and superstition, many even of the true people of God, became so bewildered that while they observed the Sabbath, they refrained from labor also on the Sunday. But this did not satisfy the papal leaders. They demanded not only that Sunday be hallowed, but that the Sabbath be profaned; and they denounced in the strongest language those who dared to show it honor. It was only by fleeing from the power of Rome that any could obey God's law in peace.

The Waldenses were the first of all the peoples of Europe to obtain a translation of the Scriptures. Hundreds of years before the Reformation, they possessed the entire Bible in manuscript in their native tongue. They had the truth unadulterated, and this rendered them the special objects of hatred and persecution. They declared the Church of Rome to be the apostate Babylon of the Apocalypse, and at the peril of their lives they stood up to resist her corruptions. While, under the pressure of long-continued persecution, some compromised their faith, little by little yielding its distinctive principles, others held fast the truth. Through ages of darkness and apostasy, there were Waldenses who denied the supremacy of Rome, who rejected image worship as idolatry, and who kept the true Sabbath. Under the fiercest tempests of opposition they maintained their faith. Though gashed by the Savoyard spear, and scorched by the Romish fagot, they stood unflinchingly for God's word and his honor. They would not yield one iota of the truth.

Behind the lofty bulwarks of the mountains,— in all ages the refuge of the persecuted and oppressed,— the Waldenses found a hiding-place. Here the lamp of truth was kept burning during the long night that descended upon Christendom. Here for a thousand years they maintained their ancient faith.

God had provided for his people a sanctuary of awful grandeur, befitting the mighty truths committed to their trust. To those faithful exiles the mountains were an emblem of the immutable righteousness of Jehovah. They pointed their children to the heights towering above them in unchanging majesty, and spoke to them of Him with whom there is no variableness nor shadow of turning, whose word is as enduring as the everlasting hills. God had set fast the mountains, and girded them with strength; no arm but that of infinite power could move them out of their place. In like manner had he established his law, the foundation of his government in Heaven and upon earth. The arm of man might reach his fellow-men and destroy their lives; but that arm could as readily uproot the mountains from their foundations, and hurl them into the sea, as it could change one precept of the law of Jehovah, or blot out one of his promises to those who do his will. In their fidelity to his law, God's servants should be as firm as the unchanging hills.

The mountains that girded their lowly valleys were a constant witness of God's creative power, and a never-failing assurance of his protecting care. Those pilgrims learned to love the silent symbols of Jehovah's presence. They indulged no repining because of the hardships of their lot; they were never lonely amid the mountain solitudes. They thanked God that he had provided for them an asylum from the wrath and cruelty of men. They rejoiced in their freedom to worship before him. Often when pursued by their enemies, the strength of the hills proved a sure defense. From many a lofty cliff they chanted the praise of God, and the armies of Rome could not silence their songs of thanksgiving.

Pure, simple, and fervent was the piety of these followers of Christ. The principles of truth they valued above houses and lands, friends, kindred, even life itself. These principles they earnestly sought to impress upon the hearts of the young. From earliest childhood the youth were instructed in the Scriptures, and taught to sacredly regard the claims of the law of God. Copies of the Bible were rare; therefore its precious words were committed to memory. Many were able to repeat large portions of both the Old and the New Testament. Thoughts of God were associated alike with the sublime scenery of nature and with the humble blessings of daily life. Little children learned to look with gratitude to God as the giver of every favor and every comfort.

Parents, tender and affectionate as they were, loved their children too wisely to accustom them to self-indulgence. Before them was a life of trial and hardship, perhaps a martyr's death. They were educated from childhood to endure hardness, to submit to control, and yet to think and act for themselves. Very early they were taught to bear responsibilities, to be guarded in speech, and to understand the wisdom of silence. One indiscreet word let fall in the hearing of their enemies, might imperil not only the life of the speaker, but the lives of hundreds of his brethren; for as wolves hunting their prey did the enemies of truth pursue those who dared to claim freedom of religious faith.

The Waldenses had sacrificed their worldly prosperity for the truth's sake, and with persevering patience they toiled for their bread. Every spot of tillable land among the mountains was carefully improved; the valleys and the less fertile hillsides were made to yield their increase.

Economy and severe self-denial formed a part of the education which the children received as their only legacy. They were taught that God designs life to be a discipline, and that their wants could be supplied only by personal labor, by forethought, care, and faith. The process was laborious and wearisome, but it was wholesome, just what man needs in his fallen state, the school which God has provided for his training and development.

While the youth were injured to toil and hardship, the culture of the intellect was not neglected. They were taught that all their powers belonged to God, and that all were to be improved and developed for his service.

The church of the Alps, in its purity and simplicity, resembled the church in the first centuries. The shepherds of the flock led their charge to the fountain of living waters,— the word of God. On the grassy slopes of the valleys, or in some sheltered glen among the hills, the people gathered about the servants of Christ to listen to the words of truth.

Here the youth received instruction. The Bible was their text-book. They studied and committed to memory the words of Holy Writ. A considerable portion of their time was spent, also, in reproducing copies of the Scriptures. Some manuscripts contained the whole Bible, others only brief selections, to which some simple explanations of the text were added by those who were able to expound the Scriptures. Thus were brought forth the treasures of truth so long concealed by those who sought to exalt themselves above God.

By patient, untiring labor, sometimes in the deep, dark caverns of the earth, by the light of torches, were the Sacred Scriptures written out, verse by verse, chapter by chapter. Thus the work went on, the revealed will of God shining out like pure gold; how much brighter, clearer, and more powerful because of the trials undergone for its sake, only those could realize who were engaged in the work. Angels from Heaven surrounded these faithful workers.

Satan had urged on the papal bishops and prelates to bury the word of truth beneath the rubbish of error, heresy, and superstition; but in a most wonderful manner was it preserved uncorrupted through all the ages of darkness. It bore not the stamp of man, but the impress of God. Men have been unwearied in their efforts to obscure the plain, simple meaning of the Scriptures, and to make them contradict their own testimony; but, like the ark upon the billowy deep, the word of God outrides the storms that threaten it with destruction. As the mine has rich veins of gold and silver hidden beneath the surface, so that all must dig who would discover its precious stores, so the Holy Scriptures have treasures of truth that are unfolded only to the earnest, humble, prayerful seeker. God designed the Bible to be a lesson-book to all mankind, in childhood, youth, and manhood, and to be studied through all time. He gave his word to men as a revelation of himself. Every new truth discerned is a fresh disclosure of the character of its Author The study of the Scriptures is the means divinely ordained to bring men into closer connection with their Creator, and to give them a clearer knowledge of his will. It is the medium of communication between God and man.

When the Waldensian youth had spent some time in their schools in the mountains, some of them were sent to complete their education in the great cities, where they could have a wider range for thought and observation than in their secluded homes. The youth thus sent forth were exposed to temptation, they witnessed vice, they encountered Satan's wily agents, who urged upon them the most subtle heresies and the most dangerous deceptions. But their education from childhood had been of a character to prepare them for all this.

In the schools whither they went, they were not to make confidants of any. Their garments were so prepared as to conceal their greatest treasure,— the precious manuscripts of the Scriptures. These, the fruit of months and years of toil, they carried with them, and whenever it could be done without exciting suspicion, they cautiously placed some portion in the way of those whose hearts seemed open to receive it. From their mother's knee the Waldensian youth had been trained with this purpose in view; they understood their work, and faithfully performed it. Converts to the true faith were won in these institutions of learning, and frequently its principles were found to be permeating the entire school; yet the Papist leaders could not, by the closest inquiry, trace the so-called corrupting heresy to its source.

The Waldenses felt that God required more of them than merely to maintain the truth in their own mountains; that a solemn responsibility rested upon them to let their light shine forth to those who were in darkness; that by the mighty power of God's word, they were to break the bondage which Rome had imposed. It was a law among them that all who entered the ministry should, before taking charge of a church at home, serve three years in the missionary field. As the hands of the men of God were laid upon their heads, the youth saw before them, not the prospect of earthly wealth or glory, but possibly a martyr's fate. The missionaries began their labors in the plains and valleys at the foot of their own mountains, going forth two and two, as Jesus sent out his disciples. These co-laborers were not always together, but often met for prayer and counsel, thus strengthening each other in the faith.

To make known the nature of their mission would have insured its defeat; therefore they concealed their real character under the guise of some secular profession, most commonly that of merchants or peddlers. They offered for sale silks, jewelry, and other valuable articles, and were received as merchants where they would have been repulsed as missionaries. All the while their hearts were uplifted to God for wisdom to present a treasure more precious than gold or gems. They carried about with them portions of the Holy Scriptures concealed in their clothing or merchandise, and whenever they could do so with safety, they called the attention of the inmates of the dwelling to these manuscripts. When they saw that an interest was awakened, they left some portion with them as a gift.

With naked feet and in coarse garments, these missionaries passed through great cities, and traversed provinces far removed from their native valleys. Everywhere they scattered the precious seed. Churches sprang up in their path, and the blood of martyrs witnessed for the truth. The day of God will reveal a rich harvest of souls garnered by the labors of these faithful men. Veiled and silent, the word of God was making its way through Christendom, and meeting a glad reception in the homes and hearts of men.

To the Waldenses the Scriptures were not merely a record of God's dealings with men in the past, and a revelation of the responsibilities and duties of the present, but an unfolding of the perils and glories of the future. They believed that the end of all things was not far distant; and as they studied the Bible with prayer and tears, they were the more deeply impressed with its precious utterances, and with their duty to make known to others its saving truths. They saw the plan of salvation clearly revealed in the word of God, and they found comfort, hope, and peace in believing in Jesus. As the light illuminated their understanding and made glad their hearts, they longed to shed its beams upon those who were in the darkness of papal error.

They saw that under the guidance of pope and priests, multitudes were vainly endeavoring to obtain pardon, by afflicting their bodies for the sin of their souls. Taught to trust their good works to save them, they were ever looking to themselves, their minds dwelling upon their sinful condition, seeing themselves exposed to the wrath of God, afflicting soul and body, yet finding no relief. Thus were conscientious souls bound by the doctrines of Rome. Thousands abandoned friends and kindred, and spent their lives in convent cells. By oft-repeated fasts and cruel scourgings, by midnight vigils, by prostration for weary hours upon the cold, damp stones of their dreary abode, by long pilgrimages, by humiliating penance and fearful torture, many vainly sought to obtain peace of conscience. Oppressed with a sense of sin, and haunted with the fear of God's avenging wrath, they suffered on, until exhausted nature gave way, and without one ray of light or hope, they sank into the tomb.

The Waldenses longed to break to those starving souls the bread of life, to open to them the messages of peace in the promises of God, and to point them to Christ as their only hope of salvation. The doctrine that good works can make satisfaction for transgression of

God's law, they held to be based upon falsehood. Reliance upon human merits intercepts the view of Christ's infinite love. Jesus died as men's sacrifice, because they can do nothing to recommend themselves to God. The merits of a crucified and risen Saviour are the foundation of the Christian's faith. The union of the soul to Christ by faith is as real, as close, as that of a limb to the body, or of a branch to the vine.

The teachings of popes and priests had led men to look upon the character of God, and even of Christ, as stern, gloomy, and forbidding. The Saviour of the world was represented as so far devoid of all sympathy with man in his fallen state that the mediation of priests and saints must be invoked. How those whose minds had been enlightened by the word of God longed to point these souls to Jesus as their compassionate, loving Saviour, standing with outstretched arms, inviting all to come to him with their burden of sin, their care and weariness. They longed to clear away the obstructions which Satan had piled up that men might not see the promises, and come directly to God, confessing their sins, and obtaining pardon and peace.

Eagerly did the Vaudois missionary unfold to the inquiring mind the precious truths of the gospel. Cautiously he produced the carefully written portions of the word of God. It was his greatest joy to give hope to the conscientious, sin-stricken soul, who could see only a God of vengeance, waiting to execute justice. With quivering lip and tearful eye did he, often on bended knees, open to his brethren the precious promises that reveal the sinner's only hope. Thus the light of truth penetrated many a darkened mind, rolling back the cloud of gloom, until the Sun of Righteousness shone into the heart with healing in his beams. Some portions of Scripture were read again and again, the hearer desiring them to be often repeated, as if he would assure himself that he had heard aright. Especially was the repetition of these words eagerly desired: "The blood of Jesus Christ his Son cleanseth us from all sin." [1 JOHN 1:7.] "As Moses lifted up the serpent in the wilderness, even so must the Son of man be lifted up, that whosoever believeth in him should not perish, but have eternal life." [JOHN 3:14, 15.]

Many were undeceived in regard to the claims of Rome. They saw how vain is the mediation of men or angels in behalf of the sinner. As the true light dawned upon their minds, they exclaimed with rejoicing, "Christ is my priest; his blood is my sacrifice; his altar is my confessional." They cast themselves wholly upon the merits of Jesus, repeating the words, "Without faith it is impossible to please God." [HEB. 11:6.] "There is none other name under heaven given among men, whereby we must be saved." [ACTS 4:12.]

The assurance of a Saviour's love seemed too much for some of these poor tempest-tossed souls to realize. So great was the relief which it brought, such a flood of light was shed upon them, that they seemed transported to Heaven. Their hand was laid confidingly in the hand of Christ; their feet were planted upon the Rock of Ages. All fear of death was banished. They could now covet the prison and the fagot if they might thereby honor the name of their Redeemer.

In secret places the word of God was thus brought forth and read, sometimes to a single soul, sometimes to a little company who were longing for light and truth. Often the entire night was spent in this manner. So great would be the wonder and admiration of the listeners that the messenger of mercy was not infrequently compelled to cease his reading until the understanding could grasp the tidings of salvation. Often would words like these be uttered: "Will God indeed accept *my* offering? Will he smile upon *me*? Will he pardon *me*?" The answer was read, "Come unto me, all ye that labor and are heavy-laden, and I will give you rest." [MATT. 11:23.]

Faith grasps the promise, and the glad response is heard, "No more long pilgrimages to make; no more painful journeys to holy shrines. I may come to Jesus just as I am, sinful and unholy, and he will not spurn the penitential prayer. 'Thy sins be forgiven thee.' Mine, even mine, may be forgiven."

A tide of sacred joy would fill the heart, and the name of Jesus would be magnified by praise and thanksgiving. Those happy souls returned to their homes to diffuse light, to repeat to others, as well as they could, their new experience; that they had found the true and living Way. There was a strange and solemn power in the words of Scripture that spoke directly to the hearts of those who were longing for the truth. It was the voice of God, and it carried conviction to those who heard.

The messenger of truth went on his way; but his appearance of humility, his sincerity, his earnestness and deep fervor, were subjects of frequent remark. In many instances his hearers had not asked him whence he came, or whither he went. They had been so overwhelmed, at first with surprise, and afterward with gratitude and joy, that they had not thought to question him. When they had urged him to accompany them to their homes, he had replied that he must visit the lost sheep of the flock. Could he have been an angel from Heaven? they queried.

In many cases the messenger of truth was seen no more. He had made his way to other lands, he was wearing out his life in some unknown dungeon, or perhaps his bones were whitening on the spot where he had witnessed for the truth. But the words he had left behind could not be destroyed. They were doing their work in the hearts of men: the blessed results will be fully known only in the Judgment.

The Waldensian missionaries were invading the kingdom of Satan, and the powers of darkness aroused to greater vigilance. Every effort to advance the truth was watched by the prince of evil, and he excited the fears of his agents. The papal leaders saw a portent of danger to their cause from the labors of those humble itinerants. If the light of truth were allowed to shine unobstructed, it would sweep away the heavy clouds of error that enveloped the people; it would direct the minds of men to God alone, and would eventually destroy the supremacy of Rome.

The very existence of this people, holding the faith of the ancient church, was a constant testimony to Rome's apostasy, and therefore excited the most bitter hatred and persecution. Their refusal to surrender the Scriptures was also an offense that Rome could not tolerate. She determined to blot them from the earth. Now began the most terrible crusades against God's people in their mountain homes. Inquisitors were put upon their track, and the scene of innocent Abel falling before the murderous Cain was often repeated.

Again and again were their fertile lands laid waste, their dwellings and chapels swept away, so that where once were flourishing fields and the homes of an innocent, industrious people, there remained only a desert. As the ravenous beast is rendered more furious by the taste of blood, so was the rage of the Papists kindled to greater intensity by the sufferings of their victims. Many of these witnesses for a pure faith were pursued across the mountains, and hunted down in the valleys where they were hidden, shut in by mighty forests, and pinnacles of rock.

No charge could be brought against the moral character of this proscribed class. Even their enemies declared them to be a peaceable, quiet, pious people. Their grand offense was that they would not worship God according to the will of the pope. For this crime, every humiliation, insult, and torture that men or devils could invent was heaped upon them.

When Rome at one time determined to exterminate the hated sect, a bull was issued by the pope condemning them as heretics, and delivering them to slaughter. They were not accused as idlers, or dishonest, or disorderly; but it was declared that they had an appearance of piety and sanctity that seduced "the sheep of the true fold." Therefore the pope ordered "that the malicious and abominable sect of malignants," if they refuse to abjure, "be crushed like venomous snakes." Did this haughty potentate expect to meet those words again? Did he know that they were registered in the books of Heaven, to confront him at the Judgment? "Inasmuch as ye have done it unto one of the least of these my brethren," said Jesus, "ye have done it unto me." [MATT. 25:40.]

This bull invited all Catholics to take up the cross against the heretics. In order to stimulate them in this cruel work, it absolved them from all ecclesiastical pains and penalties, it released all who joined the crusade from any oaths they might have taken; it legalized their title to any property which they might have illegally acquired, and promised remission of all their sins to such as should kill any heretic. It annulled all contracts made in favor of the Vaudois, ordered their domestics to abandon them, forbade all persons to give them any aid whatever, and empowered all persons to take possession of their property How clearly does this document reveal the master spirit behind the scenes! It is the roar of the dragon, and not the voice of Christ, that is heard therein.

The papal leaders would not conform their characters to the great standard of God's law, but erected a standard to suit themselves, and determined to compel all to conform to this because Rome willed it. The most horrible tragedies were enacted. Corrupt and blasphemous priests and popes were doing the work which Satan appointed them. Mercy had no place in their natures. The same spirit that crucified Christ, and that slew the apostles, the same that moved the blood-thirsty Nero against the faithful in his day, was at work to rid the earth of those who were beloved of God.

The persecutions visited for many centuries upon this God-fearing people were endured by them with a patience and constancy that honored their Redeemer. Notwithstanding the crusades against them, and the inhuman butchery to which they were subjected, they continued to send out their missionaries to scatter the precious truth. They were hunted to the death; yet their blood watered the seed sown, and it failed not of yielding fruit. Thus the Waldenses witnessed for God, centuries before the birth of Luther. Scattered over many lands, they planted the seeds of the Reformation that began in the time of Wycliffe, grew broad and deep in the days of Luther, and is to be carried forward to the close of time by those who also are willing to suffer all things for "the word of God and for the testimony of Jesus Christ." [REV. 1:9.]

Chapter 5

Early Reformers

So Bitter had been the war waged upon the Bible, that at times there were very few copies in existence; but God had not suffered his word to be wholly destroyed. Its truths were not to be forever hidden. He could as easily unchain the words of life as he could open prison doors and unbolt iron gates to set his servants free. In the different countries of Europe, men were moved by the Spirit of God to search for the truth as for hidden treasure. Providentially guided to the Holy Scriptures, they studied the sacred pages with intense interest. They were willing to accept the light, at any cost to themselves. Though they did not see all things clearly, they were enabled to perceive many long-buried truths. As Heaven-sent messengers they went forth, rending asunder the chains of error and superstition, and calling upon those who had been so long enslaved to arise and assert their liberty.

Except among the Waldenses, the word of God had for ages been locked up in languages known only to the learned; but the time had come for the Scriptures to be translated, and given to the people of different lands in their native tongue. The world had passed its midnight. The hours of darkness were wearing away, and in many lands appeared tokens of the coming dawn.

In the fourteenth century arose in England the "morning star of the Reformation." John Wycliffe was the herald of reform, not for England alone, but for all Christendom. He was the progenitor of the Puritans; his era was an oasis in the desert.

Wycliffe received a liberal education, and with him the fear of the Lord was the beginning of wisdom. He was noted at college for his fervent piety as well as for his remarkable talents and sound scholarship. He was educated in the civil and the canon law, and sought to become acquainted with every branch of knowledge. In his after-labors the value of this early discipline was apparent. While he could wield the sword of the Spirit, he was acquainted also with the practice of the schools. This combination of accomplishments won for him the respect of all parties. His followers saw with satisfaction that heir teacher was foremost among the sages and doctors of his time. The Lord saw fit to entrust the work of reform to one whose intellectual ability would give character and dignity to his labors. This silenced the voice of contempt, and prevented the adversaries of truth from attempting to put discredit upon his cause by ridiculing the ignorance of the advocate.

When Wycliffe had mastered the learning of the schools, he entered upon the study of the Scriptures. Every subject to which he turned his attention he was accustomed to investigate thoroughly, and he pursued the same course with the Bible. Heretofore he had felt a great want, which neither his scholastic studies nor the teachings of the church could satisfy. In the Scriptures he found that which he had before sought in vain. Here he saw the plan of salvation revealed, and Christ set forth as the only advocate for man. He saw that Rome had forsaken the Biblical paths for human traditions. He gave himself to the service of Christ, and determined to proclaim the truths which he had discovered.

He commenced with great prudence, but as he discerned more clearly the errors of the papacy, he taught more earnestly the doctrine of faith. His knowledge of theology, his penetrating mind, the purity of his life, and his unbending courage and integrity, won for him general confidence and esteem. He was an able and earnest teacher, and an eloquent preacher, and his daily life was a demonstration of the truths he preached. He accused the clergy of having banished the Holy Scriptures, and demanded that the authority of the Bible should be re-established in the church. Many of the people had become dissatisfied with their former faith as they saw the iniquity that prevailed in the Roman Church, and they hailed with unconcealed joy the truths brought to view in these discussions; but the Papist leaders trembled with rage when they perceived that this reformer was gaining an influence greater than their own.

Wycliffe was a clear thinker and a keen detector of error, and he struck boldly against many of the abuses sanctioned by the authority of Rome. Thus he brought upon himself the enmity of the pope and his supporters. Repeated attempts were made to condemn and execute him for heresy; but God had given him favor with princes, who stood in his defense. While acting as chaplain for the king, he had taken a bold stand against the payment of the tribute claimed by the pope from the English monarch, and had declared the papal assumption of authority over secular rulers to be contrary to both reason and revelation. A few years later, he ably defended the rights of the English crown against the encroachments of the Romish power. The people and the nobility of England sided with him, and his enemies could accomplish nothing against him. Upon one occasion, when he was brought to trial before a synod of bishops, the people surrounded the building where the synod met, and, rushing in, stood between him and all harm.

About this time, strife was caused in the church by the conflicting claims of two rival popes. Each professed infallibility, and demanded obedience. Each called upon the faithful to assist him to make war upon the other, enforcing his demand by terrible anathemas against his adversaries, and promises of rewards in Heaven to his supporters. This occurrence greatly weakened the power of the papacy, and saved Wycliffe from further persecution.

God had preserved his servant for more important labors. Wycliffe, like his Master, preached the gospel to the poor. As a professor of theology, he presented the truth to the students under his instruction, and received the title of "The Gospel Doctor." In his parish he addressed the people as a friend and pastor.

But the greatest work of his life was the translation of the Scriptures into the English language. This was the first complete English translation ever made. The art of printing being still unknown, it was only by slow and wearisome labor that copies of the work could be multiplied; yet this was done, and the people of England received the Bible in their own tongue. Thus the light of God's word began to shed its bright beams athwart the darkness. A divine hand was preparing the way for the Great Reformation.

The appeal to men's reason aroused them from their passive submission to papal dogmas. The Scriptures were received with favor by the higher classes, who alone in that age possessed a knowledge of letters. Wycliffe now taught the distinctive doctrines of Protestantism,— salvation through faith in Christ, and the sole infallibility of the Scriptures. Many priests joined him in circulating the Bible and in preaching the gospel; and so great was the effect of these labors and of Wycliffe's writings, that the new faith was accepted by nearly one-half of the people of England. The kingdom of darkness trembled. Mendicant friars, who swarmed in England, listened in anger and amazement to his bold, eloquent utterances. The hatred of Rome was kindled to greater intensity, and again she plotted to silence the Reformer's voice. But the Lord covered with his shield the messenger of truth. The efforts of his enemies to stop his work and to destroy his life were alike unsuccessful, and in his sixty-first year he died in peace in the very service of the altar.

The doctrines which had been taught by Wycliffe continued for a time to spread; but soon the pitiless storm of persecution burst upon those who had dared to accept the Bible as their guide and standard. Martyrdom succeeded martyrdom. The advocates of truth, proscribed and tortured, could only pour their suffering cries into the ear of the Lord of Sabaoth. The hunted reformers found shelter as best they could among the lower classes, preaching in secret places, and hiding away even in dens and caves. Many bore fearless witness to the truth in massive dungeons and Lollard towers.

The Papists had failed to work their will with Wycliffe during his life, and their hatred could not be satisfied while his body rested quietly in the grave. More than forty years after his death, his bones were disinterred and publicly burned, and the ashes were thrown into a neighboring brook. "The brook," says an old writer, "did convey his ashes into Avon, Avon into Severn, Severn into the narrow seas, and they into the main ocean, and thus the ashes of Wycliffe are the emblem of his doctrine, which now is dispersed all the world over." Little did his enemies realize the significance of their malicious act.

It was through the writings of Wycliffe that John Huss of Bohemia was led to renounce many of the errors of Romanism, and to enter upon the work of reform. Like Wycliffe, Huss was a noble Christian, a man of learning and of unswerving devotion to the truth. His appeals to the Scriptures and his bold denunciations of the scandalous and immoral lives of the clergy, awakened wide-spread interest, and thousands gladly accepted a purer faith. This excited the ire of pope and prelates, priests and friars, and Huss was summoned to appear before the Council of Constance to answer to the charge of heresy.

A safe-conduct was granted him by the German emperor, and upon his arrival at Constance he was personally assured by the pope that no injustice should be done him. In a short time, however, he was placed under arrest, by order of the pope and cardinals, and thrust into a loathsome dungeon. Some of the nobles and people of Bohemia addressed to the council earnest protests against this outrage. The emperor, who was loath to permit the violation of a safe-conduct, opposed the proceedings against him. But the enemies of the Reformer were malignant and determined. They appealed to the emperor's prejudices, to his fears, to his zeal for the church. They brought forward arguments of great length to prove that he was *perfectly at liberty not to keep faith with a heretic;* and that the council, being above the emperor, *could free him from his word*. Thus they prevailed.

After a long trial, in which he firmly maintained the truth, Huss was required to choose whether he would recant his doctrines or suffer death. He chose the martyr's fate, and after seeing his books given to the flames, he was himself burned at the stake. In the presence of the assembled dignitaries of Church and State, the servant of God had uttered a solemn and faithful protest against the corruptions of the papal hierarchy. His execution, in shameless violation of the most solemn and public promise of protection, exhibited to the whole world the perfidious cruelty of Rome. The enemies of truth, though they knew it not, were furthering the cause which they sought vainly to destroy.

In the gloom of his dungeon, John Huss had foreseen the triumph of the true faith. Returning, in his dreams, to the humble parish where he had preached the gospel, he saw the pope and his bishops effacing the pictures of Christ which he had painted on the walls of his chapel. The sight caused him great distress; but the next day he was filled with joy as he beheld many artists busily engaged in replacing the figures in greater numbers and brighter colors. When their work was completed, the painters exclaimed to the immense crowd surrounding them, "Now let the popes and bishops come! They shall never efface them more!" Said the Reformer, as he related his dream, "I am certain that the image of Christ will never be effaced. They have wished to destroy it, but it shall be painted in all hearts by much better preachers than myself."

Soon after the death of Huss, his faithful friend Jerome, a man of the same fervent piety and of greater learning, was also condemned, and he met his fate in the same manner. So perished God's faithful light-bearers. But the light of the truths which they proclaimed,— the light of their heroic example,— could not be extinguished. As well might men attempt to turn back the sun in its course, as to prevent the dawning of that day which was even then breaking upon the world.

Notwithstanding the rage of persecution, a calm, devout, earnest, patient protest against the prevailing corruption of religious faith continued to be uttered after the death of Wycliffe. Like the believers in apostolic days, many freely sacrificed their worldly possessions for the cause of Christ. Those who were permitted to dwell in their homes, gladly received their brethren who had been banished from home and kindred. When they too were driven forth, they accepted the lot of the outcast, and rejoiced that they were permitted to suffer for the truths sake.

Strenuous efforts were made to strengthen and extend the power of the papacy; but while the popes still claimed to be Christ's representatives, their lives were so corrupt as to disgust the people. By the aid of the invention of printing, the Scriptures were more widely circulated, and many were led to see that the papal doctrines were not sustained by the word of God.

When one witness was forced to let fall the torch of truth, another seized it from his hand, and with undaunted courage held it aloft. The struggle had opened that was to result in the emancipation, not only of individuals and churches, but of nations. Across the gulf of a hundred years, men stretched their hands to grasp the hands of the Lollards of the time of Wycliffe. Under Luther began the Reformation in Germany; Calvin preached the gospel in France, Zwingle in Switzerland. The world was awakened from the slumber of ages, as from land to land were sounded the magic words, "Religious Liberty."

Chapter 6

Luther's Separation from Rome

Foremost among those who were called to lead the church from the darkness of Popery into the light of a purer faith, stood Martin Luther. Zealous, ardent, and devoted, knowing no fear but the fear of God, and acknowledging no foundation for religious faith but the Holy Scriptures, Luther was the man for his time; through him, God accomplished a great work for the reformation of the church and the enlightenment of the world.

Like the first heralds of the gospel, Luther sprung from the ranks of poverty. His early years were spent in the humble home of a German peasant. By daily toil as a miner, his father earned the means for his education. He intended him for a lawyer; but God designed to make him a builder in the great temple that was rising so slowly through the centuries. Hardship, privation, and severe discipline were the school in which Infinite Wisdom prepared Luther for the important mission of his life.

Luther's father was a man of strong and active mind, and great force of character, honest, resolute, and straightforward. He was true to his convictions of duty, let the consequences be what they might. His sterling good sense led him to regard the monastic system with distrust. He was highly displeased when Luther, without his consent, entered a monastery; and it was two years before the father was reconciled to his son, and even then his opinions remained the same.

Luther's parents bestowed great care upon the education and training of their children. They endeavored to instruct them in the knowledge of God and the practice of Christian virtues. The father's prayer often ascended in the hearing of his son, that the child might remember the name of the Lord, and one day aid in the advancement of his truth. Every advantage for moral or intellectual culture which their life of toil permitted them to enjoy, was eagerly improved by these parents. Their efforts were earnest and persevering to prepare their children for a life of piety and usefulness. With their firmness and strength of character they sometimes exercised too great severity; but the Reformer himself, though conscious that in some respects they had erred, found in their discipline more to approve than to condemn.

At school, where he was sent at an early age, Luther was treated with harshness and even violence. So great was the poverty of his parents, that for a time he was obliged to obtain his food by singing from door to door, and he often suffered from hunger. The gloomy, superstitious ideas of religion then prevailing filled him with fear. He would lie down at night with a sorrowful heart, looking forward with trembling to the dark future, and in constant terror at the thought of God as a stern, unrelenting judge, a cruel tyrant, rather than a kind heavenly Father. Yet under so many and so great discouragements, Luther pressed resolutely forward toward the high standard of moral and intellectual excellence which he had determined to attain.

He thirsted for knowledge, and the earnest and practical character of his mind led him to desire the solid and useful rather than the showy and superficial. When, at the age of eighteen, he entered the University of Erfurth, his situation was more favorable and his prospects brighter than in his earlier years. His parents having by thrift and industry acquired a competence, they were able to render him all needed assistance. And the influence of judicious friends had somewhat lessened the gloomy effects of his former training. He now diligently applied himself to the study of the best authors, enriching his understanding with their most weighty thoughts, and making the wisdom of the wise his own. A retentive memory, a vivid imagination, strong reasoning powers, and energetic application to study, soon won for him the foremost rank among his associates.

The fear of the Lord dwelt in the heart of Luther, enabling him to maintain his steadfastness of purpose, and leading him to deep humility before God. He had an abiding sense of his dependence upon divine aid, and he did not fail to begin each day with prayer, while his heart was continually breathing a petition for guidance and support. "To pray well," he often said, "is the better half of study."

While one day examining the books in the library of the university, Luther discovered a Latin Bible. He had before heard fragments of the Gospels and Epistles at public worship, and he thought that they were the whole of God's word. Now, for the first time, he looked upon the whole Bible. With mingled awe and wonder he turned the sacred pages; with quickened pulse and throbbing heart he read for himself the words of life, pausing now and then to exclaim, "Oh, if God would give me such a book for my own!" Angels of Heaven were by his side, and rays of light from the throne of God revealed the treasures of truth to his understanding. He had ever feared to offend God, but now the deep conviction of his condition as a sinner took hold upon him as never before.

An earnest desire to be free from sin and to find peace with God, led him at last to enter a cloister, and devote himself to a monastic life. Here he was required to perform the lowest drudgery, and to beg from house to house. He was at an age when respect and appreciation are most eagerly craved, and these menial offices were deeply mortifying to his natural feelings; but he patiently endured this humiliation, believing that it was necessary because of his sins.

Every moment that could be spared from his daily duties, he employed in study, robbing himself of sleep, and grudging even the moments spent at his humble meals. Above everything else he delighted in the study of God's word. He had found a Bible chained to the convent wall, and to this he often repaired. As his convictions of sin deepened, he sought by his own works to obtain pardon and peace. He led a most rigorous life, endeavoring to crucify the flesh by fastings, watchings, and scourgings. He shrank from no sacrifice to become holy and gain Heaven. As the result of this painful discipline, he lost strength, and suffered from fainting spasms, from the effects of which he never fully recovered. But with all his efforts, his burdened soul found no relief. He was at last driven to the verge of despair.

When it appeared to Luther that all was lost, God raised up a friend and helper for him. The pious Staupitz opened the word of God to Luther's mind, and bade him look away from himself, cease the contemplation of infinite punishment for the violation of God's law, and look to Jesus, his sin-pardoning Saviour. "Instead of torturing yourself on account of your sins, cast yourself into the arms of your Redeemer. Trust in him,— in the righteousness of his life,— in the atonement of his death. Listen to the Son of God. He became man to give you the assurance of divine favor. Love him who has first loved you." Thus spoke this messenger of mercy. His words made a deep impression upon Luther's mind. After many a struggle with long-cherished errors, he was enabled to grasp the truth, and peace came to his troubled soul.

Luther was ordained a priest, and was called from the cloister to a professorship in the University of Wittemberg. Here he applied himself to the study of the Scriptures in the original tongues. He began to lecture upon the Bible; and the book of Psalms, the Gospels, and the Epistles were opened to the understanding of crowds of delighted listeners. Staupitz, his friend and superior, urged him to ascend the pulpit, and preach the word of God. Luther hesitated, feeling himself unworthy to speak to the people in Christ's stead. It was only after a long struggle that he yielded to the solicitations of his friends. Already he was mighty in the Scriptures, and the grace of God rested upon him. His eloquence captivated his hearers, the clearness and power with which he presented the truth convinced their understanding, and his deep fervor touched their hearts.

Luther was still a true son of the papal church, and had no thought that he would ever be anything else. In the providence of God he decided to visit Rome. He pursued his journey on foot, lodging at the monasteries on the way. At a convent in Italy he was filled with wonder as he saw the splendor of the apartments, the richness of the dresses, the luxury of the table, the extravagance everywhere. With painful misgivings he contrasted this scene with the self-denial and hardship of his own life. His mind was becoming perplexed.

At last he beheld in the distance the seven-hilled city. With deep emotion he prostrated himself upon the earth, exclaiming, "Holy Rome, I salute thee!" He entered the city, visited the churches, listened to the marvelous tales repeated by priests and monks, and performed all the ceremonies required. Everywhere he looked upon scenes that filled him with astonishment and horror. He saw that iniquity existed among all classes of the clergy. He heard indecent jokes from prelates, and was filled with horror at their awful profanity, even during mass. As he mingled with the monks and citizens, he met dissipation, debauchery. Turn where he would, in the place of sanctity he found profanation. "It is incredible," he wrote, "what sins and atrocities are committed in Rome." "If there be a hell, Rome is built above it. It is an abyss whence all sins proceed."

An indulgence had been promised by the pope to all who should ascend on their knees what was known as Pilate's staircase. Luther was one day performing this act, when suddenly a voice like thunder seemed to say to him, "The just shall live by faith!" He sprung upon his feet in shame and horror, and fled from the scene of his folly. That text never lost its power upon his soul. From that time he saw more clearly than ever before the fallacy of trusting to human works for salvation, and the necessity of constant faith in the merits of Christ. His eyes had been opened, and were never again to be closed, to the Satanic delusions of the papacy. When he turned his face from Rome, he had turned away also in heart, and from that time the separation grew wider, until he severed all connection with the papal church.

After his return from Rome, Luther received at the University of Wittemberg the degree of doctor of divinity. Now he was at liberty to devote himself, as never before, to the Scriptures that he loved. He had taken a solemn vow to study carefully and to preach with fidelity the word of God, not the sayings and doctrines of the popes, all the days of his life. He was no longer the mere monk or professor, but the authorized herald of the Bible. He had been called as a shepherd to feed the flock of God, that were hungering and thirsting for the truth. He firmly declared that Christians should receive no other doctrines than those which rest on the authority of the Sacred Scriptures. These words struck at the very foundation of papal supremacy. They contained the vital principle of the Reformation.

Luther saw the danger of exalting human theories above the word of God. He fearlessly attacked the speculative infidelity of the schoolmen, and opposed the philosophy and theology which had so long held a controlling influence upon the people. He denounced such studies as not only worthless but pernicious, and sought to turn the minds of his hearers from the sophistries of philosophers and theologians to the eternal truths set forth by prophets and apostles.

Precious was the message which he bore to the eager crowds that hung upon his words. Never before had such teachings fallen upon their ears. The glad tidings of a Saviour's love, the assurance of pardon and peace through his atoning blood, rejoiced their hearts, and inspired within them an immortal hope. At Wittemberg a light was kindled whose rays should extend to the uttermost parts of the earth, and which was to increase in brightness to the close of time.

But light and darkness cannot harmonize. Between truth and error there is an irrepressible conflict. To uphold and defend the one is to attack and overthrow the other. Our Saviour himself declared, "I came not to send peace, but a sword." [MATT. 10:34.] Said Luther, a few years after the opening of the Reformation, "God does not conduct, but drives me forward. I am not master of my own actions. I would gladly live in repose, but I am thrown into the midst of tumults and revolutions." He was now about to be urged into the contest.

The Roman Church had made merchandise of the grace of God. The tables of the money-changers were set up beside her altars, and the air resounded with the shouts of buyers and sellers. Under the plea of raising funds for the erection of St. Peter's church at Rome, indulgences for sin were publicly offered for sale by the authority of the pope. By the price of crime a temple was to be built up for God's worship,— the corner-stone laid with the wages of iniquity. But the very means of Rome's aggrandizement provoked the deadliest blow to her power and greatness. It was this that aroused the most determined and successful of the enemies of Popery, and led to the battle which shook the papal throne to its foundation, and jostled the triple crown upon the pontiff's head.

The official appointed to conduct the sale of indulgences in Germany— Tetzel by name— had been convicted of the basest offenses against society and against the law of God; but having escaped the punishment due to his crimes, he was employed to further the mercenary and unscrupulous projects of the Romish Church. With great effrontery he repeated the most glaring falsehoods, and related marvelous tales to deceive an ignorant, credulous, and superstitious people. Had they possessed the word of God, they would not have been thus deceived. It was to keep them under the control of the papacy, that they might swell the power and wealth of her ambitious leaders, that the Bible had been withheld from them.

As Tetzel entered a town, a messenger went before him, announcing, "The grace of God and of the holy father is at your gates." And the people welcomed the blasphemous pretender as if he were God himself come down from Heaven to them. The infamous traffic was set up in the church, and Tetzel, ascending the pulpit, extolled indulgences as the most precious gift of God. He declared that by virtue of his certificates of pardon, all the sins which the purchaser should afterward desire to commit would be forgiven him, and that even repentance was not indispensable. More than this, he assured his hearers that the indulgences had power to save not only the living but the dead; that the very moment the money should clink against the bottom of his chest, the soul in whose behalf it had been paid would escape from purgatory and make its way to Heaven.

When Simon Magus offered to purchase of the apostles the power to work miracles, Peter answered him, "Thy money perish with thee, because thou hast thought that the gift of God may be purchased with money." [ACTS 8:20.] But Tetzel's offer was grasped by eager thousands. Gold and silver flowed into his treasury. A salvation that could be bought with money was more easily obtained than that which requires repentance, faith, and diligent effort to resist and overcome sin.

The doctrine of indulgences had been opposed by men of learning and piety in the Romish Church, and there were many who had no faith in pretensions so contrary to both reason and revelation. Yet no bishop dared lift his voice against the fraud and corruption of this iniquitous traffic. The minds of men were becoming disturbed and uneasy, and many eagerly inquired if God would not work through some instrumentality for the purification of his church.

Luther, though still a Papist of the straitest sort, was filled with horror at the blasphemous assumptions of the indulgence-mongers. Many of his own congregation had purchased certificates of pardon, and they soon began to come to their pastor, confessing their various sins, and expecting absolution, not because they were penitent and wished to reform, but on the ground of the indulgence. Luther refused them absolution, and warned them that unless they should repent, and reform their lives, they must perish in their sins. In great perplexity they sought out Tetzel, and informed him that an Augustine monk had treated his letters with contempt. The friar was filled with rage. He uttered the most terrible curses, caused fires to be lighted in the public square, and declared that he had orders from the pope to burn the heretics who dared oppose his most holy indulgences.

Luther now entered boldly upon his work as a champion of the truth. His voice was heard from the pulpit in earnest, solemn warning. He set before the people the offensive character of sin, and taught them that it is impossible for man, by his own works, to lessen its guilt or evade its punishment. Nothing but repentance toward God and faith in Christ can save the sinner. The grace of Christ cannot be purchased; it is a free gift. He counseled the people not to buy the indulgences, but to look in faith to a crucified Redeemer. He related his own painful experience in vainly seeking by humiliation and penance to secure salvation, and assured his hearers that it was by looking away from himself and believing in Christ that he found peace and joy.

As Tetzel continued his traffic and his impious pretensions, Luther determined upon a more effectual protest against these crying abuses. The festival of All-Saints was an important day for Wittemberg. The costly relics of the church were then displayed, and remission of sin was granted to all who visited the church and made confession. Accordingly on this day the people in great numbers resorted thither. On the day preceding the festival, Luther went boldly to the church, to which crowds of worshipers were already repairing, and affixed to the door ninety-five propositions against the doctrine of indulgences. These theses he declared himself ready to defend against all opposers.

His propositions attracted universal attention. They were read and re-read and repeated in every direction. Great excitement was created in the university and in the whole city. By these theses it was shown that the power to grant the pardon of sin, and to remit its penalty, had never been committed to the pope or to any other man. The whole scheme was a farce,— an artifice to extort money by playing upon the superstitions of the people,— a device of Satan to destroy the souls of all who should trust to its lying pretensions. It was also clearly shown that the gospel of Christ is the most valuable treasure of the church, and that the grace of God, therein revealed, is freely bestowed upon all who seek it by repentance and faith.

Luther's theses challenged discussion; but no one dared accept the challenge The questions which he proposed had in a few days spread through all Germany, and in a few weeks they had sounded throughout Christendom. Many devoted Romanists, who had seen and lamented the terrible iniquity prevailing in the church, but had not known how to arrest its progress, read the propositions with great joy, recognizing in them the voice of God. They felt that the Lord had graciously set his hand to arrest the rapidly swelling tide of corruption that was issuing from the see of Rome. Princes and magistrates secretly rejoiced that a check was to be put upon the arrogant power from which there was no appeal.

But the sin-loving and superstitious multitudes were terrified as the sophistries that had soothed their fears were swept away. Crafty ecclesiastics, interrupted in their work of sanctioning crime, and seeing their gains endangered, were enraged, and rallied to uphold their pretensions. The Reformer had bitter accusers to meet. Some charged him with acting hastily and from impulse. Others accused him of presumption, declaring that he was not directed of God, but was acting from pride and forwardness. "Who does not know," he responded, "that one can seldom advance a new idea without having some appearance of pride, and without being accused of exciting quarrels? Why were Christ and all the martyrs put to death?— Because they appeared proud despisers of the wisdom of the times in which they lived, and because they brought forward new truths without having first consulted the oracles of the old opinions."

Again he declared: "What I am doing will not be effected by the prudence of man, but by the counsel of God. If the work be of God, who shall stop it? If it be not, who shall forward it? Not my will, not theirs, not ours, but thy will, holy Father who art in Heaven!"

Though Luther had been moved by the Spirit of God to begin his work, he was not to carry it forward without severe conflicts. The reproaches of his enemies, their misrepresentation of his purposes, and their unjust and malicious reflections upon his character and motives, came in upon him like an overwhelming flood; and they were not without effect. He had felt confident that the leaders in the church and the philosophers of the nation, would gladly unite with him in efforts for reform. Words of encouragement from those in high position had inspired him with joy and hope. Already in anticipation he had seen a brighter day dawning for the church. But encouragement had changed to reproach and condemnation. Many dignitaries, both of Church and State, were convicted of the truthfulness of his theses; but they soon saw that the acceptance of these truths would involve great changes. To enlighten and reform the people would be virtually to undermine the papal authority, to stop thousands of streams now flowing into her treasury, and thus greatly to curtail the extravagance and luxury of the Romish leaders. Furthermore, to teach the people to think and act as responsible beings, looking to Christ alone for salvation, would overthrow the pontiff's throne, and eventually destroy their own authority. For this reason they refused the knowledge tendered them of God, and arrayed themselves against Christ and the truth by their opposition to the man whom he had sent to enlighten them.

Luther trembled as he looked upon himself,—one man opposed to the mightiest powers of earth. He sometimes doubted whether he had indeed been led of God to set himself against the authority of the church. "Who was I," he writes, "to oppose the majesty of the pope, before whom the kings of the earth and the whole world trembled?" "No one can know what I suffered in those first two years, and into what dejection and even despair I was sunk." But he was not left to become utterly disheartened. When human support failed, he looked to God alone, and learned that he could lean in perfect safety upon that all-powerful arm.

To a friend of the Reformation Luther wrote: "We cannot attain to the understanding of Scripture either by study or strength of intellect. Therefore your first duty must be to begin with prayer. Entreat the Lord to deign to grant you, in his rich mercy, rightly to understand his word. There is no other interpreter of the word but the Author of that word himself. Even as he has said, 'They shall be all taught of God.' Hope nothing from your study and strength of intellect; but simply put your trust in God, and in the guidance of his Spirit. Believe one who has made trial of this matter." Here is a lesson of vital importance to those who feel that God has called them to present to others the solemn truths for this time. These truths will stir the enmity of Satan, and of men who love the fables that he has devised. In the conflict with the powers of evil, there is need of something more than intellect and human wisdom.

When enemies appealed to custom and tradition, or to the assertions and authority of the pope, Luther met them with the Bible and the Bible alone. Here were arguments which they could not answer; therefore the slaves of formalism and superstition clamored for his blood, as the Jews had clamored for the blood of Christ. "He is a heretic," cried the Roman zealots; "it is a sin to allow him to live an hour longer! Away with him at once to the scaffold!" But Luther did not fall a prey to their fury. God had a work for him to do, and angels of Heaven were sent to protect him. Many, however, who had received from Luther the precious light, were made the objects of Satan's wrath, and for the truth's sake fearlessly suffered torture and death.

Luther's teachings attracted the attention of thoughtful minds throughout all Germany. From his sermons and writings issued beams of light which awakened and illuminated thousands. A living faith was taking the place of the dead formalism in which the church had so long been held. The people were daily losing confidence in the superstitions of Romanism. The barriers of prejudice were giving way. The word of God, by which Luther tested every doctrine and every claim, was like a two-edged sword, cutting its way to the hearts of the people. Everywhere there was awakening a desire for spiritual progress. Everywhere was such a hungering and thirsting after righteousness as had not been known for ages. The eyes of the people, so long directed to human rites and human mediators, were now turning, in penitence and faith, to Christ and him crucified.

This wide-spread interest aroused still further the fears of the papal authorities. Luther received a summons to appear at Rome to answer to the charge of heresy. The command filled his friends with terror. They knew full well the danger that threatened him in that corrupt city, already drunk with the blood of the martyrs of Jesus. They protested against his going to Rome, and requested that he receive his examination in Germany.

This arrangement was finally effected, and the pope's legate was appointed to hear the case. In the instructions communicated by the pontiff to this official, it was stated that Luther had already been declared a heretic. The legate was therefore charged to prosecute and reduce him to submission without delay. If he should remain steadfast, and the legate should fail to gain possession of his person, he was empowered to proscribe him in all places in Germany, to put away, curse, and excommunicate all who were attached to him. And further, the pope called upon his legate, in order entirely to root out the pestilent heresy, to excommunicate all, of whatever dignity in Church or State, except the emperor, who should neglect to seize Luther and his adherents, and deliver them up to suffer the vengeance of Rome.

Here is displayed the true spirit of Popery. Not a trace of Christian principle, or even of common justice, is to be seen in the whole document. Luther was at a great distance from Rome; he had had no opportunity to explain or defend his position; yet before his case had been investigated, he was summarily pronounced a heretic, and in the same day, exhorted, accused, judged, and condemned; and all this by the self-styled holy father, the only supreme, infallible authority in Church or State!

Augsburg had been fixed upon as the place of trial, and the Reformer set out on foot to perform the journey thither. Serious fears were entertained in his behalf. Threats had been made openly that he would be waylaid and murdered on the way, and his friends begged him not to venture. They even entreated him to leave Wittemberg for a time, and find safety with those who would gladly protect him. But he would not leave the position where God had placed him. He must continue faithfully to maintain the truth, notwithstanding the storms that were beating upon him. His language was: "I am like Jeremiah, a man of strife and contention; but the more they increase their threatenings, the more they multiply my joy... They have already torn to pieces my honor and my good name. All I have left is my wretched body; let them have it; they will then shorten my life by a few hours. But as to my soul, they shall not have that. He who resolves to bear the word of Christ to the world, must expect death at every hour."

The tidings of Luther's arrival at Augsburg gave great satisfaction to the papal legate. The troublesome heretic who was exciting the attention of the whole world seemed now in the power of Rome, and the legate determined that he should not leave the city as he had entered. The Reformer had failed to provide himself with a safe-conduct. His friends urged him not to appear before the legate without one, and they themselves undertook to procure it from the emperor. The legate intended to force Luther, if possible, to retract, or, failing in this, to cause him to be conveyed to Rome, to share the fate of Huss and Jerome. Therefore through his agents he endeavored to induce Luther to appear without a safe-conduct, trusting himself to his mercy. This the Reformer firmly declined to do. Not until he had received the document pledging him the emperor's protection, did he appear in the presence of the papal ambassador.

As a matter of policy, the Romanists had decided to attempt to win Luther by an appearance of gentleness. The legate, in his interviews with him, professed great friendliness; but he demanded that Luther submit implicitly to the authority of the church, and yield every point without argument or question. He had not rightly estimated the character of the man with whom he had to deal. Luther, in reply, expressed his regard for the church, his desire for the truth, his readiness to answer all objections to what he had taught, and to submit his doctrines to the decision of certain leading universities. But at the same time he protested against the cardinal's course in requiring him to retract without having proved him in error.

The only response was, "Recant, recant." The Reformer showed that his position was sustained by the Scriptures, and firmly declared that he could not renounce the truth.

When the prelate saw that Luther's reasoning was unanswerable, he lost all self-control, and in a rage cried out: "Retract, or I will send you to Rome, there to appear before the judges commissioned to take cognizance of your case. I will excommunicate you and all your partisans, and all who shall at any time countenance you, and will cast them out of the church." And he finally declared, in a haughty and angry tone, "Retract, or return no more."

The Reformer retired with his friends, leaving the cardinal and his supporters to look at one another in utter confusion at the unexpected result of the conference.

Luther's efforts on this occasion were not without good results. The large assembly present had opportunity to compare the two men, and to judge for themselves of the spirit manifested by them, as well as of the strength and truthfulness of their positions. How marked the contrast! The Reformer, simple, humble, firm, stood up in the strength of God, having truth on his side; the pope's representative, self-important, overbearing, haughty, and unreasonable, was without a single argument from the Scriptures yet vehemently crying, "Retract, or be sent to Rome for punishment."

Notwithstanding Luther had secured a safe-conduct, the Romanists were plotting to seize and imprison him. His friends urged that as it was useless for him to prolong his stay, he should return to Wittemberg without delay, and that the utmost caution should be observed in order to conceal his intentions. He accordingly left Augsburg before daybreak, on horseback, accompanied only by a guide furnished him by the magistrate. With many forebodings he secretly made his way through the dark and silent streets of the city. Enemies, vigilant and cruel, were plotting his destruction. Would he escape the snares prepared for him? Those were moments of anxiety and earnest prayer. He reached a small gate in the wall of the city. It was opened for him, and with his guide he passed through without hindrance. Once beyond the limits, he soon left the city far behind. Satan and his emissaries were defeated. The man whom they had thought in their power was gone, escaped as a bird from the snare of the fowler.

At the news of Luther's departure, the legate was overwhelmed with surprise and anger. He had expected to receive great honor for his wisdom and firmness in dealing with this disturber of the church; but his hope was disappointed. He gave expression to his wrath in a letter to Frederick, the elector of Saxony, bitterly denouncing Luther, and demanding that Frederick send the Reformer to Rome or banish him from Saxony.

In defense, Luther urged that the legate or the pope show him his errors from the Scriptures, and pledged himself in the most solemn manner to renounce his doctrines if they could be shown to contradict the word of God. And he expressed his gratitude to God that he had been counted worthy to suffer in so holy a cause. These words made a deep impression upon the elector, and he resolved to stand as Luther's protector. He refused to send him to Rome, or to expel him from his territories.

The elector saw that there was a general breaking down of the moral restraints of society. A great work of reform was needed. The complicated and expensive arrangements to restrain and punish crime would be unnecessary if men but acknowledged and obeyed the requirements of God and the dictates of an enlightened conscience. He saw that Luther was laboring to secure this object, and he secretly rejoiced that a better influence was making itself felt in the church.

He saw also that as a professor in the university, Luther was eminently successful. From all parts of Germany, students crowded to Wittemberg to listen to his teachings. Young men, coming in sight of the city for the first time, would raise their hands toward heaven, and thank God that he had caused the light of his truth to shine forth from that place as in former ages from Jerusalem.

Luther was as yet but partially converted from the errors of Romanism. But as he compared the holy oracles with the papal decrees and constitutions, he was filled with wonder. "I am reading," he wrote, "the decretals of the popes, and …I know not whether the pope is antichrist himself, or whether he is his apostle, so misrepresented and even crucified does Christ appear in them." Yet at this time Luther was still a supporter of the Roman Church, and had no thought that he would ever separate from her communion.

The Reformer's writings and his doctrine were extending to every nation in Christendom. The work spread to Switzerland and Holland. Copies of his writings found their way to France and Spain. In England his teachings were received as the word of life. To Belgium and Italy also the truth had extended. Thousands were awakening from their deathlike stupor to the joy and hope of a life of faith.

Rome became more and more exasperated by the attacks of Luther, and it was secretly declared by some of his fanatical opponents, that he who should take his life would be without sin. One day a stranger, with a pistol concealed under his cloak, approached the Reformer, and inquired why he went thus alone. "I am in the hands of God," answered Luther. "He is my help and my shield. What can men do unto me?" Upon hearing these words, the stranger turned pale, and fled away, as from the presence of the angels of Heaven.

Rome was bent upon the destruction of Luther; but God was his defense. His doctrines were heard everywhere,— in convents, in cottages, in the castles of the nobles, in the universities, in the palaces of kings; and noble men were rising on every hand to sustain his efforts.

In an appeal to the emperor and nobility of Germany in behalf of the Reformation of Christianity, Luther wrote concerning the pope: "It is monstrous to see him who is called the vicar of Christ, displaying a magnificence unrivaled by that of any emperor. Is this to represent the poor and lowly Jesus or the humble St. Peter? The pope, say they, is the lord of the world! But Christ, whose vicar he boasts of being, said, 'My kingdom is not of this world.' Can the dominions of a vicar extend beyond those of his superior?"

He wrote thus of the universities: "I fear much that the universities will be found to be great gates leading down to hell, unless they take diligent care to explain the Holy Scriptures, and to engrave them in the hearts of youth. I advise no one to place his child where the Holy Scriptures are not regarded as the rule of life. Every institution where the word of God is not diligently studied, must become corrupt."

This appeal was rapidly circulated throughout Germany, and exerted a powerful influence upon the people. The whole nation was roused to rally around the standard of reform. Luther's opponents, burning with a desire for revenge, urged the pope to take decisive measures against him. It was decreed that his doctrines should be condemned immediately. Sixty days were granted the Reformer and his adherents, after which, if they did not recant, they were all to be excommunicated.

That was a terrible crisis for the Reformation. For centuries Rome's sentence of excommunication had been swiftly followed by the stroke of death. Luther was not blind to the tempest about to burst upon him; but he stood firm, trusting in Christ to be his support and shield. With a martyr's faith and courage he wrote: "What is about to happen I know not, and I care not to know." "Wherever the blow may reach me, I fear not. Not so much as a leaf falls without the will of our

Father; how much rather will he care for us! It is a little matter to die for the Word, since his Word, that was made flesh for us, hath himself died. If we die with him, we shall live with him; and, passing through that which he has passed through before us, we shall be where he is, and dwell with him forever."

When the papal bull reached Luther, he said: "I despise it, and resist it, as impious and false. It is *Christ* himself who is condemned therein." "I glory in the prospect of suffering for the best of causes. Already I feel greater liberty; for I know now that the pope is antichrist, and that his throne is that of Satan himself."

Yet the word of the pontiff of Rome still had power. Prison, torture, and sword were weapons potent to enforce submission. Everything seemed to indicate that the Reformer's work was about to close. The weak and superstitious trembled before the decree of the pope, and while there was general sympathy for Luther, many felt that life was too dear to be risked in the cause of reform.

But Luther proceeded to publicly burn the pope's bull, with the canon laws, the decretals, and certain writings sustaining the papal power. By this action he boldly declared his final separation from the Roman Church. He accepted his excommunication, and proclaimed to the world that between himself and the pope there must hereafter be war. The great contest was now fully entered upon. Soon after, a new bull appeared, and the excommunication which had before been threatened, was finally pronounced against the Reformer and all who should receive his doctrines.

Opposition is the lot of all whom God employs to present truths specially applicable to their time. There was a present truth,— a truth at that time of special importance,— in the days of Luther; there is a present truth for the church to-day. But truth is no more desired by the majority to-day than it was by the Papists who opposed Luther. There is the same disposition to accept the theories and traditions of men for the word of God as in former ages. Those who present truth for this time should not expect to be received with greater favor than were earlier reformers. The great controversy between truth and error, between Christ and Satan, is to increase in intensity to the close of this world's history.

Chapter 7

Luther Before the Diet

A new emperor, Charles the Fifth, had ascended the throne of Germany, and the emissaries of Rome hastened to present their congratulations, and induce the monarch to employ his power against the Reformation. On the other hand, the Elector of Saxony, to whom Charles was in great degree indebted for his crown, entreated him to take no step against Luther until he should have granted him a hearing. The emperor was thus placed in a position of great perplexity and embarrassment. The Papists would be satisfied with nothing short of an imperial edict sentencing Luther to death. The elector had declared firmly that neither his imperial majesty nor any one else had yet made it appear to him that the Reformer's writings had been refuted; therefore he requested that Doctor Luther be furnished with a safe-conduct, so that he might answer for himself before a tribunal of learned, pious, and impartial judges.

The attention of all parties was now directed to the assembly of the German States which convened at Worms soon after the accession of Charles to the empire. There were important political questions and interests to be considered by this national council; but these appeared of little moment when contrasted with the cause of the monk of Wittemberg.

Charles had previously directed the elector to bring Luther with him to the Diet, assuring him that the Reformer should be protected from all violence, and should be allowed a free conference with one competent to discuss the disputed points. Luther was anxious to appear before the emperor. His health was at this time much impaired; yet he wrote to the elector: "If I cannot perform the journey to Worms in good health, I will be carried there, sick as I am. For, since the emperor has summoned me, I cannot doubt that it is the call of God himself. If they intend to use violence against me, as they probably do, for assuredly it is with no view of gaining information that they require me to appear before them, I place the matter in the Lord's hands. He still lives and reigns who preserved the three Israelites in the fiery furnace. If it be not his will to save me, my life is of little consequence. Let us only take care that the gospel be not exposed to the scorn of the ungodly, and let us shed our blood in its defense rather than allow them to triumph. Who shall say whether my life or my death would contribute most to the salvation of my brethren?" "Expect anything from me but flight or recantation. Fly I cannot; still less can I recant."

As the news was circulated at Worms that Luther was to appear before the Diet, a general excitement was created. Aleander, the papal legate to whom his case had been specially entrusted, was alarmed and enraged. He saw that the result would be disastrous to the papal cause. To institute inquiry into a case in which the pope had already pronounced sentence of condemnation, would be to cast contempt upon the authority of the sovereign pontiff. Furthermore, he was apprehensive that the eloquent and powerful arguments of this man might turn away many of the princes from the cause of the pope. He therefore, in the most urgent manner, remonstrated with Charles against Luther's appearance at Worms. He warned, entreated, and threatened, until the emperor yielded, and wrote to the elector that if Luther would not retract, he must remain at Wittemberg.

Not content with this victory, Aleander labored with all the power and cunning at his command to secure Luther's condemnation. With a persistence worthy of a better cause, he urged the matter upon the attention of princes, prelates, and other members of the assembly, accusing the Reformer of sedition, rebellion, impiety, and blasphemy. But the vehemence and passion manifested by the legate plainly revealed that he was actuated by hatred and revenge rather than by zeal for religion. It was the prevailing sentiment of the assembly that Luther was innocent.

With redoubled zeal, Aleander urged upon the emperor the duty of executing the papal edicts. Overcome at last by this importunity, Charles bade the legate present his case to the Diet. Rome had few advocates better fitted, by nature and education, to defend her cause. The friends of the Reformer looked forward with some anxiety to the result of Aleander's speech.

There was no little excitement when the legate, with great dignity and pomp, appeared before the national assembly. Many called to mind the scene of our Saviour's trial, when Annas and Caiaphas, before the judgment-seat of Pilate, demanded the death of him "that perverted the people."

With all the power of learning and eloquence, Aleander set himself to overthrow the truth. Charge after charge he hurled against Luther as an enemy of the Church and the State, the living and the dead, clergy and laity, councils and private Christians. "There is enough in the errors of Luther." he declared, "to warrant the burning of a hundred thousand heretics."

In conclusion, he endeavored to cast contempt upon the adherents of the reformed faith: "What are all these Lutherans?— A motley rabble of insolent grammarians, corrupt priests, dissolute monks, ignorant lawyers, and degraded nobles, with the common people whom they have misled and perverted. How greatly superior is the Catholic party in numbers, intelligence, and power! A unanimous decree from this illustrious assembly will open the eyes of the simple, show the unwary their danger, determine the wavering, and strengthen the weak-hearted."

With such weapons have the advocates of truth in every age been attacked. The same arguments are still urged against all who dare to present, in opposition to established errors, the plain and direct teachings of God's word. "Who are these preachers of new doctrines?" exclaim those who desire a popular religion. "They are unlearned, few in numbers, and of the poorer class. Yet they claim to have the truth, and to be the chosen people of God. They are ignorant and deceived. How greatly superior in numbers and influence are our denominations! How many great and learned men are in our churches! How much more power is on our side!" These are the arguments that have a telling influence upon the world; but they are no more conclusive now than in the days of the Reformer.

The Reformation did not, as many suppose, end with Luther. It is to be continued to the close of this world's history. Luther had a great work to do in reflecting to others the light which God had permitted to shine upon him; yet he did not receive all the light which was to be given to the world. From that time to this, new light has been continually shining upon the Scriptures, and new truths have been constantly unfolding.

The legate's address made a deep impression upon the Diet. There was no Luther present, with the clear and convincing truths of God's word, to vanquish the papal champion. No attempt was made to defend the Reformer. There was manifest a general impulse to root out the Lutheran heresy from the empire. Rome had enjoyed the most favorable opportunity to defend her cause. The greatest of her orators had spoken. All that she could say in her own vindication had been said. But the apparent victory was the signal of defeat. Henceforth the contrast between truth and error would be more clearly seen, as they should take the field in open warfare. Never from that day would Rome stand as secure as she had stood.

The majority of the assembly were ready to sacrifice Luther to the demands of the pope; but many of them saw and deplored the existing depravity in the church, and desired a suppression of the abuses suffered by the German people in consequence of Rome's corruption and greed of gain. The legate had presented the papal rule in the most favorable light. Now the Lord moved upon a member of the Diet to give a true delineation of the effects of papal tyranny. With noble firmness, Duke George of Saxony stood up in that princely assembly, and specified with terrible exactness the deceptions and abominations of Popery, and their dire results. In closing he said:—

"These are but a few of the abuses which cry out against Rome for redress. All shame is laid aside, and one object alone incessantly pursued: money! evermore money! so that the very men whose duty it is to teach the truth, utter nothing but falsehoods, and are not only tolerated but rewarded; because the greater their lies, the greater are their gains. This is the foul source from which so many corrupt streams flow out on every side. Profligacy and avarice go hand in hand. Alas! it is the scandal caused by the clergy that plunges so many poor souls into everlasting perdition. A thorough reform must be effected."

A more able and forcible denunciation of the papal abuses could not have been made by Luther himself; and the fact that the speaker was a determined enemy of the Reformer, gave greater influence to his words.

Had the eyes of the assembly been opened, they would have beheld angels of God in the midst of them, shedding beams of light athwart the darkness of error, and opening minds and hearts to the reception of truth. It was the power of the God of truth and wisdom that controlled even the adversaries of the Reformation, and thus prepared the way for the great work about to be accomplished. Martin Luther was not present; but the voice of One greater than Luther had been heard in that assembly.

The council now demanded the Reformer's appearance before them. Notwithstanding the entreaties, protests, and threats of Alean-der, the emperor at last consented, and Luther was summoned to appear before the Diet. With the summons was issued a safe-conduct, insuring his return to a place of security. These were borne to Wittemberg by a herald, who was commissioned to conduct him to Worms.

The friends of Luther were terrified and distressed. Knowing the prejudice and enmity against him, they feared that even his safe-conduct would not be respected, and they entreated him not to imperil his life. He replied: "The Papists have little desire to see me at Worms, but they long for my condemnation and death. It matters not. Pray not for me, but for the word of God... Christ will give me his Spirit to overcome these ministers of Satan. I despise them while I live; I will triumph over them by my death. They are busy at Worms about compelling me to recant. My recantation shall be this: I said formerly that the pope was Christ's vicar; now I say that he is the adversary of the Lord, and the apostle of the devil."

Luther was not to make his perilous journey alone. Besides the imperial messenger, three of his firmest friends determined to accom-pany him. A multitude of students and citizens, to whom the gospel was precious, bade him farewell with weeping, as he departed. Thus the Reformer and his companions set out from Wittemberg.

On the journey they saw that the minds of the people were oppressed by gloomy forebodings. At some towns no honors were proffered them. As they stopped for the night, a friendly priest expressed his fears by holding up before Luther the portrait of an

Italian reformer who had suffered martyrdom for the truth's sake. The next day they learned that Luther's writings had been condemned at Worms. Imperial messengers were proclaiming the emperor's decree, and urging all men to bring the proscribed works to the magistrates. The herald, in alarm, asked the Reformer if he still wished to go forward. He answered, "I will go on, though I should be put under interdict in every town."

At Erfurth, Luther was received with honor. Surrounded by admiring crowds, he entered the city where, in his earlier years, he had often begged a morsel of bread. He was urged to preach. This he had been forbidden to do; but the herald gave his consent, and the monk whose duty it once was to unclose the gates and sweep the aisles, now ascended the pulpit, while the people listened to his words as if spell-bound. The bread of life was broken to those starving souls. Christ was lifted up before them as above popes, legates, emperors, and kings. Luther made no reference to his own perilous position. He did not seek to make himself the object of thought or sympathy. In the contemplation of Christ, he had lost sight of self. He hid behind the Man of Calvary, seeking only to present Jesus as the sinner's Redeemer.

As the Reformer proceeded on his journey, he was everywhere regarded with great interest. An eager multitude thronged about him; and friendly voices warned him of the purpose of the Romanists. "You will be burned alive," said they, "and your body reduced to ashes, as was that of John Huss." Luther answered, "Though they should kindle a fire all the way from Worms to Wittemberg, whose flames should rise up to heaven, I would go through it in the name of the Lord, and stand before them; I would enter the jaws of this behemoth, and break his teeth, confessing the Lord Jesus Christ."

The news of his approach to Worms created great commotion. His friends trembled for his safety; his enemies feared for the success of their cause. Strenuous efforts were made to dissuade him from entering the city. The Papists urged him to repair to the castle of a friendly knight, where, they declared, all difficulties could be amicably adjusted. The advocates of truth endeavored to excite his fears by describing the dangers that threatened him. All their efforts failed. Luther, still unshaken, declared, "Though there should be as many devils at Worms as there are tiles on its roofs, I would enter."

Upon his arrival at Worms, the crowd that flocked to the gates to welcome him was even greater than at the public entry of the emperor himself. The excitement was intense, and from the midst of the throng a shrill and plaintive voice chanted a funeral dirge, as a warning to Luther of the fate that awaited him. "God will be my defense," said he, as he alighted from his carriage.

The emperor immediately convoked his council to consider what course should be pursued toward Luther. One of the bishops, a rigid Papist, declared: "We have long consulted on this matter. Let your majesty get rid of this man at once. Did not Sigismund bring John Huss to the stake? We are under no obligation either to give or to observe the safe-conduct of a heretic." "Not so," said the emperor; "we must keep our promise." It was therefore decided that the Reformer should be heard.

All the city were eager to see this remarkable man, and he had enjoyed but a few hours' rest when noblemen, knights, priests, and citizens gathered about him. Even his enemies marked his firm, courageous bearing, the kindly and joyous expression upon his countenance, and the solemn elevation and deep earnestness that gave to his words an irresistible power. Some were convinced that a divine influence attended him; others declared, as had the Pharisees concerning Christ, "He hath a devil."

On the following day, Luther was summoned to attend the Diet. An imperial officer was appointed to conduct him to the hall of audience; yet it was with difficulty that he reached the place. Every avenue was crowded with spectators, eager to look upon the monk who had dared resist the authority of the pope.

As he was about to enter the presence of his judges, an old general, the hero of many battles, said to him kindly, "Poor monk! poor monk! thou art now going to make a nobler stand than I, or any other captains, have ever made in our most bloody battles. But if thy cause is just, and thou art sure of it, go forward in God's name, and fear nothing! He will not forsake thee."

At length Luther stood before the council. The emperor occupied the throne. He was surrounded by the most illustrious personages in the empire. Never had any man appeared in the presence of a more imposing assembly than that before which Martin Luther was to answer for his faith.

The very fact of that appearance was a signal victory for the truth. That a man whom the pope had condemned should be judged by another tribunal, was virtually a denial of the pontiff's supreme authority. The Reformer, placed under ban, and denounced from human fellowship by the pope, had been assured protection, and was granted a hearing, by the highest dignitaries of the nation. Rome had commanded him to be silent; but he was about to speak in the presence of thousands from all parts of Christendom.

In the presence of that powerful and titled assembly, the lowly-born Reformer seemed awed and embarrassed. Several of the princes, observing his emotion, approached him, and one of them whispered, "Fear not them which kill the body, but are not able to kill the soul." Another said, "When ye shall be brought before governors and kings for my sake, it shall be given you, by the Spirit of your Father, what ye shall say." Thus the words of Christ were brought by the world's great men to strengthen his servant in the hour of trial.

Luther was conducted to a position directly in front of the emperor's throne. A deep silence fell upon the crowded assembly. Then an imperial officer arose, and, pointing to a collection of Luther's writings, demanded that the Reformer answer two questions,— whether he acknowledged them as his, and whether he proposed to retract the opinions which he had therein advanced. Luther replied that as to the first question, he acknowledged the books to be his. "As to the second," he said, "seeing it is a question which concerns faith, the salvation of souls, and the word of God, which is the greatest and most precious treasure either in Heaven or earth, it would be rash and perilous for me to reply without reflection. I might affirm less than the circumstances demand, or more than truth requires; in either case I should fall under the sentence of Christ: 'Whosoever shall deny me before men, him will I also deny before the Father which is in Heaven.' For this reason I entreat your imperial majesty, with all humility, to allow me time, that I may answer without offending against the word of God."

In making this request, Luther moved wisely. His course convinced the assembly that he did not act from passion or impulse. Such calmness and self-command, unexpected in one who had shown himself bold and uncompromising, added to his power, and enabled him afterward to answer with a prudence, decision, wisdom, and dignity, that surprised and disappointed his adversaries, and rebuked their insolence and pride.

The next day he was to appear to render his second answer. For a time his heart sunk within him as he contemplated the forces that were combined against the truth. His faith faltered as his enemies seemed to multiply before him, and the powers of darkness to prevail. Clouds gathered about him, and seemed to separate him from God. He longed for the assurance that the Lord of hosts would be with him. In anguish of spirit he threw himself with his face upon the earth, and poured out those broken, heart-rending cries which none but God can fully understand. In his helplessness, his soul fastened upon Christ, the mighty deliverer. It was not for his own safety, but for the success of the truth, that he wrestled with God; and he prevailed. He was strengthened with the assurance that he would not appear alone before the council. Peace returned to his soul, and he rejoiced that he was permitted to uphold and defend the word of God before the rulers of the nation. An all-wise providence had permitted Luther to realize his peril, that he might not trust to his own strength and wisdom, and rush presumptuously into danger. God was preparing his servant for the great work before him.

As the time for his appearance drew near, Luther approached a table on which lay the Holy Scriptures, placed his left hand upon the sacred volume, and, raising his right hand to Heaven, he vowed to adhere constantly to the gospel, and to confess his faith freely, even though he should be called to seal his testimony with his blood.

When he was again ushered into the presence of the Diet, his countenance bore no trace of fear or embarrassment. Calm and peaceful, yet grandly brave and noble, he stood as God's witness among the great ones of the earth. The imperial officer now demanded his decision as to whether he desired to retract his doctrines. Luther made his answer in a subdued and humble tone, without violence or passion. His demeanor was diffident and respectful; yet he manifested a confidence and joy that surprised the assembly.

He stated that his published works were not all of the same character. In some he had treated of faith and good works, and even his enemies declared them not only harmless but profitable. To retract these would be to condemn truths which all parties confessed. The second class consisted of writings exposing the corruptions and abuses of the papacy. To revoke these works would strengthen the tyranny of Rome, and open a wider door to many and great impieties. In the third class of his books he had attacked individuals who had defended existing evils. Concerning these he freely confessed that he had been more violent than was becoming. He did not claim to be free from fault; but even these books he could not revoke, for such a course would embolden the enemies of truth, and they would then take occasion to crush God's people with still greater cruelty.

"But as I am a mere man, and not God," he continued, "I will defend myself as did Christ, who said, 'If I have spoken evil, bear witness of the evil.' By the mercy of God, I implore your imperial majesty, or any one else who can, whoever he may be, to prove to me from the writings of the prophets that I am in error. As soon as I shall be convinced, I will instantly retract all my errors, and will be the first to cast my books into the fire. What I have just said, will show that I have considered and weighed the dangers to which I am exposing myself; but far from being dismayed by them, I rejoice exceedingly to see the gospel this day, as of old, a cause of trouble and dissension. This is the character, the destiny, of God's word. Said Christ, 'I came not to send peace, but a sword.' God is wonderful and terrible in his counsels. Let us have a care lest in our endeavors to arrest discords we be found to fight against the holy word of God, and bring down upon our heads a frightful deluge of inextricable dangers, present disaster, and everlasting desolation… I might cite examples drawn from the oracles of God. I might speak of Pharaohs, of kings of Babylon or of Israel, who were never more contributing to their own ruin than when, by measures in appearance most prudent, they thought to establish their authority. God 'removeth the mountains, and they know not.'"

Luther had spoken in German; he was now requested to repeat the same words in Latin. Though exhausted by the previous effort, he complied, and again delivered his speech, with the same clearness and energy as at the first. God's providence directed in this matter. The minds of many of the princes were so blinded by error and superstition that at the first delivery they did not see the force of Luther's reasoning; but the repetition enabled tem clearly to perceive the points presented.

Those who stubbornly closed their eyes to the light, and determined not to be convinced of the truth, were enraged at the power of Luther's words. As he ceased speaking, the spokesman of the Diet said angrily, "You have not answered the question. A clear and express reply is demanded. Will you or will you not retract?"

The Reformer answered: "Since your most serene majesty and the princes require a simple answer, I will give it thus: Unless I shall be convinced by proofs from Scripture or by evident reason (for I believe neither in popes nor in councils, since they have frequently erred and contradicted themselves), I cannot choose but adhere to the word of God, which has possession of my conscience. Nor can I possibly nor will I ever make any recantation, since it is neither safe nor honest to act contrary to conscience. Here I take my stand; I cannot do otherwise. God be my help! Amen."

Thus stood this righteous man, upon the sure foundation of the word of God. The light of Heaven illuminated his countenance. His greatness and purity of character, his peace and joy of heart, were manifest to all as he testified against the power of error, and witnessed to the superiority of that faith that overcomes the world.

The whole assembly were for a time speechless with amazement. The emperor himself and many of the princes were struck with admiration. The partisans of Rome had been worsted; their cause appeared in a most unfavorable light. They sought to maintain their power, not by appealing to the Scriptures, but by a resort to threats, Rome's unfailing argument. Said the spokesman of the Diet, "If you do not retract, the emperor and the States of the empire will proceed to consider how to deal with an obstinate heretic."

Luther's friends, who had with great joy listened to his noble defense, trembled at these words; but the doctor himself said calmly, "May God be my helper! for I can retract nothing."

Firm as a rock he stood, while the fiercest billows of worldly power beat harmlessly against him. The simple energy of his words, his fearless bearing, his calm, speaking eye, and the unalterable determination expressed in every word and act, made a deep impression upon the assembly. It was evident that he could not be induced, either by promises or threats, to yield to the mandate of Rome.

The Papist leaders were chagrined that their power, which had caused kings and nobles to tremble, should be thus despised by a humble monk; they longed to make him feel their wrath by torturing his life away. But Luther, understanding his danger, had spoken to all with Christian dignity and calmness. His words had been free from pride, passion, and misrepresentation. He lost sight of himself, and of the great men surrounding him, and felt only that he was in the presence of One infinitely superior to popes, prelates, kings, and emperors. Christ had spoken through Luther's testimony with a power and grandeur that for the time inspired both friends and foes with awe and wonder. The Spirit of God had been present in that council, impressing the hearts of the chiefs of the empire. Several of the princes openly acknowledged the justice of Luther's cause. Many were convinced of the truth; but with some the impressions received were not lasting. There was another class who did not at the time express their convictions, but who, having searched the Scriptures for themselves, at a future time declared with great boldness for the Reformation.

The elector Frederick had looked forward with anxiety to Luther's appearance before the Diet, and with deep emotion he listened to his speech. He rejoiced at the doctor's courage, firmness, and self-possession, and was proud of being his protector. He contrasted the parties in contest, and saw that the wisdom of popes, kings, and prelates had been brought to naught by the power of truth. The papacy had sustained a defeat which would be felt among all nations and in all ages.

As the legate perceived the effect produced by Luther's speech, he feared, as never before, for the security of the Romish power, and resolved to employ every means at his command to effect the Reformer's overthrow. With all the eloquence and diplomatic skill for which he was so eminently distinguished, he represented to the youthful emperor the folly and danger of sacrificing, in the cause of an insignificant monk, the friendship and support of the powerful see of Rome.

His words were not without effect. On the day following Luther's answer, Charles Fifth caused a message to be presented to the Diet, announcing his determination to carry out the policy of his predecessors to maintain and protect the Catholic religion. Since Luther had refused to renounce his errors, the most vigorous measures should be employed against him and the heresies he taught. Nevertheless, the safe-conduct granted him must be respected, and before proceedings against him could be instituted, he must be allowed to reach his home in safety.

"I am firmly resolved to tread in the footsteps of my ancestors," wrote the monarch. He had decided that he would not step out of the path of the custom, even to walk in the ways of truth and righteousness. Because his fathers did, he would uphold the papacy, with all its cruelty and corruption. Thus he took his position, refusing to accept any light in advance of what his fathers had received, or to perform any duty that they had not performed.

He seemed to feel that a change of religious views would be inconsistent with the dignity of a king. There are many at the present day thus clinging to the customs and traditions of their fathers. When the Lord sends them additional light, they refuse to accept it, because, not having been granted to their fathers, it was not received by them. We are not placed where our fathers were; consequently our duties and responsibilities are not the same as theirs. We shall not be approved of God in looking to the example of our fathers to determine our duty instead of searching the word of truth for ourselves. Our responsibility is greater than was that of our ancestors. We are accountable for the light which they received, and which was handed down as an inheritance for us, and we are accountable also for the additional light which is now shining upon us from the word of God.

Said Christ of the unbelieving Jews, "If I had not come and spoken unto them, they had not had sin; but now they have no cloak for their sin." [JOHN 15:22] The same divine power had spoken through Luther to the emperor and princes of Germany. And as the light shone forth from God's word, his Spirit pleaded for the last time with many in that assembly. As Pilate, centuries before, permitted pride and popularity to close his heart against the world's Redeemer; as the trembling Felix bade the messenger of truth, "Go thy way for this time; when I have a convenient season I will call for thee;" as the proud Agrippa confessed, "Almost thou persuadest me to be a Christian," yet turned away from the Heaven-sent message,— so had Charles Fifth, yielding to the dictates of worldly pride and policy, decided to reject the light of truth.

Several of the pope's adherents demanded that Luther's safe-conduct should not be respected. "The Rhine," they said, "should receive his ashes, as it received those of John Huss a century ago." Rumors of the designs against Luther were widely circulated, causing great excitement throughout the city. The Reformer had made many friends, who, knowing the treacherous cruelty of Rome toward all that dared expose her corruptions, resolved that he should not be sacrificed. Hundreds of nobles pledged themselves to protect him. Not a few openly denounced the royal message as evincing a weak submission to the controlling power of Rome. On the gates of houses and in public places, placards were posted, some condemning and others sustaining Luther. On one of them were written merely the significant words of the wise man, "Woe to thee, O land, when thy king is a child." The popular enthusiasm in Luther's favor throughout all Germany convinced both the emperor and the Diet that any injustice shown him would endanger the peace of the empire, and even the stability of the throne.

Frederick of Saxony maintained a studied reserve, carefully concealing his real feelings toward the Reformer, while at the same time he guarded him with tireless vigilance, watching all his movements and all those of his enemies. But there were many who made no attempt to conceal their sympathy. Princes, knights, gentlemen, ecclesiastics, and common people surrounded Luther's lodgings, entering and gazing upon him as though he were more than human. Even those who believed him to be in error could not but admire that nobility of soul which led him to imperil his life rather than violate his conscience.

Earnest efforts were made to obtain Luther's consent to a compromise with Rome. Nobles and princes represented to him that if he persisted in setting up his own judgment against that of the church and the councils, he would soon be banished from the empire, and then would have no defense. To this appeal Luther answered: "It is impossible to preach the gospel of Christ without offense. Why, then, should the fear of danger separate me from the Lord and that divine word which alone is truth? No; I would rather give up my body, my blood, and my life."

Again he was urged to submit to the judgment of the emperor, and then he would have nothing to fear. "I consent," said he in reply, "with all my heart, that the emperor, the princes, and even the humblest Christian, should examine and judge my writings; but on one condition, that they take God's word for their guide. Men have nothing to do but render obedience to that. My conscience is in dependence upon that word, and I am the subject of its authority."

To another appeal he said, "I consent to forgo my safe-conduct, and resign my person and my life to the emperor's disposal; but as to the word of God — never!" He stated his willingness to submit to the decision of a general council, but only on condition that the council be required to decide according to the Scriptures. Both friends and foes were at last convinced that further effort for reconciliation would be useless.

Had the Reformer yielded a single point, Satan and his hosts would have gained the victory. But his unwavering firmness was the means of emancipating the church, and beginning a new and better era. The influence of this one man, who dared to think and act for himself in religious matters, was to affect the church and the world, not only in his own time, but in all future generations. His firmness and fidelity would strengthen all, to the close of time, who should pass through a similar experience. The power and majesty of God stood forth above the counsel of men, above the mighty power of Satan.

Luther was soon commanded by the authority of the emperor to return home, and he knew that this notice would be speedily followed by his condemnation. Threatening clouds overhung his path; but as he departed from Worms, his heart was filled with joy and praise. "Satan himself," said he, "kept the pope's citadel; but Christ has made a wide breach in it, and the devil has been compelled to confess that Christ is mightier than he." On this journey the Reformer received the most flattering attentions from all classes. Dignitaries of the church welcomed the monk upon whom the pope's curse rested, and secular officers honored the man who was under the ban of the empire.

He had not been long absent from Worms, when the Papists prevailed upon the emperor to issue an edict against him. In this decree Luther was denounced as "Satan himself under the semblance of a man in a monk's hood." It was commanded that as soon as his safe-conduct should expire, measures be taken to stop his work. All persons were forbidden to harbor him, to give him food or drink, or by word or act, in public or private, to aid or abet him. He was to be seized wherever he might be, and delivered to the authorities. His adherents also were to be imprisoned, and their property confiscated. His writings were to be destroyed, and finally, all who should dare to act contrary to this decree were included in its condemnation. The emperor had spoken, and the Diet had given its sanction to the decree. The Romanists were jubilant. Now they considered the fate of the Reformation sealed.

God had provided a way of escape for his servant in this hour of peril. A vigilant eye had followed Luther's movements, and a true and noble heart had resolved upon his rescue. It was plain that Rome would be satisfied with nothing short of his death; only by concealment could he be preserved from the jaws of the lion. God gave wisdom to Frederick of Saxony to devise a plan for the Reformer's preservation. With the co-operation of true friends, the elector's purpose was carried out, and Luther was effectually hidden from friends and foes. Upon his homeward journey, he was seized, separated from his attendants, and hurriedly conveyed through the forests to the castle of Wartburg, an isolated mountain fortress. Both his seizure and his concealment were so involved in mystery that even Frederick himself for a long time knew not whither he had been conducted. This ignorance was not without design: so long as the elector knew nothing of Luther's whereabouts, he could reveal nothing. He satisfied himself that the Reformer was safe, and with this knowledge he was content.

Spring, summer, and autumn passed, and winter came, and Luther still remained a prisoner. Aleander and his partisans rejoiced that the light of the gospel seemed about to be extinguished. But instead of this, the Reformer was filling his lamp from the store-house of truth, to shine forth in due time with brighter radiance.

In the friendly security of the Wartburg, Luther for a time rejoiced in his release from the heat and turmoil of battle. But he could not long find satisfaction in quiet and repose. Accustomed to a life of activity and stern conflict, he could ill endure to remain inactive. In those solitary days, the condition of the church rose up before him, and he cried in despair, "Alas! there is no one in this latter day of His anger to stand like a wall before the Lord, and save Israel!" Again, his thoughts returned to himself, and he feared being charged with cowardice in withdrawing from the contest. Then he reproached himself for his indolence and self-indulgence. Yet at the same time he was daily accomplishing more than it seemed possible for one man to do. His pen was never idle. While his enemies flattered themselves that he was silenced, they were astonished and confused by tangible proof that he was still active. A host of tracts, issuing from his pen, circulated throughout Germany. He also performed a most important service for his countrymen by translating the New Testament into the German tongue. From his rocky Patmos he continued for nearly a whole year to proclaim the gospel, and rebuke the sins and errors of the times.

But it was not merely to preserve Luther from the wrath of his enemies, nor even to afford him a season of quiet for these important labors, that God had withdrawn his servant from the stage of public life. There were results more precious than these to be secured. In the solitude and obscurity of his mountain retreat, Luther was removed from earthly supports, and shut out from human praise. He was thus saved from the pride and self-confidence that are so often caused by success. By suffering and humiliation he was prepared again to walk safely upon the dizzy heights to which he had been so suddenly exalted.

As men rejoice in the freedom which the truth brings them, they are inclined to extol those whom God has employed to break the chains of error and superstition. Satan seeks to divert men's thoughts and affections from God, and fix them upon human agencies; to honor the mere instrument, and to ignore the Hand that directs all the events of providence. Too often, religious leaders who are thus praised and reverenced lose sight of their dependence upon God, and are led to trust in themselves. As a result, they seek to control the minds and consciences of the people, who are disposed to look to them for guidance instead of looking to the word of God. The work of reform is often retarded because of this spirit indulged by its supporters. From this danger, God would guard the cause of the Reformation. He desired that work to receive, not the impress of man, but of God. The eyes of men had been turned to Luther as the expounder of the truth; he was removed that all eyes might be directed to the eternal Author of truth.

Chapter 8

Progress of the Reformation

Luther's mysterious disappearance excited consternation throughout all Germany. Inquiries concerning him were heard everywhere. Even his enemies were more agitated by his absence than they could have been by his presence. The wildest rumors were circulated, and many believed that he had been murdered. There was great lamentation, not only by his avowed friends, but by thousands who had not openly taken their stand with the Reformation. Many bound themselves by a solemn oath to avenge his death.

The Romanists saw with terror to what a pitch had risen the feeling against them. Though at first exultant at the supposed death of Luther, they now desired to hide from the wrath of the people. Those who were enraged against him when he was at large, were filled with fear now that he was in captivity. "The only way of extricating ourselves," said one, "is to light our torches, and go searching through the earth for Luther, till we can restore him to a nation that *will* have him." The edict of the emperor seemed to fall powerless. The papal legates were filled with indignation as they saw that it commanded far less attention than did the fate of Luther.

The tidings that he was safe, though a prisoner, calmed the fears of the people, while it still further aroused their enthusiasm in his favor. His writings were read with greater eagerness than ever before. Increasing numbers joined the cause of the heroic man who had, at such fearful odds, defended the word of God. The Reformation was constantly gaining in strength. The seed which Luther had sown sprung up everywhere. His absence accomplished a work which his presence would have failed to do. Other laborers felt a new responsibility, now that their great leader was removed. With new faith and earnestness they pressed forward to do all in their power, that the work so nobly begun might not be hindered.

But Satan was not idle. He now attempted what he has attempted in every other reformatory movement,— to deceive and destroy the people by palming off upon them a counterfeit in place of the true work. As there were false Christs in the first century of the Christian church, so there arose false prophets in the sixteenth century.

A few men, deeply affected by the excitement in the religious world, imagined themselves to have received special revelations from Heaven, and claimed to have been divinely commissioned to carry forward to its completion the Reformation but feebly begun by Luther. In truth, they were undoing the very work which he had accomplished. They rejected the fundamental principle of the Reformation,— the word of God as the all-sufficient rule of faith and practice; and for that unerring guide they substituted the changeable, uncertain standard of their own feelings and impressions. By this act of setting aside the great detector of error and falsehood, the way was opened for Satan to control minds as best pleased himself.

One of these prophets claimed to have been instructed by the angel Gabriel. A student who united with him abandoned his studies, declaring that he had received from God himself the ability to explain the Scriptures. Others who were naturally inclined to fanaticism united with them. The proceedings of these enthusiasts created no little excitement. The preaching of Luther had aroused the people everywhere to feel the necessity of reform, and now some really honest persons were misled by the pretensions of the new prophets.

The leaders of the movement repaired to Wittemberg, and urged their claims upon Melancthon and his co-laborers. Said they: "We are sent by God to teach the people. We have received special revelations from God himself, and therefore know what is coming to pass. We are apostles and prophets, and appeal to Doctor Luther as to the truth of what we say."

The Reformers were astonished and perplexed. This was such an element as they had never before encountered, and they knew not what course to pursue. Said Melancthon: "There are indeed spirits of no ordinary kind in these men; but what spirits?" "On the one hand, let us beware of quenching the Spirit of God, and on the other, of being seduced by the spirit of Satan."

The fruit of the new teaching soon became apparent. The minds of the people were diverted from the word of God, or decidedly prejudiced against it. The schools were thrown into confusion. Students, spurning all restraint, abandoned their studies. The men who thought themselves competent to revive and control the work of the Reformation, succeeded only in bringing it to the very brink of ruin. The Romanists now regained their confidence, and exclaimed exultingly, "One more effort, and all will be ours."

Luther at the Wartburg, hearing of what had occurred, said with deep concern, "I always expected that Satan would send us this plague." He perceived the true character of those pretended prophets, and saw the danger that threatened the cause of truth. The opposition of the pope and the emperor had not caused him so great perplexity and distress as he now experienced. From the professed friends of the Reformation had risen its worst enemies. The very truths which had brought peace to his troubled heart had been made the cause of dissension in the church.

In the work of reform, Luther had been urged forward by the Spirit of God, and had been carried beyond himself. He had not purposed to take such positions as he did, or to make so radical changes. He had been but the instrument in the hands of infinite power. Yet he often trembled for the result of his work. He had once said, "If I knew that my doctrine had injured one human being, however poor and unknown,— which it could not, for it is the very gospel,— I would rather face death ten times over than not retract it."

And now a whole city, and that city Wittemberg itself, was fast sinking into confusion. The doctrines taught by Luther had not caused this evil; but throughout Germany his enemies were charging it upon him. In bitterness of soul he sometimes asked, "Can such be the end of this great work of the Reformation?" Again, as he wrestled with God in prayer, peace flowed into his heart. "The work is not mine, but thine own," he said; "thou wilt not suffer it to be corrupted by superstition or fanaticism." But the thought of remaining longer from the conflict in such a crisis, became insupportable. He determined to return to Wittemberg.

Without delay he set out on his perilous journey. He was under the ban of the empire. Enemies were at liberty to take his life; friends were forbidden to aid or shelter him. The imperial government was adopting the most stringent measures against his adherents. But he saw that the work of the gospel was imperiled, and in the name of the Lord he went forth once more to battle for the truth.

With great caution and humility, yet with decision and firmness, he entered upon his work. "By the word," said he, "we must refute and expel what has gained a place and influence by violence. I would not resort to force against the superstitious and unbelieving." "Let there be no compulsion. I have been laboring for liberty of conscience. Liberty is the very essence of faith." Ascending the pulpit, he with great wisdom and gentleness instructed, exhorted, and reproved, and by the power of the gospel brought back the misguided people into the way of truth.

Luther had no desire to encounter the fanatics whose course had been productive of so great evil. He knew them to be men of hasty and violent temper, who, while claiming to be especially illuminated from Heaven, would not endure the slightest contradiction, or even the kindest admonition. Arrogating to themselves supreme authority, they required every one, without a question, to acknowledge their claims. But as they demanded an interview with him, he consented to meet them; and so successfully did he expose their pretensions, that the impostors at once departed from Wittemberg.

The fanaticism was checked for a time; but several years later it broke out with greater violence and more terrible results. Said Luther, concerning the leaders in this movement: "To them the Holy Scriptures were but a dead letter, and they all began to cry, 'The Spirit! the Spirit!' But most assuredly I will not follow where their spirit leads them. May God in his mercy preserve me from a church in which there are none but saints. I wish to be in fellowship with the humble, the feeble, the sick, who know and feel their sins, and who sigh and cry continually to God from the bottom of their hearts to obtain his consolation and support."

Thomas Munzer, the most active of the fanatics, was a man of considerable ability, which, rightly directed, would have enabled him to do good; but he had not learned the first principles of true religion. He imagined himself ordained of God to reform the world, forgetting, like many other enthusiasts, that the reform should begin with himself. He was ambitious to obtain position and influence, and unwilling to be second, even to Luther. He charged the Reformers with establishing, by their adherence to the Bible alone, a species of Popery. He considered himself called of God to remedy the evil, and held that manifestations of the Spirit were the means by which this was to be accomplished, and that he who had the Spirit possessed the true faith, though he might never see the written word.

The fanatical teachers gave themselves up to be governed by impressions, calling every thought of the mind the voice of God; consequently they went to great extremes. Some even burned their Bibles, exclaiming, "The letter killeth, but the Spirit giveth life." Men naturally love the marvelous, and whatever flatters their pride, and many were ready to accept Munzer's teachings. He soon denounced all order in public worship, and declared that to obey princes was to attempt to serve both God and Belial.

The minds of the people, already beginning to throw off the yoke of the papacy, were also becoming impatient under the restraints of civil authority. Munzer's revolutionary teachings, claiming divine sanction, led them to break away from all control, and give the rein to their prejudices and passions. The most terrible scenes of sedition and strife followed, and the fields of Germany were drenched with blood.

The agony of soul which Luther had so long before experienced in his cell at Erfurth, now pressed upon him with redoubled power as he saw the results of fanaticism charged upon the Reformation. The Papist princes declared, and many believed, that Luther's doctrine had been the cause of the rebellion. Although this charge was without the slightest foundation, it could not but cause the Reformer great distress. That the work of Heaven should be thus degraded by being classed with the basest fanaticism, seemed more than he could endure. On the other hand, the leaders in the revolt hated Luther because he had not only opposed their doctrines and denied their claims to divine inspiration, but had pronounced them rebels against the civil authority. In retaliation they denounced him as a base pretender. He seemed to have brought upon himself the enmity of both princes and people.

The Romanists exulted, expecting to witness the speedy downfall of the Reformation; and they blamed Luther, even for the errors which he had been most earnestly endeavoring to correct. The fanatical party, by falsely claiming to have been treated with great injustice, succeeded in gaining the sympathies of a large class of the people, and, as is usually the case with those who take the wrong side, they came to be regarded as martyrs. Thus the ones who were exerting every energy in opposition to the Reformation were pitied and lauded as the victims of cruelty and oppression. This was the work of Satan, prompted by the same spirit of rebellion which was first manifested in Heaven.

Satan is constantly seeking to deceive men, and lead them to call sin righteousness, and righteousness sin. How successful has been his work! How often are censure and reproach cast upon God's faithful servants because they will stand fearlessly in defense of the truth! Men who are but agents of Satan are praised and flattered, and even looked upon as martyrs, while those who should be respected and sustained for their fidelity to God, are left to stand alone, under suspicion and distrust.

Counterfeit holiness, spurious sanctification, is still doing its work of deception. Under various forms it exhibits the same spirit as in the days of Luther, diverting minds from the Scriptures, and leading men to follow their own feelings and impressions rather than to yield obedience to the law of God. This is one of Satan's most successful devices to cast reproach upon purity and truth.

Fearlessly did Luther defend the gospel from the attacks which came from every quarter. The word of God proved itself a weapon mighty in every conflict. With that word he warred against the usurped authority of the pope, and the rationalistic philosophy of the school-men, while he stood firm as a rock against the fanaticism that sought to ally itself with the Reformation.

Each of these opposing elements was in its own way setting aside the Holy Scriptures, and exalting human wisdom as the source of religious truth and knowledge. Rationalism idolizes reason, and makes this the criterion for religion. Romanism, claiming for her sovereign pontiff an inspiration descended in unbroken line from the apostles, and unchangeable through all time, gives ample opportunity for every species of extravagance and corruption to be concealed under the sanctity of the apostolic commission. The inspiration claimed by Munzer and his associates proceeded from no higher source than the vagaries of the imagination, and its influence was subversive of all authority, human or divine. True Christianity receives the word of God as the great treasure-house of inspired truth, and the test of all inspiration.

Upon his return from the Wartburg, Luther completed his translation of the New Testament, and the gospel was soon after given to the people of Germany in their own language. This translation was received with great joy by all who loved the truth; but it was scornfully rejected by those who chose human traditions and the commandments of men.

The priests were alarmed at the thought that the common people would now be able to discuss with them the precepts of God's word, and that their own ignorance would thus be exposed. The weapons of their carnal reasoning were powerless against the sword of the Spirit. Rome summoned all her authority to prevent the circulation of the Scriptures; but decrees, anathemas, and tortures were alike in vain. The more she condemned and prohibited the Bible, the greater was the anxiety of the people to know what it really taught. All who could read were eager to study the word of God for themselves. They carried it about with them, and read and re-read, and could not be satisfied until they had committed large portions to memory. Seeing the favor with which the New Testament was received, Luther immediately began the translation of the Old, and published it in parts as fast as completed.

Luther's writings were welcomed alike in city and in hamlet. At night the teachers of the village schools read them aloud to little groups gathered at the fireside. With every effort, some souls would be convicted of the truth, and, receiving the word with gladness, would in their turn tell the good news to others.

The words of inspiration were verified: "The entrance of thy words giveth light; it giveth understanding unto the simple." [PS. 119:130.] The study of the Scriptures was working a mighty change in the minds and hearts of the people. The papal rule had placed upon its subjects an iron yoke which held them in ignorance and degradation. A superstitious observance of forms had been scrupulously maintained; but in all their service the heart and intellect had had little part. The preaching of Luther, setting forth the plain truths of God's word, and then the word itself, placed in the hands of the common people, had aroused their dormant powers, not only purifying and ennobling the spiritual nature, but imparting new strength and vigor to the intellect.

Persons of all ranks were to be seen with the Bible in their hands, defending the doctrines of the Reformation. The Papists who had left the study of the Scriptures to the priests and monks, now called upon them to come forward and refute the new teachings. But, ignorant alike of the Scriptures and of the power of God, priests and friars were totally defeated by those whom they had denounced as unlearned and heretical. "Unhappily," said a Catholic writer, "Luther had persuaded his followers that their faith ought only to be founded on the oracles of Holy Writ." Crowds would gather to hear the truth advocated by men of little education, and even discussed by them with learned and eloquent theologians. The shameful ignorance of these great men was made apparent as their arguments were met by the simple teachings of God's word. Women and children, artisans and soldiers, had a better knowledge of the Scriptures than had learned doctors or surpliced priests.

As the Romish clergy saw their congregations diminishing, they invoked the aid of the magistrates, and by every means in their power endeavored to bring back their hearers. But the people had found in the new teachings that which supplied the wants of their souls, and they turned away from those who had so long fed them with the worthless husks of superstitious rites and human traditions.

When persecution was kindled against the teachers of the truth, they gave heed to the words of Christ, "When they persecute you in this city, flee ye into another. [MATT. 10:23.] The light penetrated everywhere. The fugitives would find somewhere a hospitable door opened to them, and there abiding, they would preach Christ, sometimes in the church, or, if denied that privilege, in private houses or in the open air. Wherever they could obtain a hearing was a consecrated temple. The truth, proclaimed with such energy and assurance, spread with irresistible power.

In vain were both ecclesiastical and civil authorities invoked to crush the heresy. In vain they resorted to imprisonment, torture, fire, and sword. Thousands of believers sealed their faith with their blood, and yet the work went on. Persecution served only to extend the truth; and the fanaticism which Satan endeavored to unite with it, resulted in making more clear the contrast between the work of Satan and the work of God.

Chapter 9

Protest of the Princes

One of the noblest testimonies ever uttered for the Reformation was the Protest offered by the Christian princes of Germany at the Diet of Spires. The courage, faith, and firmness of these men of God, gained for succeeding ages liberty of thought and of conscience. Their Protest gave to the reformed church the name of Protestant; its principles are the very essence of Protestantism.

A dark and threatening day had come for the Reformation. For a season religious toleration had prevailed in the empire; God's providence had held opposing elements in check, that the gospel might obtain a firmer foothold; but Rome had now summoned her forces to crush out the truth. At Spires the Papists openly manifested their hostility toward the Reformers and all who favored them. Said Melancthon, "We are the execration and the sweepings of the earth; but Christ will look down on his poor people, and will preserve them." The evangelical princes in attendance at the Diet were forbidden even to have the gospel preached in their dwellings. But the people of Spires thirsted for the word of God, and, notwithstanding the prohibition, thousands flocked to the morning and evening worship still held in the chapel of the Elector of Saxony.

This hastened the crisis. An imperial message announced to the Diet that as the resolution granting liberty of conscience had given rise to great disorders, the emperor declared it to be annulled. This arbitrary act excited the indignation and alarm of the evangelical Christians. Said one, "Christ has again fallen into the hands of Caiaphas and Pilate." The Romanists became more violent. A bigoted Papist declared, "The Turks are better than the Lutherans; for the Turks observe fast-days, and the Lutherans violate them. If we must choose between the Holy Scriptures of God and the old errors of the church, we should reject the former." Said Melancthon, "Every day, in full assembly, Faber casts some new stone against the Gospellers."

Religious toleration had been legally established, and the evangelical States were resolved to oppose the infringement of their rights. Luther, being still under the ban imposed by the edict of Worms, was not permitted to be present at Spires; but his place was supplied by his co-laborers and the princes whom God had raised up to defend his cause in this emergency. The noble Frederick of Saxony, Luther's former protector, had been removed by death; but Duke John his brother, who succeeded to the throne, had joyfully welcomed the Reformation, and while a friend of peace, he displayed great energy and courage in all matters relating to the interests of the faith.

The priests demanded that the States which had accepted the Reformation submit implicitly to Romish jurisdiction. The Reformers, on the other hand, claimed the liberty which had previously been granted. They could not consent that Rome should again bring under her control those nations that had with so great joy received the word of God. The Diet finally decreed, that where the Reformation had not become established, the edict of Worms should be rigorously enforced; and that in the evangelical States, where there would be danger of revolt, no new reform should be introduced, there should be no preaching upon disputed points, the celebration of the mass should not be opposed, and no Roman Catholic should be permitted to embrace Lutheranism.

If this decree became a law, the Reformation could neither be extended where as yet it had not reached, nor be established on a firm foundation where it already existed. Liberty of speech would be prohibited. No conversions would be allowed. And to these restrictions and prohibitions the friends of the Reformation were required at once to submit. The hopes of the world seemed about to be extinguished. The re-establishment of the papal hierarchy would inevitably cause a revival of the ancient abuses; and an occasion would readily be found for completing the destruction of a work that had already been shaken by fanaticism and dissension.

As the evangelical party met for consultation, one looked to another in blank dismay. From one to another passed the inquiry, "What is to be done?" Mighty issues for the world were at stake. Had these men been controlled by ambition or selfishness, they might have accepted the decree. They themselves were apparently left free to maintain their faith. Ought they not to be satisfied with this? Should they throw themselves into the conflict to wrestle for liberty of conscience in all the world? Should they expose themselves to the vengeance of Rome?

Never were these men placed in a more trying position; but they came forth from the test with principles unsullied. As the mist that had hovered over their minds cleared away, they saw what would be the result of this decree. Should they lend their influence to restore the stake and the torture? Should they oppose the advancement of truth,— oppose the Spirit of God in its work of calling men to Christ? Could they refuse obedience to the Saviour's command, "Go ye into all the world, and preach the gospel to every creature"? [MARK 16:15.] Ought they to consent that those who might desire to renounce error should be denied the privilege? Having entered the kingdom of Heaven themselves, should they bar the way so that others could not enter? Rather would they sacrifice their dominions, their titles, and their own lives.

"Let us reject this decree," said the princes. "In matters of conscience the majority has no power." The deputies declared that

Germany was indebted to the decree of toleration for the peace which she enjoyed, and that its abolition would fill the empire with troubles and divisions. "The Diet is incompetent," said they, "to do more than preserve religious liberty until a council meets." To protect liberty of conscience is the duty of the State, and this is the limit of its authority in matters of religion. Every secular government that attempts to regulate or enforce religious observances by civil authority is sacrificing the very principle for which the evangelical Christians so nobly struggled.

The Papists determined to put down what they termed daring obstinacy. They began by endeavoring to cause divisions among the supporters of the Reformation, and to intimidate all who had not openly declared in its favor. The princes were at last summoned before the Diet. They pleaded for delay, but in vain. Those who still refused to sacrifice liberty of conscience and the right of individual judgment well knew that their position marked them for future criticism, condemnation, and persecution. Said one of the Reformers, "We must either deny the word of God or— be burned."

King Ferdinand, the emperor's representative at the Diet, saw that the decree would cause serious divisions unless the princes could be induced to accept and sustain it. He therefore tried the art of persuasion, well knowing that to employ force with such men would only render them more determined. He begged them to accept the decree, assuring them that such an act would be highly gratifying to the emperor. But these faithful men acknowledged an authority above that of earthly rulers, and they answered calmly, "We will obey the emperor in everything that may contribute to maintain peace and the honor of God."

In the presence of the Diet, the king at last announced to the elector and his friends that their only remaining course was to submit to the majority. Having thus spoken, he withdrew from the assembly, giving the Reformers no opportunity for deliberation or reply. In vain they sent messengers entreating him to return. To their remonstrances he answered only, "It is a settled affair; submission in all that remains."

The imperial party were convinced that the Christian princes would adhere to the Holy Scriptures as superior to human doctrines and requirements; and they knew that an acceptance of this principle would eventually overthrow the papacy. But they flattered themselves that weakness was on the side of the Reformation, while strength was with the emperor and the pope. Had the Reformers made flesh their arm, they would have been as powerless as the Papists supposed. But though weak in numbers, and at variance with Rome, they had their strength. They appealed from the decision of the Diet to the word of God, and from the emperor of Germany to the King of kings and Lord of lords.

As Ferdinand had refused to regard their conscientious convictions, the princes decided not to heed his absence, but to bring their Protest before the national council without delay. A solemn declaration was therefore drawn up, and presented to the Diet:—

"We protest by these presents, before God, our only Creator, Preserver, Redeemer, and Saviour, and who will one day be our Judge, as well as before all men and all creatures, that we, for us and our people, neither consent nor adhere in any manner whatever to the proposed decree in anything that is contrary to God, to his word, to our right conscience, or to the salvation of our souls... We cannot assert that when Almighty God calls a man to his knowledge, he dare not embrace that divine knowledge... There is no true doctrine but that which conforms to the word of God. The Lord forbids the teaching of any other faith. The Holy Scriptures, with one text explained by other and plainer texts, are, in all things necessary for the Christian, easy to be understood, and adapted to enlighten. We are therefore resolved by divine grace to maintain the pure preaching of God's only word, as it is contained in the scriptures of the Old and New Testaments, without anything added thereto. This word is the only truth. It is the sure rule of all doctrine and life, and can never fail or deceive us. He who builds on this foundation shall stand against all the powers of hell, whilst all the vanities that are set up against it shall fall before the face of God." "We therefore reject the yoke that is imposed upon us."

A deep impression was made upon the Diet. The majority were filled with amazement and alarm at the boldness of the protesters. The future appeared to them stormy and uncertain. Dissension, strife, and bloodshed seemed inevitable. But the Reformers, assured of the justice of their cause, and relying upon the arm of Omnipotence, were full of courage and firmness.

The Protest denied the right of civil rulers to legislate in matters between the soul and God, and declared with prophets and apostles, "We ought to obey God rather than men." It rejected also the arbitrary power of the church, and set forth the unerring principle that all human teaching should be in subjection to the oracles of God. The protesters had thrown off the yoke of man's supremacy, and had exalted Christ as supreme in the church, and his word in the pulpit. The power of conscience was set above the State, and the authority of the Holy Scriptures above the visible church. The crown of Christ was uplifted above the pope's tiara and the emperor's diadem. The protesters had moreover affirmed their right to freely utter their convictions of truth. They would not only believe and obey, but teach what the word of God presents, and they denied the right of priest or magistrate to interfere. The Protest of Spires was a solemn witness against religious intolerance, and an assertion of the right of all men to worship according to the dictates of their own consciences.

The declaration had been made. It was written in the memory of thousands, and registered in the books of Heaven, where no effort of man could erase it. All evangelical Germany adopted the Protest as the expression of its faith. Everywhere men beheld in this declaration the promise of a new and better era. Said one of the princes to the Protestants of Spires, "May the Almighty, who has given you grace to confess energetically, freely, and fearlessly, preserve you in that Christian firmness until the day of eternity."

Had the Reformation, after attaining a degree of success, consented to temporize to secure favor with the world, it would have been untrue to God and to itself, and would thus have insured its own destruction. The experience of those early reformers contains a lesson for all succeeding ages. Satan's manner of working against God and his word has not changed; he is still as much opposed to the Scriptures being made the guide of life as in the sixteenth century. In our time there is a wide departure from its doctrines and precepts, and there is need of a return to the great Protestant principle,— the Bible and the Bible only as the rule of faith and duty. Satan is still working through every means which he can control to destroy religious liberty. The anti-christian power which the protesters of Spires repudiated, is now with renewed vigor seeking to re-establish its lost supremacy. The same unswerving adherence to the word of God manifested at that crisis of the Reformation, is the only hope of reform today.

There appeared tokens of danger to the Protestants. There were tokens, also, that the divine hand was stretched out to protect the faithful. It was about this time that Melancthon hurried his friend Grynaeus through the streets of Spires to the Rhine, and urged him to cross the river without delay. Grynaeus, in astonishment, desired to know the reason for this sudden flight. Said Melancthon, "An old man of grave and solemn aspect, but who is unknown to me, appeared before me, and said, 'In a minute the officers of justice will be sent by Ferdinand to arrest Grynaeus.'" On the banks of the Rhine, Melancthon waited until the waters of that stream interposed between his beloved friend and those who sought his life. When he saw him on the other side at last, he said, "He is torn from the cruel jaws of those who thirst for innocent blood."

Grynaeus had been on intimate terms with a leading Papist doctor; but, having been shocked at one of his sermons, he went to him, and entreated that he would no longer war against the truth. The papist concealed his anger, but immediately repaired to the king, and obtained from him authority to arrest the protester. When Melancthon returned to his house, he was informed that after his departure officers in pursuit of Grynaeus had searched it from top to bottom. He ever believed that the Lord had saved his friend by sending a holy angel to give him warning.

The Reformation was to be brought into greater prominence before the mighty ones of the earth. The evangelical princes had been denied a hearing by King Ferdinand; but they were to be granted an opportunity to present their cause in the presence of the emperor and the assembled dignitaries of Church and State. To quiet the dissensions which disturbed the empire, Charles Fifth convoked a Diet at Augsburg, over which he announced his intention to preside in person. Thither the Protestant leaders were summoned.

Great dangers threatened the Reformation; but its advocates still trusted their cause with God, and pledged themselves to be firm to the gospel. They determined to prepare a statement of their views in systematic form, with the evidence from the Scriptures, to present before the Diet; and the task was committed to Luther, Melancthon, and their associates. The Confession thus prepared was accepted by the Protestants as an exposition of their faith, and they assembled to affix their names to the important document. It was a solemn and trying time, The Reformers were solicitous that their cause should not be confounded with political questions; they felt that the Reformation should exercise no other influence than that which proceeds from the word of God. As the Christian princes advanced to sign the Confession, Melancthon interposed, saying, "It is for the theologians and ministers to propose these things, while the authority of the mighty ones of earth is to be reserved for other matters." "God forbid," replied John of Saxony, "that you should exclude me. I am resolved to do my duty without being troubled about my crown. I desire to confess the Lord. My electoral hat and robes are not so precious to me as the cross of Jesus Christ." Having thus spoken, he wrote down his name. Said another of the princes as he took the pen, "If the honor of my Lord Jesus Christ requires it, I am ready to leave my goods and life behind me." "Rather would I renounce my subjects and my States, rather would I quit the country of my fathers, staff in hand," he continued, "than to receive any other doctrine than is contained in this Confession." Such was the faith and daring of those men of God.

The appointed time came to appear before the emperor. Charles Fifth, seated upon his throne, surrounded by the electors and the princes, gave audience to the Protestant Reformers. The confession of their faith was read. In that august assembly the truths of the gospel were clearly set forth, and the errors of the papal church were pointed out. Well has that day been pronounced "the greatest day of the Reformation, and one of the most glorious in the history of Christianity and of the world."

But a few years had passed since the monk of Wittemberg stood alone at Worms before the national council. Now in his stead were the noblest and most powerful princes of the empire. Luther had been forbidden to appear at Augsburg, but he had been present by his words and prayers. "I am overjoyed," he wrote, "that I have lived until this hour, in which Christ has been publicly exalted by such illustrious confessors, and in so glorious an assembly. Herein is fulfilled what the Scripture saith, 'I will declare thy testimony in the presence of kings.'"

In the days of Paul, the gospel for which he was imprisoned was thus brought before the princes and nobles of the imperial city. So on this occasion, that which the emperor had forbidden to be preached from the pulpit, was proclaimed in the palace; what many had regarded as unfit even for servants to listen to, was heard with wonder by the masters and lords of the empire. "Kings and great men were the auditory, crowned princes were the preachers, and the sermon was the royal truth of God." "Since the apostolic age," says a writer, "there has never been a greater work, or a more magnificent confession of Jesus Christ."

"All that the Lutherans have said is true, and we cannot deny it," declared a papist bishop. "Can you by sound reasons refute the Confession made by the elector and his allies?" asked another, of Doctor Eck. "Not with the writings of the apostles and prophets," was the reply; "but with the Fathers and councils I can." "I understand, then," responded the questioner, "that the Lutherans are entrenched in the Scriptures, and we are only outside." Some of the princes of Germany were won to the reformed faith. The emperor himself declared that the Protestant articles were but the truth. The Confession was translated into many languages, and circulated through all Europe, and it has been accepted by millions in succeeding generations as the expression of their faith.

God's faithful builders were not toiling alone. While "principalities and powers and wicked spirits in high places" were leagued against them, the Lord did not forsake his people. Could their eyes have been opened, they would have seen as marked evidence of divine presence and aid as was granted to a prophet of old. When Elisha's servant pointed his master to the hostile army surrounding them, and cutting off all opportunity for escape, the prophet prayed, "Lord, I pray thee, open his eyes, that he may see." [2 KINGS 6:17] And, lo, the mountain was filled with chariots and horses of fire, the army of Heaven stationed to protect the man of God. Thus did angels guard the workers in the cause of the Reformation. God had commanded his servants to build, and no opposing force could drive them from the walls.

From the secret place of prayer came the power that shook the world in the Great Reformation. There, with holy calmness, the servants of the Lord set their feet upon the rock of his promises. During the struggle at Augsburg, Luther did not fail to devote three hours each day to prayer; and these were taken from that portion of the day most favorable to study. In the privacy of his chamber he was heard to pour out his soul before God in words full of adoration, fear, and hope, as if speaking to a friend. "I know that thou art our Father and our God," he said, "and that thou wilt scatter the persecutors of thy children; for thou art thyself endangered with us. All this matter is thine, and it is only by thy constraint that we have put our hands to it. Defend us then, O Father!" To Melancthon, who was crushed under the burden of anxiety and fear, he wrote: "Grace and peace in Christ! In Christ, I say, and not in the world, Amen! I hate with exceeding hatred those extreme cares which consume you. If the cause is unjust, abandon it; if the cause is just, why should we belie the promises of Him who commands us to sleep without fear?" "Christ will not be wanting to the work of justice and truth. He lives, he reigns; what fear, then, can we have?"

God did listen to the cries of his servants. He gave to princes and ministers grace and courage to maintain the truth against the rulers of the darkness of this world. Saith the Lord, "Behold, I lay in Zion a chief corner-stone, elect, precious, and he that believeth on him shall not be confounded." [1 PETER 2:6] The Protestant Reformers had built on Christ, and the gates of hell could not prevail against them.

Chapter 10

Later Reformers

While Luther was opening a closed Bible to the people of Germany, Tyndale was impelled by the Spirit of God to do the same for England. He was a diligent student of the Scriptures, and fearlessly preached his convictions of truth, urging that all doctrines be brought to the test of God's word. His zeal could not but excite opposition from the Papists. A learned Catholic doctor who engaged in controversy with him exclaimed, "It were better for us to be without God's law than without the pope's." Tyndale replied, "I defy the pope and all his laws; and if God spare my life, ere many years I will cause a boy who driveth the plow to know more of the Scriptures than you do."

The purpose which he had begun to cherish, of giving to the people the New-Testament Scriptures in their own language, was now confirmed, and he immediately applied himself to the work. Driven from his home by persecution, he went to London, and there for a time pursued his labors undisturbed. But again the violence of the Papists forced him to flee. All England seemed closed against him, and he resolved to seek shelter in Germany. Here he began the printing of the English New Testament. Twice the work was stopped; but when forbidden to print in one city, he went to another. At last he made his way to Worms, where, a few years before, Luther had defended the gospel before the Diet. In that ancient city were many friends of the Reformation, and Tyndale there prosecuted his work without further hindrance. Three thousand copies of the New Testament were soon finished, and another edition followed in the same year.

With great earnestness and perseverance he continued his labors. Notwithstanding the English authorities had guarded their ports with the strictest vigilance, the word of God was in various ways secretly conveyed to London, and thence circulated throughout the country. The Papists attempted to suppress the truth, but in vain. The bishop of Durham at one time bought of a bookseller who was a friend of Tyndale, his whole stock of Bibles, for the purpose of destroying them, supposing that this would greatly hinder the work. But, on the contrary, the money thus furnished, purchased material for a new and better edition, which, but for this, could not have been published. When Tyndale was afterward made a prisoner, his liberty was offered him on condition that he would reveal the names of those who had helped him meet the expense of printing his Bibles. He replied that the bishop of Durham had done more than any other person; for by paying a large price for the books left on hand, he had enabled him to go on with good courage.

Tyndale was betrayed into the hands of his enemies, and at one time suffered imprisonment for many months. He finally witnessed for his faith by a martyr's death; but the weapons which he prepared have enabled other soldiers to do battle through all the centuries even to our time.

In Scotland the gospel found a champion in the person of John Knox. This true-hearted reformer feared not the face of man. The fires of martyrdom, blazing around him, served only to quicken his zeal to greater intensity. With the tyrant's ax held menacingly over his head, he stood his ground, striking sturdy blows on the right hand and on the left, to demolish idolatry. Thus he kept to his purpose, praying and fighting the battles of the Lord, until Scotland was free.

In England, Latimer maintained from the pulpit that the Bible ought to be read in the language of the people. "The Author of Holy Scripture," said he, "is God himself, and this Scripture partakes of the might and eternity of its Author. There is neither king nor emperor that is not bound to obey it. Let us beware of those by-paths of human tradition, full of stones, brambles, and uprooted trees. Let us follow the straight road of the word. It does not concern us what the Fathers have done, but rather what they ought to have done."

Barnes and Frith, the faithful friends of Tyndale, arose to defend the truth. The Ridleys and Cranmer followed. These leaders in the English Reformation were men of learning, and most of them had been highly esteemed for zeal or piety in the Romish communion. Their opposition to the papacy was the result of their knowledge of the errors of the holy see. Their acquaintance with the mysteries of Babylon, gave greater power to their testimonies against her.

"Do you know," said Latimer, "who is the most diligent bishop in England? I see you listening and hearkening that I should name him. I will tell you It is the devil. He is never out of his diocese; you shall never find him idle. Call for him when you will, he is ever at home, he is ever at the plow. You shall never find him remiss, I warrant you. Where the devil is resident, there away with books, and up with candles; away with Bibles, and up with beads; away with the light of the gospel, and up with the light of wax tapers, yea, at noonday; down with Christ's cross, up with the purgatory pick-purse; away with clothing the naked, the poor, the impotent; up with the decking of images and the gay garnishing of stones and stocks; down with God and his most holy word; up with traditions, human councils, and a blinded pope. Oh that our prelates would be as diligent to sow the corn of good doctrine as Satan is to sow cockle and darnel!"

The grand principle maintained by Tyndale, Frith, Latimer, and the Ridleys, was the divine authority and sufficiency of the Sacred Scriptures. They rejected the assumed authority of popes, councils, Fathers, and kings to rule the conscience in matters of religious faith.

The Bible was their standard, and to this they brought all doctrines and all claims.

Faith in God and his word sustained these holy men as they yielded up their lives at the stake. "Be of good comfort," exclaimed Latimer to his fellow-martyr as the flames were about to silence their voices, "we shall this day light such a candle in England as, I trust, by God's grace shall never be put out."

The Church of England, following in the steps of Rome, persecuted dissenters from the established faith. In the seventeenth century thousands of godly pastors were expelled from their positions. The people were forbidden, on pain of heavy fines, imprisonment, and banishment, to attend any religious meetings except such as were sanctioned by the church. Those faithful souls who could not refrain from gathering to worship God, were compelled to meet in dark alleys, in obscure garrets, and at some seasons in the woods at midnight. In the sheltering depths of the forest, a temple of God's own building, those scattered and persecuted children of the Lord assembled to pour out their souls in prayer and praise. But despite all their precautions, many suffered for their faith. The jails were crowded. Families were broken up. Many were banished to foreign lands. Yet God was with his people, and persecution could not prevail to silence their testimony. Many were driven across the ocean to America, and here laid the foundations of civil and religious liberty which have been the bulwark and glory of our country.

As in apostolic days, the persecution turned out rather to the furtherance of the gospel. In a loathsome dungeon crowded with profligates and felons, John Bunyan breathed the very atmosphere of Heaven, and there he wrote his wonderful allegory of the pilgrim's journey from the land of destruction to the celestial city. For two hundred years that voice from Bedford jail has spoken with thrilling power to the hearts of men. Bunyan's "Pilgrim's Progress" and "Grace Abounding to the Chief Sinners," have guided many feet into the path of life.

Baxter, Flavel, Alleine, and other men of talent, education, and deep Christian experience, stood up in valiant defense of "the faith once delivered to the saints." The work accomplished by these men, proscribed and outlawed by the rulers of this world, can never perish. Flavel's "Fountain of Life" and "Method of Grace" have taught thousands how to commit the keeping of their souls to Christ. Baxter's "Reformed Pastor" has proved a blessing to many who desire a revival of the work of God, and his "Saints' Everlasting Rest" has done its work in leading souls to the "rest that remaineth for the people of God."

A hundred years later, in a day of great spiritual darkness, Whitefield and the Wesleys appeared as light-bearers for God. Under the rule of the established church, the people of England had lapsed into a state of religious declension hardly to be distinguished from heathenism. Natural religion was the favorite study of the clergy, and included most of their theology. The higher classes sneered at piety, and prided themselves on being above what they called its fanaticism. The lower classes were grossly ignorant, and abandoned to vice, while the church had no courage or faith to any longer support the down-fallen cause of truth.

Whitefield and the Wesleys were prepared for their work by long and sharp personal convictions of their own lost condition; and that they might be able to endure hardness as good soldiers of Christ, they were subjected to the fiery ordeal of scorn, derision, and persecution, both in the university and as they were entering the ministry. They and a few others who sympathized with them were contemptuously called Methodists by their ungodly fellow-students,— a name which is at the present time regarded as honorable by one of the largest denominations in England and America.

They were members of the Church of England, and were strongly attached to her forms of worship; but the Lord had presented before them in his word a higher standard. The Holy Spirit urged them to preach Christ and him crucified. The power of the Highest attended their labors. Thousands were convicted and truly converted. It was necessary that these sheep be protected from ravening wolves. Wesley had no thought of forming a new denomination, but he organized them under what was called the Methodist Connection.

Mysterious and trying was the opposition which these preachers encountered from the established church; yet God, in his wisdom, had overruled events to cause the reform to begin where it did. Had it come wholly from without, it would not have penetrated where it was so much needed. As the revival preachers were churchmen, and labored within the pale of the church wherever they could find opportunity, the truth had an entrance where the doors would other-wise have remained closed. Some of the clergy were roused from their moral stupor, and became zealous preachers in their own parishes. The churches that had been petrified by formalism were quickened into life.

Men of different gifts performed their appointed work. They did not harmonize upon every point of doctrine, but all were moved by the Spirit of God, and united in the absorbing aim to win souls to Christ. The differences between Whitefield and the Wesleys threatened at one time to create alienation; but as they learned meekness in the school of Christ, mutual forbearance and charity reconciled them. They had no time to dispute, while error and iniquity were teeming every-where, and sinners were going down to ruin. They labored and prayed together, and their friendship was strengthened as they sowed the gospel seed in the same fields.

The servants of God trod a rugged path. Men of influence and learning employed their powers against them. After a time many of the clergy manifested determined hostility, and the doors of the churches were closed against a pure faith and those who proclaimed it. The course of the clergy in denouncing them from the pulpit, aroused the elements of darkness, ignorance, and iniquity. Again and again did John Wesley escape death by a miracle of God's mercy. When the rage of the mob was excited against him, and there seemed no way of escape, an angel in human form came to his side, the mob fell back, and the servant of Christ passed in safety from the place of danger.

The Methodists of those early days— people as well as preachers— endured ridicule and persecution, alike from church-members and from the openly irreligious who were inflamed by their misrepresentations. They were arraigned before courts of justice— such only in name, for justice had no place in the courts of that time. Often they suffered violence from their persecutors. Mobs went from house to house, destroying furniture and goods, plundering whatever they chose, and brutally abusing men, women, and children. In some instances, public notices were posted, calling upon those who desired to assist in breaking the windows and robbing the houses of the Methodists to assemble at a given time and place. These open violations of all law, human and divine, were allowed to pass without a reprimand. A systematic persecution was carried on against a people whose only fault was that of seeking to turn the feet of sinners from the path of destruction to the path of holiness.

Said John Wesley, referring to the charges against himself and his associates: "Some allege that the doctrines of these men are false, erroneous, and enthusiastic; that they are new and unheard-of till of late; that they are Quakerism, fanaticism, Popery. This whole pretense has been already cut up by the roots, it having been shown at large that every branch of this doctrine is the plain doctrine of Scripture interpreted by our own church. Therefore it cannot be false or erroneous, provided the Scripture be true." "Others allege that their doctrines are too strict; they make the way to Heaven too narrow; and this is in truth the original objection, as it was almost the only one for some time, and is secretly at the bottom of a thousand more which appear in various forms. But do they make the way to Heaven any narrower than our Lord and his apostles made it? Is their doctrine stricter than that of the Bible? Consider only a few plain texts: 'Thou shalt love the Lord thy God with all thy heart, and with all thy soul, and with all thy strength, and with all thy mind; and thy neighbor as thyself.' [LUKE 10:27.] 'Every idle word that men shall speak, they shall give account thereof in the day of Judgment.' [MATT. 12:36.] 'Whether therefore ye eat, or drink, or whatsoever ye do, do all to the glory of God.' [1 COR. 10:31.]

"If their doctrine is stricter than this, they are to blame; but you know in your conscience it is not. And who can be one jot less strict without corrupting the word of God? Can any steward of the mysteries of God be found faithful if he change any part of that sacred deposition?— No; he can abate nothing; he can soften nothing; he is constrained to declare to all men, I may not bring down the Scriptures to your taste. You must come up to it, or perish forever. The popular cry is, The uncharitableness of these men! Uncharitable, are they? In what respect? Do they not feed the hungry and clothe the naked? No; that is not the thing; they are not wanting in this, but they are so uncharitable in judging; they think none can be saved but those who are of their own way."

How similar are the arguments urged against those who present the truths of God's word applicable to this time.

Among the reformers of the church an honorable place should be given to those who stood in vindication of a truth generally ignored, even by Protestants,— those who maintained the validity of the fourth commandment, and the obligation of the Bible Sabbath. When the Reformation swept back the darkness that had rested down on all Christendom, Sabbath-keepers were brought to light in many lands. No class of Christians have been treated with greater injustice by popular historians than have those who honored the Sabbath. They have been stigmatized as semi-Judaizers, or denounced as superstitious and fanatical. The arguments which they presented from the Scriptures in support of their faith were met as such arguments are still met, with the cry, The Fathers, the Fathers! ancient tradition, the authority of the church!

Luther and his co-laborers accomplished a noble work for God; but, coming as they did from the Roman Church, having themselves believed and advocated her doctrines, it was not to be expected that they would discern all these errors. It was their work to break the fetters of Rome, and to give the Bible to the world; yet there were important truths which they failed to discover, and grave errors which they did not renounce. Most of them continued to observe the Sunday with other papal festivals. They did not, indeed, regard it as possessing divine authority, but believed that it should be observed as a generally accepted day of worship.

There were some among them, however, who honored the Sabbath of the fourth commandment. Such was the belief and practice of Carlstadt, and there were others who united with him. John Frith, who aided Tyndale in the translation of the Scriptures, and who was martyred for his faith, thus states his views respecting the Sabbath: "The Jews have the word of God for their Saturday, since it is the seventh day, and they were commanded to keep the seventh day solemn. And we have not the word of God for us, but rather against us; for we keep not the seventh day, as the Jews do, but the first, which is not commanded by God's law."

A hundred years later, John Trask acknowledged the obligation of the true Sabbath, and employed voice and pen in its defense. He was soon called to account by the persecuting power of the Church of England. He declared the sufficiency of the Scriptures as a guide for religious faith, and maintained that civil authorities should not control the conscience in matters which concern salvation. He was brought for trial before the infamous tribunal of the Star Chamber, where a long discussion was held respecting the Sabbath. Trask would not depart from the injunctions and commandments of God to obey the commandments of men. He was therefore condemned, and sentenced to be set upon the pillory, and thence to be publicly whipped to the fleet, there to remain a prisoner. This cruel sentence was executed, and after a time his spirit was broken. He endured his sufferings in the prison for one year, and then recanted. Oh that he had suffered on, and won a martyr's crown!

The wife of Trask was also a Sabbath-keeper. She was declared, even by her enemies, to be a woman endowed with many virtues worthy the imitation of all Christians. She was a school-teacher of acknowledged excellence, and was noted for her carefulness in dealing with the poor. "This," said her enemies, "she professed to do out of conscience, as believing she must one day come to be judged for all things done in the flesh. Therefore she resolved to go by the safest rule, rather against than for her private interest." Yet it was declared that she possessed a spirit of strange, unparalleled obstinacy in adhering to her own opinions, which spoiled her. In truth, she chose to obey the word of God in preference to the traditions of men. At last this noble woman was seized and thrust into prison. The charge brought against her was that she taught only five days in the week, and rested on Saturday, it being known that she did it in obedience to the fourth commandment. She was accused of no crime; the motive of her act was the sole ground of complaint.

She was often visited by her persecutors, who employed their most wily arguments to induce her to renounce her faith. In reply, she begged them to show from the Scriptures that she was in error, and urged that if Sunday were really a holy day, the fact must be stated in the word of God. But in vain she asked for Bible testimony. She was exhorted to smother her convictions, and believe what the church declared to be right.

She refused to purchase liberty by renouncing the truth. The promises of God sustained her faith: "Fear none of those things which thou shalt suffer. Behold, the devil shall cast some of you into prison that ye may be tried." "Be thou faithful unto death, and I will give thee a crown of life." [REV. 2:10.] For nearly sixteen years this feeble woman remained a prisoner, in privation and great suffering. The book of God alone can testify what she endured during those weary years. Faithfully she witnessed for the truth; her patience and fortitude failed not until she was released by death.

Her name was cast out as evil on earth, but it is honored in the heavenly records. She was registered among the number who have been hunted, maligned, cast out, imprisoned, martyred; "of whom the world was not worthy." "And they shall be mine, saith the Lord of hosts, in that day when I make up my jewels." [MAL. 3:17.]

God has, in his providence, preserved the history of a few of those who suffered for their obedience to the fourth commandment; but there were many, of whom the world knows nothing, who for the same truth endured persecution and martyrdom. Those who oppressed these followers of Christ called themselves Protestants; but they abjured the fundamental principle of Protestantism,— the Bible and the Bible only as the rule of faith and practice. The testimony of the Scriptures they thrust from them with disdain. This spirit still lives, and it will increase more and more as we near the close of time. Those who honor the Bible Sabbath are even now pronounced willful and stubborn by a large share of the Christian world, and the time is not far distant when the spirit of persecution will be manifested against them.

In the seventeenth century there were several Sabbatarian churches in England, while there were hundreds of Sabbath-keepers scattered throughout the country. Through their labors this truth was planted in America at an early date. Less than half a century after the landing of the pilgrims at Plymouth, the Sabbath-keepers of London sent one of their number to raise the standard of Sabbath reform in the new world. This missionary held that the ten commandments as they were delivered from Mount Sinai are moral and immutable, and that it was the anti-christian power which thought to change times and laws, that had changed the Sabbath from the seventh to the first day. In Newport, R. I., several church-members embraced these views, yet continued for some years in the church with which they had previously been connected. Finally there arose difficulty between the Sabbatarians and the Sunday observers, and the former were compelled to withdraw from the church, that they might peaceably keep God's holy day. Soon after, they entered into an organization, thus forming the first Sabbath-keeping church in America. These Sabbath-keepers had flattered themselves that they could obey the fourth commandment and yet remain connected with Sunday observers. It was a blessing to them and to after-generations that such a union could not exist; for had it continued, it would eventually have caused the light of God's holy Sabbath to go out in darkness.

Some years later, a church was formed in New Jersey. A zealous observer of Sunday, having reproved a person for laboring on that day, was asked for his authority from the Scriptures. On searching for this he found, instead, the divine command for keeping the seventh day, and he began at once to observe it. Through his labors a Sabbatarian church was raised up.

From that time the work gradually extended, until thousands began the observance of the Sabbath. Among the Seventh-day Baptists of this country have been men eminent for talent, learning, and piety. They have accomplished a great and good work as they have stood for two hundred years in defense of the ancient Sabbath.

In the present century few have taken a nobler stand for this truth than was taken by Eld. J. W. Morton, whose labors and writings in favor of the Sabbath have led many to its observance. He was sent as a missionary to Haiti by the Reformed Presbyterians. Sabbatarian publications fell into his hands, and after giving the subject a careful examination, he became satisfied that the fourth commandment requires the observance of the seventh-day Sabbath. Without waiting to consider his own interests, he immediately determined to obey God. He returned home, made known his faith, was tried for heresy, and expelled from the Reformed Presbyterian Church without being allowed to present the reasons for his position.

The course of the Presbyterian synod in condemning Eld. Morton without granting him a hearing, is an evidence of the spirit of intolerance which still exists, even among those claiming to be Protestant reformers. The infinite God, whose throne is in the heavens, condescends to address his people, "Come now, and let us reason together;" [ISA. 1:18.] but frail, erring men proudly refuse to reason with their brethren. They stand ready to censure one who accepts any light which they have not received— as though God had pledged himself to give no more light to any one than he had given to them. This is the course pursued by opposers of the truth in every age. They forget the declaration of the Scriptures, "Light is sown for the righteous." [PS. 97:11.] "The path of the just is as the shining light, that shineth more and more unto the perfect day." [PROV. 4:18.] It is a sad thing when a people claiming to be reformers cease to reform.

If professed Christians would but carefully and prayerfully compare their views with the Scriptures, laying aside all pride of opinion and desire for the supremacy, a flood of light would be shed upon the churches now wandering in the darkness of error. As fast as his people can bear it, the Lord reveals to them their errors in doctrine and their defects of character. From age to age he has raised up men and qualified them to do a special work needed in their time. But to none of these did he commit all the light which was to be given to the world. Wisdom does not die with them. It was not the will of God that the work of reform should cease with the going out of Luther's life; it was not his will that at the death of the Wesleys the Christian faith should become stereotyped. The work of reform is progressive. Go forward, is the command of our great Leader,— forward unto victory.

We shall not be accepted and honored of God in doing the same work that our fathers did. We do not occupy the position which they occupied in the unfolding of truth. In order to be accepted and honored as they were, we must improve the light which shines upon us, as they improved that which shone upon them; we must do as they would have done, had they lived in our day. Luther and the Wesleys were reformers in their time. It is our duty to continue the work of reform. If we neglect to heed the light, it will become darkness; and the degree of darkness will be proportionate to the light rejected.

The prophet of God declares that in the last days knowledge shall be increased. There are new truths to be revealed to the humble seeker. The teachings of God's word are to be freed from the errors and superstition with which they have been encumbered. Doctrines that are not sanctioned by the Scriptures have been widely taught, and many have honestly accepted them; but when the truth is revealed, it becomes the duty of every one to accept it. Those who allow worldly interests, desire for popularity, or pride of opinion, to separate them from the truth, must render an account to God for their neglect.

Chapter 11

The Two Witnesses

The suppression of the Scriptures under the dominion of Rome, the terrible results of that suppression, and the final exaltation of the word of God, are vividly portrayed by the prophetic pencil. To John the exile on lonely Patmos was given a view of the 1260 years during which the papal power was permitted to trample upon God's word and oppress his people. Said the angel of the Lord: "The holy city [the true church] shall they tread under foot forty and two months. And I will give power unto my two witnesses, and they shall prophesy a thousand two hundred and threescore days, clothed in sackcloth." [REV. 11:2, 3.] The periods here mentioned are the same, alike representing the time in which God's faithful witnesses remained in a state of obscurity.

The two witnesses represent the Old and New Testament Scriptures. Both are important testimonies to the origin and perpetuity of the law of God. Both are witnesses also to the plan of salvation. The types, sacrifices, and prophecies of the Old Testament point forward to a Saviour to come. The Gospels and Epistles of the New Testament tell of a Saviour who has come in the exact manner foretold by type and prophecy.

"These are the two olive trees, and the two candlesticks standing before the God of the earth." [REV. 11:4.] Said the psalmist, "Thy word is a lamp unto my feet, and a light unto my path." [PS. 119:105.]

The papal power sought to hide from the people the word of truth, and set before them false witnesses to contradict its testimony. When the Bible was proscribed by religious and secular authority; when its testimony was perverted, and every effort made that men and demons could invent to turn the minds of the people from it; when those who dared proclaim its sacred truths were hunted, betrayed, tortured, buried in dungeon cells, martyred for their faith, or compelled to flee to mountain fastnesses and to dens and caves of the earth,— then indeed did the faithful witnesses prophesy in sackcloth.

But men cannot with impunity trample upon the word of God. The Lord had declared concerning his two witnesses, "If any man will hurt them, fire proceedeth out of their mouth, and devoureth their enemies; and if any man will hurt them, he must in this manner be killed." [REV. 11:5.] The meaning of this fearful denunciation is set forth in the closing chapter of the book of Revelation: "I testify unto every man that heareth the words of the prophecy of this book, If any man shall add unto these things, God shall add unto him the plagues that are written in this book. And if any man shall take away from the words of the book of this prophecy, God shall take away his part out of the book of life, and out of

the holy city, and from the things which are written in this book."
[REV. 22:18, 19.]

Such are the warnings which God has given to guard men against changing in any manner that which he has revealed or commanded. These solemn denunciations apply to all who by their influence lead men to lightly regard the law of God. They should cause those to fear and tremble who flippantly declare it a matter of little consequence whether we obey God's law or not. All who exalt their own opinions above the written word, all who would change the plain meaning of Scripture to suit their own convenience, or for the sake of conformity to the world, are taking upon themselves a fearful responsibility. The written word, the law of God, will measure the character of every man, and condemn all whom this unerring test shall declare wanting.

Notwithstanding the Lord's witnesses were clothed in sackcloth, they continued to prophesy throughout the entire period of 1260 years. In the darkest times there were faithful men who loved God's word, and were jealous for his honor. To these loyal servants were given wisdom, power, and authority to declare his truth during the whole of this time.

"And when they shall have finished their testimony, the beast that ascendeth out of the bottomless pit shall make war against them, and shall overcome them, and kill them. And their dead bodies shall lie in the street of the great city, which spiritually is called Sodom and Egypt, where also our Lord was crucified." [REV. 11:7, 8.]

These events were to take place near the close of the period in which the witnesses testified in sackcloth. Through the medium of the papacy, Satan had long controlled the powers that ruled in Church and State. The fearful results were specially apparent in those countries that rejected the light of the Reformation. There was a state of moral debasement and corruption similar to the condition of Sodom just prior to its destruction, and to the idolatry and spiritual darkness that prevailed in Egypt in the days of Moses.

In no land had the spirit of enmity against Christ and the truth been more strikingly displayed than in giddy and godless France. Nowhere had the gospel encountered more bitter and cruel opposition. In the streets of Paris, Christ had indeed been crucified in the person of his saints. The world still recalls with shuddering horror the scenes of that most cowardly and cruel onslaught, the Massacre of St. Bartholomew. The king of France, urged on by Romish priests and prelates, lent his sanction to the dreadful work. The palace bell, tolling at midnight, gave the signal for the slaughter to begin. Protestants by thousands, sleeping quietly in their homes, trusting to the plighted honor of their king, were dragged forth without a warning, and murdered in cold blood.

Satan, in the person of the Roman zealots, led the van. As Christ was the invisible leader of his people from Egyptian bondage, so was Satan the unseen leader of his subjects in this horrible work of multiplying martyrs. For three days the butchery went on; more than thirty thousand perished. The result caused great joy to the hosts of darkness. The Roman pontiff, sharing in the diabolical rejoicing, proclaimed a jubilee to be observed throughout his dominions, to celebrate the event.

The same master-spirit that urged in the Massacre of St. Bartholomew, led also in the scenes of the French Revolution. Satan seemed to triumph. Notwithstanding the labors of the Reformers, he had succeeded in holding vast multitudes in ignorance concerning God and his word. Now he appeared in a new guise. In France arose an atheistical power that openly declared war against the authority of Heaven. Men threw off all restraint. The law of God was trampled under foot. Those who could engage in the most Heaven-daring blasphemy and the most abominable wickedness were most highly exalted. Fornication was sanctioned by law. Profanity and corruption seemed deluging the earth. In all this, supreme homage was paid to Satan, while Christ, in his characteristics of truth, purity, and unselfish love, was crucified. The Bible was publicly burned. The Sabbath was blotted out. Romanism had enjoined image worship; now divine honors were paid to the vilest objects. The work which the papacy had begun, atheism completed. The one withheld from the people the truths of the Bible; the other taught them to reject both the Bible and its Author. The seed sown by priests and prelates was yielding its evil fruit.

Terrible indeed was the condition of infidel France. The word of truth lay dead in her streets, and those who hated the restrictions and requirements of God's law were jubilant. But transgression and rebellion were followed by the sure result. Unhappy France reaped in blood the harvest she had sown. The war against the Bible and the law of God banished peace and happiness from the hearts and homes of men. No one was secure: he who triumphed to-day was suspected, condemned, to-morrow. Violence and terror reigned supreme. The land was filled with crimes too horrible for pen to trace.

God's faithful witnesses were not long to remain silent. "The Spirit of life from God entered into them, and they stood upon their feet, and great fear fell upon them which saw them." [REV. 11:11.] The world stood aghast at the enormity of guilt which had resulted from a rejection of the Sacred Oracles, and men were glad to return once more to faith in God and his word.

Concerning the two witnesses the prophet declares further, "And they heard a great voice from Heaven saying unto them, Come up hither. And they ascended up to heaven in a cloud; and their enemies beheld them." [REV. 11:12.] Since the French Revolution the word of God has been honored as never before. The Bible has been translated into nearly every language spoken by men, and scattered over every part of the globe. After being, as it were, thrust down to hell, it has, in truth, been exalted to heaven.

Chapter 12

God Honors the Humble

Those who received the great blessings of the Reformation did not go forward in the path so nobly entered upon by Luther. A few faithful men arose from time to time, to proclaim new truth, and expose long-cherished error; but the majority, like the Jews in Christ's day, or the Papists in the time of Luther, were content to believe as their fathers believed, and to live as they lived. Therefore religion again degenerated into formalism; and errors and superstitions which would have been cast aside had the church continued to walk in the light of God's word, were retained and cherished. Thus the spirit inspired by the Reformation gradually died out, until there was almost as great need of reform in the Protestant churches as in the Roman Church in the time of Luther. There was the same spiritual stupor, the same respect for the opinions of men, the same spirit of worldliness, the same substitution of human theories for the teachings of God's word. Pride and extravagance were fostered under the guise of religion. The churches became corrupted by allying themselves with the world. Thus were degraded the great principles for which Luther and his fellow-laborers had done and suffered so much.

As Satan saw that he had failed to crush out the truth by persecution, he again resorted to the same plan of compromise which had led to the great apostasy and the formation of the church of Rome. He induced Christians to ally themselves, not now with pagans, but with those who, by their worship of the god of this world, as truly proved themselves idolaters. Satan could no longer keep the Bible from the people; it had been placed within the reach of all. But he led thousands to accept false interpretations and unsound theories, without searching the Scriptures to learn the truth for themselves. He had corrupted the doctrines of the Bible, and traditions which were to ruin millions were taking deep root. The church was upholding and defending these traditions, instead of contending for the faith once delivered to the saints.

And while wholly unconscious of their condition and their peril, the church and the world were rapidly approaching the most solemn and momentous period of earth's history,— the period of the revelation of the Son of man. Already had the signs which Christ himself had promised,— the sun clothed in darkness by day and the moon by night,— declared his coming near. When Jesus pointed his followers to these signs, he foretold also the existing state of worldliness and backsliding, and gave warning of the result to those who refused to arouse from their careless security: "Thou hast a name that thou livest, and art dead." "If therefore thou shalt not watch, I will come on thee

as a thief, and thou shalt not know what hour I will come upon thee."
[REV. 3:1, 3.]

He who knows the end from the beginning, and who inspired
prophets and apostles to write the future history of churches and of
nations, was about to accomplish another reform similar to that of the
days of Luther. The Lord raised up men to investigate his word, to
examine the foundation upon which the Christian world were building, and to raise the solemn inquiry, What is truth? Are we building
upon the rock, or upon shifting sand?

God saw that many of his professed people were not building for
eternity; and in his care and love he was about to send a message of
warning to arouse them from their stupor, and prepare them for the
coming of their Lord. The warning was not to be entrusted to learned
doctors of divinity or popular ministers of the gospel. Had these been
faithful watchmen, diligently and prayerfully searching the Scriptures,
they would have known the time of night; the prophecies of Daniel
and John would have revealed to them the great events about to take
place. If they had faithfully followed the light already given, some star
of heavenly radiance would have been sent to guide them into all truth.

At the time of Christ's first advent, the priests and scribes of the
holy city, to whom were entrusted the oracles of God, should have
discerned the signs of the times, and proclaimed the coming of the
Promised One. The prophecy of Micah designated his birthplace;
[MICAH 5:2.] Daniel specified the time of his advent. [DAN. 9:25.]
God had committed these prophecies to the Jewish leaders; therefore
they were without excuse if they did not know and declare to the
people that the Messiah's coming was at hand. Their ignorance was
the result of sinful neglect.

God did not send his messengers to the palaces of kings, to the
assemblies of philosophers, or to the schools of the rabbis, to make
known the wonderful fact that the Redeemer of men was about to
appear upon the earth. The Jews were building monuments for the
slain prophets of God, while by their deference to the great men of
the earth they were paying homage to the servants of Satan. Absorbed
in their ambitious strife for place and power among men, they lost
sight of the divine honors proffered them by the King of Heaven.

With what profound and reverent interest should the elders of
Israel have been studying the place, the time, the circumstances, of
the greatest event in the world's history,— the coming of the Son of
God to accomplish the redemption of man! Oh, why were not the
people watching and waiting that they might be among the first to
welcome the world's Redeemer! But lo, at Bethlehem two weary
travelers from the hills of Nazareth traverse the whole length of the
narrow street to the eastern extremity of the town, vainly seeking a
place of rest and shelter for the night. No doors are open to receive

them. In a wretched hovel prepared for cattle, they at last find refuge, and there the Saviour of the world is born.

Heavenly angels had seen the glory which the Son of God shared with the Father before the world was, and they had looked forward with intense interest to his appearance on earth as an event fraught with the greatest joy to all people. Angels were appointed to carry the glad tidings to those who were prepared to receive it, and who would joyfully make it known to the inhabitants of the earth. Christ has stooped to take upon himself man's nature; he is to bear an infinite weight of woe as he shall make his soul an offering for sin; yet angels desire that even in his humiliation, the Son of the Highest may appear before men with a dignity and glory befitting his character. Will the great men of earth assemble at Israel's capital to greet his coming? Will legions of angels present him to the expectant company?

An angel visits the earth to see who are prepared to welcome Jesus. But he can discern no tokens of expectancy. He hears no voice of praise and triumph that the period of the Messiah's coming is at hand. The angel hovers for a time over the chosen city and the temple where the divine presence was manifested for ages; but even here is the same indifference. The priests, in their pomp and pride, are offering polluted sacrifices in the temple. The Pharisees are with loud voices addressing the people, or making boastful prayers at the corners of the streets. There is no evidence that Christ is expected, and no preparation for the Prince of life.

In amazement the celestial messenger is about to return to Heaven with the shameful tidings, when he discovers a group of shepherds who are watching their flocks by night, and, as they gaze into the starry heavens, are contemplating the prophecy of a Messiah to come to earth, and longing for the advent of the world's Redeemer. Here is a company that can be trusted with the heavenly message. And suddenly the angel of the Lord appeared, declaring the good tidings of great joy. Celestial glory flooded all the plain, an innumerable company of angels were revealed, and as if the joy were too great for one messenger to bring from Heaven, a multitude of voices broke forth in the anthem which all the nations of the saved shall one day sing, "Glory to God in the highest, and on earth peace, good will toward men."

Oh, what a lesson is this wonderful story of Bethlehem! How it rebukes our unbelief, our pride and self-sufficiency. How it warns us to beware, lest by our criminal indifference we also fail to discern the signs of the times, and therefore know not the day of our visitation. It is "unto them that look for him" that Christ is to "appear the second time without sin unto salvation." [HEB. 9:28.]

Jesus sends his people a message of warning to prepare them for his coming. To the prophet John was made known the closing work in the great plan of man's redemption. He beheld an angel flying "in the midst of heaven, having the everlasting gospel to preach unto them that dwell on the earth, and to every nation, and kindred, and tongue, and people, saying with a loud voice, Fear God, and give glory to him; for the hour of his Judgment is come; and worship him that made heaven, and earth, and the sea, and the fountains of waters." [REV. 14:6, 7.]

The angel represented in prophecy as delivering this message, symbolizes a class of faithful men, who, obedient to the promptings of God's Spirit and the teachings of his word, proclaim this warning to the inhabitants of earth. This message was not to be committed to the religious leaders of the people. They had failed to preserve their connection with God, and had refused the light from Heaven; therefore they were not of the number described by the apostle Paul: "But ye, brethren, are not in darkness, that that day should overtake you as a thief. Ye are all the children of light, and the children of the day; we are not of the night nor of darkness." [1 THESS. 5:4, 5.]

The watchmen upon the walls of Zion should be the first to catch the tidings of the Saviour's advent, the first to lift their voices to proclaim him near, the first to warn the people to prepare for his coming. But they were at ease, dreaming of peace and safety, while the people were asleep in their sins. Jesus saw his church, like the barren fig-tree, covered with pretentious leaves, yet destitute of precious fruit. There was a boastful observance of the forms of religion, while the spirit of true humility, penitence and faith— which alone could render the service acceptable to God— was lacking. Instead of the graces of the Spirit, there were manifested pride, formalism, vainglory, selfishness, oppression. A backsliding church closed their eyes to the signs of the times. God did not forsake them, or suffer his faithfulness to fail; but they departed from him, and separated themselves from his love. As they refused to comply with the conditions, his promises were not fulfilled to them.

Love for Christ and faith in his coming waxed cold. Such is the sure result of neglect to appreciate and improve the light and privileges which God bestows. Unless the church will follow on in his opening providence, accepting every ray of light, performing every duty which may be revealed, religion will inevitably degenerate into the observance of forms, and the spirit of vital godliness will disappear. This truth has been repeatedly illustrated in the history of the church. God requires of his people works of faith and obedience corresponding to the blessings and privileges bestowed. Obedience requires a sacrifice and involves a cross; and this is why so many of the professed followers of Christ refused to receive the light from Heaven, and, like the Jews of old, knew not the time of their visitation. [LUKE 19:44.] Because of their pride and unbelief, the Lord passed them by, and

revealed his truth to men in humble life, who had given heed to all
the light they had received.

Chapter 13

William Miller

An upright, honest-hearted farmer, who had been led to doubt the divine authority of the Scriptures, yet who sincerely desired to know the truth, was the man chosen of God to proclaim the nearness of Christ's second coming. Like many other reformers, William Miller had in early life battled with poverty, and had thus learned the great lessons of energy and self-denial. His mind was active and well-developed, and he had a keen thirst for knowledge. Though he had not enjoyed the advantages of a collegiate education, his love of study and a habit of careful thought and close criticism rendered him a man of sound judgment and comprehensive views.

He possessed an irreproachable moral character and an enviable reputation, being generally esteemed for his integrity, thrift, and benevolence. In childhood he had been subject to religious impressions; but in early manhood, being thrown almost exclusively into the society of deists, he was led to adopt their sentiments, which he continued to hold for about twelve years. At the age of thirty-four, however, the Holy Spirit impressed his heart with a sense of his condition as a sinner. He found in his former belief no assurance of happiness beyond the grave. The future was dark and gloomy. Referring afterward to his feelings at this time, he said:—

"Annihilation was a cold and chilling thought, and accountability was sure destruction to all. The heavens were as brass over my head, and the earth as iron under my feet. Eternity—what was it? And death— why was it? The more I reasoned, the further I was from demonstration. The more I thought, the more scattered were my conclusions. I tried to stop thinking; but my thoughts would not be controlled. I was truly wretched, but did not understand the cause. I murmured and complained, but knew not of whom. I knew that there was a wrong, but knew not where or how to find the right. I mourned, but without hope."

In this state he continued for some months. "Suddenly," he says, "the character of a Saviour was vividly impressed upon my mind. It seemed that there might be a being so good and compassionate as to himself atone for our transgressions, and thereby save us from suffering the penalty of sin. I immediately felt how lovely such a being must be, and imagined that I could cast myself into the arms of, and trust in the mercy of, such a One. But the question arose, How can it be proved that such a being does exist? Aside from the Bible, I found that I could get no evidence of the existence of such a Saviour, or even of a future state."

"I saw that the Bible did bring to view just such a Saviour as I needed; and I was perplexed to find how an uninspired book should develop principles so perfectly adapted to the wants of a fallen world. I was constrained to admit that the Scriptures must be a revelation from God. They became my delight; and in Jesus I found a friend. The Saviour became to me the chiefest among ten thousand; and the Scriptures, which before were dark and contradictory, now became a lamp to my feet and a light to my path. My mind became settled and satisfied. I found the Lord God to be a Rock in the midst of the ocean of life. The Bible now became my chief study, and I can truly say, I searched it with great delight. I found the half was never told me. I wondered why I had not seen its beauty and glory before, and marveled that I could ever have rejected it. I found everything revealed that my heart could desire, and a remedy for every disease of the soul. I lost all taste for other reading, and applied my heart to get wisdom from God."

He now publicly professed his faith in the religion which he had despised. But his infidel associates were not slow to bring forward all those arguments which he himself had often urged against the divine authority of the Scriptures. He was not then prepared to answer them; but he reasoned, that if the Bible is a revelation from God, it must be consistent with itself; and that as it was given for man's instruction, it must be adapted to his understanding. He determined to study the Scriptures for himself, and ascertain if every apparent contradiction could not be harmonized.

Endeavoring to lay aside all preconceived opinions, and dispensing with commentaries, he compared scripture with scripture by the aid of the marginal references and the concordance. He pursued his study in a regular and methodical manner; beginning with Genesis, and reading verse by verse, he proceeded no faster than the meaning of the several passages so unfolded as to leave him free from all embarrassment. When he found anything obscure, it was his custom to compare it with every other text which seemed to have any reference to the matter under consideration. Every word was permitted to have its proper bearing upon the subject of the text, and if his view of it harmonized with every collateral passage, it ceased to be a difficulty. Thus whenever he met with a passage hard to be understood, he found an explanation in some other portion of the Scriptures. As he studied with earnest prayer for divine enlightenment, that which had before appeared dark to his understanding was made clear. He experienced the truth of the psalmist's words, "The entrance of thy words giveth light; it giveth understanding unto the simple." [PS. 119:130.]

After two years of careful investigation, he was fully satisfied, that the Bible is its own interpreter; that it is a system of revealed truths so clearly and simply given that the wayfaring man, though a fool, need not err therein; that "all Scripture is given by inspiration of God, and is profitable for doctrine, for reproof, for correction, for instruction in righteousness;" [2 TIM. 3:16.] that "prophecy came not in old time by the will of man; but holy men of God spake as they were moved by the Holy Ghost;" [2 PET. 1:21.] that it was written "for our learning, that we through patience and comfort of the Scriptures might have hope." [ROM. 15:4.]

With intense interest he studied the books of Daniel and the Revelation, employing the same principles of interpretation as in the other scriptures, and found, to his great joy, that the prophetic symbols could be understood. Angels of Heaven were guiding his mind, and opening to his understanding prophecies which had ever been dark to God's people. Link after link of the chain of truth rewarded his efforts; step by step he traced down the great lines of prophecy, until he reached the solemn conclusion that in a few years the Son of God would come the second time, in power and glory, and that the events connected with that coming and the close of human probation would take place about the year 1843. [For a statement of Wm. Miller's position and an explanation of his disappointment, see Appendix, Note 1]

Deeply impressed by these momentous truths, he felt that it was his duty to give the warning to the world. He expected to encounter opposition from the ungodly, but was confident that all Christians would rejoice in the hope of meeting the Saviour whom they professed to love. His only fear was, that in their great joy at the prospect of glorious deliverance, so soon to be consummated, many would receive the doctrine without sufficiently examining the Scriptures in demon-stration of its truth. He therefore hesitated to present it, lest he should be in error, and be the means of misleading others. He was thus led to review the evidences in support of the conclusions at which he had arrived, and to consider carefully every difficulty which presented itself to his mind. He found that objections vanished before the light of God's word, as mist before the rays of the sun. Five years spent thus, left him fully convinced of the correctness of his position. And now the duty of making known to others what he believed to be so clearly taught in the Scriptures, urged itself with new force upon him. "When I was about my business," he said, "it was continually ringing in my ears, Go and tell the world of their danger. This text was constantly occurring to me: 'When I say unto the wicked, O wicked man, thou shalt surely die; if thou dost not speak to warn the wicked from his way, that wicked man shall die in his iniquity; but his blood will I require at thine hand. Nevertheless, if thou warn the wicked of his way to turn from it; if he do not turn from his way, he shall die in his iniquity; but thou hast delivered thy soul.' [EZE. 33:8, 9.] I felt that if the wicked could be effectually warned, multitudes of them would repent; and that if they were not warned, their blood might be required at my hand."

He began to present his views in private as he had opportunity, praying that some minister might feel their force and devote himself to their promulgation. But he could not banish the conviction that he had a personal duty to perform in giving the warning. The words were ever recurring to his mind, "Go and tell it to the world; their blood will I require at thy hand." For nine years he waited, the burden still pressing upon his soul, until in 1831 he for the first time publicly gave the reasons of his faith.

As Elisha was called from following his oxen in the field, to receive the mantle of consecration to the prophetic office, so was Wm. Miller called to leave his plow, and open to the people the mysteries of the kingdom of God. With trembling he entered upon his work, leading his hearers down, step by step, through the prophetic periods to the second appearing of Christ. With every effort he gained strength and courage as he saw the wide-spread interest excited by his words.

Though he had little of the learning of the schools, he became wise because he connected himself with the Source of wisdom. He possessed strong mental powers, united with true kindness of heart, Christian humility, calmness, and self-control. He was a man of sterling worth, who could not but command respect and esteem wherever integrity of character and moral excellence were valued. He was attentive and affable to all, ready to listen to the opinions of others, and to weigh their arguments. Without passion or excitement he tested all theories and doctrines by the word of God; and his sound reasoning, and intimate knowledge of the Scriptures, enabled him to refute error and expose falsehood.

The Lord, in his great mercy, does not bring judgments upon the earth without giving warning to its inhabitants by the mouth of his servants. Says the prophet Amos, "Surely the Lord God will do nothing, but he revealeth his secret unto his servants the prophets." [AMOS 3:7.] When the iniquity of the antediluvians moved him to bring a flood of waters upon the earth, he first made known to them his purpose, that they might have opportunity to turn from their evil ways. For a hundred and twenty years was sounded in their ears the warning to repent, lest the wrath of God be manifested in their destruction. But the message seemed to them an idle tale, and they believed it not. From unbelief they proceeded to scorn and contempt, ridiculing the warning as highly improbable, and unworthy of their notice. Emboldened in their wickedness, they mocked the messenger of God, made light of his entreaties, and even accused him of presumption. How dare one man stand up against all the great men of the earth? If Noah's message were true, why did not all the world see it and believe it? One man's assertion against the wisdom of thousands!

They would not credit the warning, nor would they seek shelter in the ark.

Scoffers pointed to the things of nature,— to the unvarying succession of the seasons, to the blue skies that had never poured out rain, to the green fields refreshed by the soft dews of night,— and they cried out, "Doth he not speak parables?" In contempt they declared the preacher of righteousness to be a wild enthusiast; and they went on, more eager in their pursuit of pleasure, more intent upon their evil ways, than ever before. But their unbelief did not hinder the predicted event. God bore long with their wickedness, giving them ample opportunity for repentance; but at the appointed time his judgments were visited upon the rejecters of his mercy.

Christ declares that there will exist similar unbelief concerning his second coming. As the people of Noah's day "knew not until the flood came and took them all away, so," in the words of our Saviour, "shall also the coming of the Son of man be." [MATT. 24:39.] When the professed people of God are uniting with the world, living as they live, and joining with them in forbidden pleasure; when the luxury of the world becomes the luxury of the church; when the marriage bells are chiming, and all are looking forward to many years of worldly prosperity,— then, suddenly as the lightning flashes from the heavens, will come the end of their bright visions and delusive hopes.

As God sent his servant to warn the world of the coming flood, so he sent chosen messengers to make known the nearness of the day of final judgment. But as Noah's contemporaries laughed to scorn the predictions of the solitary preacher of righteousness, so did many in Miller's day treat his words of warning.

In their labors for the Protestant churches, Wm. Miller and his companions encountered a spirit of hatred and opposition little less bitter than that which Luther experienced from Rome. By Romanists in Luther's time, and by Protestants in the time of Miller, fables, false theories, human forms and customs, were received and honored in place of the teachings of the word of truth. In the sixteenth century the Roman Church withheld the Scriptures from the people; in the nineteenth century, when Bibles are scattered everywhere like leaves of autumn, the Protestant churches teach that an important part of the sacred word— and that portion which brings to view truths especially applicable to our time— is sealed, and cannot be understood.

Ministers and people have declared the prophecies of Daniel and John to be a collection of mysteries which no one could understand or explain. But the very title of the book of Revelation contradicts these assertions: "The Revelation of Jesus Christ, which God gave unto him, to show unto his servants things which must shortly come to pass; and he sent and signified it by his angel unto his servant John, who bare record of the word of God, and of the testimony of Jesus Christ, and of all things that he saw. *Blessed* is he that *readeth,* and they that *hear* the words of this prophecy, and *keep* those things which are written therein; for the time is at hand." [REV. 1:1-3.]

Says the prophet, "Blessed is he that readeth"— there are some who will not read; the blessing is not for them. "And they that hear"— there are some, also, who refuse to hear anything concerning the prophecies; the blessing is not for this class. "And keep those things that are written therein"— many refuse to heed the warnings and instructions contained in the Revelation. None of these can claim the blessing promised. All who ridicule the subjects of the prophecy, and mock at the symbols here solemnly given, all who refuse to reform their lives, and prepare for the coming of the Son of man, will be unblest.

In view of the testimony of Inspiration, how dare ministers teach that the Revelation is a mystery beyond the reach of human understanding? It is a mystery revealed, a book opened. The study of the Revelation directs the mind to the prophecies of Daniel, and both present most important instruction, given of God to men, concerning events to take place at the close of this world's history.

To John were opened scenes of deep and thrilling interest in the experience of the church. He saw the position, dangers, conflicts, and final deliverance of the people of God. He records the closing messages which are to ripen the harvest of the earth, either as sheaves for the heavenly garner or as fagots for the fires of the last day. Subjects of vast importance were revealed to him especially for the last church, that those who should turn from error to truth might be instructed concerning the perils and conflicts before them. None need be in darkness in regard to what is coming upon the earth.

Why, then, this wide-spread ignorance concerning an important part of Holy Writ? Why this general reluctance to investigate its teachings? It is the result of a studied effort of the prince of darkness to conceal from men that which reveals his deceptions. For this reason, Christ the Revelator, foreseeing the warfare that would be waged against the study of the Revelation, pronounced a blessing upon all who should read, hear, and observe the words of the prophecy.

Those who believed that the Advent movement was of God, went forth as did Luther and his co-laborers, with their Bibles in their hands, and with fearless firmness met the opposition of the world's great teachers. Many to whom the people had looked for instruction in divine things were proved to be ignorant both of the Scriptures and of the power of God. Yet their very ignorance rendered them more determined; they could not maintain their position by the Scriptures, and they were driven to resort to the sayings and doctrines of men, to the traditions of the Fathers.

But the word of God was the only testimony accepted by the advocates of truth. "The Bible and the Bible only," was their watchword. The weakness of all arguments brought against them, revealed to Adventists the strength of the foundation upon which they stood. At the same time it angered their opponents, who, for want of stronger weapons, resorted to personal abuse. Grave doctors of divinity sneered at Wm. Miller as an unlearned and feeble adversary. Because he explained the visions of Daniel and John, he was denounced as a man of fanciful ideas, who made visions and dreams his hobby. The plainest statements of Bible facts, which could not be controverted, were met with the cry of heresy, ignorance, stupidity, insolence.

Many churches were thrown open to the enemies of the Advent faith, while they were closed against its friends. The sentiments expressed by Doctor Eck concerning Luther were the same that inspired ministers and people to refuse Adventists a hearing. Said the papal champion: "I am surprised at the humility and modesty with which the reverend doctor [Luther] undertakes to oppose, alone, so many illustrious Fathers, thus affirming that he knows more of these things than the sovereign pontiffs, the councils, the doctors, and the universities." "It would be surprising, no doubt, if God had hidden the truth from so many saints and martyrs until the advent of the reverend father." Thus thought great and wise men in the days of Noah, thus argued the opponents of Wm. Miller, and thus still argue those who oppose the proclamation of the Advent faith and the commandments of God.

When Luther was accused of preaching novelties, he declared: "These are not novelties that I preach. But I affirm that the doctrines of Christianity have been lost sight of by those whose special duty it was to preserve them; by the learned, by the bishops. I doubt not indeed that the truth has still found an abode in some few hearts." "Poor husbandmen and simple children in these days understand more of Jesus Christ than the pope, the bishops, or the doctors." When Wm. Miller was charged with showing contempt for the doctors of divinity, he pointed to the word of God as the standard by which all doctrines and theories must be tested; and, knowing that he had truth on his side, he went forward in his work undismayed.

In every age, God has called his servants to lift up their voices against the prevailing errors and sins of the multitude. Noah was called to stand alone to warn the antediluvian world. Moses and Aaron were alone against king and princes, magicians and wise men, and the multitudes of Egypt. Elijah was alone when he testified against an apostate king and a backsliding people. Daniel and his fellows stood alone against the decrees of mighty monarchs. The majority are usually to be found on the side of error and falsehood. The fact that doctors of divinity have the world on their side does not prove them to be on the side of truth and of God. The wide gate and the broad road attract the multitudes, while the strait gate and the narrow way are sought only by the few.

If ministers and people had really desired to know the truth, and had given to the Advent doctrine the earnest, prayerful attention which its importance demands, they would have seen that it was in harmony with the Scriptures. Had they united with its advocates in their labors, there would have resulted such a revival of the work of God as the world has never witnessed. As Whitefield and the Wesleys were urged by the Holy Spirit to arouse the formal and world-loving churches of their time, so was Wm. Miller moved to proclaim the coming of Christ and the necessity of a work of preparation. His only offense was that of opening to the world the "sure word of prophecy, whereunto," says the apostle Peter, "ye do well that ye take heed, as unto a light that shineth in a dark place." [2 PET. 1:19.] He urged its truths upon the people, not with harshness, but in a more mild and persuasive manner than was employed by other reformers.

The opposition which he encountered was very similar to that which had been experienced by Wesley and his fellow-laborers. Let the popular churches of to-day remember that the men whose memory they cherish with reverence endured the same hatred, scorn, and abuse from the press and the pulpit that were heaped upon Wm. Miller.

Why were the doctrine and preaching of Christ's second coming so offensive to the churches? When Jesus made known to his disciples that he must be separated from them, he said, "I go to prepare a place for you; and if I go and prepare a place for you, I will come again, and receive you unto myself, that where I am, there ye may be also." [JOHN 14:2, 3.] When he ascended from Olivet, the compassionate Saviour, anticipating the loneliness and sorrow of his followers, commissioned angels to comfort them with the assurance that he would come again in person, even as he went into heaven. As the disciples stood gazing intently upward to catch the last glimpse of him whom they loved, their attention was arrested by the words, "Ye men of Galilee, why stand ye gazing up into heaven? This same Jesus which is taken up from you into heaven, shall so come in like manner as ye have seen him go into heaven." [ACTS 1:11.] Hope was kindled afresh by the angels' message. The disciples "returned to Jerusalem with great joy, and were continually in the temple, praising and blessing God." [LUKE 24:52, 53.] They were not rejoicing because Jesus had been separated from them and they were left to struggle with the trials and temptations of the world, but because of the angels' assurance that he would come again.

Those who really love the Saviour cannot but hail with joy a message founded upon the word of God, the He in whom their hopes of eternal life are centered is coming again, not to be insulted, despised, and rejected, as at his first advent, but in power and glory, to redeem his people. The proclamation of Christ's coming should now be, as when made by the angels to the shepherds of Bethlehem, good tidings of great joy. There can be no more conclusive evidence that the churches have departed from God than the irritation and animosity excited by this Heaven-sent message.

It is those who do not love the Saviour that desire him to remain away, and such eagerly receive the testimony borne by unfaithful servants, "My Lord delayeth his coming." [MATT. 24:48.] While they refuse to search the Scriptures to learn if these things are so, they grasp every fable which will put off the coming of Christ into the distant future, or make it spiritual, fulfilled at the destruction of Jerusalem, or taking place at death.

Again and again did Wm. Miller urge that if his doctrine were false, he should be shown his error from the Scriptures. In an address to Christians of all denominations he wrote: "What have we believed that we have not been commanded to believe by the word of God, which you yourselves allow is the rule and the only rule of our faith and practice? What have we done that should call down such virulent denunciations against us from pulpit and press, and give you just cause to exclude us (Adventists) from your churches and fellowship?" "If we are wrong, pray show us wherein consists our wrong. Show us from the word of God that we are in error; we have had ridicule enough; that can never convince us that we are in the wrong; the word of God alone can change our views. Our conclusions have been formed deliberately and prayerfully, as we have seen the evidence in the Scriptures."

At a later date he stated: "I have candidly weighed the objections advanced against these views; but I have seen no arguments that were sustained by the Scriptures that, in my opinion, invalidated my position. I cannot, therefore, conscientiously refrain from looking for my Lord, or from exhorting my fellow-men, as I have opportunity, to be in readiness for that event."

In a letter to a friend and fellow-laborer, he spoke thus: "I could not see that I should harm my fellowmen, even supposing the event should not take place at the time specified; for it is a command of our Saviour to look for it, watch, expect it, and be ready. Then, if I could by any means, in accordance with God's word, persuade men to believe in a crucified, risen, and coming Saviour, I felt it would have a bearing on the everlasting welfare and happiness of such. I had not a distant thought of disturbing our churches, ministers, religious editors, or departing from the best biblical commentaries or rules which had been recommended for the study of the Scriptures. And even to this day, my opposers have not been able to show where I have departed from any rule laid down by our old standard writers of the Protestant faith. I have only interpreted Scripture in accordance with their rules."

Instead of arguments from the Scriptures, the opponents of the Advent faith chose to employ ridicule and scoffing. The careless and ungodly, emboldened by the position of religious teachers, resorted to opprobrious epithets, to base and blasphemous witticisms, in their efforts to heap contumely upon Wm. Miller and his work. The gray-headed man who had left a comfortable home to travel at his own expense from city to city, from town to village, toiling unceasingly to bear to the world the solemn warning of the Judgment near, was sneeringly denounced as a fanatic, a liar, a speculating knave.

Time, means, and talents were employed in misrepresenting and maligning Adventists, in exciting prejudice against them, and holding them up to public contempt. Ministers occupied themselves in gathering up damaging reports, absurd and malicious fabrications, and dealing them out from the pulpit. Earnest were the efforts put forth to draw away the minds of the people from the subject of the second advent. But in seeking to crush out Adventism, the popular ministry undermined faith in the word of God. It was made to appear a sin, something of which men should be ashamed, to study the prophecies which relate to the coming of Christ and the end of the world. This teaching made men infidels, and many took license to walk after their own ungodly lusts. Then the authors of the evil charged it all upon Adventists.

The Wesleys encountered similar accusations from the ease-loving, godless ministers who were constantly intercepting their labors, and seeking to destroy their influence. They were pronounced uncharitable, and accused of pride and vanity, because they did not pay homage to the popular teachers of their time. They were accused of skepticism, of disorderly practices, and of contempt of authority. John Wesley fearlessly threw back these charges upon those who framed them, showing that they themselves were responsible for the very evils of which they accused the Methodists. In a similar manner may the charges against Adventism be refuted.

The great controversy between truth and error has been carried forward from century to century since the fall of man. God and angels, and those united with them, have been inviting, urging men to repentance and holiness and Heaven; while Satan and his angels, and men inspired by them, have been opposing every effort to benefit and save the fallen race. Wm. Miller was disturbing Satan's kingdom, and the arch-enemy sought not only to counteract the effect of the message, but to destroy the messenger himself. As Father Miller made a practical application of Scripture truth to the hearts of his hearers, the rage of professed Christians was kindled against him, even as the anger of the Jews was excited against Christ and his apostles. Church-members stirred up the baser classes, and upon several occasions enemies plotted to take his life as he should leave the place of meeting. But holy angels were in the throng, and one of these, in the form of a man, took the arm of this servant of the Lord, and led him in safety from the angry mob. His work was not yet done, and Satan and his emissaries were disappointed in their purpose.

Comparing his own expectations as to the effect of his preaching with the manner in which it had been received by the religious world, Wm. Miller said: "It is true, but not wonderful, when we become acquainted with the state and corruption of the present age, ... that I have met with great opposition from the pulpit and professed religious press; and I have been instrumental, through the preaching of the Advent doctrine, of making it quite manifest that not a few of our theological teachers are infidels in disguise. I cannot for a moment believe that denying the resurrection of the body, or the return of Christ to this earth, or a judgment day yet future, is any the less infidelity now than it was in the days of infidel France; and yet who does not know that these things are as common as pulpits and presses are? And which of these questions are not publicly denied in our pulpits, and by the writers and editors of the public papers?

"Surely, we have fallen on strange times. I expected of course the doctrine of Christ's speedy coming would be opposed by infidels, blasphemers, drunkards, gamblers, and the like; but I did not expect that ministers of the gospel and professors of religion would unite with characters of the above description, at stores and public places, in ridiculing the solemn doctrine of the second advent. Many who were not professors of religion have affirmed to me these facts, and say they have seen them and have felt their blood chilled at the sight.

"These are some of the effects which are produced by preaching this solemn and soul-stirring doctrine among our Pharisees of the present day. Is it possible that such ministers and members are obeying God, and watching and praying for his glorious appearing, while they join these scoffers in their unholy and ungodly remarks? If Christ does come, where must they appear? and what a dreadful account they will meet in that tremendous hour!"

It is the lot of God's servants to suffer opposition and reproach from their contemporaries. Now, as in the time of our Saviour, men build the sepulchers and sound the praises of the dead prophets, while they persecute the living messengers of the Most High. Wm. Miller was despised and hated by the ungodly and unbelieving; but his influence and his labors were a blessing to the world. Under his preaching, thousands of sinners were converted, backsliders were reclaimed, and multitudes were led to study the Scriptures and to find in them a beauty and glory before unknown.

Chapter 14

The First Angel's Message

The prophecy of the first angel's message, brought to view in Revelation 14, found its fulfillment in the Advent movement of 1840-1844. In both Europe and America, men of faith and prayer were deeply moved as their attention was called to the prophecies, and, tracing down the inspired record, they saw convincing evidence that the end of all things was at hand. The Spirit of God urged his servants, to give the warning. Far and wide spread the message of the everlasting gospel, "Fear God, and give glory to him; for the hour of his Judgment is come." [REV. 14:7.]

Wherever missionaries had penetrated, were sent the glad tidings of Christ's speedy return. In different lands were found isolated bodies of Christians, who, solely by the study of the Scriptures, had arrived at the belief that the Saviour's advent was near. In some portions of Europe, where the laws were so oppressive as to forbid the preaching of the Advent doctrine, little children were impelled to declare it, and many listened to the solemn warning.

To Wm. Miller and his co-laborers it was given to preach the message in America, and the light kindled by their labors shone out to distant lands. The testimony of the Scriptures pointing to the coming of Christ in 1843, awakened wide-spread interest. Many were convinced that the arguments from the prophetic periods were correct, and, sacrificing their pride of opinion, they joyfully received the truth. Some ministers laid aside their sectarian views and feelings, left their salaries and their churches, and united in proclaiming the coming of Jesus. There were but few ministers, however, who would accept this message; therefore it was largely committed to humble laymen. Farmers left their fields, mechanics their tools, traders their merchandise, professional men their positions; and yet the number of workers was small in comparison with the work to be accomplished. The condition of an ungodly church and a world lying in wickedness burdened the souls of the true watchmen, and they willingly endured toil, privation, and suffering that they might call men to repentance unto salvation. Though opposed by Satan, the work went steadily forward, and the Advent truth was accepted by many thousands.

Everywhere was heard the searching testimony warning sinners, both worldlings and church-members, to flee from the wrath to come. Like John the Baptist, the forerunner of Christ, the preachers laid the ax at the root of the tree, and urged all to bring forth fruit meet for repentance. Their stirring appeals were in marked contrast to the assurances of peace and safety that were heard from popular pulpits; and wherever the message was given, it moved the people. The simple, direct testimony of the Scriptures, set home by the power of the Holy Spirit, brought a weight of conviction which few were able wholly to resist. Professors of religion were roused from their false security. They saw their backslidings, their worldliness and unbelief, their pride and selfishness. Many sought the Lord with repentance and humiliation. The affections that had so long clung to earthly things they now fixed upon Heaven. The Spirit of God rested upon them, and with hearts softened and subdued they joined to sound the cry, "Fear God, and give glory to him; for the hour of his Judgment is come."

Sinners inquired with weeping, "What must I do to be saved?" Those whose lives had been marked with dishonesty were anxious to make restitution. All who found peace in Christ longed to see others share the blessing. The hearts of parents were turned to their children, and the hearts of children to their parents. The barriers of pride and reserve were swept away. Heartfelt confessions were made, and the members of the household labored for the salvation of those who were nearest and dearest. Often was heard the sound of earnest intercession. Everywhere were souls in deep anguish, pleading with God. Many wrestled all night in prayer for the assurance that their own sins were pardoned, or for the conversion of their relatives or neighbors. That earnest, determined faith gained its object. Had the people of God continued to be thus importunate in prayer, pressing their petitions at the mercy-seat, they would be in possession of a far richer experience than they now have. There is too little prayer, too little real conviction of sin; and the lack of living faith leaves many destitute of the grace so richly provided by our gracious Redeemer.

All classes flocked to the Adventist meetings. Rich and poor, high and low, were, from various causes, anxious to hear for themselves the doctrine of the second advent. The Lord held the spirit of opposition in check while his servants explained the reasons of their faith. Sometimes the instrument was feeble; but the Spirit of God gave power to his truth. The presence of holy angels was felt in these assemblies, and many were daily added to the believers. As the evidences of Christ's soon coming were repeated, vast crowds listened in breathless silence to the solemn words. Heaven and earth seemed to approach each other. The power of God would be felt upon old and young and middle-aged. Men sought their homes with praises upon their lips, and the glad sound rang out upon the still night air. None who attended those meetings can ever forget those scenes of deepest interest.

The proclamation of a definite time for Christ's coming called forth great opposition from many of all classes, from the minister in the pulpit down to the most reckless, Heaven-daring sinner. "No man knoweth the day nor the hour!" [See Appendix, Note 2] was heard alike from the hypocritical minister and the bold scoffer. They closed their ears to the clear and harmonious explanation of the text by those who were pointing to the close of the prophetic periods and to the signs which Christ himself had foretold as tokens of his advent. Many who professed to love the Saviour, declared that they had no opposition to the preaching of his coming; they merely objected to the definite time. God's all-seeing eye read their hearts. They did not wish to hear of Christ's coming to judge the world in righteousness. They had been unfaithful servants, their works would not bear the inspection of the heart-searching God, and they feared to meet their Lord. Like the Jews at the time of Christ's first advent, they were not prepared to welcome Jesus. Satan and his angels exulted and flung the taunt in the face of Christ and holy angels, that his professed people had so little love for him that they did not desire his appearing.

Unfaithful watchmen hindered the progress of the work of God. As the people were roused, and began to inquire the way of salvation, these leaders stepped in between them and the truth, seeking to quiet their fears by falsely interpreting the word of God. In this work, Satan and unconsecrated ministers united, crying, Peace, peace, when God had not spoken peace. Like the Pharisees in Christ's day, many refused to enter the kingdom of Heaven themselves, and those who were entering in, they hindered. The blood of these souls will be required at their hand.

Wherever the message of truth was proclaimed, the most humble and devoted in the churches were the first to receive it. Those who studied the Bible for themselves could not but see the unscriptural character of the popular views of prophecy, and wherever the people were not deceived by the efforts of the clergy to misstate and pervert the faith, wherever they would search the word of God for themselves, the Advent doctrine needed only to be compared with the Scriptures to establish its divine authority.

Many were persecuted by their unbelieving brethren. In order to retain their position in the church, some consented to be silent in regard to their hope; but others felt that loyalty to God forbade them thus to hide the truths which he had committed to their trust. Not a few were cut off from the fellowship of the church for no other reason than expressing their belief in the coming of Christ. Very precious to those who bore the trial of their faith were the words of the prophet, "Your brethren that hated you, that cast you out for my name's sake, said, Let the Lord be glorified. But he shall appear to your joy, and they shall be ashamed." [ISA. 66:5.]

Angels of God were watching with the deepest interest the result of the warning. When the churches as a body rejected the message, angels turned away from them in sadness. Yet there were in the churches many who had not yet been tested in regard to the Advent truth. Many were deceived by husbands, wives, parents, or children, and were made to believe it a sin even to listen to such heresies as were taught by the Adventists. Angels were bidden to keep faithful watch over these souls; for another light was yet to shine upon them from the throne of God.

With unspeakable desire those who had received the message watched for the coming of their Saviour. The time when they expected to meet him was at hand. They approached this hour with a calm solemnity. They rested in sweet communion with God, an earnest of the peace that was to be theirs in the bright hereafter. None who experienced this hope and trust can forget those precious hours of waiting. Worldly business was for the most part laid aside for a few weeks. Believers carefully examined every thought and emotion of their hearts as if upon their death-beds and in a few hours to close their eyes upon earthly scenes. There was no making of "ascension robes;" [See Appendix, Note 3] but all felt the need of internal evidence that they were prepared to meet the Saviour; their white robes were purity of soul,— characters cleansed from sin by the atoning blood of Christ.

God designed to prove his people. His hand covered a mistake in the reckoning of the prophetic periods. [See Appendix, Note 1] Adventists did not discover the error, nor was it discovered by the most learned of their opponents. The latter said, "Your reckoning of the prophetic periods is correct. Some great event is about to take place; but it is not what Mr. Miller predicts; it is the conversion of the world, and not the second advent of Christ."

The time of expectation passed, and Christ did not appear for the deliverance of his people. Those who with sincere faith and love had looked for their Saviour, experienced a bitter disappointment. Yet the Lord had accomplished his purpose: he had tested the hearts of those who professed to be waiting for his appearing. There were among them many who had been actuated by no higher motive than fear. Their profession of faith had not affected their hearts or their lives. When the expected event failed to take place, these persons declared that they were not disappointed; they had never believed that Christ would come. They were among the first to ridicule the sorrow of the true believers.

But Jesus and all the heavenly host looked with love and sympathy upon the tried and faithful yet disappointed ones. Could the veil separating the visible from the invisible world have been swept back, angels would have been seen drawing near to these steadfast souls, and shielding them from the shafts of Satan.

Chapter 15

The Second Angel's Message

The churches that refused to receive the first angel's message, rejected light from Heaven. That message was sent in mercy to arouse them to see their true condition of worldliness and backsliding, and to seek a preparation to meet their Lord. God has ever required his people to remain separate from the world, that they might not be allured from their allegiance to him. He delivered the Israelites from bondage in Egypt because he would not have them corrupted by the idolatry with which they were there surrounded. The children of this world are the children of darkness. Their attention is not directed to the Sun of Righteousness, but is centered upon themselves and the treasures of earth. Blinded by the god of this world, they have no just perception of the glory and majesty of the true God. While they enjoy his gifts, they forget the claims of the Giver. Such have chosen to walk in darkness, and they are led by the prince of the powers of darkness. They do not love and enjoy divine things, because they do not discern their value or loveliness. They have alienated themselves from the light of God, and their understanding becomes so confused in regard to that which is right, true, and holy, that the things of the Spirit of God are foolishness to them.

It was to separate the church of Christ from the corrupting influence of the world that the first angel's message was given. But with the multitude, even of professed Christians, the ties which bound them to earth were stronger than the attractions heavenward. They chose to listen to the voice of worldly wisdom, and turned away from the heart-searching message of truth.

Peter, writing as he was inspired by the Holy Spirit, described the manner in which the message of Christ's second coming would be received: "There shall come in the last days scoffers, walking after their own lusts, and saying, Where is the promise of his coming? for since the fathers fell asleep, all things continue as they were from the beginning of the creation. For this they willingly are ignorant of, that by the word of God the heavens were of old, and the earth standing out of the water and in the water; whereby the world that then was, being overflowed with water, perished; but the heavens and the earth which are now, by the same word are kept in store, reserved unto fire against the day of judgment and perdition of ungodly men." [2 PETER 3:3-7.]

Those who perished in the waters of the flood had an opportunity to escape. All were urged to find refuge in the ark; but the multitudes refused to heed the warning. So when the first angel's message was given, all who heard were invited to receive it, and share the blessing to follow its acceptance; but many scorned and rejected the call. One turned to his farm, another to his merchandise, and they cared for none of these things. Inspiration declares that when the antediluvians rejected Noah's words, the Spirit of God ceased to strive with them. So when men now despise the warnings which God in mercy sends them, his Spirit after a time ceases to arouse conviction in their hearts. God gives light to be cherished and obeyed, not to be despised and rejected. The light which he sends becomes darkness to those who disregard it. When the Spirit of God ceases to impress the truth upon the hearts of men, all hearing is vain, and all preaching also is vain.

When the churches spurned the counsel of God by rejecting the Advent message, the Lord rejected them. The first angel was followed by a second, proclaiming, "Babylon is fallen, is fallen, that great city, because she made all nations drink of the wine of the wrath of her fornication." [REV. 14:8] This message was understood by Adventists to be an announcement of the moral fall of the churches in consequence of their rejection of the first message. The proclamation, "Babylon is fallen," was given in the summer of 1844, and as the result, about fifty thousand withdrew from these churches.

The term Babylon, derived from Babel, and signifying confusion, is applied in Scripture to the various forms of false or apostate religion. But the message announcing the fall of Babylon must apply to some religious body that was once pure, and has become corrupt. It cannot be the Romish Church which is here meant; for that church has been in a fallen condition for many centuries. But how appropriate the figure as applied to the Protestant churches, all professing to derive their doctrines from the Bible, yet divided into almost innumerable sects. The unity for which Christ prayed does not exist. Instead of one Lord, one faith, one baptism, there are numberless conflicting creeds and theories. Religious faith appears so confused and discordant that the world know not what to believe as truth. God is not all in this; it is the work of man,— the work of Satan.

In Revelation 17, Babylon is represented as a woman, a figure which is used in the Scriptures as the symbol of a church. A virtuous woman represents a pure church, a vile woman an apostate church. Babylon is said to be a harlot; and the prophet beheld her drunken with the blood of saints and martyrs. The Babylon thus described represents Rome, that apostate church which has so cruelly persecuted the followers of Christ. But Babylon the harlot is the mother of daughters who follow her example of corruption. Thus are represented those churches that cling to the doctrines and traditions of Rome and follow her worldly practices, and whose fall is announced in the second angel's message.

The close relation of the church to Christ is represented under the figure of marriage. The Lord had joined his people to himself by a solemn covenant, he promising to be their God, and they pledging themselves to be his, and his alone. Said Paul, addressing the church, "I have espoused you to one husband, that I may present you as a chaste virgin to Christ." [2 COR. 11:2] but when her confidence and affection were turned away from him, and she sought after vanity, and allowed the love of worldly things to separate her from God, she forfeited the privileges included in this peculiar and sacred relation. By the apostle James those who assimilate to the world are addressed as "adulterers and adulteresses." [JAS. 4:4.]

A profession of religion has become popular with the world. Rulers, politicians, lawyers, doctors, merchants, join the church as a means of securing the respect and confidence of society, and advancing their own worldly interests. Thus they seek to cover all their unrighteous transactions under a profession of Christianity. The various religious bodies, re-enforced by the wealth and influence of these baptized worldlings, make a still higher bid for popularity and patronage. Splendid churches, embellished in the most extravagant manner, are erected on popular avenues. The worshipers array themselves in costly and fashionable attire. A high salary is paid for a talented minister to entertain and attract the people. His sermons must not touch popular sins, but be made smooth and pleasing for fashionable ears. Thus fashionable sinners are enrolled on the church-records, and fashionable sins are concealed under a pretense of godliness. God looks down upon these apostate bodies, and declares them daughters of a harlot. To secure the favor and support of the great men of earth, they have broken their solemn vows of allegiance and fidelity to the King of Heaven.

The great sin charged against Babylon is, that she "made all nations drink of the wine of the wrath of her fornication." This cup of intoxication which she presents to the world, represents the false doctrines which she has accepted as the result of her unlawful connection with the great ones of the earth. Friendship with the world corrupts her faith, and in her turn she exerts a corrupting influence upon the world by teaching doctrines which are opposed to the plainest statements of the word of God.

Prominent among these false doctrines is that of the temporal millennium,— a thousand years of spiritual peace and prosperity, in which the world is to be converted, before the coming of Christ. This siren song has lulled thousands of souls to sleep over the abyss of eternal ruin.

The doctrine of the natural immortality of the soul has opened the way for the artful working of Satan through modern Spiritualism; and besides the Romish errors, purgatory, prayers for the dead, invocation of saints, etc., which have sprung from this source, it has led many Protestants to deny the resurrection and the Judgment, and has given rise to the revolting heresy of eternal torment, and the dangerous delusion of Universalism.

And even more dangerous and more widely held than these are the assumptions that the law of God was abolished at the cross, and that the first day of the week is now a holy day, instead of the Sabbath of the fourth commandment.

When faithful teachers expound the word of God, there arise men of learning, ministers professing to understand the Scriptures, who denounce sound doctrine as heresy, and thus turn away inquirers after truth. Were it not that the world is hopelessly intoxicated with the wine of Babylon, multitudes would be convicted and converted by the plain, cutting truths of the word of God. The sin of the world's impenitence lies at the door of the church.

God sent his professed people a message that would have corrected the evils which separated them from his favor. A state of union, faith, and love had been produced among those who from every denomination in Christendom received the Advent doctrine; and had the churches in general accepted the same truth, the same blessed results would have followed. But Babylon scornfully rejected the last means which Heaven had in reserve for her restoration, and then, with greater eagerness, she turned to seek the friendship of the world.

Those who preached the first message had no purpose or expectation of causing divisions in the churches, or of forming separate organizations. "In all my labors," said Wm. Miller, "I never had the desire or thought to establish any separate interest from that of existing denominations, or to benefit one at the expense of another. I thought to benefit all. Supposing that all Christians would rejoice in the prospect of Christ's coming, and that those who could not see as I did would not love any the less those who should embrace this doctrine, I did not conceive there would ever be any necessity for separate meetings. My whole object was a desire to convert souls to God, to notify the world of a coming Judgment, and to induce my fellow-men to make that preparation of heart which will enable them to meet their God in peace. The great majority of those who were converted under my labors united with the various existing churches. When individuals came to me to inquire respecting their duty, I always told them to go where they would feel at home; and I never favored any one denomination in my advice to such."

For a time many of the churches welcomed his labors; but as they decided against the Advent truth, they desired to suppress all agitation of the subject. Those who had accepted the doctrine were thus placed in a position of great trial and perplexity. They loved their churches, and were loath to separate from them; but as they were ridiculed and oppressed, denied the privilege of speaking of their hope, or of attending preaching upon the Lord's coming, many at last arose and cast off the yoke which had been imposed upon them.

In the days of the Reformation, the gentle and pious Melancthon declared, "There is no other church than the assembly of those who have the word of God, and who are purified by it." Adventists, seeing that the churches rejected the testimony of God's word, could no longer regard them as constituting the church of Christ, "the pillar and ground of the truth;" and as the message, "Babylon is fallen," began to be proclaimed, they felt themselves justified in separating from their former connection.

Since the rejection of the first message, a sad change has taken place in the churches. As truth is spurned, error is received and cherished. Love for God, and faith in his word, have grown cold. The churches have grieved the Spirit of the Lord, and it has been in a great measure withdrawn. The words of the prophet Ezekiel are fearfully applicable: "Son of man, these men have set up their idols in their heart, and put the stumbling-block of their iniquity before their face. Should I be inquired of at all by them?" "I the Lord will answer him that cometh according to the multitude of his idols." [EZE. 14:3, 4.] Men may not bow down to idols of wood and stone, but all who love the things of the world and take pleasure in unrighteousness have set up idols in their hearts. The majority of professed Christians are serving other gods besides the Lord. Pride and luxury are cherished, idols are set up in the sanctuary, and her holy places are polluted.

Anciently the Lord declared to his servants concerning Israel: "The leaders of this people cause them to err, and they that are led of them are destroyed." [ISA. 9:16.] "The prophets prophesy falsely, and the priests bear rule by their means, and my people love to have it so; and what will ye do in the end thereof?" [JER. 5:31.] "For from the least of them even unto the greatest of them, every one is given to covetousness; and from the prophet even unto the priest, every one dealeth falsely." [JER. 6:13.] The Jewish church, once so highly favored of the Lord, became an astonishment and a reproach through neglect to improve the blessings granted them. Pride and unbelief led to their ruin. But these scriptures do not apply to ancient Israel only. The character and condition of many nominally Christian churches are here portrayed. Though in possession of far greater blessings than were granted to the Jews, they are following in the steps of that people; and the greater the light and privileges bestowed, the greater the guilt of those who permit them to pass unimproved.

The picture which the apostle Paul has drawn of the professed people of God in the last days is a sad but faithful delineation of the popular churches of our time. "Having a form of godliness, but denying the power thereof," "lovers of pleasures more than lovers of

God," "lovers of their own selves, covetous, boasters, proud," [2 TIM. 3:2-7.]— such are a few specifications from the dark catalogue which he has given. And in view of the frequent and startling revelations of crime, even among those that minister in holy things, who dare affirm that there is one sin enumerated by the apostle which is not concealed under a profession of Christianity?

"But what fellowship hath righteousness with unrighteousness?" "And what concord hath Christ with Belial?" "And what agreement hath the temple of God with idols? For ye are the temple of the living God; as God hath said, I will dwell in them, and walk in them; and I will be their God, and they shall be my people. Wherefore come out from among them, and be ye separate, saith the Lord, and touch not the unclean, and I will receive you, and will be a Father unto you, and ye shall be my sons and daughters, saith the Lord Almighty." [2 COR. 6:14-18.]

At the proclamation of the first angel's message, the people of God were in Babylon; and many true Christians are still to be found in her communion. Not a few who have never seen the special truths for this time are dissatisfied with their present position, and are longing for clearer light. They look in vain for the image of Christ in the church. As the churches depart more and more widely from the truth, and ally themselves more closely with the world, the time will come when those who fear and honor God can no longer remain in connection with them. Those that "believed not the truth, but had pleasure in unrighteousness," will be left to receive "strong delusion," and to "believe a lie." [2 THESS. 2:11, 12.] Then the spirit of persecution will again be revealed. But the light of truth will shine upon all whose hearts are open to receive it, and all the children of the Lord still in Babylon, will heed the call, "Come out of her, my people."

Chapter 16

The Tarrying Time

When the year 1843 [See Appendix, Note 4] entirely passed away unmarked by the advent of Jesus, those who had looked in faith for his appearing were for a time left in doubt and perplexity. But notwithstanding their disappointment, many continued to search the Scriptures, examining anew the evidences of their faith, and carefully studying the prophecies to obtain further light. The Bible testimony in support of their position seemed clear and conclusive. Signs which could not be mistaken pointed to the coming of Christ as near. The believers could not explain their disappointment; yet they felt assured that God had led them in their past experience.

Their faith was greatly strengthened by the direct and forcible application of those scriptures which set forth a tarrying time. As early as 1842, the Spirit of God had moved upon Charles Fitch to devise the prophetic chart, which was generally regarded by Adventists as a fulfillment of the command given by the prophet Habakkuk, "to write the vision and make it plain upon tables." No one, however, then saw the tarrying time, which was brought to view in the same prophecy. After the disappointment, the full meaning of this scripture became apparent. Thus speaks the prophet: "Write the vision, and make it plain upon tables, that he may run that readeth it. For the vision is yet for an appointed time, but at the end it shall speak, and not lie: though it tarry, wait for it; because it will surely come, it will not tarry." [HAB. 2:2, 3.]

A portion of Ezekiel's prophecy also was a source of much strength and comfort to believers: "And the word of the Lord came unto me, saying, Son of man, what is that proverb that ye have in the land of Israel, saying, The days are prolonged, and every vision faileth? Tell them therefore, Thus saith the Lord God:" "The days are at hand, and the effect of every vision." "I will speak, and the word that I shall speak shall come to pass; it shall be no more prolonged." "They of the house of Israel say, The vision that he seeth is for many days to come, and he prophesieth of the times that are far off. Therefore say unto them, Thus saith the Lord God: There shall none of my words be prolonged any more, but the word which I have spoken shall be done." [EZE. 12:21-25, 27, 28.]

The waiting ones rejoiced that He who knows the end from the beginning had looked down through the ages, and, foreseeing their disappointment, had given them words of courage and hope. Had it not been for such portions of Scripture, showing that they were in the right path, their faith would have failed in that trying hour.

In the parable of the ten virgins, Matthew 25, the experience of Adventists is illustrated by the incidents of an Eastern marriage. "Then shall the kingdom of Heaven be likened unto ten virgins, which took their lamps, and went forth to meet the bridegroom." "While the bridegroom tarried, they all slumbered and slept." The wide-spread movement under the proclamation of the first message, answered to the going forth of the virgins, while the passing of the time of expectation, the disappointment, and the delay, were represented by the tarrying of the bridegroom. After the definite time had passed, the true believers were still united in the belief that the end of all things was at hand; but it soon became evident that they were losing, to some extent, their zeal and devotion, and were falling into the state denoted in the parable by the slumbering of the virgins during the tarrying time.

About this time, fanaticism began to appear. Some who professed to be zealous believers in the message rejected the word of God as the one infallible guide, and, claiming to be led by the Spirit, gave themselves up to the control of their own feelings, impressions, and imaginations. There were some who manifested a blind and bigoted zeal, denouncing all who would not sanction their course. Their fanatical ideas and exercises met with no sympathy from the great body of Adventists; yet they served to bring reproach upon the cause of truth.

Satan was seeking by this means to oppose and destroy the work of God. The people had been greatly stirred by the Advent movement, thousands of sinners had been converted, and faithful men were giving themselves to the work of proclaiming the truth, even in the tarrying time. The prince of evil was losing his subjects; and in order to bring reproach upon the cause of God, he sought to deceive those who professed the faith, and to drive them to extremes. Then his agents stood ready to seize upon every error, every failure, every unbecoming act, and hold it up before the people in the most exaggerated light, to render Adventists and their faith odious. Thus the greater the number whom he could crowd in to make a profession of the Advent faith while his power controlled their hearts, the greater advantage would he gain by calling attention to them as representatives of the whole body of believers.

Satan is an accuser of the brethren, and it is his spirit which inspires men to watch for the errors and defects of the Lord's people, and to hold them up to notice, while their good deeds are passed by without a mention. He is always active when God is at work for the salvation of souls. When the sons of God come to present themselves before the Lord, Satan comes also among them. In every revival he is ready to bring in those who are unsanctified in heart and unbalanced in mind. When they have accepted some points of truth, and gained a place with believers, he works through them to introduce theories that will deceive the unwary. No man is proved to be a true Christian because he is found in company with the children of God, even in the house of worship and around the table of the Lord. Satan is frequently there upon the most solemn occasions, in the form of those whom he can use as his agents.

The great deceiver will profess anything, in order to gain adherents. But should he claim to be converted, should he, if it were possible, enter Heaven and associate with the angels, he would not be changed in character. While the true worshipers would be bowed in adoration before their Maker, he would be plotting mischief against God's cause and people, devising means to ensnare souls, considering the most successful method of sowing tares.

Satan contests every inch of ground over which God's people advance in their journey toward the heavenly city. In all the history of the church, no reformation has been carried forward without encountering serious obstacles. Thus it was in Paul's day. Wherever the apostle would raise up a church, there were some who professed to receive the faith, but who brought in heresies, that, if received, would eventually crowd out the love of the truth. Luther suffered great perplexity and distress from the course of fanatical persons who claimed that God had spoken directly through them, and who therefore set their own ideas and opinions above the testimony of the Scriptures. Many who were lacking in faith and experience, but who had considerable self-sufficiency, and who loved to hear and tell some new thing, were beguiled by the pretensions of the new teachers, and they joined the agents of Satan in their work of tearing down what God had moved Luther to build up. The Wesleys also, and others who blessed the world by their influence and their faith, encountered at every step the wiles of Satan in pushing over-zealous, unbalanced, and unsanctified ones into fanaticism of every grade.

Wm. Miller had no sympathy with those influences that led to fanaticism. He declared, with Martin Luther, that every spirit should be tested by the word of God: "The devil has great power over the minds of some at the present day. And how shall we know what manner of spirit they are of? The Bible answers: 'By their fruits ye shall know them.'" "There are many spirits gone out into the world; and we are commanded to try the spirits. The spirit that does not cause us to live soberly, righteously, and godly, in this present world, is not the spirit of Christ. I am more and more convinced that Satan has much to do in these wild movements." "Many among us, who pretend to be wholly sanctified, are following the traditions of men, and apparently are as ignorant of truth as others who make no such pretensions, and are not half so modest." "The spirit of error will lead us from the truth; and the Spirit of God will lead us into truth. But, say you, a man may be in error, and think he has the truth. What then? We answer, The

Spirit and word agree. If a man judges himself by the word of God, and finds a perfect harmony through the whole word, then he must believe he has the truth; but if he finds the spirit by which he is led does not harmonize with the whole tenor of God's law or book, then let him walk carefully, lest he be caught in the snare of the devil." "I have often obtained more evidence of inward piety from a kindling eye, a wet cheek, and a choked utterance, than from all the noise in Christendom."

The enemies of the Reformation charged all the evils of fanaticism upon the very ones who were laboring most earnestly against it. A similar course was pursued by the opposers of the Advent movement. And not content with misrepresenting and exaggerating the errors of extremists and fanatics, they circulated unfavorable reports that had not the slightest semblance of truth. These persons were actuated by prejudice and hatred. Their peace was disturbed by the proclamation of Christ at the door. They feared it might be true, yet hoped it was not, and this was the secret of their warfare against Adventists and their faith.

The fact that a few fanatics worked their way into the ranks of Adventists is no more a reason to decide that the movement was not of God, than is the presence of fanatics and deceivers in the church in Paul's or Luther's day a sufficient excuse for discarding or ridiculing their work. Let the people of God arouse out of sleep, and begin in earnest the work of repentance and reformation, let them search the Scriptures to learn the truth as it is in Jesus, let them make an entire consecration to God, and evidence will not be wanting that Satan is still active and vigilant. With all possible deception will he manifest his power, calling to his aid all the fallen angels of his realm.

It was not the proclamation of the Advent message that created fanaticism and division. These appeared in the summer of 1844, when Adventists were in a state of doubt and perplexity concerning their real position. The preaching of the first message in 1843, and of the midnight cry in 1844, tended directly to repress fanaticism and dissension. Those who participated in these solemn movements were in harmony; their hearts were filled with love for one another, and for Jesus, whom they expected soon to see. The one faith, the one blessed hope, lifted them above the control of any human influence, and proved a shield against the assaults of Satan.

Chapter 17

The Midnight Cry

"While the bridegroom tarried, they all slumbered and slept. And at midnight there was a cry made, Behold, the bridegroom cometh; go ye out to meet him. Then all those virgins arose, and trimmed their lamps." [MATT. 25:5-7.]

In the summer of 1844, Adventists discovered the mistake in their former reckoning of the prophetic periods, and settled upon the correct position. The 2300 days of Dan. 8:14, which all believed to extend to the second coming of Christ, had been thought to end in the spring of 1844; but it was now seen that this period extended to the autumn of the same year, [See Appendix, Note 1.] and the minds of Adventists were fixed upon this point as the time for the Lord's appearing. The proclamation of this time message was another step in the fulfillment of the parable of the marriage, whose application to the experience of Adventists had already been clearly seen. As in the parable the cry was raised at midnight announcing the approach of the bridegroom, so in the fulfillment, midway between the spring of 1844, when it was first supposed that the 2300 days would close, and the autumn of 1844, at which time it was afterward found that they were really to close, such a cry was raised, in the very words of Scripture: "Behold, the Bridegroom cometh; go ye out to meet him."

Like a tidal wave the movement swept over the land. From city to city, from village to village, and into remote country places it went, until the waiting people of God were fully aroused. Before this proclamation, fanaticism disappeared, like early frost before the rising sun. Believers once more found their position, and hope and courage animated their hearts. The work was free from those extremes which are ever manifested when there is human excitement without the controlling influence of the word and Spirit of God. It was similar in character to those seasons of humiliation and returning unto the Lord which among ancient Israel followed messages of reproof from his servants. It bore the characteristics which mark the work of God in every age. There was little ecstatic joy, but rather deep searching of heart, confession of sin, and forsaking of the world. A preparation to meet the Lord was the burden of agonizing spirits. There was persevering prayer, and unreserved consecration to God.

Said Wm. Miller, in describing that work: "There is no great expression of joy; that is, as it were, suppressed for a future occasion, when all Heaven and earth will rejoice together with joy unspeakable and full of glory. There is no shouting; that, too, is reserved for the shout from Heaven. The singers are silent; they are waiting to join the angelic hosts, the choir from Heaven. No arguments are used or needed; all seem convinced that they have the truth. There is no clashing of sentiments; all are of one heart and of one mind."

Of all the great religious movements since the days of the apostles, none have been more free from human imperfection and the wiles of Satan than was that of the autumn of 1844. Even now, after the lapse of forty years, all who shared in that movement and who have stood firm upon the platform of truth, still feel the holy influence of that blessed work, and bear witness that it was of God.

At the call, "The Bridegroom cometh; go ye out to meet him," the waiting ones "arose and trimmed their lamps;" they studied the word of God with an intensity of interest before unknown. Angels were sent from Heaven to arouse those who had become discouraged, and prepare them to receive the message. The work did not stand in the wisdom and learning of men, but in the power of God. It was not the most talented, but the most humble and devoted, who were the first to hear and obey the call. Farmers left their crops standing in the fields, mechanics laid down their tools, and with tears and rejoicing went out to give the warning. Those who had formerly led in the cause were among the last to join in this movement. The churches in general closed their doors against it, and a large company who had the living testimony withdrew from their connection. In the providence of God, this cry united with the second angel's message, and gave power to that work.

The midnight cry was not so much carried by argument, though the Scripture proof was clear and conclusive. There went with it an impelling power that moved the soul. There was no doubt, no questioning. Upon the occasion of Christ's triumphal entry into Jerusalem, the people who were assembled from all parts of the land to keep the feast, flocked to the Mount of Olives, and as they joined the throng that were escorting Jesus, they caught the inspiration of the hour, and helped to swell the shout, "Blessed is he that cometh in the name of the Lord!" [MATT. 21:9.] In like manner did unbelievers who flocked to the Adventist meetings— some from curiosity, some merely to ridicule— feel the convincing power attending the message, "Behold, the Bridegroom cometh!"

At that time there was faith that brought answers to prayer,— faith that had respect to the recompense of reward. Like showers of rain upon the thirsty earth, the Spirit of grace descended upon the earnest seekers. Those who expected soon to stand face to face with their Redeemer felt a solemn joy that was unutterable. The softening, subduing power of the Holy Spirit melted the heart, as wave after wave of the glory of God swept over the faithful, believing ones.

Carefully and solemnly those who received the message came up to the time when they hoped to meet their Lord. Every morning they felt that it was their first duty to secure the evidence of their acceptance with

God. Their hearts were closely united, and they prayed much with and for one another. They often met together in secluded places to commune with God, and the voice of intercession ascended to Heaven from the fields and groves. The assurance to the Saviour's approval was more necessary to them than their daily food, and if a cloud darkened their minds, they did not rest until it was swept away. As they felt the witness of pardoning grace, they longed to behold Him whom their souls loved.

But again they were destined to disappointment. The time of expectation passed, and their Saviour did not appear. With unwavering confidence they had looked forward to his coming, and now they felt as did Mary, when, coming to the Saviour's tomb and finding it empty, she exclaimed with weeping, "They have taken away my Lord, and I know not where they have laid him." [JOHN 20:13.]

A feeling of awe, a fear that the message might be true, had for a time served as a restraint upon the unbelieving world. After the passing of the time, this did not at once disappear; they dared not triumph over the disappointed ones; but as no tokens of God's wrath were seen, they recovered from their fears, and resumed their reproach and ridicule. A large class who had professed to believe in the Lord's soon coming, renounced their faith. Some who had been very confident were so deeply wounded in their pride that they felt like fleeing from the world. Like Jonah, they complained of God, and chose death rather than life. Those who had based their faith upon the opinions of others, and not upon the word of God, were now as ready to again exchange their views. The scoffers won the weak and cowardly to their ranks, and all united in declaring that there could be no more fears or expectations now. The time had passed, the Lord had not come, and the world might remain the same for thousands of years.

The earnest, sincere believers had given up all for Christ, and had shared his presence as never before. They had, as they believed, given their last warning to the world, and, expecting soon to be received into the society of their divine Master and the heavenly angels, they had, to a great extent, withdrawn from the unbelieving multitude. With intense desire they had prayed, "Come, Lord Jesus, and come quickly." But he had not come. And now to take up again the heavy burden of life's cares and perplexities, and to endure the taunts and sneers of a scoffing world, was indeed a terrible trial of faith and patience.

Yet this disappointment was not so great as was that experienced by the disciples at the time of Christ's first advent. When Jesus rode triumphantly into Jerusalem, his followers believed that he was about to ascend the throne of David, and deliver Israel from her oppressors. With high hopes and joyful anticipations they vied with one another in showing honor to their King. Many spread their outer garments as a carpet in his path, or strewed before him the leafy branches of the palm. In their enthusiastic joy they united in the glad acclaim, "Hosanna to the Son of David!" When the Pharisees, disturbed and angered by this outburst of rejoicing, wished Jesus to rebuke his disciples, he replied, "If these should hold their peace, the stones would immediately cry out." [LUKE 19:40.] Prophecy must be fulfilled. The disciples were accomplishing the purpose of God; yet they were doomed to a bitter disappointment. But a few days had passed ere they witnessed the Saviour's agonizing death, and laid him in the tomb. Their expectations had not been realized in a single particular, and their hopes died with Jesus. Not till their Lord had come forth triumphant from the grave could they perceive that all had been foretold by prophecy, and "that Christ must needs have suffered, and risen again from the dead." [ACTS 17:3.] In like manner was prophecy fulfilled in the first and second angels' messages. They were given at the right time, and accomplished the work which God designed to accomplish by them.

The world had been looking on, expecting that if the time passed and Christ did not appear, the whole system of Adventism would be given up. But while many, under strong temptation, yielded their faith, there were some who stood firm. They could detect no error in their reckoning of the prophetic periods. The ablest of their opponents had not succeeded in overthrowing their position. True, there had been a failure as to the expected event, but even this could not shake their faith in the word of God. When Jonah proclaimed in the streets of Nineveh that within forty days the city would be overthrown, the Lord accepted the humiliation of the Ninevites, and extended their period of probation; yet the message of Jonah was sent of God, and Nineveh was tested according to his will. Adventists believed that God had in like manner led them to warn the world of the coming Judgment, and notwithstanding their disappointment, they felt assured that they had reached a most important crisis.

The parable of the wicked servant was regarded as applying to those who desired to put off the coming of the Lord: "If that evil servant shall say in his heart, My lord delayeth his coming; and shall begin to smite his fellow-servants, and to eat and drink with the drunken; the lord of that servant shall come in a day when he looketh not for him, and in an hour that he is not aware of, and shall cut him asunder, and appoint him his portion with the hypocrites." [MATT. 24:48-51.]

The feelings of those who held fast the Advent truth are expressed in the words of Wm. Miller: "Were I to live my life over again, with the same evidence that I then had, to be honest with God and men I should have to do as I have done." "I hope I have cleansed my garments from the blood of souls; I feel that, as far as possible, I have freed myself from all guilt in their condemnation." "Although I have been twice disappointed," wrote this man of God, "I am not yet cast down or discouraged." "My hope in the coming of Christ is as strong as ever. I have done only what, after years of sober consideration, I felt it my solemn duty to do. If I have erred, it has been on the side of charity, the love of my fellow-man, and my conviction of duty to God." "One thing I do know, I have preached nothing but what I believed; and God's hand has been with me, his power has been manifested in the work, and much good has been effected." "Many thousands, to all human appearance, have been made to study the Scriptures by the preaching of the time; and by that means, through faith and the sprinkling of the blood of Christ, have been reconciled to God." "I have never courted the smiles of the proud, nor quailed when the world frowned. I shall not now purchase their favor, nor shall I go beyond duty to tempt their hate. I shall never seek my life at their hands, nor shrink, I hope, from losing it, if God in his good providence so orders."

God did not forsake his people; his Spirit still abode with those who did not rashly deny the light which they had received, and denounce the Advent movement. The apostle Paul, looking down through the ages, had written words of encouragement and warning for the tried, waiting ones at this crisis: "Cast not away therefore your confidence, which hath great recompense of reward. For ye have need of patience, that, after ye have done the will of God, ye might receive the promise. For yet a little while, and He that shall come will come, and will not tarry. Now the just shall live by faith; but if any man draw back, my soul shall have no pleasure in him. But we are not of them who draw back unto perdition, but of them that believe to the saving of the soul." [HEB. 10:35-39.]

The people here addressed were in danger of making ship-wreck of faith. They had done the will of God in following the guidance of his Spirit and his word; yet they could not understand his purpose in their past experience, nor could they discern the pathway before them, and they were tempted to doubt whether God had indeed been leading them. At this time the words were specially applicable, "Now the just shall live by faith." As the bright light of the midnight cry had shone upon their pathway, and they had seen the prophecies unsealed, and the rapidly fulfilling signs telling that the coming of Christ was near, Adventists had walked, as it were, by sight. But now, bowed down by disappointed hopes, they could stand only by faith in God and in his word. The scoffing world were saying, "You have been deceived. Give up your faith, and say that the Advent movement was of Satan." But God's word declared, "If any man draw back, my soul shall have no pleasure in him." To renounce their faith now, and deny the power of the Holy Spirit which had attended the message, would be drawing back toward perdition. They were encouraged to steadfastness by the words of Paul, "Cast not away therefore your confidence;" "ye have need of patience;" "for yet a little while, and He that shall come will come, and will not tarry." Their only safe course was to cherish the light which they had already received of God, hold fast to his promises, and continue to search the Scriptures, and patiently wait and watch to receive further light.

Chapter 18

The Sanctuary

The scripture which above all others had been both the foundation and central pillar of the Advent faith was the declaration, "Unto two thousand and three hundred days; then shall the sanctuary be cleansed." [DAN. 8:14.] These had been familiar words to all believers in the Lord's soon coming. By the lips of thousands was this prophecy joyfully repeated as the watchword of their faith. All felt that upon the events therein brought to view depended their brightest expectations and most cherished hopes. These prophetic days had been shown to terminate in the autumn of 1844. In common with the rest of the Christian world, Adventists then held that the earth, or some portion of it, was the sanctuary, and that the cleansing of the sanctuary was the purification of the earth by the fires of the last great day. This they understood would take place at the second coming of Christ. Hence the conclusion that Christ would return to the earth in 1844.

But the appointed time came, and the Lord did not appear. The believers knew that God's word could not fail; their interpretation of the prophecy must be at fault; but where was the mistake? Many rashly cut the knot of difficulty by denying that the 2300 days ended in 1844. No reason could be given for this position, except that Christ had not come at the time of expectation. They argued that if the prophetic days had ended in 1844, Christ would then have come to cleanse the sanctuary by the purification of the earth by fire; and that since he had not come, the days could not have ended.

To accept this conclusion was to renounce the former reckoning of the prophetic periods, and involve the whole question in confusion. It was a deliberate surrender of positions which had been reached through earnest, prayerful study of the Scriptures, by minds enlightened by the Spirit of God, and hearts burning with its living power; positions which had withstood the most searching criticism and the most bitter opposition of popular religionists and worldly-wise men, and which had stood firm against the combined forces of learning and eloquence, and the taunts and revilings alike of the honorable and the base. And all this sacrifice was made in order to maintain the theory that the earth is the sanctuary.

God had led his people in the great Advent movement; his power and glory had attended the work, and he would not permit it to end in darkness and disappointment, to be reproached as a false and fanatical excitement. He would not leave his word involved in doubt and uncertainty. Though the majority of Adventists abandoned their former reckoning of the prophetic periods, and consequently denied the correctness of the movement based thereon, a few were unwilling to renounce points of faith and experience that were sustained by the Scriptures and by the special witness of the Spirit of God. They believed that they had adopted sound principles of interpretation in their study of the Scriptures, and that it was their duty to hold fast the truths already gained, and to still pursue the same course of Biblical research. With earnest prayer they reviewed their position, and studied the Scriptures to discover their mistake. As they could see no error in their explanation of the prophetic periods, they were led to examine more closely the subject of the sanctuary. [See Appendix, Note 5]

In their investigation they learned, that the earthly sanctuary, built by Moses at the command of God, according to the pattern shown him in the mount, was "a figure for the time then present, in which were offered both gifts and sacrifices;" that its two holy places were "patterns of things in the heavens;" that Christ, our great High Priest, is "a minister of the sanctuary, and of the true tabernacle, which the Lord pitched, and not man;" that "Christ is not entered into the holy places made with hands, which are the figures of the true, but into Heaven itself, now to appear in the presence of God for us." [HEB. 9:9, 23; 8:2, 9:24.]

The sanctuary in Heaven, in which Jesus ministers in our behalf, is the great original, of which the sanctuary built by Moses was a copy. God placed his Spirit upon the builders of the earthly sanctuary. The artistic skill displayed in its construction was a manifestation of divine wisdom. The walls had the appearance of massive gold, reflecting in every direction the light of the seven lamps of the golden candlestick. The table of show-bread and the altar of incense glittered like burnished gold. The gorgeous curtain which formed the ceiling, inwrought with figures of angels in blue and purple and scarlet, added to the beauty of the scene. And beyond the second veil was the holy shekinah, the visible manifestation of God's glory, before which none but the high priest could enter and live. The matchless splendor of the earthly tabernacle reflected to human vision the glories of that heavenly temple where Christ our forerunner ministers for us before the throne of God.

As the sanctuary on earth had two apartments, the holy and the most holy, so there are two holy places in the sanctuary in Heaven. And the ark containing the law of God, the altar of incense, and other instruments of service found in the sanctuary below, have also their counterpart in the sanctuary above. In holy vision the apostle John was permitted to enter Heaven, and he there beheld the candlestick and the altar of incense, and as "the temple of God was opened," he beheld also "the ark of his testament." [REV. 4:5; 8:3; 11:19.]

Those who were seeking for the truth found indisputable proof of the existence of a sanctuary in Heaven. Moses made the earthly sanctuary after a pattern which was shown him. Paul declares that that pattern was the true sanctuary which is in Heaven. John testifies that he saw it in Heaven.

In the temple in Heaven, the dwelling-place of God, his throne is established in righteousness and judgment. In the most holy place is his law, the great rule of right by which all mankind are tested. The ark that enshrines the tables of the law is covered with the mercy-seat, before which Christ pleads his blood in the sinner's behalf. Thus is represented the union of justice and mercy in the plan of human redemption. This union infinite wisdom alone could devise, and infinite power accomplish; it is a union that fills all Heaven with wonder and adoration. The cherubim of the earthly sanctuary looking reverently down upon the mercy-seat, represent the interest with which the heavenly host contemplate the work of redemption. This is the mystery of mercy into which angels desire to look,— that God can be just while he justifies the repenting sinner, and renews his intercourse with the fallen race; that Christ could stoop to raise unnumbered multitudes from the abyss of ruin, and clothe them with the spotless garments of his own righteousness, to unite with angels who have never fallen, and to dwell forever in the presence of God.

At the termination of the 2300 days, in 1844, no sanctuary had existed on earth for many centuries; therefore the sanctuary in Heaven must be the one brought to view in the declaration, "Unto two thousand and three hundred days; then shall the sanctuary be cleansed." But how could a sanctuary in Heaven need cleansing? Turning again to the Scriptures, the students of prophecy learned that the cleansing was not a removal of physical impurities, for it was to be accomplished with blood, and therefore must be a cleansing from sin. Thus says the apostle: "It was therefore necessary that the patterns of things in the Heavens should be purified with these [the blood of animals]; but the heavenly things themselves with better sacrifices than these [even the precious blood of Christ]." [HEB. 9:23.] To obtain a further knowledge of the cleansing to which the prophecy points, it was necessary to understand the ministration of the heavenly sanctuary. This could be learned only from the ministration of the earthly sanctuary; for Paul declares that the priests who officiated there served "unto the example and shadow of heavenly things." [HEB. 8:5.]

The ministration of the earthly sanctuary consisted of two divisions: the priests ministered daily in the holy place, while once a year the high priest performed a special work of atonement in the most holy, for the cleansing of the sanctuary. Day by day the repentant sinner brought his offering to the door of the tabernacle, and, placing his hand upon the victim's head, confessed his sins, thus in figure transferring them to the innocent sacrifice. The animal was then slain, and the blood or the flesh was carried by the priest into the holy place.

Thus the sin was, in figure, transferred to the sanctuary. Such was the work that went forward throughout the year. The continual transfer of sins to the sanctuary, rendered a further work of ministration necessary in order for their removal. On the tenth day of the seventh month the high priest entered the inner apartment, or most holy place, which he was forbidden, on pain of death, to enter at any other time. The cleansing of the sanctuary then performed completed the yearly round of service.

On the great day of atonement, two kids of the goats were brought to the door of the tabernacle, and lots were cast upon them, "one lot for the Lord, and the other lot for the scape-goat." The goat upon which fell the lot for the Lord was to be slain as a sin-offering for the people. And the priest was to bring his blood within the veil, and sprinkle it upon the mercy-seat, and before the mercy-seat. "And he shall make an atonement for the holy place, because of the uncleanness of the children of Israel, and because of their transgressions in all their sins; and so shall he do for the tabernacle of the congregation, that remaineth among them in the midst of their uncleanness." [LEV. 16:8, 16.]

"And Aaron shall lay both his hands upon the head of the live goat, and confess over him all the iniquities of the children of Israel, and all their transgressions in all their sins, putting them upon the head of the goat, and shall send him away by the hand of a fit man into the wilderness; and the goat shall bear upon him all their iniquities unto a land not inhabited." [LEV. 16:21, 22.] The scape-goat came no more into the camp of Israel, and the man who led him away was required to wash himself and his clothing with water before returning to the camp.

The whole ceremony was designed to impress the Israelites with the holiness of God and his abhorrence of sin, and, further, to show them that they could not come in contact with sin without becoming polluted. Every man was required to afflict his soul while this work of atonement was going forward. All business was laid aside, and the whole congregation of Israel spent the day in solemn humiliation before God, with prayer, fasting, and deep searching of heart.

Important truths concerning the atonement may be learned from the typical service. A substitute was accepted in the sinner's stead; but the sin was not canceled by the blood of the victim. A means was thus provided by which it was transferred to the sanctuary. By the offering of blood, the sinner acknowledged the authority of the law, confessed his guilt in transgression, and expressed his desire for pardon through faith in a Redeemer to come; but he was not yet entirely released from the condemnation of the law. On the day of atonement the high priest, having taken an offering from the congregation, went into the most holy place with the blood of this general offering, and sprinkled it upon the mercy-seat, directly over the law, to make satisfaction for its claims. Then, in his character of mediator, he took the sins upon himself, and bore them from the sanctuary. Placing his hands upon the head of the scape-goat, he confessed over him all these sins, thus in figure transferring them from himself to the goat. The goat then bore them away, and they were regarded as forever separated from the people.

Such was the service performed "unto the example and shadow of heavenly things." And what was done in type in the ministration of the earthly, is done in reality in the ministration of the heavenly. After his ascension, our Saviour began his work as our high priest. Says Paul, "Christ is not entered into the holy places made with hands, which are the figures of the true; but into Heaven itself, now to appear in the presence of God for us." [HEB. 9:24.] In harmony with the typical service, he began his ministration in the holy place, and at the termination of the prophetic days in 1844, as foretold by Daniel the prophet, he entered the most holy to perform the last division of his solemn work,— to cleanse the sanctuary.

As the sins of the people were anciently transferred, in figure, to the earthly sanctuary by the blood of the sin-offering, so our sins are, in fact, transferred to the heavenly sanctuary by the blood of Christ. And as the typical cleansing of the earthly was accomplished by the removal of the sins by which it had been polluted, so the actual cleansing of the heavenly is to be accomplished by the removal, or blotting out, of the sins which are there recorded. This necessitates an examination of the books of record to determine who, through repentance of sin and faith in Christ, are entitled to the benefits of his atonement. The cleansing of the sanctuary therefore involves a work of investigative Judgment. This work must be performed prior to the coming of Christ to redeem his people; for when he comes, his reward is with him to give to every man according to his works. [REV. 22:12.]

Thus those who followed in the advancing light of the prophetic word saw that instead of coming to the earth at the termination of the 2300 days in 1844, Christ then entered the most holy place of the heavenly sanctuary, into the presence of God, to perform the closing work of atonement, preparatory to his coming.

It was seen, also, that while the sin-offering pointed to Christ as a sacrifice, and the high priest represented Christ as a mediator, the scape-goat typified Satan, the author of sin, upon whom the sins of the truly penitent will finally be placed. When the high priest, by virtue of the blood of the sin-offering, removed the sins from the sanctuary, he placed them upon the scape-goat. When Christ, by virtue of his own blood, removes the sins of his people from the heavenly sanctuary at the close of his ministration, he will place them upon Satan, who, in the execution of the judgment, must bear the final penalty. The scape-goat was sent away into a land not inhabited, never to come again into the congregation of Israel. So will Satan be forever banished from the presence of God and his people, and he will be blotted from existence in the final destruction of sin and sinners.

Chapter 19

An Open and a Shut Door

The subject of the sanctuary was the key which unlocked the mystery of the disappointment, showing that God had led his people in the great Advent movement. It opened to view a complete system of truth, connected and harmonious, and revealed present duty as it brought to light the position and work of God's people.

After the passing of the time of expectation, in 1844, Adventists still believed the Saviour's coming to be very near; they held that they had reached an important crisis, and that the work of Christ as man's intercessor before God, had ceased. Having given the warning of the Judgment near, they felt that their work for the world was done, and they lost their burden of soul for the salvation of sinners, while the bold and blasphemous scoffing of the ungodly seemed to them another evidence that the Spirit of God had been withdrawn from the rejecters of his mercy. All this confirmed them in the belief that probation had ended, or, as they then expressed it, "the door of mercy was shut." [See Appendix, Note 6]

But clearer light came with the investigation of the sanctuary question. Now was seen the application of those words of Christ in the Revelation, addressed to the church at this very time: "These things saith he that is holy, he that is true, he that hath the key of David, he that openeth and no man shutteth, and shutteth and no man openeth; I know thy works; behold, I have set before thee an open door, and no man can shut it." [REV. 3:7, 8.] Here an open as well as a shut door is brought to view. At the termination of the 2300 prophetic days in 1844, Christ changed his ministration from the holy to the most holy place. When, in the ministration of the earthly sanctuary, the high priest on the day of atonement entered the most holy place, the door of the holy place was closed, and the door of the most holy was opened. So, when Christ passed from the holy to the most holy of the heavenly sanctuary, the door, or ministration, of the former apartment was closed, and the door, or ministration, of the latter was opened. Christ had ended one part of his work as our intercessor, to enter upon another portion of the work; and he still presented his blood before the Father in behalf of sinners. "Behold," he declares, "I have set before thee an open door, and no man can shut it."

Those who by faith follow Jesus in the great work of the atonement, receive the benefits of his mediation in their behalf; but those who reject the light that brings to view this work of ministration, are not benefited thereby. The Jews who rejected the light given at Christ's first advent, and refused to believe in him as the Saviour of the world, could not receive pardon through him. When Jesus at his ascension entered by his own blood into the heavenly sanctuary to shed upon his disciples the blessings of his mediation, the Jews were left in total darkness, to continue their useless sacrifices and offerings. The ministration of types and shadows had ceased. That door by which men had formerly found access to God, was no longer open. The Jews had refused to seek him in the only way whereby he could then be found, through the ministration in the sanctuary in Heaven. Therefore they found no communion with God. To them the door was shut. They had no knowledge of Christ as the true sacrifice and the only mediator before God; hence they could not receive the benefits of his mediation.

The condition of the unbelieving Jews illustrates the condition of the careless and unbelieving among professed Christians, who are willingly ignorant of the work of our merciful High Priest. In the typical service, when the high priest entered the most holy place, all Israel were required to gather about the sanctuary, and in the most solemn manner humble their souls before God, that they might receive the pardon of their sins, and not be cut off from the congregation. How much more essential in this anti-typical day of atonement that we understand the work of our High Priest, and know what duties are required of us.

Men cannot with impunity reject the warnings which God in mercy sends them. A message was sent from Heaven to the world in Noah's day, and their salvation depended upon the manner in which they treated that message. Because they rejected the warning, the Spirit of God was withdrawn from that sinful race, and they perished in the waters of the flood. In the time of Abraham, mercy ceased to plead with the guilty inhabitants of Sodom, and all but Lot with his wife and two daughters were consumed by the fire sent down from heaven. So in the days of Christ. The Son of God declared to the unbelieving Jews of that generation, "Your house is left unto you desolate." [MATT. 23:38.] Looking down to the last days, the same infinite power declares, concerning those who "received not the love of the truth, that they might be saved," "For this cause God shall send them strong delusion, that they should believe a lie; that they all might be damned who believed not the truth, but had pleasure in unrighteousness." [2 THESS. 2:10-12.] As they reject the teachings of his word, God withdraws his Spirit, and leaves them to the deceptions which they love.

But Christ still intercedes in man's behalf, and light will be given to those who seek it. Though this was not at first understood by Adventists, it was afterward made plain as the scriptures which define their true position began to open before them.

The passing of the time in 1844 was followed by a period of great trial to those who still held the Advent faith. Their only relief, so far as ascertaining their true position was concerned, was the light which directed their minds to the sanctuary above. As has been stated, Adventists were for a short time united in the belief that the door of mercy was shut. This position was soon abandoned. Some renounced their faith in their former reckoning of the prophetic periods, and ascribed to human or Satanic agencies the powerful influence of the Holy Spirit which had attended the Advent movement. Another class firmly held that the Lord had led them in their past experience; and as they waited and watched and prayed to know the will of God, they saw that their great High Priest had entered upon another work of ministration, and, following him by faith, they were led to understand also the closing work of the church, and were prepared to receive and give to the world the warning of the third angel of Revelation 14.

Chapter 20

The Third Angel's Message

When Christ entered the most holy place of the heavenly sanctuary to perform the closing work of the atonement, he committed to his servants the last message of mercy to be given to the world. Such is the warning of the third angel of Revelation 14. Immediately following its proclamation, the Son of man is seen by the prophet coming in glory to reap the harvest of the earth.

As foretold in the Scriptures, the ministration of Christ in the most holy place began at the termination of the prophetic days in 1844. To this time apply the words of the Revelator, "The temple of God was opened in Heaven, and there was seen in his temple the ark of his testament." [REV. 11:19] The ark of God's testament is in the second apartment of the sanctuary. As Christ entered there, to minister in the sinner's behalf, the inner temple was opened, and the ark of God was brought to view. To those who by faith beheld the Saviour in his work of intercession, God's majesty and power were revealed. As the train of his glory filled the temple, light from the holy of holies was shed upon his waiting people on the earth.

They had by faith followed their High Priest from the holy to the most holy, and they saw him pleading his blood before the ark of God. Within that sacred ark is the Father's law, the same that was spoken by God himself amid the thunders of Sinai, and written with his own finger on the tables of stone. Not one command has been annulled; not a jot or tittle has been changed. While God gave to Moses a copy of his law, he preserved the great original in the sanctuary above. Tracing down its holy precepts, the seekers for truth found, in the very bosom of the Decalogue, the fourth commandment, as it was first proclaimed: "Remember the Sabbath day, to keep it holy. Six days shalt thou labor, and do all thy work; but the seventh day is the Sabbath of the Lord thy God: in it thou shalt not do any work, thou, nor thy son, nor thy daughter, thy man-servant, nor thy maid-servant, nor thy cattle, nor thy stranger that is within thy gates: for in six days the Lord made heaven and earth, the sea, and all that in them is, and rested the seventh day; wherefore the Lord blessed the Sabbath day, and hallowed it." [EX. 20:8-11.]

The Spirit of God impressed the hearts of these students of his word. The conviction was urged upon them, that they had ignorantly transgressed the fourth commandment by disregarding the Creator's rest-day. They began to examine the reasons for observing the first day of the week instead of the day which God had sanctified. They could find no evidence in the Scriptures that the fourth commandment had been abolished, or that the Sabbath had been changed; the blessing which first hallowed the seventh day had never been removed. They had been honestly seeking to know and do God's will, and now, as they saw themselves transgressors of his law, sorrow filled their hearts. They at once evinced their loyalty to God by keeping his Sabbath holy.

Many and earnest were the efforts made to overthrow their faith. None could fail to see that if the earthly sanctuary was a figure or pattern of the heavenly, the law deposited in the ark on earth was an exact transcript of the law in the ark in Heaven, and that an acceptance of the truth concerning the heavenly sanctuary involved an acknowledgment of the claims of God's law, and the obligation of the Sabbath of the fourth commandment. Here was the secret of the bitter and determined opposition to the harmonious exposition of the Scriptures that brought to view the ministration of Christ in the heavenly sanctuary. How hard men tried to close the door which God had opened, and to open the door which he had closed! But "He that openeth and no man shutteth, and shutteth and no man openeth," had declared, "Behold, I have set before thee an open door, and no man can shut it." [REV. 3:7, 8.] Christ had opened the door, or ministration, of the most holy place, light was shining from that open door of the sanctuary in Heaven, and the fourth commandment was shown to be included in the law within the ark; what God had established, no man could overthrow.

Those who had accepted the light concerning the mediation of Christ and the perpetuity of the law of God, found that these were the truths brought to view in the third message. [See Appendix, Note 7] The angel declares, "Here are they that keep the commandments of God, and the faith of Jesus." This statement is preceded by a solemn and fearful warning: "If any man worship the beast and his image, and receive his mark in his forehead, or in his hand, the same shall drink of the wine of the wrath of God, which is poured out without mixture into the cup of his indignation." [REV. 14:9, 10.] An interpretation of the symbols employed was necessary to an understanding of this message. What was represented by the beast, the image, and the mark? Again those who were seeking for the truth returned to the study of the prophecies.

In the book of the Revelation, under the symbols of a great red dragon, a leopard-like beast, and a beast with lamb-like horns, [REV. 12; 13.] are brought to view those earthly governments which are especially engaged in trampling upon God's law and persecuting his people. Their war is carried forward to the close of time. The people of God, symbolized by a holy woman and her children, are greatly in the minority. In the last days only a remnant exists. John speaks of them as those that "keep the commandments of God, and have the testimony of Jesus Christ." [REV. 12:17.]

Through the great powers controlled by paganism and the papacy, symbolized by the dragon and the leopard-like beast, Satan for many centuries destroyed God's faithful witnesses. Under the dominion of Rome, they were tortured and slain for more than a thousand years; but the papacy was at last deprived of its strength, and forced to desist from persecution. [REV. 13:3, 10.] At that time the prophet beheld a new power coming up, represented by the beast with lamb-like horns. The appearance of this beast and the manner of its rise seem to indicate that the power which it represents is unlike those brought to view under the preceding symbols. The great kingdoms that have ruled the world obtained their dominion by conquest and revolution, and they were presented to the prophet Daniel as beasts of prey, rising when the "four winds of the heaven strove upon the great sea." [DAN. 7:2.] But the beast with horns like a lamb is seen "coming up out of the earth;" [REV. 13:11.] signifying that instead of overthrowing other powers to establish itself, the nation thus represented arose in territory previously unoccupied, and grew up gradually and peacefully.

Here is a striking figure of the rise and growth of our own nation. And the lamb-like horns, emblems of innocence and gentleness, well represent the character of our government, as expressed in its two fundamental principles, Republicanism and Protestantism. The Christian exiles who first fled to America, sought an asylum from royal oppression and priestly intolerance, and they determined to establish a government upon the broad foundation of civil and religious liberty. These principles are the secret of our power and prosperity as a nation. Millions from other lands have sought our shores, and the United States has risen to a place among the most powerful nations of the earth.

But the stern tracings of the prophetic pencil reveal a change in this peaceful scene. The beast with lamb-like horns speaks with the voice of a dragon, and "exerciseth all the power of the first beast before him." The spirit of persecution manifested by paganism and the papacy is again to be revealed. Prophecy declares that this power will say "to them that dwell on the earth, that they should make an image to the beast." [REV. 13:14.] The image is made to the first or leopard-like beast, which is the one brought to view in the third angel's message. By this first beast is represented the Roman Church, an ecclesiastical body clothed with civil power, having authority to punish all dissenters. The image to the beast represents another religious body clothed with similar power. The formation of this image is the work of that beast whose peaceful rise and mild professions render it so striking a symbol of the United States. Here is to be found an image of the papacy. When the churches of our land, uniting upon such points of faith as are held by them in common, shall influence the State to enforce their decrees and sustain their institutions, then will Protestant America have formed an image of the Roman hierarchy. Then the true church will be assailed by persecution, as were God's ancient people. Almost every century furnishes examples of what bigotry and malice can do under a plea of serving God by protecting the rights of Church and State. Protestant churches that have followed in the steps of Rome by forming alliance with worldly powers have manifested a similar desire to restrict liberty of conscience. In the seventeenth century thousands of nonconformist ministers suffered under the rule of the Church of England. Persecution always follows religious favoritism on the part of secular governments.

The beast with lamb-like horns commands "all, both small and great, rich and poor, free and bond, to receive a mark in their right hand, or in their foreheads; and that no man might buy or sell, save he that had the mark, or the name of the beast, or the number of his name." [REV. 13:16, 17.] This is the mark concerning which the third angel utters his warning. It is the mark of the first beast, or the papacy, and is therefore to be sought among the distinguishing characteristics of that power. The prophet Daniel declared that the Roman Church, symbolized by the little horn, was to think to change times and laws, [DAN. 7:25.] while Paul styled it the man of sin, [2 THESS. 2:3, 4.] who was to exalt himself above God. Only by changing God's law could the papacy exalt itself above God; whoever should understandingly keep the law as thus changed would be giving supreme honor to that power by which the change was made. Such an act of obedience to papal laws would be a mark of allegiance to the pope in the place of God.

The papacy has attempted to change the law of God. The second commandment, forbidding image worship, has been dropped from the law, and the fourth commandment has been so changed as to authorize the observance of the first instead of the seventh day as the Sabbath. But Papists urge as a reason for omitting the second commandment, that it is unnecessary, being included in the first, and that they are giving the law exactly as God designed it to be understood. This cannot be the change foretold by the prophet. An intentional, deliberate change is brought to view: "He shall *think* to change times and laws." The change in the fourth commandment exactly fulfills the prophecy. For this change the only authority claimed is that of the church. Here the papal power openly sets itself above God.

The claim so often put forth, that Christ changed the Sabbath, is disproved by his own words. In his sermon on the mount he declared: "Think not that I am come to destroy the law or the prophets; I am not come to destroy, but to fulfill. For verily I say unto you, Till heaven and earth pass, one jot or one tittle shall in no wise pass from the law, till all be fulfilled. Whosoever therefore shall break one of these least commandments, and shall teach men so, he shall be called the least in the kingdom of Heaven; but whosoever shall do and teach them, the same shall be called great in the kingdom of Heaven." [MATT. 5:17-19.]

Roman Catholics acknowledge that the change of the Sabbath was made by their church; and they cite this change as evidence of the authority of the church to legislate in divine things, and declare that Protestants, by observing the Sabbath as thus changed, are recognizing her power. The Roman Church has not relinquished her claim to supremacy; and when the world and the Protestant churches accept a Sabbath of her creating, while they reject the Bible Sabbath, they virtually admit this assumption. They may claim the authority of apostles and Fathers for the change; but in so doing they ignore the very principle which separates them from Rome,— that "the Bible, and the Bible only, is the religion of Protestants." The papist can see that they are deceiving themselves, willingly closing their eyes to the facts in the case. As the Sunday institution gains favor, he rejoices, feeling assured that it will eventually bring the whole Protestant world under the banner of Rome.

The fourth commandment, which Rome has endeavored to set aside, is the only precept of the Decalogue that points to God as the Creator of the heavens and the earth, and thus distinguishes the true God from all false gods. The Sabbath was instituted to commemorate the work of creation, and thus to direct the minds of men to the true and living God. The fact of his creative power is cited throughout the Scriptures as proof that the God of Israel is superior to heathen deities. Had the Sabbath always been kept, man's thoughts and affections would have been led to his Maker as the object of reverence and worship, and there would never have been an idolater, an atheist, or an infidel.

That institution which points to God as the Creator is a sign of his rightful authority over the beings he has made. The change of the Sabbath is the sign, or mark, of the authority of the Romish Church. Those who, understanding the claims of the fourth commandment, choose to observe the false in place of the true Sabbath, are thereby paying homage to that power by which alone it is commanded. The change in the fourth commandment is the change pointed out in the prophecy, and the keeping of the counterfeit Sabbath is the reception of the mark. But Christians of past generations observed the first day, supposing that they were keeping the Bible Sabbath, and there are in the churches of to-day many who honestly believe that Sunday is the Sabbath of divine appointment. None of these have received the mark of the beast. There are true Christians in every church, not excepting the Roman Catholic communion. The test upon this question does not come until Sunday observance is enforced by law, and the world is enlightened concerning the obligation of the true Sabbath. Not until the issue is thus plainly set before the people, and they are brought to choose between the commandments of God and the command- ments of men, will those who continue in transgression receive the mark of the beast.

The most fearful threatening ever addressed to mortals is con- tained in the third angel's message. That must be a terrible sin which calls down the wrath of God unmingled with mercy. Men are not to be left in darkness concerning this important matter; the warning against this sin is to be given to the world before the visitation of God's judgments, that all may know why they are to be inflicted, and have opportunity to escape them.

In the issue of the great contest, two distinct, opposite classes are developed. One class "worship the beast and his image, and receive his mark," and thus bring upon themselves the awful judgments threatened by the third angel. The other class, in marked contrast to the world, "keep the commandments of God and the faith of Jesus." [REV. 14:9, 12.] Though the powers of earth summon their forces to compel "all, both small and great, rich and poor, free and bond," to receive the mark of the beast, yet the people of God do not receive it. The prophet of Patmos beholds "them that had gotten the victory over the beast, and over his image, and over his mark, and over the number of his name, stand on the sea of glass, having the harps of God," [REV. 15:2.] and singing the song of Moses and the Lamb.

Such were the momentous truths that opened before those who received the third angel's message. As they reviewed their experience from the first proclamation of the second advent to the passing of the time in 1844, they saw their disappointment explained, and hope and joy again animated their hearts. Light from the sanctuary illuminated the past, the present, and the future, and they knew that God had led them by his unerring providence. Now with new courage and firmer faith, they joined in giving the warning of the third angel.

The work of Sabbath reform to be accomplished in the last days is clearly brought to view in the prophecy of Isaiah: "Thus saith the Lord, Keep ye judgment, and do justice; for my salvation is near to come, and my righteousness to be revealed. Blessed is the man that doeth this, and the son of man that layeth hold on it; that keepeth the Sabbath from polluting it, and keepeth his hand from doing any evil." "The sons of the stranger, that join themselves to the Lord, to serve him, and to love the name of the Lord, to be his servants, every one that keepeth the Sabbath from polluting it, and taketh hold of my covenant; even them will I bring to my holy mountain, and make them joyful in my house of prayer." [ISA. 56:1, 2, 6, 7.]

These words apply in the Christian age, as is shown by the context: "The Lord God which gathereth the outcasts of Israel saith, Yet will I gather others to him, beside those that are gathered unto him." [ISA. 56:8.] Here is foreshadowed the gathering in of the Gentiles by the gospel. And upon those who then honor the Sabbath, a blessing is pronounced. Thus the obligation of the fourth command-ment extends past the crucifixion, resurrection, and ascension of Christ, to the time when his servants should preach to all nations the message of glad tidings.

The Lord commands by the same prophet, "Bind up the testi-mony, seal the law among my disciples." [ISA. 8:16.] The seal of God's law is found in the fourth commandment. This only, of all the ten, brings to view both the name and the title of the Lawgiver. It declares him to be the Creator of the heavens and the earth, and thus shows his claim to reverence and worship above all others. Aside from this precept, there is nothing in the Decalogue to show by whose authority the law is given. When the Sabbath was changed by the papal power, the seal was taken from the law. The disciples of Jesus are called upon to restore it, by exalting the Sabbath of the fourth commandment to its rightful position as the Creator's memorial and the sign of his authority.

"To the law and to the testimony." While conflicting doctrines and theories abound, the law of God is the one unerring standard to which all opinions, doctrines, and theories are to be brought. Says the prophet, "If they speak not according to this word, it is because there is no light in them." [ISA. 8:20.]

Again, the command is given, "Cry aloud, spare not, lift up thy voice like a trumpet, and show my people their transgression, and the house of Jacob their sins." It is not the wicked world, but those whom the Lord designates as "my people," that are to be reproved for their transgressions. He declares further, "Yet they seek me daily, and delight to know my ways, as a nation that did righteousness, and forsook not the ordinance of their God." [ISA. 58:1, 2.] Here is brought to view a class who think themselves righteous, and appear to manifest great interest in the service of God; but the stern and solemn rebuke of the Searcher of hearts proves them to be trampling upon the divine precepts.

The prophet thus points out the ordinance which has been for-saken: "Thou shalt raise up the foundations of many generations; and thou shalt be called, The repairer of the breach, the restorer of paths to dwell in. If thou turn away thy foot from the Sabbath, from doing thy pleasure on my holy day; and call the Sabbath a delight, the holy of the Lord, honorable; and shalt honor him, not doing thine own ways, nor finding thine own pleasure, nor speaking thine own words; then shalt thou delight thyself in the Lord." [ISA. 58:12, 13.] This prophecy also applies in our time. The breach was made in the law of God when the Sabbath was changed by the Romish power. But the time has come for that divine institution to be restored. The breach is to be repaired, and the foundation of many generations to be raised up.

With peculiar fitness may the Sabbath be called the foundation of many generations. Hallowed by the Creator's rest and blessing, it was kept by Adam in his innocence in holy Eden; by Adam, fallen yet repentant, when he was driven from his happy estate. It was kept by all the patriarchs, from Abel to righteous Noah, to Abraham, to Jacob. When the chosen people were in bondage in Egypt, many, in the midst of prevailing idolatry, lost their knowledge of God's law; but when the Lord delivered Israel, he proclaimed his law in awful grandeur to the assembled multitude, that they might know his will, and fear and obey him forever.

From that day to the present, the knowledge of God's law has been preserved in the earth, and the Sabbath of the fourth commandment has been kept. Though the man of sin succeeded in trampling the Sabbath under foot, yet even in the period of his supremacy there were, hidden in secret places, faithful souls who honored the Creator's rest-day.

Since the Reformation, there have been in every generation witnesses for God to uphold the standard of the ancient Sabbath. Though often in the midst of reproach and persecution, a constant testimony has been borne to this truth. Since 1844, in fulfillment of the prophecy of the third angel's message, the attention of the world has been called to the true Sabbath, and a constantly increasing number are returning to the observance of God's holy day.

Chapter 21

The Third Message Rejected

As those who first received the third angel's message saw the beauty and harmony of the system of truth that opened to their understanding, they desired that the light which appeared to them so precious might be imparted to all Christians; and they could not but believe that it would be joyfully accepted. But truths that would place them at variance with the world were not welcome to many who claimed to be followers of Christ. Obedience to the fourth commandment required a sacrifice from which the majority, even of Adventists, drew back.

As the claims of the Sabbath were presented, many who had endured reproach and persecution for the Advent faith, began to reason from the worldling's standpoint. Said they: "We have always kept Sunday, our fathers kept it, and many good and pious men have died happy while keeping it. If they were right, so are we. The keeping of this new Sabbath would throw us out of harmony with the world, and we would have no influence over them. What can a little company keeping the seventh day hope to accomplish against all the world who are keeping Sunday?" It was by similar arguments that the Jews endeavored to justify their rejection of Christ. Their fathers had been accepted of God in presenting the sacrificial offerings, and why could not the children find salvation in pursuing the same course? So, in the time of Luther, Papists reasoned that true Christians had died in the Catholic faith, and therefore that religion was sufficient for salvation. Such reasoning would prove an effectual barrier to all advancement in religious faith or practice.

Many urged that Sunday-keeping had been an established doctrine and a wide-spread custom of the church for many centuries. Against this argument it was shown that the Sabbath and its observance were more ancient and wide-spread, even as old as the world itself, and bearing the sanction both of angels and of God. When the foundations of the earth were laid, when the morning stars sang together, and all the sons of God shouted for joy, then was laid the foundation of the Sabbath. [JOB 38:6, 7; GEN. 2:1-3.] Well may this institution demand our reverence: it was ordained by no human authority, and rests on no human tradition; it was established by the Ancient of days, and commanded by his eternal word.

As the attention of the people was called to the subject of Sabbath reform, popular ministers perverted the word of God, placing such interpretations upon its testimony as would best quiet inquiring minds. And those who did not search the Scriptures for themselves were content to accept the ministers' conclusions. By argument, sophistry, the traditions of the Fathers, and the authority of the church, opposers endeavored to overthrow the truth. Its advocates were driven to their Bibles to defend the validity of the fourth commandment. Humble men, armed with the word of truth alone, met and withstood the attacks of men of learning. With surprise and anger, popular ministers found their eloquent sophistry powerless against the simple, straight-forward reasoning of men who had but little of the learning of the schools.

In the absence of Scripture testimony in their favor, many with unwearying persistency inquired,— forgetting how the same reasoning had been employed against Christ and his apostles,— "Why do not our great men understand this Sabbath question? But few believe as you do, and even these are uneducated persons. It cannot be that you are right, and that all the men of learning in the world are wrong."

To refute such arguments it was needful only to cite the teachings of the Scriptures and the history of the Lord's dealings with his people in all ages. God works through those who hear and obey his voice, those who will, if need be, speak unpalatable truths, those who do not fear to reprove popular sins. The reason why he does not oftener choose men of learning and high position is, that they trust to their creeds, theories, and theological systems, and feel no need to be taught of God. Only those who have a personal connection with the Source of wisdom are able to understand or explain the Scriptures. Men who have little of the learning of the schools are called to declare the truth, not because they are unlearned, but because they are not too self-sufficient to be taught of God. They learn in the school of Christ, and their humility and obedience make them great. In committing to them a knowledge of his truth, God confers upon them an honor, in comparison with which earthly honor and human greatness sink into insignificance.

As the majority of Adventists rejected the truths concerning the sanctuary and the law of God, many also renounced their faith in the Advent movement, and adopted unsound and conflicting views of the prophecies which applied to that work. Some were led into the error of repeated time-setting. The light of the third message would have shown them that no prophetic period extends to the coming of Christ; that the exact time of his coming is not foretold. But, turning from the light, they continued to set time after time for the Lord to come, and as often were disappointed.

When the Thessalonian church received erroneous views concerning the coming of Christ, the apostle Paul counseled them to carefully test their hopes and anticipations by the word of God. He cited them to prophecies revealing the events to take place before Christ should come, and showed that they had no ground to expect him in their day. "Let no man deceive you by any means," are his words of warning. Should they indulge expectations that were not sanctioned by the Scriptures, they would be led to a mistaken course of action; disappointment would expose them to the derision of unbelievers, and they would be in danger of yielding to discourage-ment, and would be tempted to doubt the truths essential for their salvation. The apostle's admonition to the Thessalonians contains an important lesson for those who live in the last days. Many Adventists have felt that unless they could fix their faith upon a definite time for the Lord's coming, they could not be zealous and diligent in the work of preparation. But as their hopes are again and again excited, only to be destroyed, their faith receives such a shock that it becomes well-nigh impossible for them to be impressed by the great truths of prophecy. The more frequently a definite time is set for the second advent, and the more widely it is taught, the better it suits the purposes of Satan. After the time has passed, he excites ridicule and contempt of its advocates, and thus casts reproach upon the true time movement of 1843 and 1844. Those who persist in this error will at last fix upon a date too far in the future for the coming of Christ. Thus they will be led to rest in a false security, and many will not be undeceived until it is too late.

The history of ancient Israel is a striking illustration of the past experience of the Adventist body. God led his people in the Advent movement, even as he led the children of Israel from Egypt. In the great disappointment their faith was tested as was that of the Hebrews at the Red Sea. Had they still trusted to the guiding hand that had been with them in their past experience, they would have seen of the salvation of God. If all who had labored unitedly in the work in 1844 had received the third angel's message, and proclaimed it in the power of the Holy Spirit, the Lord would have wrought mightily with their efforts. A flood of light would have been shed upon the world. Years ago the inhabitants of the earth would have been warned, the closing work completed, and Christ would have come for the redemption of his people.

It was not the will of God that Israel should wander forty years in the wilderness; he desired to lead them directly to the land of Canaan, and establish them there, a holy, happy people. But "they could not enter in because of unbelief." [HEB. 3:19.] Because of their backsliding and apostasy, they perished in the desert, and others were raised up to enter the promised land. In like manner, it was not the will of God that the coming of Christ should be so long delayed, and his people should remain so many years in this world of sin and sorrow. But unbelief separated them from God. As they refused to do the work which he had appointed them, others were raised up to proclaim the message. In mercy to the world, Jesus delays his coming, that sinners may have an opportunity to hear the warning, and find in him a shelter before the wrath of God shall be poured out.

Now, as in former ages, the presentation of a truth that reproves the errors and sins of the times, will call forth a storm of opposition. "Every one that doeth evil hateth the light, neither cometh to the light, lest his deeds should be reproved." [2 JOHN 3:20.] Those who cannot sustain their position by the Scriptures are stubbornly determined that it shall be sustained at all hazards, and with a malicious spirit they attack the character and motives of those who stand in defense of unpopular truth. Though very unbelieving in regard to the sure word of prophecy, they manifest the utmost credulity in accepting anything detrimental to the Christian integrity of those who dare to reprove fashionable sins. This spirit will increase more and more as we near the close of time.

And what is our duty in view of this? Shall we conclude that the truth ought not to be presented, since its effect is so often to arouse men to evade or resist its claims?— No; we have no more reason for withholding the testimony of God's word because it excites opposition than had Martin Luther. Luther declared himself to have been urged on, compelled by the Spirit of God, to battle against the evils of his time; and in the same manner must those labor who still carry forward the work of reform. To the servants of God at this time is the command addressed, "Lift up thy voice like a trumpet, and show my people their transgression, and the house of Jacob their sins."

The true followers of Christ do not wait for truth to become popular. Being convinced of their duty, they deliberately accept the cross, and thus remove the greatest obstacle to the reception of truth,— the only argument which its advocates have never been able to refute. It is weak, inefficient world-servers that think it praiseworthy to have no principle in religious things. We should choose the right because it is right, and leave consequences with God. To men of principle, faith, and daring, is the world indebted for its great reforms. By such men must the work of reform for this time be carried forward.

Thus saith the Lord: "Hearken unto me, ye that know righteousness, the people in whose heart is my law; fear ye not the reproach of men, neither be ye afraid of their revilings. For the moth shall eat them up like a garment, and the worm shall eat them like wool; but my righteousness shall be forever, and my salvation from generation to generation." [ISA. 51:7, 8.]

Chapter 22

Modern Revivals

The character and tendency of modern revivals has awakened no little anxiety in thoughtful minds among all denominations. Many of the revivals which have occurred during the last forty years have given no evidence of the work of the Spirit of God. The light which flames up for a time, soon dies out; leaving the darkness more dense than before. Popular revivals are too often carried by appeals to the imagination, by exciting the emotions, by pandering to the love for what is new and startling. Converts thus gained have no more desire to listen to Bible truths, no more interest in the testimony of prophets and apostles, than has the novel-reader. Unless a religious service has something of a sensational character, it has no attractions for them. A message which appeals to unimpassioned reason, awakens no response. The plain warnings of God's word, relating directly to their eternal interests, fall as upon the ears of the dead.

The converts are not renewed in heart or changed in character. They do not renounce their pride and love of the world. They are no more willing to deny self, to take up the cross, and follow the meek and lowly Jesus, than before their conversion. In a genuine revival, when the Spirit of God convicts the conscience, the earnest, anxious inquiry will be heard, "What must I do to be saved?" And this not merely for a day. With every truly converted soul the relation to God and to eternal things will be the great topic of life. But where, in the popular churches of to-day, is the deep conviction of sin? where is the spirit of consecration to God? The spirit that controls the world rules in the church. Religion has become the sport of infidels and skeptics because so many who bear its name are ignorant of its principles. The power of godliness has well-nigh departed from the churches. Heart union with Christ is a rare thing now. The majority of church-members know no tie but that which joins them to an organized body of professed Christians. Love of pleasure and thirst for excitement are everywhere prevalent. Picnics, church theatricals, church fairs, fine houses, personal display, have banished thoughts of God. Lands and goods and worldly occupations engross the mind, and things of eternal interest receive hardly a passing notice.

Pleasure-lovers may have their names upon the church-records, they may stand high as worldly-wise men; but they have no connection with Christ of Calvary. The apostle Paul describes a class who are "lovers of pleasures more than lovers of God; having a form of godliness, but denying the power thereof." Concerning them he says, "From such turn away." [2 TIM. 3:4, 5.] Be not deceived by them, do not imitate their practices.

Notwithstanding the wide-spread declension of faith and piety in the churches, the Lord still has honest children among them; and before his judgments shall be visited upon the earth, many ministers and lay-members will separate from these bodies, and gladly receive the special truths for this time. The enemy of souls desires to hinder this work, and before the time shall come for such a movement, he will arouse what appears to be great religious interest in the churches. They will exult that God is working marvelously for them, when the work is that of another spirit. Under a religious guise, Satan will spread his influence over the land. He hopes to deceive many by leading them to think that God is still with the churches.

Many of the revivals which have occurred since 1844, in the churches that have rejected the Advent truth, are similar in character to those more extensive movements to be witnessed in the future. The excitement manifested is well adapted to mislead the unwary; yet none need be deceived. In the light of God's word it is not difficult to determine the nature of these religious movements. The history of God's dealings with his people in the past testifies that his Spirit is not poured out upon those who neglect or oppose the warnings sent them by his servants. And by the rule which Christ himself has given, "Ye shall know them by their fruits," it is evident that these movements are not the work of the Spirit of God.

The scriptural doctrine of conversion has been almost wholly lost sight of Christ declared to Nicodemus, "Except a man be born again, he cannot see the kingdom of God." The heart must be renewed by divine grace, man must have a new life from above, or his profession of godliness will avail nothing.

The apostle Paul, in relating his experience, presents an important truth concerning the work to be wrought in conversion. He says, "I was alive without the law once,"— he felt no condemnation; "but when the commandment came," when the law of God was urged upon his conscience, "sin revived, and I died." [ROM. 7:9.] Then he saw himself a sinner, condemned by the divine law. Mark, it was Paul, and not the law, that died. He says, further, "I had not known sin, but by the law; for I had not known lust, except the law had said, Thou shalt not covet." [ROM. 7:7.] "The commandment which was ordained to life, I found to be unto death." [ROM. 7:10.] The law which promised life to the obedient, pronounced death upon the transgressor. "Wherefore," he says, "the law is holy, and the commandment holy, and just, and good." [ROM. 7:12.]

How wide the contrast between these words of Paul and those that come from many of the pulpits of to-day. The people are taught that obedience to God's law is not necessary to salvation; that they have only to believe in Jesus, and they are safe. Without the law, men have no conviction of sin, and feel no need of repentance. Not seeing their lost condition as violators of God's law, they do not feel their need of the atoning blood of Christ as their only hope of salvation.

The law of God is an agent in every genuine conversion. There can be no true repentance without conviction of sin. The Scriptures declare that "sin is the transgression of the law," [1 JOHN 3:4.] and that "by the law is the knowledge of sin." [ROM. 3:20.] In order to see his guilt, the sinner must test his character by God's great standard of righteousness. To discover his defects, he must look into the mirror of the divine statutes. But while the law reveals his sins, it provides no remedy. The gospel of Christ alone can offer pardon. In order to stand forgiven, the sinner must exercise repentance toward God, whose law has been transgressed, and faith in Christ, his atoning sacrifice. Without true repentance, there can be no true conversion. Many are deceived here, and too often their entire experience proves to be a deception. This is why so many who are joined to the church have never been joined to Christ.

"The carnal mind is enmity against God; for it is not subject to the law of God, neither indeed can be." [ROM. 8:7.] In the new birth, the heart is renewed by divine grace, and brought into harmony with God as it is brought into subjection to his law. When this mighty change has taken place in the sinner, he has passed from death unto life, from sin unto holiness, from transgression and rebellion to obedience and loyalty. The old life of alienation from God has ended; the new life of reconciliation, of faith and love, has begun. Then will "the righteousness of the law" "be fulfilled in us who walk not after the flesh, but after the Spirit." [ROM. 8:4.]

The doctrine of sanctification, or perfect holiness, which fills a prominent place in some of the religious movements of the day, is among the causes that have rendered modern revivals so ineffectual. True sanctification is a Bible doctrine. The apostle Paul declared to the Thessalonian church, "This is the will of God, even your sanctification." [1 THESS. 4:3.] And again he prayed, "The very God of peace sanctify you wholly; and I pray God your whole spirit and soul and body be preserved blameless unto the coming of our Lord Jesus Christ." [1 THESS. 5:23.] But the sanctification now so widely advocated is not that brought to view in the Scriptures. It is false in theory, and dangerous in its practical results.

Its advocates teach that the law of God is a grievous yoke. and that by faith in Christ, men are released from all obligation to keep his Father's commandments. Bible sanctification is a conformity to the will of God, attained by rendering obedience to his law, through faith in his Son. Our Saviour prayed for his disciples, "Sanctify them through thy truth; thy word is truth." [JOHN 17:17.] There is no genuine sanctification except through obedience to the truth; and the psalmist declares, "Thy law is the truth." [PS. 119:142.] The law of

God is the only standard of moral perfection. That law was exemplified in the life of Christ. He says, "I have kept my Father's commandments." [JOHN 15:10.] And the apostle John affirms, "He that saith he abideth in Him ought himself also so to walk, even as he walked." And again, "This is the love of God, that we keep his commandments." [1 JOHN 2:6; 5:3.] Those who love God will love his commandments also. The truly sanctified heart is in harmony with the divine precepts; for they are "holy, and just, and good."

It is only when the law of God is set aside, and men have no standard of right, no means to detect sin, that erring mortals can claim perfect holiness. But let none deceive themselves with the belief that God will accept and bless them while they are willfully violating one of his requirements. The commission of a known sin silences the witnessing voice of the Spirit, and separates the soul from God. Jesus cannot abide in the heart that disregards the divine law. God will honor those only who honor him. "Whosoever committeth sin transgresseth also the law; for sin is the transgression of the law." "Whosoever abideth in Him sinneth not; whosoever sinneth [transgresseth the law] hath not seen him, neither known him." [1 JOHN 3:4, 6.] Though John in his epistles treats so fully upon love, yet he does not hesitate to reveal the true character of that class who claim to be sanctified while living in transgression of the law of God: "He that saith, I know Him, and keepeth not his commandments, is a liar, and the truth is not in him." [1 JOHN 2:4.]

Sanctification is believed by many to be instantaneously accomplished. "Only believe," say they, "and the blessing is yours." No further effort on the part of the receiver is supposed to be required. But the Bible teaches that sanctification is progressive. The Christian will feel the promptings of sin, but he will keep up a constant warfare against it. Here is where Christ's help is needed. Human weakness becomes united to divine strength, and faith exclaims, "Thanks be to God, which giveth us the victory through our Lord Jesus Christ." [1 COR. 15:57.] Paul exhorts his brethren, "Work out your own salvation with fear and trembling;" [PHIL. 2:12.] and concerning himself he declares, "I press toward the mark for the prize of the high calling of God in Christ Jesus." [PHIL. 3:14.] The successive steps in the attainment of Bible sanctification are set before us in the words of Peter: "Giving all diligence, add to your faith, virtue; and to virtue, knowledge; and to knowledge, temperance; and to temperance, patience; and to patience, godliness; and to godliness, brotherly kindness; and to brotherly kindness, charity." "Wherefore the rather, brethren, give diligence to make your calling and election sure; for if ye do these things, ye shall never fall." [2 PET. 1:5-7, 10.] This is a daily work, continuing as long as life shall last.

Spurious sanctification carries with it a boastful, self-righteous spirit which is foreign to the religion of the Bible. Meekness and humility are the fruits of the Spirit. The prophet Daniel was an example of true sanctification. His long life was filled up with noble service for his Master. He was a man "greatly beloved" [DAN. 10:11.] of Heaven, and was granted such honors as have rarely been vouch-safed to mortals. Yet his purity of character and unwavering fidelity were equaled only by his humility and contrition. Instead of claiming to be pure and holy, this honored prophet identified himself with the really sinful of Israel, as he pleaded before God in behalf of his people: "We do not present our supplications before thee for our righteous-ness, but for thy great mercies." "We have sinned, we have done wickedly." And "for our sins, and for the iniquities of our fathers, Jerusalem and thy people are become a reproach." He declares, "I was speaking, and praying, and confessing my sin and the sin of my people." [DAN. 9:18, 15, 16, 20.] And when at a later time the Son of God appeared in answer to his prayers to give him instruction, he declares, "My comeliness was turned in me into corruption, and I retained no strength." [DAN. 10:8.]

Those who are truly seeking to perfect Christian character will never indulge the thought that they are sinless. The more their minds dwell upon the character of Christ, and the nearer they approach to his divine image, the more clearly will they discern its spotless perfec-tion, and the more deeply will they feel their own weakness and defects. Those who claim to be without sin, give evidence that they are far from holy. It is because they have no true knowledge of Christ that they can look upon themselves as reflecting his image. The greater the distance between them and their Saviour, the more righteous they appear in their own eyes.

The sanctification set forth in the Scriptures embraces the entire being,— spirit, soul, and body. Paul prayed for the Thessalonians, that their "whole spirit and soul and body be preserved blameless unto the coming of our Lord Jesus Christ." Again he writes to believers, "I beseech you therefore, brethren, by the mercies of God, that ye present your bodies a living sacrifice, holy, acceptable unto God." [ROM. 12:1.] The Jews were commanded to offer in sacrifice to God only such animals as were free from disease or blemish. So Christians are required to preserve all their powers in the best possible condition for the Lord's service. Says Peter, "Abstain from fleshly lusts, which war against the soul." [1 PET. 2:11.] The word of God will make but a feeble impression upon those whose faculties are benumbed by any sinful gratification. The heart cannot preserve consecration to God while the animal appetites and passions are indulged at the expense of health and life. Paul writes to the Corinthians, "Let us cleanse ourselves from all filthiness of the flesh and spirit, perfecting holiness

in the fear of God." [2 COR. 7:1.] And with the fruits of the Spirit—
"love, joy, peace, long-suffering, gentleness, goodness, faith, meekness,"— he classes temperance. [GAL. 5:22, 23.]

Notwithstanding these inspired declarations, how many professed Christians are enfeebling their powers in the pursuit of gain or
the worship of fashion; how many are debasing their godlike manhood by gluttony, by wine-drinking, by forbidden pleasure. And the
church, instead of rebuking, too often encourages the evil by appealing to appetite, to desire for gain, or love of pleasure, to replenish her
treasury, which love for Christ is too feeble to supply. Were Jesus to
enter the churches of to-day, and behold the feasting and unholy
traffic there conducted in the name of religion, would he not drive
out those desecrators, as he banished the money-changers from the
temple?

The apostle James declares that the wisdom from above is
"first pure." Had he encountered those who take the precious name
of Jesus upon lips defiled by tobacco, those whose breath and
person are contaminated by its foul odor, and who pollute the air
of heaven and force all about them to inhale the poison,— had the
apostle come in contact with a practice so opposed to the purity of
the gospel, would he not have denounced it as "earthly, sensual,
devilish"? Slaves of tobacco, claiming the blessing of entire sanctification, talk of their hope of Heaven; but God's word plainly
declares that "there shall in no wise enter into it anything that
defileth." [REV. 21:27.]

"Know ye not that your body is the temple of the Holy Ghost,
which is in you, which ye have of God, and ye are not your own? For
ye are bought with a price; therefore glorify God in your body, and in
your spirit, which are God's." [1 COR. 6:19, 20.] He whose body is the
temple of the Holy Spirit will not be enslaved by a pernicious habit. His
powers belong to Christ, who has bought him with the price of blood.
His property is the Lord's. How could he be guiltless in squandering
this entrusted capital? Professed Christians yearly expend an immense
sum upon useless and pernicious indulgences, while souls are perishing
for the word of life. God is robbed in tithes and offerings, while they
offer upon the altar of destroying lust more than they give to relieve
the poor or for the support of the gospel. If all who profess to be
followers of Christ were truly sanctified, every channel of needless
expense would be turned into the Lord's treasury, and Christians would
set an example of temperance, self-denial, and self-sacrifice. Then they
would be the light of the world.

The world is given up to self-indulgence. The lust of the flesh,
the lust of the eye, and the pride of life, control the masses of the
people. But Christ's followers have a holier calling. "Come out from
among them, and be ye separate, saith the Lord, and touch not the

unclean; and I will receive you, and will be a Father unto you, and ye shall be my sons and daughters, saith the Lord Almighty." [2 COR. 6:17, 18.]

It is the privilege and the duty of every Christian to maintain a close union with Christ, and to have a rich experience in the things of God. Then his life will be fruitful in good works. When we read the lives of men who have been eminent for their piety, we often regard their experiences and attainments as beyond our reach. But this is not the case. Said Christ: "Herein is my Father glorified, that ye bear much fruit." "As the branch cannot bear fruit of itself, except it abide in the vine, no more can ye, except ye abide in me." "He that abideth in me, and I in him, the same bringeth forth much fruit." [JOHN 15:8, 4, 5.] The prophets and apostles did not perfect Christian character by a miracle. They used the means which God had placed within their reach, and all who will put forth a like effort will secure a like result.

Paul addressed his Corinthian brethren as "them that are sanctified in Christ Jesus;" and he thanked God that in everything they were enriched by him, "in all utterance and in all knowledge," so that they came behind in no gift. [1 COR. 1:2, 5, 7.] In his epistle to the Colossians he set forth the glorious privileges granted to the children of God. Said the apostle: We "do not cease to pray for you, and to desire that ye might be filled with the knowledge of his will in all wisdom and spiritual understanding; that ye might walk worthy of the Lord unto all pleasing, being fruitful in every good work, and increasing in the knowledge of God; strengthened with all might, according to his glorious power, unto all patience and long-suffering with joyfulness." [COL. 1:9-11.] Such are the fruits of Bible sanctification.

In setting aside the claims of the law of God, the church has lost sight of the blessings of the gospel. Bible conversion and sanctification,— a radical change of heart and transformation of character,— is the great need of the churches of to-day. Revivals in which men become members of the church without real conviction of sin, without repentance, and without acknowledging the claims of the law of God, are a cause of weakness to the church, and an occasion of stumbling to the world.

Chapter 23

The Investigative Judgment

"I Beheld," says the prophet Daniel, "till the thrones were cast down, and the Ancient of days did sit, whose garment was white as snow, and the hair of his head like the pure wool; his throne was like the fiery flame, and his wheels as burning fire. A fiery stream issued and came forth from before him; thousand thousands ministered unto him, and ten thousand times ten thousand stood before him; the Judgment was set, and the books were opened." "And, behold, one like the Son of man came with the clouds of heaven, and came to the Ancient of days, and they brought him near before him. And there was given him dominion, and glory, and a kingdom, that all people, nations, and languages should serve him; his dominion is an everlasting dominion, which shall not pass away." [DAN. 7:9, 10, 13, 14.]

Thus was presented to the prophet's vision the opening of the investigative Judgment. The coming of Christ here described is not his second coming to the earth. He comes to the Ancient of days in Heaven to receive dominion, and glory, and a kingdom, which will be given him at the close of his mediatorial work. It is this coming, and not his second advent to the earth, that was foretold in prophecy to take place at the termination of the 2300 days, in 1844. Attended by a cloud of heavenly angels, our great High Priest enters the holy of holies, and there appears in the presence of God to engage in the last acts of his ministration in behalf of man,— to perform the work of investigative Judgment, and to make an atonement for all who are shown to be entitled to its benefits.

"The dead were judged," says John, "out of those things which were written in the books, according to their works." [REV. 20:12.] Angels of God have kept a faithful record of the lives of all, and they are to be judged according to their deeds. In view of this Judgment, Peter exhorted the men of Israel: "Repent ye therefore, and be converted, that your sins may be blotted out, when the times of refreshing shall come from the presence of the Lord; and he shall send Jesus," "whom the heaven must receive until the times of restitution of all things, which God hath spoken by the mouth of all his holy prophets since the world began." [ACTS 3:19-21.]

Christ himself declares: "He that overcometh, the same shall be clothed in white raiment; and I will not blot out his name out of the book of life, but I will confess his name before my Father, and before his angels." [REV. 3:5.] Again he said to his disciples: "Whosoever therefore shall confess me before men, him will I confess also before my Father which is in Heaven. But whosoever shall deny me before men, him will I also deny before my Father which is in Heaven." [MATT. 10:32, 33.]

The lives of all who have believed on Jesus pass in solemn review before God. Beginning with those who first lived upon the earth, our Advocate examines the cases of each successive generation, and closes with the living. Every name is mentioned, every case closely investigated. Names are accepted, names rejected. From age to age, all who have truly repented of sin, and by faith claimed the blood of Christ as their atoning sacrifice, have had pardon written against their names in the books of Heaven, and in the closing work of Judgment their sins are blotted out, and they themselves are accounted worthy of eternal life.

The deepest interest manifested among men in the decisions of earthly tribunals but faintly represents the interest evinced in the heavenly courts when the names entered in the book of life come up in review before the Judge of all the earth. The divine Intercessor presents the plea that all who from among the fallen sons of men have overcome through faith in his blood, be forgiven their transgressions, that they be restored to their Eden home, and crowned as joint-heirs with himself to the "first dominion." [MICAH 4:8.] Satan, in his efforts to deceive and tempt our race, had thought to frustrate the divine plan in man's creation; but Christ now asks that this plan be carried into effect as if man had never fallen. He asks for his people not only pardon and justification, full and complete, but a share in his glory and a seat upon his throne.

While Jesus is pleading for the subjects of his grace, Satan accuses them before God as transgressors. The great deceiver has sought to lead them into skepticism, to cause them to lose confidence in God, to separate from his love, and to break his law. Now he points to their defective characters, to their unlikeness to Christ which has dishonored their Redeemer, to all the sins which he has tempted them to commit, and because of these he claims them as his subjects.

Jesus does not excuse their sins, but shows their penitence and faith, and, claiming for them forgiveness, he lifts his wounded hands before the Father and the holy angels, saying, "I know them by name. I have graven them on the palms of my hands. 'The sacrifices of God are a broken spirit; a broken and a contrite heart, O God, thou wilt not despise.'" [PS. 51:17.] And to the accuser of his people he declares, "The Lord rebuke thee, O Satan; even the Lord that hath chosen Jerusalem rebuke thee. Is not this a brand plucked out of the fire?" [ZECH. 3:2.] Christ will place his own signet upon his faithful ones, that he may present them to his Father "a glorious church, not having spot, or wrinkle, or any such thing." Their names stand enrolled in the book of life, and concerning them it is written, "They shall walk with me in white; for they are worthy."

Those who are owned and approved of God are not therefore recognized and honored by the world. The very names that are taken upon the lips of Jesus as belonging to his own sons and daughters, joint-heirs with the King of glory, honored among the heavenly angels, are often those that are spoken with contempt and mockery by the ungodly. Steadfast souls whom Jesus delights to honor are for his sake defamed, imprisoned, mobbed, hunted, and slain. God's people must live by faith. They must look over into the great beyond, and choose divine honors and the recompense of the reward above every earthly gain or preferment. While probation continues, they must expect that the world will know them not, "because it knew Him not."

Great and small, high and low, rich and poor, are to be judged "out of those things which were written in the books, according to their works." Day after day, passing into eternity, bears its burden of records for the books of Heaven. Words once spoken, deeds once done, can never be recalled. Angels of God have registered both the good and the evil. The mightiest conqueror upon the earth cannot call back the record of even a single day. Our acts, our words, even our most secret motives, all have their weight in deciding our destiny for weal or woe. Though they may be forgotten by us, they will bear their testimony to justify or condemn. They go before us to the Judgment.

The use made of every talent will be scrutinized. Have we improved the capital entrusted us of God? Will the Lord at his coming receive his own with usury? No value is attached to the mere profession of faith in Christ; nothing is counted as genuine but that love which is shown by works.

As the features of the countenance are reproduced with marvelous exactness in the camera of the artist, so is the character faithfully delineated in the books above. If Christians were as solicitous to stand faultless in the heavenly records as they are to be represented without a blemish in the picture, how different would their life-history appear.

Could the veil which separates the visible from the invisible world be swept back, and the children of men behold an angel recording every word and deed to meet them again in the Judgment, how many words that are daily uttered would remain unspoken; how many deeds would remain undone. When all the details of life appear in the books that never contain a false entry, many will find too late that the record testifies against them. There their hidden selfishness stands revealed. There is the record of unfulfilled duties to their fellow-men, of forgetfulness of the Saviour's claims. There they will see how often were given to Satan the time, thought, and strength that belonged to Christ. Sad is the record which angels bear to Heaven. Intelligent beings, professed followers of Christ, are absorbed in the acquirement of worldly possessions or the enjoyment of earthly pleasures. Money, time, and strength are sacrificed for display and self-indulgence; but few are the moments devoted to prayer, to the searching of the Scriptures, to humiliation of soul and confession of sin.

Satan invents unnumbered schemes to occupy our minds that they may not dwell upon the very work with which we ought to be best acquainted. The arch-deceiver hates the great truths that bring to view an atoning sacrifice and an all-powerful Mediator. He knows that with him everything now depends on his diverting minds from Jesus and his truth.

Those who would share the benefits of the Saviour's mediation should permit nothing to interfere with their duty to perfect holiness in the fear of God. The hours heretofore given to pleasure, to display, or to gain-seeking, should now be devoted to an earnest, prayerful study of the word of truth. The subject of the sanctuary and the investigative Judgment should be clearly understood by the people of God. All need a knowledge for themselves of the position and work of their great High Priest. Otherwise, it will be impossible for them to exercise the faith essential at this time, or to occupy the position which God designs them to fill.

We are to bear testimony of the great truths which God has committed to us. The sanctuary in Heaven is the very center of Christ's work in behalf of men. It concerns every soul living upon the earth. It opens to our view the plan of redemption, bringing us down to the very close of time, and revealing the triumphant issue of the contest between righteousness and sin. It is of the utmost importance that all who have received the light, both old and young, should thoroughly investigate these subjects, and be able to give an answer to every one that asketh them a reason of the hope that is in them.

The intercession of Christ in man's behalf in the sanctuary above is as essential to the plan of salvation as was his death upon the cross. By his death he began that work which after his resurrection he ascended to complete in Heaven. We must by faith enter within the veil, "whither the forerunner is for us entered." There the light from the cross of Calvary is reflected. There we may gain a clearer insight into the mysteries of redemption. The salvation of man is accomplished at an infinite expense to Heaven; the sacrifice made is equal to the broadest demands of the broken law of God. Jesus has opened the way to the Father's throne, and through his mediation the sincere desire of all who come to him in faith may be presented before God.

"He that covereth his sins shall not prosper; but whoso confesseth and forsaketh them shall have mercy." [PROV. 28:13.] If those who hide and excuse their faults could see how Satan exults over them how he taunts Christ and holy angels with them, they would make haste to confess their sins and to put them away. Satan is continually seeking to deceive the followers of Christ with his fatal sophistry that their defective traits of character render it impossible for them to overcome. But Jesus pleads in their behalf his wounded hands, his bruised body; and he declares to all who would follow him, "My grace is sufficient for thee." "Take my yoke upon you, and learn of me; for I am meek and lowly in heart, and ye shall find rest unto your souls. For my yoke is easy, and my burden is light." [MATT. 11:29, 30.] Let none, then, regard their defects as incurable. God will give faith and grace to overcome them.

All who would have their names retained in the book of life, should now, in the few remaining days of their probation, afflict their souls before God by sorrow for sin, and true repentance. There must be deep, faithful searching of heart. The light, frivolous spirit indulged by the majority of professed Christians must be put away. There is earnest warfare before all who would subdue the evil tendencies that strive for the mastery.

Solemn are the scenes connected with the closing work of the atonement. Momentous are the interests therein involved. The Judgment is now passing in the sanctuary above. Forty years has this work been in progress. Soon— none know how soon— it will pass to the cases of the living. In the awful presence of God our lives are to come up in review. At this time above all others it behooves every soul to heed the Saviour's admonition, "Watch and pray, for ye know not when the time is." "Watch ye therefore, ... lest coming suddenly he find you sleeping." [MARK 13:33, 35, 36.]

"If therefore thou shalt not watch, I will come on thee as a thief; and thou shalt not know what hour I will come upon thee." [REV. 3:3.] How perilous is the condition of those, who, growing weary of their watch, turn to the attractions of the world. While the man of business is absorbed in the pursuit of gain, while the pleasure-lover is seeking indulgence, while the daughter of fashion is arranging her adornments,— it may be in that hour the Judge of all the earth will pronounce the sentence, "Thou art weighed in the balances, and art found wanting."

Every soul that has named the name of Christ has a case pending at the heavenly tribunal. It is court week with us, and the decision passed upon each case will be final.

Chapter 24

Origin of Evil

To many minds the origin of sin and the reason for its existence are a source of great perplexity. In their interest in these questions, the truths plainly revealed in God's word and essential to salvation are neglected; and the fact that the Scriptures furnish no explanation, is seized upon as an excuse for rejecting the words of Holy Writ.

It is impossible to explain the origin of sin, or to give a reason for its existence. It is an intruder, for whose existence no reason can be given. It is mysterious, unaccountable; to excuse it, is to defend it. Could it be excused, could a cause be shown for its existence, it would cease to be sin. Our only definition of sin is that given in the word of God; it is "the transgression of the law."

Sin originated with him, who, next to Christ, stood highest in the favor of God, and highest in power and glory among the inhabitants of Heaven. Before his fall, Lucifer was the covering cherub, holy and undefiled. The prophet of God declares, "Thou wast perfect in thy ways from the day that thou wast created, till iniquity was found in thee." [EZE. 28:15.] Peace and joy, in perfect submission to the will of Heaven, existed throughout the angelic host. Love to God was supreme, love for one another impartial. Such was the condition that existed for ages before the entrance of sin.

But over this happy state there came a change. Says the prophet, addressing the prince of evil, "Thine heart was lifted up because of thy beauty, thou hast corrupted thy wisdom by reason of thy brightness." [EZE. 28:17.] Though God had created Lucifer noble and beautiful, and had exalted him to high honor among the angelic host, yet he had not placed him beyond the possibility of evil. It was in Satan's power, did he choose to do so, to pervert these gifts. He might have remained in favor with God, beloved and honored by all the angelic throng, presiding in his exalted position with generous, unselfish care, exercising his noble powers to bless others and to glorify his Maker. But, little by little, he began to seek his own honor, and to employ his powers to attract attention and win praise to himself. He also gradually led the angels over whom he ruled to do him service, instead of devoting all their powers to the service of their Creator. This course perverted his own imagination, and perverted those who yielded implicitly to his authority.

The heavenly councils admonished Lucifer to change his course. The Son of God warned and entreated him not to venture thus to dishonor his Maker, and bring ruin upon himself. But instead of yielding, Satan represented to those who loved him, that he had been wrongly judged, that his dignity was not respected, and that his liberty was to be abridged.

That Christ should regard him as needing to be corrected, and should presume to take the position of a superior, aroused in him a spirit of resistance, and he charged the Son of God with a design to humble him before the angels. By misrepresentation of the words of Christ, by prevarication and direct falsehood, Satan secured the sympathy of the angels under his control, and they united with him in revolt against Heaven's authority.

To the last, he refused to acknowledge his own course to be deserving of censure. When the consequence of his disaffection became apparent, and it was decreed that with all his sympathizers he must be forever banished from the abode of bliss, the arch-deceiver threw the blame wholly upon Christ. With one accord, Satan and his hosts declared that had they not been reproved, the rebellion would never have occurred, thus making Christ responsible for their course. Thus stubborn and defiant in their disloyalty, seeking vainly to overthrow the government of God, yet blasphemously claiming to be themselves the innocent victims of oppressive power, the arch-rebel and all his sympathizers were at last banished from Heaven.

The rebellion in Heaven was prompted by the same spirit which inspires rebellion on earth. Satan has continued with men the same policy which he pursued with the angels. His spirit now reigns in the children of disobedience. There is a constant hatred of reproof, and a disposition to rebel against it. When God sends to wrong-doers a message of warning or correction, Satan leads them to justify themselves, and to seek the sympathy of others. Instead of changing their wrong course, they manifest great indignation against the reprover, as if he were the sole cause of difficulty. From the days of righteous Abel to our own time, such is the spirit which has been displayed toward those who dare to condemn sin.

Satan had excited sympathy in his favor by representing that God had dealt unjustly with him in bestowing supreme honor upon Christ. Before he was sentenced to banishment from Heaven, his course was with convincing clearness shown to be wrong, and he was granted an opportunity to confess his sin, and submit to God's authority as just and righteous. But he chose to carry his points at all hazards. To sustain his charge of God's injustice toward him, he resorted to misrepresentation, even of the words and acts of the Creator.

Here, for a time, Satan had the advantage; and he exulted in his arrogated superiority, in this one respect, to the angels of Heaven, and even to God himself. While Satan can employ fraud and sophistry to accomplish his objects, God cannot lie; while Lucifer, like the serpent, can choose a tortuous course, turning, twisting, gliding, to conceal himself, God moves only in a direct, straight-forward line.

Satan had disguised himself in a cloak of falsehood, and for a time it was impossible to tear off the covering, so that the hideous deformity of his character could be seen. He must be left to reveal himself in his cruel, artful, wicked works.

He was not immediately dethroned when he first ventured to indulge the spirit of discontent and insubordination, nor even when he began to present his false claim and lying representations before the loyal angels. Long was he retained in Heaven. Again and again was he offered pardon on condition of repentance and submission. Such efforts as God alone could make, were made to convince him of his error, and restore him to the path of rectitude. God would preserve the order of the heavens, and had Lucifer been willing to return to his allegiance, humble and obedient, he would have been re-established in his office as covering cherub. But as he stubbornly justified his course, and maintained that he had no need of repentance, it became necessary for the Lord of Heaven to vindicate his justice and the honor of his throne; and Satan and all who sympathized with him were cast out.

By the same misrepresentation of the character of God as he had practiced in Heaven, causing him to be regarded as severe and tyrannical, Satan induced man to sin. And having succeeded thus far, he declared that God's unjust restrictions had led to man's fall, as they had led to his own rebellion.

But the Eternal One himself proclaims his character: "The Lord God, merciful and gracious, long-suffering, and abundant in goodness and truth, keeping mercy for thousands, forgiving iniquity and transgression and sin, and that will by no means clear the guilty." [EX. 34:6, 7.]

In the banishment of Satan from Heaven, God declared his justice, and maintained the honor of his throne. But when man had sinned through yielding to the deceptions of this apostate spirit, God gave an evidence of his love by yielding up his only begotten Son to die for the fallen race. In the atonement the character of God stands revealed. The mighty argument of the cross demonstrates to the whole universe that God was in no wise responsible for the course of sin that Lucifer had chosen; that it was no arbitrary withdrawal of divine grace, no deficiency in the divine government, which inspired in him the spirit of rebellion.

In the contest between Christ and Satan, during the Saviour's earthly ministry, the character of the great deceiver was unmasked. Nothing could so effectually have uprooted Satan from the minds and affections of the heavenly angels and the whole loyal universe as did his cruel warfare upon the world's Redeemer. The daring blasphemy of his demand that Christ should pay him homage, his presumptuous boldness in bearing him to the mountain summit and the pinnacle of the temple, the malicious intent betrayed in urging him to cast himself down from the dizzy height, the unsleeping malice that hunted him from place to place, inspiring the hearts of priests and people to reject his love, and at the last to raise the cry "Crucify him! crucify him!"—all this excited the amazement and indignation of the universe.

It was Satan that prompted the world's rejection of Christ. The prince of evil exerted all his power and cunning to destroy Jesus; for he saw that the Saviour's mercy and love, his compassion and pitying tenderness, were representing to the world the character of God. Satan contested every claim put forth by the Son of God, and employed men as his agents to fill the Saviour's life with suffering and sorrow. The sophistry and falsehood by which he had sought to hinder the work of Jesus, the hatred manifested through the children of disobedience, his cruel accusations against Him whose life was one of unexampled goodness, all sprang from deep-seated revenge. The pent up fires of envy and malice, hatred and revenge, burst forth on Calvary against the Son of God, while all Heaven gazed upon the scene in silent horror.

When the great sacrifice had been consummated, Christ ascended on high, refusing the adoration of angels until he had preferred the request, "I will that they also whom thou hast given me, be with me where I am." [JOHN 17:24.] Then with inexpressible love and power came forth the answer from the Father's throne, "Let all the angels of God worship him." [HEB. 1:6.] Not a stain rested upon Jesus. His humiliation ended, his sacrifice completed, there was given unto him a name that is above every name.

Now the guilt of Satan stood forth without excuse. His lying charges against the divine character and government appeared in their true light. He had accused God of seeking merely the exaltation of himself in requiring submission and obedience from his creatures, and had declared that while the Creator exacted self-denial from all others, he himself practiced no self-denial, and made no sacrifice. Now it was seen that for the salvation of a fallen and sinful race, the Ruler of the universe had made the greatest sacrifice which God could make. It was seen, also, that while Lucifer had opened the door for the entrance of sin, by his desire for honor and supremacy, Christ had, in order to destroy sin, humbled himself, and become obedient unto death.

God had manifested his abhorrence of the principles of rebellion. All Heaven saw his justice revealed, both in the condemnation of Satan and in the redemption of man. Lucifer had declared God's law to be of such a character that its penalty could not be remitted, and therefore every transgressor must be forever debarred from the Creator's favor. He had claimed that the sinful race were placed beyond redemption, and were therefore his rightful prey. But the death of Christ was an argument in man's behalf that could not be turned aside. He suffered the penalty of the law. God was just in permitting his wrath to fall upon Him who was equal with himself, and man was set free to accept the righteousness of Christ, and by a life of penitence and humiliation to triumph as the Son of God had triumphed over the power of Satan.

God's law stands fully vindicated. He is just, and yet the justifier of all who believe in Jesus. Nothing less than this plan of atonement could convince the whole universe of God's justice.

In the final execution of the judgment it will be seen that no cause for sin exists. When the Judge of all the earth shall demand of Satan, "Why hast thou rebelled against me, and robbed me of the subjects of my kingdom?" the originator of evil can render no excuse. Every mouth will be stopped, and all the hosts of rebellion will be speechless before the great tribunal.

Chapter 25

Enmity Between Man and Satan

"I will put enmity between thee and the woman, and between thy seed and her seed; it shall bruise thy head, and thou shalt bruise his heel." [GEN. 3:15.] The divine sentence pronounced against Satan after the fall of man, was also a prophecy, embracing all the ages to the close of time, and foreshadowing the great conflict to engage all the races of men who should live upon the earth.

God declares, "I will put enmity." This enmity is not naturally entertained. When man transgressed the divine law, his nature became evil, and he was in harmony, and not at variance, with Satan. There exists naturally no enmity between sinful man and the originator of sin. Both became evil through apostasy. The apostate is never at rest, except as he obtains sympathy and support by inducing others to follow his example. For this reason, fallen angels and wicked men unite in desperate companionship. Had not God specially interposed, Satan and man would have entered into an alliance against Heaven; and instead of cherishing enmity against Satan, the whole human family would have been united in opposition to God.

Satan tempted man to sin, as he had caused angels to rebel, that he might thus secure co-operation in his warfare against Heaven. There was no dissension between himself and the fallen angels as regards their hatred of Christ; while on all other points there was discord, they were firmly united in opposing the authority of the Ruler of the universe. But when Satan heard the declaration that enmity should exist between himself and the woman, and between his seed and her seed, he knew that his efforts to deprave human nature would be interrupted; that by some means man was to be enabled to resist his power.

The grace that Christ implants in the soul creates the enmity against Satan. Without this converting grace and renewing power, man would continue the captive of Satan, a servant ever ready to do his bidding. But the new principle in the soul creates conflict where hitherto had been peace. The power which Christ imparts, enables man to resist the tyrant and usurper. Whoever is seen to abhor sin instead of loving it, whoever resists and conquers those passions that have held sway within, displays the operation of a principle wholly from above.

The antagonism that exists between the spirit of Christ and the spirit of Satan was most strikingly displayed in the world's reception of Jesus. It was not so much because he appeared without worldly wealth, pomp, or grandeur, that the Jews were led to reject him. They saw that he possessed power which would more than compensate for the lack of these outward advantages. But the purity and holiness of Christ called forth against him the hatred of the ungodly. His life of self-denial and sinless devotion was a perpetual reproof to a proud, sensual people. It was this that evoked enmity against the Son of God. Satan and evil angels joined with evil men. All the energies of apostasy conspired against the champion of truth.

The same enmity is manifested toward Christ's followers as was manifested toward their Master. Whoever sees the repulsive character of sin, and, in strength from above, resists temptation, will assuredly arouse the wrath of Satan and his subjects. Hatred of the pure principles of truth, and reproach and persecution of its advocates, will exist as long as sin and sinners remain. The followers of Christ and the servants of Satan cannot harmonize. The offense of the cross has not ceased. "All that will live godly in Christ Jesus shall suffer persecution." [2 TIM. 3:12.]

Satan's agents are constantly working under his direction to establish his authority and build up his kingdom in opposition to the government of God. To this end they seek to deceive Christ's followers, and allure them from their allegiance. Like their leader, they misconstrue and pervert the Scriptures to accomplish their object. As Satan endeavored to cast reproach upon God, so do his agents seek to malign God's people. The spirit which put Christ to death moves the wicked to destroy his followers. All this is foreshadowed in that first prophecy, "I will put enmity between thee and the woman, and between thy seed and her seed." Such is the work that will be carried forward in the great controversy between Christ and Satan to the close of time.

Satan summons all his forces, and throws his whole power into the combat. Why is it that he meets with no greater resistance? Why are the soldiers of Christ so sleepy and indifferent?— Because they do not realize their peril. There is but little enmity against Satan and his works, because there is so great ignorance concerning his power and malice, and the vast extent of his warfare against Christ and his church. Multitudes are deluded here. They do not know that their enemy is a mighty general, who controls the minds of evil angels, and that with well-matured plans and skillful movements he is warring against Christ to prevent the salvation of souls. Among professed Christians, and even among ministers of the gospel, there is heard scarcely a reference to Satan, except perhaps an incidental mention in the pulpit. They overlook the evidences of his continual activity and success; they neglect the many warnings of his subtlety; they seem to ignore his very existence.

While men are ignorant of his devices, this vigilant foe is upon their track every moment. He is intruding his presence in every department of the household, in every street of our cities, in the churches, in the councils, in the courts of justice, perplexing, deceiving, seducing, everywhere ruining the souls and bodies of men, women, and children, breaking up families, sowing hatred, emulation, strife, sedition, murder. And the Christian world seem to regard these things as though God had appointed them, and they must exist.

Satan is continually seeking to overcome the people of God by breaking down the barriers which separate them from the world. Ancient Israel were enticed into sin when they ventured into forbidden association with the heathen. In a similar manner are modern Israel led astray. "The god of this world hath blinded the minds of them which believe not, lest the light of the glorious gospel of Christ, who is the image of God, should shine unto them." [2 COR. 4:4.] All who are not decided followers of Christ are servants of Satan. In the unregenerate heart there is love of sin, and a disposition to cherish and excuse it. In the renewed heart there is hatred of sin, and determined resistance against it. When Christians choose the society of the ungodly and unbelieving, they expose themselves to temptation. Satan conceals himself from view, and stealthily draws his bandage across their eyes. They cannot see that such company is calculated to do them harm, and while all the time assimilating to the world in character, words, and actions, they are becoming more and more blinded. Familiarity with sin inevitably causes it to appear less repulsive. He who chooses to associate with the servants of Satan soon ceases to fear their master.

The tempter often works most successfully through those who are least suspected of being under his control. The opinion prevails with many that all which appears like courtesy or refinement must, in some sense, pertain to Christ. Never was there a greater mistake. These qualities should grace the character of every Christian, for they would exert a powerful influence in favor of true religion; but they must be consecrated to God, or they are a power for evil. Many who are affable and intelligent, and who would not stoop to what is commonly regarded as an immoral act, are but polished instruments in the hands of Satan. The insidious, deceptive character of their influence and example renders them more dangerous enemies to the cause of Christ than are those who are unattractive, coarse, rough, and degraded.

By earnest prayer and dependence upon God, Solomon obtained the wisdom which excited the wonder and admiration of the world. But when he turned from the Source of his strength, and went forward relying upon himself, he fell a prey to temptation. Then the marvelous powers bestowed on this wisest of kings, only rendered him a more efficient agent of the adversary of souls.

While Satan is constantly seeking to blind their minds to the fact, let Christians never forget that they "wrestle not against flesh and blood, but against principalities, against powers, against the rulers of the darkness of this world, against wicked spirits [margin] in high places." [EPH. 6:12.] The inspired warning is sounding down the centuries to our time: "Be sober, be vigilant; because your adversary the devil, as a roaring lion, walketh about, seeking whom he may devour." [1 PET. 5:8.] "Put on the whole armor of God, that ye may be able to stand against the wiles of the devil." [EPH. 6:11.]

From the days of Adam to our own time, our great enemy has been exercising his power to oppress and destroy. He is now preparing for his last campaign against the church. All who seek to follow Jesus will be brought into conflict with this relentless foe. The more nearly the Christian imitates the divine Pattern, the more surely will he make himself a mark for the attacks of Satan. All who are actively engaged in the cause of God, seeking to unveil the deceptions of the evil one and to present Christ before the people, will be able to join in the testimony of Paul, in which he speaks of serving the Lord with all humility of mind, with many tears and temptations.

Satan assailed Christ with his fiercest and most subtle temptations; but he was repulsed in every conflict. Those battles were fought in our behalf; those victories make it possible for us to conquer. Christ will give strength to all who seek it. No man without his own consent can be overcome by Satan. The tempter has no power to control the will or to force the soul to sin. He may distress, but he cannot contaminate. He can cause agony, but not defilement. The fact that Christ has conquered should inspire his followers with courage to fight manfully the battle against sin and Satan.

Chapter 26

Agency of Evil Spirits

The existence of Satan and the agency of evil spirits are facts fully established by both the Old and the New Testament. From the days of Adam to Moses, and through all the succeeding ages to John, the latest gospel writer, Satan is recognized as an active, personal agent, the originator of evil, the enemy of God and man. It is true that imagination and superstition have given their own coloring to these facts, and have linked them with legends and traditions of heathen, Jewish, and even Christian nations; but as revealed in the word of God they are of the utmost solemnity and importance. The connection of the visible with the invisible world, the ministration of angels of God, and the agency of evil angels, are inseparably interwoven with human history. We are told of the fall of the angels from their purity, of Lucifer their leader, the instigator of rebellion, of their confederacy and government, of their various orders, of their great intelligence and subtlety, and of their malicious designs against the innocence and happiness of men. We are told of One mightier than the fallen foe,— One by whose authority Satan's power is limited and controlled; and we are told, also, of the punishment prepared for the originator of iniquity.

During the time when Christ was upon the earth, evil spirits manifested their power in a most striking manner. And why was this?— Christ had come to enter upon the plan devised for man's redemption, and Satan therefore determined to assert his right to control the world. He had succeeded in establishing idolatry in every part of the earth except the land of Palestine. To the only land that had not fully yielded to the tempter's sway, Christ came to shed upon the people the light of Heaven. Here two rival powers claimed supremacy. Jesus was stretching out his arms of love, inviting all who would to find pardon and peace in him. The hosts of darkness understood that if his mission should be successful, their rule was soon to end. Satan raged like a chained lion, and defiantly exhibited his power over the bodies as well as the souls of men.

The fact that men have been possessed with demons is clearly stated in the New Testament. The persons thus afflicted were not merely suffering with disease from natural causes. Christ had perfect understanding of that with which he was dealing, and he recognized the direct presence and agency of evil spirits.

A striking example of their number, power, and malignity, and also of the power and mercy of Christ, is given in the Scripture account of the healing of the demoniacs at Gadara. Those wretched maniacs, spurning all restraint, writhing, foaming, raging, were filling the air with their cries, doing violence to themselves, and endangering all who should approach them. Their bleeding and disfigured bodies and distracted minds presented a spectacle well-pleasing to the prince of darkness. One of the demons controlling the sufferers declared, "My name is Legion; for we are many." [MARK 5:9.] In the Roman army a legion consisted of from three to five thousand men. Satan's hosts also are marshaled into companies, and the single company to which these demons belonged numbered no less than a legion.

At the command of Jesus, the evil spirits departed from their victims, leaving them calmly sitting at the Saviour's feet, subdued, intelligent, and gentle. But the demons were permitted to sweep a herd of swine into the sea; and to the dwellers of Gadara their loss outweighed the blessings which Christ had bestowed, and the divine Healer was entreated to depart. This was the result which Satan designed to secure. By casting the blame upon Jesus, he aroused the selfish fears of the people, and prevented them from listening to his words. Satan is constantly accusing Christians as the cause of loss, misfortune, and suffering, instead of allowing the reproach to fall where it belongs, upon himself and his agents.

But the purposes of Christ were not thwarted. He allowed the evil spirits to destroy the herd of swine as a rebuke to those Jews, who, by raising these unclean beasts for the sake of gain, had transgressed the command of God. Had not Christ restrained the demons, they would have plunged into the sea, not only the swine, but also their keepers and owners. The preservation of both the keepers and the owners was due alone to his merciful interposition for their deliverance. Furthermore, this scene was permitted to take place that the disciples might witness the cruel power of Satan upon both man and beast. The Saviour desired his followers to have a knowledge of the foe whom they were to meet, that they might not be deceived and overcome by his devices. It was also his will that the people of that region should behold his power to break the bondage of Satan and release his captives. And though Jesus himself departed, the men so marvelously delivered, remained to declare the mercy of their Benefactor.

Other instances of a similar nature are recorded in the Scriptures. The daughter of the Syrophenician woman was grievously vexed with a devil, whom Jesus cast out by his word. [MARK 7:26-30.] One "possessed with a devil, blind and dumb," [MATT. 12:22.] a youth who had a dumb spirit, that ofttimes "cast him into the fire, and into the waters, to destroy him," [MARK 9:17-27.] the maniac, who, tormented by "a spirit of an unclean devil," [LUKE 4:33-36.] disturbed the Sabbath quiet of the synagogue at Capernaum, were all healed by the compassionate Saviour. In nearly every instance, Christ addressed the demon as an intelligent entity, commanding him to come out of his victim and to torment him no more. The worshipers at Capernaum, beholding his mighty power, "were all amazed, and spake among themselves, saying, What a word is this! for with authority and power he commandeth the unclean spirits, and they come out."

Those possessed with devils are usually represented as being in a condition of great suffering; yet there were exceptions to this rule. For the sake of obtaining supernatural power, some welcomed the Satanic influence. These of course had no conflict with the demons. Of this class were those who possessed the spirit of divination,— Simon Magus, Elymas the sorcerer, and the damsel who followed Paul and Silas at Philippi.

None are in greater danger from the influence of evil spirits than are those who, notwithstanding the direct and ample testimony of the Scriptures, deny the existence and agency of the devil and his angels. So long as we are ignorant of their wiles, they have almost inconceivable advantage; many give heed to their suggestions while they suppose themselves to be following the dictates of their own wisdom. This is why, as we approach the close of time, when Satan is to work with greatest power to deceive and destroy, he spreads everywhere the belief that he does not exist. It is his policy to conceal himself and his manner of working.

There is nothing that the great deceiver fears so much as that we shall become acquainted with his devices. The better to disguise his real character and purposes, he has caused himself to be so represented as to excite no stronger emotion than ridicule or contempt. He is well pleased to be painted as a ludicrous or loathsome object, misshapen, half animal and half human. He is pleased to hear his name used in sport and mockery by those who consider themselves intelligent and well-informed.

It is because he has masked himself with consummate skill that the question is so widely asked, "Does such a being really exist?" It is an evidence of his success that theories giving the lie to the plainest testimony of the Scriptures are so generally received in the religious world. And it is because Satan can most readily control the minds of those who are unconscious of his influence that the word of God gives us so many examples of his malignant work, unveiling before us his secret forces, and thus placing us on our guard against his assaults.

The power and malice of Satan and his host might justly alarm us, were it not that we may find shelter and deliverance in the superior power of our Redeemer. We carefully secure our houses with bolts and locks to protect our property and our lives from evil men; but we seldom think of the evil angels who are constantly seeking access to us, and against whose attacks we have no method of defense. If permitted, they can distract our minds, disorder, torment our bodies, destroy our possessions and our lives. Their only delight is in misery and destruction. Fearful is the condition of those who resist the divine claims and yield to Satan's temptations until God gives them up to the control of evil spirits. But those who follow Christ are ever safe under his watchcare. Angels that excel in strength are sent from Heaven to protect them. The wicked one cannot break through the guard which God has stationed about his people.

Chapter 27

The Snares of Satan

As the people of God approach the perils of the last days, Satan holds earnest consultation with his angels as to the most successful plan of overthrowing their faith. He sees that the popular churches are already lulled to sleep by his deceptive power. By pleasing sophistry and lying wonders he can continue to hold them under his control. Therefore he directs his angels to lay their snares especially for those who are looking for the second advent of Christ, and endeavoring to keep all the commandments of God.

Says the great deceiver: "We must watch those who are calling the attention of the people to the Sabbath of Jehovah; they will lead many to see the claims of the law of God; and the same light which reveals the true Sabbath, reveals also the ministration of Christ in the heavenly sanctuary, and shows that the last work for man's salvation is now going forward. Hold the minds of the people in darkness till that work is ended, and we shall secure the world and the church also.

"The Sabbath is the great question which is to decide the destiny of souls. We must exalt the Sabbath of our creating. We have caused it to be accepted by both worldlings and church-members; now the church must be led to unite with the world in its support. We must work by signs and wonders to blind their eyes to the truth, and lead them to lay aside reason and the fear of God, and follow custom and tradition.

"I will influence popular ministers to turn the attention of their hearers from the commandments of God. That which the Scriptures declare to be a perfect law of liberty shall be represented as a yoke of bondage. The people accept their ministers' explanations of Scripture, and do not investigate for themselves. Therefore by working through the ministers, I can control the people according to my will.

"But our principal concern is to silence this sect of Sabbath-keepers. We must excite popular indignation against them. We will enlist great men and worldly-wise men upon our side, and induce those in authority to carry out our purposes. Then the Sabbath which I have set up shall be enforced by laws the most severe and exacting. Those who disregard them shall be driven out from the cities and villages, and made to suffer hunger and privation. When once we have the power, we will show that we can do with those who will not swerve from their allegiance to God. We led the Romish Church to inflict imprisonment, torture, and death upon those who refused to yield to her decrees, and now that we are bringing the Protestant churches and the world into harmony with this right arm of our strength, we will finally have a law to exterminate all who will not submit to our authority. When death shall be made the penalty of violating our

Sabbath, then many who are now ranked with commandment-keepers will come over to our side.

"But before proceeding to these extreme measures, we must exert all our wisdom and subtlety to deceive and ensnare those who honor the true Sabbath. We can separate many from Christ by worldliness, lust, and pride. They may think themselves safe because they believe the truth, but indulgence of appetite or the lower passions, which will confuse judgment and destroy discrimination, will cause their fall.

"Go, make the possessors of lands and money drunk with the cares of this life. Present the world before them in its most attractive light, that they may lay up their treasure here, and fix their affections upon earthly things. We must do our utmost to prevent those who labor in God's cause from obtaining means to use against us. Keep the money in our own ranks. The more means they obtain, the more they will injure our kingdom by taking from us our subjects. Make them care more for money than for the upbuilding of Christ's kingdom and the spread of the truths we hate, and we need not fear their influence; for we know that every selfish, covetous person will fall under our power, and will finally be separated from God's people.

"Through those that have a form of godliness but know not the power, we can gain many who would otherwise do us great harm. Lovers of pleasure more than lovers of God will be our most effective helpers. Those of this class who are apt and intelligent will serve as decoys to draw others into our snares. Many will not fear their influence, because they profess the same faith. We will thus lead them to conclude that the requirements of Christ are less strict than they once believed, and that by conformity to the world they would exert a greater influence with worldlings. Thus they will separate from Christ; then they will have no strength to resist our power, and erelong they will be ready to ridicule their former zeal and devotion.

"Until the great decisive blow shall be struck, our efforts against commandment-keepers must be untiring. We must be present at all their gatherings. In their large meetings especially our cause will suffer much, and we must exercise great vigilance, and employ all our seductive arts to prevent souls from hearing the truth and becoming impressed by it.

"I will have upon the ground, as my agents, men holding false doctrines mingled with just enough truth to deceive souls. I will also have unbelieving ones present, who will express doubts in regard to the Lord's messages of warning to his church. Should the people read and believe these admonitions, we could have little hope of overcoming them. But if we can divert their attention from these warnings, they will remain ignorant of our power and cunning, and we shall secure them in our ranks at last. God will not permit his words to be slighted with impunity. If we can keep souls deceived for a time, God's mercy will be withdrawn, and he will give them up to our full control.

"We must cause distraction and division. We must destroy their anxiety for their own souls, and lead them to criticize, to judge, and to accuse and condemn one another, and to cherish selfishness and enmity. For these sins, God banished us from his presence; and all who follow our example will meet a similar fate."

The Scriptures declare that upon one occasion, when the angels of God came to present themselves before the Lord, Satan came also among them, not to bow before the Eternal King, but to further his own malicious designs against the righteous. With the same object he is in attendance when men assemble for the worship of God. Though hidden from sight, he is working with all diligence to control the minds of the worshipers. Like a skillful general, he lays his plans beforehand. As he sees the messenger of God searching the Scriptures, he takes note of the subject to be presented to the people. Then he employs all his cunning and shrewdness to so control circumstances that the message may not reach those whom he is deceiving on that very point. The one who most needs the warning will be urged into some business transaction which requires his presence, or will by some other means be prevented from hearing the words that might prove to him a savor of life unto life.

Again, Satan sees the Lord's servants burdened because of the spiritual darkness that enshrouds the people. He hears their earnest prayers for divine grace and power to break the spell of indifference, carelessness, and indolence. Then with renewed zeal he plies his arts. He tempts men to the indulgence of appetite or to some other form of self-gratification, and thus benumbs their sensibilities, so that they fail to hear the very things which they most need to learn.

Satan well knows that all whom he can lead to neglect prayer and the searching of the Scriptures will be overcome by his attacks. Therefore he invents every possible device to engross the mind. There has ever been a class professing godliness who, instead of following on to know the truth, make it their religion to seek some fault of character or error of faith in those with whom they do not agree. Such are Satan's right-hand helpers. Accusers of the brethren are not few; and they are always active when God is at work, and his servants are rendering him true homage. They will put a false coloring upon the words and acts of those who love and obey the truth. They will represent the most earnest, zealous, self-denying servants of Christ as deceived or deceivers. It is their work to misrepresent the motives of every true and noble deed, to circulate insinuations, and arouse suspicion in the minds of the inexperienced. In every conceivable manner they will seek to cause that which is pure and righteous to be regarded as foul and deceptive. And in this work the agents of Satan have their master and his angels to help them.

But none need be deceived concerning them. It may be readily seen whose children they are, whose example they follow, and whose work they do. "Ye shall know them by their fruits." [MATT. 7:16.] They closely resemble Satan, the envenomed slanderer, the accuser of the brethren.

It is Satan's plan to bring into the church insincere, unregenerate elements that will encourage doubt and unbelief, and hinder all who desire to see the work of God advance, and to advance with it. Many who have no real faith in God or in his word, assent to some principles of truth, and pass as Christians; and thus they are enabled to introduce their errors as scriptural doctrines.

The position that it is of no consequence what men believe, is one of Satan's most successful deceptions. He knows that the truth, received in the love of it, sanctifies the soul of the receiver; therefore he is constantly seeking to substitute false theories, fables, another gospel. From the beginning, the servants of God have contended against false teachers, not merely as vicious men, but as incubators of falsehoods that were fatal to the soul. Elijah, Jeremiah, Paul, firmly and fearlessly opposed those who were turning men from the word of God. That liberality which regards a correct religious faith as unimportant, found no favor with these holy defenders of the truth.

The vague and fanciful interpretations of Scripture, and the many conflicting theories concerning religious faith, that are found in the Christian world, are the work of our great adversary to so confuse minds that they shall not discern the truth. And the discord and division which exists among the churches of Christendom is in a great measure due to the prevailing custom of wresting the Scriptures to support a favorite theory. Instead of carefully studying God's word with humility of heart to obtain a knowledge of his will, many seek only to discover something odd or original.

In order to sustain erroneous doctrines or unchristian practices, they seize upon passages of Scripture separated from the context, perhaps quoting half of a single verse as proving their point, when the remaining portion would show the meaning to be quite the opposite. With the cunning of the serpent, they entrench themselves behind disconnected utterances construed to suit their carnal desires. Thus do many willfully pervert the word of God. Others, who have an active imagination, seize upon the figures and symbols of Holy Writ, interpret to suit their fancy, with little regard to the testimony of Scripture as its own interpreter, and then they present their vagaries as the teachings of God's word.

Whenever the study of the Scriptures is entered upon without a prayerful, humble, teachable spirit, the plainest and simplest as well as the most difficult passages will be wrested from their true meaning. The papal leaders select such portions of Scripture as best serve their purpose, interpret to suit themselves, and then present these to the people, while they deny them the privilege of studying the Bible, and understanding its sacred truths for themselves. Unless the whole Bible is given to the people just as it reads, it would be better for them not to have it at all.

The Bible was designed to be a guide to all who wish to become acquainted with the will of their Maker. God gave to men the sure word of prophecy; angels and even Christ himself came to make known to Daniel and John the things that must shortly come to pass. Those important matters that concern our salvation were not left involved in mystery. They were not revealed in such a way as to perplex and mislead the honest seeker after truth. Said the Lord by the prophet Habakkuk, "Write the vision, and make it plain upon tables, that he may run that readeth it." [HAB. 2:2, 3.] The word of God is plain to all who study it with a prayerful heart. Every truly honest soul will come to the light of truth. "Light is sown for the righteous." [PS. 97:11.] No church can advance in holiness unless its members are earnestly seeking for truth as for hid treasure.

By the cry of liberality, men are blinded to the devices of their adversary, while he is all the time working steadily for the accomplishment of his object. As he succeeds in supplanting the word of truth by human speculations, the law of God is set aside, and the churches are under the bondage of sin while they claim to be free.

To many, scientific research has become a curse; their finite minds are so weak that they lose their balance. They cannot harmonize their views of science with Scripture statements, and they think that the Bible is to be tested by their standard of "science falsely so called." Thus they err from the faith, and are seduced by the devil. Men have endeavored to be wiser than their Creator; human philosophy has attempted to search out and explain mysteries which will never be revealed, through the eternal ages. If men would but search and understand what God has made known of himself and his purposes, they would obtain such a view of the glory, majesty, and power of Jehovah, that they would realize their own littleness, and would be content with that which has been revealed for themselves and their children.

It is a masterpiece of Satan's deceptions to keep the minds of men searching and conjecturing in regard to that which God has not made known, and which he does not intend that we shall understand. It was thus that Lucifer himself was cast out of Heaven. He became dissatisfied because all the secrets of God's purposes were not confided to him, and he entirely disregarded that which was revealed concerning his own work in the lofty position assigned him. By arousing the same discontent in the angels under his command, he caused their fall. Now he seeks to imbue the minds of men with the same spirit, and to lead them also to disregard the direct commands of God.

Those who are unwilling to accept the plain, cutting truths of the Bible, are continually seeking for pleasing fables that will quiet their consciences. The less spiritual, self-denying, and humiliating the doctrines presented, the greater the favor with which they are received. These persons degrade the intellectual powers to serve their carnal desires. Too wise in their own conceit to search the word of God with contrition of soul and earnest prayer for divine guidance, they have no shield from delusion. Satan is ready to supply the heart's desire, and he palms off his deceptions in the place of truth. It was thus that the papacy gained its power over the minds of men; and by rejection of the truth because it involves a cross, Protestants are following the same path. All who neglect the word of God to study convenience and policy, that they may not be at variance with the world, will be left to receive damnable heresy for religious truth. The apostle Paul speaks of a class who received not the love of the truth, that they might be saved. He says of these, "For this cause God shall send them strong delusion, that they should believe a lie, that they all might be damned who believed not the truth, but had pleasure in unrighteousness." [2 THESS. 2:10-12.] With such a warning before us, it behooves us to be on our guard as to what doctrines we receive.

Every conceivable form of error will be accepted by those who willfully reject the truth. Satan has different deceptions prepared to reach different minds; and some who look with horror upon one deception will readily receive another.

Among the most successful agencies of the great deceiver are the delusive doctrines and lying wonders of Spiritualism. Disguised as an angel of light, he spreads his nets where least suspected. If men would but study the word of God with earnest prayer that they might understand its teachings, they would not be left in darkness to receive false doctrines. But as they reject the truth, they fall a prey to these deceptions.

Another dangerous heresy is the doctrine that denies the divinity of Christ. Men who have no experimental knowledge of Jesus, will yet assume an appearance of great wisdom, as though their judgment were beyond question, and boldly declare that the Son of God had no existence prior to his first advent to this world. This position directly contradicts the plainest statements of our Saviour concerning himself; yet it is received with favor by a large class who claim to believe the Scriptures. With such persons it is folly to argue. No argument, however conclusive, will convince those who reject the direct testimony of the Son of God. "The natural man receiveth not the things of the Spirit of God; for they are foolishness unto him; neither can he know them, because they are spiritually discerned." [1 COR. 2:14.] Those who persistently cling to such errors, give evidence of their own ignorance of God and of his Son.

Still another subtle and mischievous error is the fast-spreading belief that Satan has no existence as a personal being; that the name is used in Scripture merely to represent men's evil thoughts and desires.

The teaching so widely echoed from popular pulpits, that the second advent of Christ is his coming to each individual at death, is a device to divert the minds of men from his personal coming in the clouds of heaven. For years Satan has thus been saying, "Behold, he is in the secret chambers;" and many souls have been lost by accepting this deception.

Again, worldly wisdom teaches that prayer is not essential. Men of science claim that there can be no real answer to prayer; that this would be a violation of law, a miracle, and that miracles have no existence. The universe, say they, is governed by fixed laws, and God himself does nothing contrary to these laws. Thus they represent God as bound by his own laws; as if the operation of divine laws could exclude divine freedom. Such teaching is opposed to the testimony of the Scriptures. Were not miracles wrought by Christ and his apostles? The same compassionate Saviour lives to-day, and he is as willing to listen to the prayer of faith as when he walked visibly among men. The natural co-operates with the supernatural. It is a part of God's plan to grant us, in answer to the prayer of faith, that which he would not bestow, did we not thus ask.

Innumerable are the erroneous doctrines and fanciful ideas that are obtaining among the churches of Christendom. It is impossible to estimate the evil results of removing one of the landmarks fixed by the word of God. Few who venture to do this, stop with the rejection of a single truth. The majority continue to set aside one after another of its principles, until they become actual infidels.

And this is the object which Satan seeks to accomplish. There is nothing that he desires more than to destroy confidence in God and in his word. Satan stands at the head of the great army of doubters, and he works to the utmost of his power to beguile souls into his ranks. It is becoming fashionable to doubt. There are many who seem to feel that it is a virtue to stand on the side of unbelief, skepticism, and infidelity. But underneath an appearance of candor and humility, it will be found that such persons are actuated by self-confidence and pride. It is a terrible thing to lose faith in God or in his word. Unbelief strengthens as it is encouraged. There is danger in even once giving expression to doubt; a seed is sown which produces a harvest of its kind. Satan will nourish the crop every moment. Those who allow themselves to talk of their doubts will find them constantly becoming more confirmed. God will never remove every occasion for doubt. He will never work a miracle to remove unbelief when he has given sufficient evidence for faith.

God looks with displeasure upon the self-sufficient and the unbelieving, who are ever doubting his promises and distrusting the assurance of his grace. They are unproductive trees that spread their dark branches far and wide, shutting away the sunlight from other plants, and causing them to droop and die under the chilling shadow. The life-work of these persons will appear as a never-ceasing witness against them. They are sowing seeds of doubt and skepticism that will yield an unfailing harvest.

The followers of Christ know little of the plots which Satan and his hosts are forming against them. But He who sitteth in the heavens will overrule all these devices for the accomplishment of his deep designs. The Lord permits his people to be subjected to the fiery ordeal of temptation, not because he takes pleasure in their distress and affliction, but because this process is essential to their final victory. He could not, consistently with his own glory, shield them from temptation; for the very object of the trial is to prepare them to resist all the allurements of evil.

Satan is well aware that the weakest soul who abides in Christ is more than a match for the hosts of darkness, and that, should he reveal himself openly, he would be met and resisted. Therefore he seeks to draw away the soldiers of the cross from their strong fortification, while he lies in ambush with his forces, ready to destroy all who venture upon his ground. No man is safe for a day or an hour without prayer. Especially should we entreat the Lord for wisdom to understand his word. Satan is an expert in quoting Scripture, placing his own interpretation upon passages by which he hopes to cause us to stumble. We should study the Bible with humility of heart, never losing sight of our dependence upon God. While we must constantly guard against the devices of Satan, we should pray in faith continually, "Lead us not into temptation."

Chapter 28

The First Great Deception

With the earliest history of man, Satan began his efforts to deceive our race. He who had incited rebellion in Heaven desired to bring the whole creation to unite with him in his warfare against the government of God. His envy and jealousy were excited as he looked upon the beautiful home prepared for the happy, holy pair, and he immediately laid his plans to cause their fall. Had he revealed himself in his real character, he would have been repulsed at once, for Adam and Eve had been warned against this dangerous foe; but he worked in the dark, concealing his purpose, that he might more effectually accomplish his object.

Employing as his medium the serpent, then a creature of fascinating appearance, he addressed himself to Eve, "Hath God said, Ye shall not eat of every tree of the garden?" [GEN. 3:1.] Had Eve refrained from entering into argument with the tempter, she would have been safe; but she ventured to parley with him, and fell a victim to his wiles. It is thus that many are still overcome. They doubt and argue concerning the requirements of God, and instead of obeying the divine commands, they accept human theories, which but disguise the devices of Satan.

"The woman said unto the serpent, We may eat of the fruit of the trees of the garden; but of the fruit of the tree which is in the midst of the garden, God hath said, Ye shall not eat of it, neither shall ye touch it, lest ye die. And the serpent said unto the woman, Ye shall not surely die; for God doth know that in the day ye eat thereof, then your eyes shall be opened, and ye shall be as gods, knowing good and evil." [GEN. 3:2-5.] Eve yielded to temptation, and through her influence Adam also was deceived. They accepted the words of the serpent, that God did not mean what he said; they distrusted their Creator, and imagined that he was restricting their liberty, and that they might obtain great light and freedom by transgressing his law.

But what did Adam, after his sin, find to be the meaning of the words, "In the day that thou eatest thereof thou shalt surely die"? Did he find them to mean, as Satan had led him to believe, that he was to be ushered into a more exalted state of existence? Then indeed there was great good to be gained by transgression, and Satan was proved to be a benefactor of the race. But Adam did not so understand the divine sentence. God declared that as a penalty for his sin, man should return to the ground whence he was taken: "Dust thou art, and unto dust shalt thou return." [GEN. 3:19.] The words of Satan, "Your eyes shall be opened," proved to be true only in this sense: After Adam and

Eve had disobeyed God, their eyes were opened to discern their folly; they did know evil, and they tasted the bitter fruit of transgression.

Immortality had been promised on condition of obedience to the requirements of God. It was forfeited by disobedience, and Adam became subject to death. He could not transmit to his posterity that which he did not possess; and there would have been no hope for the fallen race, had not God, by the sacrifice of his Son, brought immortality within their reach. "The wages of sin is death; but the gift of God is eternal life through Jesus Christ our Lord." [ROM. 6:23.] In no other way can it be obtained. But every man may come in possession of this priceless blessing if he will comply with the conditions. All "who by patient continuance in well-doing seek for glory and honor and immortality," will receive eternal life. [ROM. 2:7.]

The one who promised Adam life in disobedience was the great deceiver. The first sermon ever preached upon the immortality of the soul was preached by the serpent to Eve in Eden,— "Ye shall not surely die;" and this declaration, resting solely upon the authority of Satan, is echoed from the pulpits of Christendom, and received by the majority of mankind as readily as it was received by our first parents. The divine sentence, "The soul that sinneth, it shall die," [EZE. 18:20.] is made to mean, The soul that sinneth, it shall not die, but live eternally. We cannot but wonder at the strange infatuation which renders men so credulous concerning the words of Satan, and so unbelieving in regard to the words of God.

The fruit of the tree of life had the power to perpetuate life. Had man after his fall been allowed free access to that tree, he would have lived forever, and thus sin would have been immortalized. But a flaming sword was placed "to keep the way of the tree of life," and not one of the family of Adam has been permitted to pass that barrier and partake of the life-giving fruit. Therefore there is not an immortal sinner.

But after the fall, Satan bade his angels make a special effort to foster the belief in man's natural immortality; and when they had induced the people to receive this error, they led them on to conclude that the sinner would live in eternal misery. Now the prince of darkness, working through his agents, represents God as a revengeful tyrant, declaring that he plunges into hell all those who do not please him, and causes them ever to feel his wrath; and that while they suffer unutterable anguish, and writhe in the eternal flames, their Creator looks down upon them with satisfaction.

Thus the archfiend clothes with his own attributes the Creator and Benefactor of mankind. Cruelty is Satanic. God is love; and all that he created was pure, holy, and lovely, until sin was brought in by the first great rebel. Satan himself is the enemy who tempts man to sin, and then destroys him if he can; and when he has made sure of his victim, then he exults in the ruin he has wrought. If permitted, he would sweep the entire race into his net. Were it not for the interposition of divine power, not one son or daughter of Adam would escape.

He is seeking to overcome men to-day, as he overcame our first parents, by shaking their confidence in their Creator, and leading them to doubt the wisdom of his government and the justice of his laws. Satan and his emissaries represent God as even worse than themselves, in order to excuse their own malignity and rebellion. The great deceiver endeavors to shift his own horrible cruelty of character upon our heavenly Father, that he may cause himself to appear as one greatly wronged because he will not submit to so unjust a governor. He presents before the world the liberty which they may enjoy under his mild sway, in contrast with the bondage imposed by the stern decrees of Jehovah. Thus he succeeds in luring souls away from their allegiance to God.

How repugnant to every emotion of love and mercy, and even to our sense of justice, is the doctrine that the wicked dead are tormented with fire and brimstone in an eternally burning hell, that for the sins of a brief earthly life they are to suffer torture as long as God shall live. Yet this doctrine has been generally embodied in the creeds of Christendom. Says a learned doctor of divinity: "The sight of hell-torments will exalt the happiness of the saints forever. When they see others who are of the same nature and born under the same circumstances, plunged in such misery, and they so distinguished, it will make them sensible of how happy they are." Another uses these words: "While the decree of reprobation is eternally executing on the vessels of wrath, the smoke of their torment will be eternally ascending in view of the vessels of mercy, who, instead of taking the part of these miserable objects, will say, Amen, Alleluia! praise ye the Lord!"

Where in the pages of God's word are such sentiments expressed? Those who present them may be learned and even honest men; but they are deluded by the sophistry of Satan. He leads them to misconstrue strong expressions of Scripture, giving to the language the coloring of bitterness and malignity which pertains to himself, but not to our Creator.

What would be gained to God should we admit that he delights in witnessing unceasing tortures; that he is regaled with the groans and shrieks and imprecations of the suffering creatures whom he holds in the flames of hell? Can these horrid sounds be music in the ear of Infinite Love? It is urged that the infliction of endless misery upon the wicked would show God's hatred of sin as an evil which is ruinous to the peace and order of the universe. Oh, dreadful blasphemy! As if God's hatred of sin is the reason why he perpetuates sin. For, according to the received theology, continued torture without hope of mercy maddens its wretched victims, and as they pour out their rage in curses and blasphemy, they are forever augmenting their load of guilt. God's glory is not enhanced by thus perpetuating continually increasing sin through ceaseless ages.

It is beyond the power of the human mind to estimate the evil which has been wrought by the heresy of eternal torment. The religion of the Bible, full of love and goodness, and abounding in compassion, is darkened by superstition and clothed with terror. When we consider in what false colors Satan has painted the character of God, can we wonder that our merciful Creator is feared, dreaded, and even hated? The appalling views of God which have spread over the world from the teachings of the pulpit have made thousands, yea, millions, of skeptics and infidels.

The theory of eternal torment is one of the false doctrines that constitute the wine of the abominations of Babylon, of which she makes all nations drink. That ministers of Christ should have accepted this heresy and proclaimed it from the sacred desk, is indeed a mystery. They received it from Rome, as they received the false Sabbath. True, it has been taught by great and good men; but the light on this subject had not come to them as it has come to us. They were responsible only for the light which shone in their time; we are accountable for that which shines in our day. If we turn from the testimony of God's word, and accept false doctrines because our fathers taught them, we fall under the condemnation pronounced upon Babylon; we are drinking of the wine of her abominations.

A large class to whom the doctrine of eternal torment is revolting are driven to the opposite error. They see that the Scriptures represent God as a being of love and compassion, and they cannot believe that he will consign his creatures to the fires of an eternally burning hell. But, holding that the soul is naturally immortal, they see no alternative but to conclude that all mankind will finally be saved. Many regard the threatenings of the Bible as designed merely to frighten men into obedience, and not to be literally fulfilled. Thus the sinner can live in selfish pleasure, disregarding the requirements of God, and yet expect to be finally received into his favor. Such a doctrine, presuming upon God's mercy, but ignoring his justice, pleases the carnal heart, and emboldens the wicked in their iniquity.

To show how believers in universal salvation wrest the Scriptures to sustain their soul-destroying dogmas, it is needful only to cite their own utterances. At the funeral of an irreligious young man, who was killed instantly by an accident, a Universalist minister selected as his text the Scripture statement concerning David, "He was comforted concerning Amnon, seeing he was dead." [2 SAM. 13:39.]

"I am frequently asked," said the speaker, "what will be the fate of those who leave the world in sin, die, perhaps, in a state of inebriation, die with the scarlet stains of crime unwashed from their robes, or die as this young man died, having never made a profession or enjoyed an experience of religion. We are content with the Scriptures; their answer shall solve the awful problem. Amnon was exceedingly sinful; he was unrepentant, he was made drunk, and while drunk was killed. David was a prophet of God; he must have known whether it would be ill or well for Amnon in the world to come. What were the expressions of his heart?— 'The soul of King David longed to go forth unto Absalom; for he was comforted concerning Amnon, seeing he was dead.'

"And what is the inference to be deduced from this language? Is it not that endless suffering formed no part of his religious belief?— So we conceive; and here we discover a triumphant argument in support of the more pleasing, more enlightened, more benevolent hypothesis of ultimate universal purity and peace. He was comforted, seeing his son was dead. And why so?— Because by the eye of prophecy he could look forward into the glorious future, and see that son far removed from all temptations, released from the bondage and purified from the corruptions of sin, and after being made sufficiently holy and enlightened, admitted to the assembly of ascended and rejoicing spirits. His only comfort was, that in being removed from the present state of sin and suffering, his beloved son had gone where the loftiest breathings of the Holy Spirit would be shed upon his darkened soul; where his mind would be unfolded to the wisdom of Heaven and the sweet raptures of immortal love, and thus prepared with a sanctified nature to enjoy the rest and society of the heavenly inheritance.

"In these thoughts we would be understood to believe that the salvation of Heaven depends upon nothing which we can do in this life; neither upon a present change of heart, nor upon present belief, or a present profession of religion."

Thus does the professed minister of Christ reiterate the falsehood uttered by the serpent in Eden,— "Ye shall not surely die." "In the day ye eat thereof, then your eyes shall be opened, and ye shall be as gods." The vilest of sinners,— the murderer, the thief, and the adulterer,— will after death be prepared to enter into immortal bliss.

And from what does this perverter of the Scriptures draw his conclusions?— From a single sentence expressing David's submission to the dispensation of Providence. His soul "longed to go forth unto Absalom; for he was comforted concerning Amnon, seeing he was dead." The poignancy of his grief having been softened by time, his thoughts turned from the dead to the living son, self-banished through fear of the just punishment of his crime. And this is the evidence that the incestuous, drunken Amnon was at death immediately transported to the abodes of bliss, there to be purified and prepared for the companionship of sinless angels! A pleasing fable indeed, well suited to gratify the carnal heart! This is Satan's own doctrine, and it does his work effectually. Should we be surprised that, with such instruction, wickedness abounds? Is there not need of contending earnestly for the faith once delivered to the saints?

The course pursued by this one false teacher illustrates that of many others. A few words of Scripture are separated from the context, which would in many cases show its meaning to be exactly opposite to the interpretation put upon it; and such disjointed passages are perverted and used in proof of doctrines that have no foundation in the word of God. The testimony cited as evidence that the drunken Amnon is in Heaven, is a mere inference, directly contradicted by the plain and positive statement of the Scriptures, that no drunkard shall inherit the kingdom of God. It is thus that doubters, unbelievers, and skeptics turn the truth into a lie. And multitudes have been deceived by their sophistry, and rocked to sleep in the cradle of carnal security.

If the souls of all men pass directly to Heaven at the hour of dissolution, then we may well covet death rather than life. Many have been led by this belief to put an end to their existence. When overwhelmed with trouble, perplexity, and disappointment, it seems an easy thing to break the brittle thread of life, and soar away into the bliss of the eternal world.

God has given in his word abundant evidence that he will punish the transgressors of his law. Witness the visitation of his judgments upon the angels who kept not their first estate, on the inhabitants of the antediluvian world, on the people of Sodom, on unbelieving Israel. Their history is placed on record for our admonition.

Let us consider what the Bible teaches further concerning the ungodly and unrepentant, whom the Universalist places in Heaven as holy, happy angels.

"I am Alpha and Omega, the beginning and the end. I will give unto him that is athirst of the fountain of the water of life freely." This promise is only to those that thirst. None but those who feel their need of the water of life, and seek it at the loss of all things else, will be supplied. "He that overcometh shall inherit all things; and I will be his God, and he shall be my son." [REV. 21:6, 7.] Here, also, conditions are specified. To inherit all things, we must resist and overcome sin.

"No fornicator, nor unclean person, nor covetous man, which is an idolater, hath any inheritance in the kingdom of Christ and God." [EPH. 5:5, REV. VER.] "Follow peace with all men, and holiness, without which no man shall see the Lord." [HEB. 12:14.] "Blessed are they that do his commandments, that they may have right to the tree of life, and may enter in through the gates into the city. For without are dogs, and sorcerers, and whoremongers, and murderers, and idolaters, and whosoever loveth and maketh a lie." [REV. 22:14, 15.]

God has given to men a declaration of his character: "The Lord God, merciful and gracious, long-suffering, and abundant in goodness and truth, keeping mercy for thousands, forgiving iniquity and transgression and sin, and that will by no means clear the guilty." [EX. 34:6, 7.] The power and authority of the divine government will be employed to put down rebellion; yet all the manifestations of retributive justice will be perfectly consistent with the character of God as a merciful, long-suffering, benevolent being.

God does not force the will or judgment of any. He takes no pleasure in a slavish obedience. He desires that the creatures of his hands shall love him because he is worthy of love. He would have them obey him because they have an intelligent appreciation of his wisdom, justice, and benevolence. And all who have a just conception of these qualities will love him because they are drawn toward him in admiration of his attributes.

The principles of kindness, mercy, and love taught and exemplified by our Saviour, are a copy of the will and character of God. Christ declared that he taught nothing except that which he had received from his Father. The principles of the divine government are in perfect harmony with the Saviour's precept, "Love your enemies." God executes justice upon the wicked, for the good of the universe, and even of those upon whom his judgments are visited. He would make them happy if he could do so in accordance with the laws of his government and the justice of his character. He surrounds them with the tokens of his love, he grants them a knowledge of his law, and follows them with the offers of his mercy; but they despise his love, make void his law, and reject his mercy. While constantly receiving his gifts, they dishonor the Giver; they hate God because they know that he abhors their sins. The Lord bears long with their perversity; but the decisive hour will come at last, when their destiny is to be decided. Will he then chain these rebels to his side? Will he force them to do his will?

Those who have chosen Satan as their leader, and have been controlled by his power, are not prepared to enter the presence of God. Pride, deception, licentiousness, cruelty, have become fixed in their characters. Can they enter Heaven to dwell forever with those whom they despised and hated on earth? Truth will never be agreeable to a liar; meekness will not satisfy self-esteem and pride; purity is not acceptable to the corrupt; disinterested love does not appear attractive to the selfish. The destiny of the wicked is fixed by their own choice. Their exclusion from Heaven is voluntary; it is just.

Like the waters of the flood, the fires of the great day declare God's verdict that the wicked are incurable. They have no disposition to submit to divine authority. Their will has been exercised in revolt; and when life is ended, it is too late to turn the current of their

thoughts in the opposite direction,— too late to turn from transgression to obedience, from hatred to love.

In mercy to the world, God blotted out its wicked inhabitants in
Noah's time. In mercy he destroyed the corrupt dwellers in Sodom.
Through the deceptive power of Satan, the workers of iniquity obtain
sympathy and admiration, and are thus constantly leading others to
rebellion. It was so in Noah's day, and in the time of Abraham and
Lot; it is so in our time. It is in mercy to the universe that God will
finally destroy the rejecters of his grace.

But the doctrine of never-ending torment has no sanction in the
Bible. John in the Revelation, describing the future joy and glory of
the redeemed, declares that he heard every voice in Heaven and earth,
and under the earth, ascribing praise to God. There will be no lost
beings in hell to mingle their shrieks with the songs of the saved.

"The wages of sin is death; but the gift of God is eternal life
through Jesus Christ our Lord." [ROM. 6:23.] While life is the inheritance of the righteous, death is the portion of the wicked. The penalty
threatened is not merely temporal death, for all must suffer this. It is
the second death, the opposite of everlasting life. God cannot save the
sinner in his sins; but he declares that the wicked, having suffered the
punishment of their guilt, shall be as though they had not been. Says
an inspired writer, "Thou shalt diligently consider his place, and it
shall not be." [PS. 37:10.] In consequence of Adam's sin, death passed
upon all mankind. All alike go down into the grave. But through the
provisions of the plan of salvation, all are to be brought forth from
their graves. Then those who have not secured the pardon of their
sins must receive the penalty of transgression. They suffer punishment
varying in duration and intensity according to their works, but finally
ending in the second death. Covered with infamy, they sink into
hopeless, eternal oblivion.

Upon the fundamental error of natural immortality rests the
doctrine of consciousness in death, a doctrine, like eternal torment,
opposed to the teachings of the Scriptures, to the dictates of reason,
and to our feelings of humanity. According to the popular belief, the
redeemed in Heaven are acquainted with all that takes place on the
earth, and especially with the lives of the friends whom they have left
behind. But how could it be a source of happiness to the dead to know
the troubles of the living, to witness the sins committed by their own
loved ones, and to see them enduring all the sorrows, disappointments, and anguish of life? How much of Heaven's bliss would be
enjoyed by those who were hovering over their friends on earth? And
how utterly revolting is the belief that as soon as the breath leaves the
body, the soul of the impenitent is consigned to the flames of hell! To
what depths of anguish must those be plunged who see their friends

passing to the grave unprepared, to enter upon an eternity of woe and sin! Many have been driven to insanity by this harrowing thought.

What say the Scriptures concerning these things? David declares that man is not conscious in death. "His breath goeth forth, he returneth to his earth; in that very day his thoughts perish." [PS. 146:4.] Solomon bears the same testimony: "The living know that they shall die; but the dead know not anything." "Their love, and their hatred, and their envy, is now perished; neither have they any more a portion forever in anything that is done under the sun." "There is no work, nor device, nor knowledge, nor wisdom, in the grave, whither thou goest." [ECCL. 9:5, 6. 10.]

When, in answer to his prayer, Hezekiah's life was prolonged fifteen years, the grateful king rendered to God a tribute of praise for his great mercy. In this song he tells the reason why he thus rejoices: "The grave cannot praise thee; death cannot celebrate thee; they that go down into the pit cannot hope for thy truth. The living, the living, he shall praise thee, as I do this day. The father to the children shall make known thy truth." [ISA. 38:18, 19.] Popular theology represents the righteous dead as in Heaven, entered into bliss, and praising God with an immortal tongue; but Hezekiah could see no such glorious prospect in death. With his words agrees the testimony of the psalmist: "In death there is no remembrance of thee; in the grave who shall give thee thanks?" "The dead praise not the Lord, neither any that go down into silence." [PS. 6:5; 115:17.]

Peter, speaking through the Holy Spirit on the day of Pentecost, said: "Men and brethren, let me freely speak unto you of the patriarch David, that he is both dead and buried, and his sepulcher is with us unto this day." "For David is not ascended into the heavens." [ACTS 2:29, 34.] The fact that David remains in the grave until the resurrection proves that the righteous do not go to Heaven at death. It is only through the resurrection, and by virtue of the fact that Christ has risen, that David can at last sit at the right hand of God.

Paul declares: "If the dead rise not, then is not Christ raised. And if Christ be not raised, your faith is vain; ye are yet in your sins. Then they also which are fallen asleep in Christ are perished." [1 COR. 15:16-18.] If for four thousand years the righteous had gone directly to Heaven at death, how could they be said to perish, even though there should never be a resurrection?

When about to leave his disciples, Jesus did not tell them that they would soon come to him. "I go to prepare a place for you," he said. "And if I go and prepare a place for you, I will come again, and receive you unto myself." [JOHN 14:2, 3.] And Paul tells us, further, that "the Lord himself shall descend from heaven with a shout, with the voice of the archangel, and with the trump of God; and the dead in Christ shall rise first. Then we which are alive and remain shall be caught up together with them in the clouds, to meet the Lord in the air; and so shall we ever be with the Lord." And he adds, "Comfort one another with these words." [1 THESS. 4:16-18.] How wide the contrast between these words of comfort and those of the minister previously quoted. The latter consoled the bereaved friends with the assurance, that, however sinful the dead might have been, he was received among the angels as soon as he breathed out his life here. Paul points his brethren to the future coming of the Lord, when the fetters of the tomb shall be broken, and the "dead in Christ" shall be raised to eternal life.

Before any can enter the mansions of the blest, their cases must be investigated, and their characters and their deeds must pass in review before God. All are to be judged according to the things written in the books, and to be rewarded as their works have been. This Judgment does not take place at death. Mark the words of Paul: "He hath appointed a day, in the which he will judge the world in righteousness by that man whom he hath ordained; whereof he hath given assurance unto all men, in that he hath raised him from the dead." [ACTS 17:31.] Here the apostle plainly stated that a specified time, then future, had been fixed upon for the Judgment of the world.

Jude refers to the same period: "The angels which kept not their first estate, but left their own habitation, he hath reserved in everlasting chains under darkness unto the Judgment of the great day." And again he quotes the words of Enoch: "Behold, the Lord cometh with ten thousands of his saints, to execute judgment upon all." [JUDE 6, 14, 15.] John declares that he "saw the dead, small and great, stand before God, and the books were opened;" "and the dead were judged out of those things which were written in the books." [REV. 20:12.]

But if the dead are already enjoying the bliss of Heaven or writhing in the flames of hell, what need of a future Judgment? The teachings of God's word on these important points are neither obscure nor contradictory; they may be understood by common minds. But what candid mind can see either wisdom or justice in the current theory? Will the righteous, after the investigation of their cases at the Judgment, receive the commendation, "Well done, good and faithful servant, enter thou into the joy of thy Lord," when they have been dwelling in his presence, perhaps for long ages? Are the wicked summoned from the place of torment to receive the sentence from the Judge of all the earth, "Depart, ye cursed, into everlasting fire?" Oh, solemn mockery! shameful impeachment of the wisdom and justice of God!

Nowhere in the Sacred Scriptures is found the statement that the righteous go to their reward or the wicked to their punishment at death. The patriarchs and prophets have left no such assurance. Christ and his apostles have given no hint of it. The Bible clearly teaches that the dead do not go immediately to Heaven. They are represented as sleeping until the resurrection. In the very day that the silver cord is loosed and the golden bowl broken, man's thoughts perish. They that go down to the grave are in silence. They know no more of anything that is done under the sun. Blessed rest for the weary righteous! Time, be it long or short, is but a moment to them. They sleep, they are awakened by the trump of God to a glorious immortality. As they are called forth from their deep slumber, they begin to think just where they ceased. The last sensation was the pang of death, the last thought that they were falling beneath the power of the grave. When they arise from the tomb, their first glad thought will be echoed in the triumphal shout, "O death, where is thy sting? O grave, where is thy victory?"

Chapter 29

Spiritualism

The doctrine of natural immortality has prepared the way for modern Spiritualism. If the dead are admitted to the presence of God and holy angels, and privileged with knowledge far exceeding what they before possessed, why should they not return to the earth to enlighten and instruct the living? How can those who believe in man's consciousness in death reject what comes to them as divine light communicated by glorified spirits? Here is a channel regarded as sacred, through which Satan works for the accomplishment of his purposes. The fallen angels who do his bidding appear as messengers from the spirit world. While professing to bring the living into communication with the dead, Satan exercises his bewitching influence upon their minds.

He has power even to bring before men the appearance of their departed friends. The counterfeit is perfect; the familiar look, the words, the tone, are reproduced with marvelous distinctness. Many are comforted with the assurance that their loved ones are enjoying the bliss of Heaven; and without suspicion of danger, they give ear to seducing spirits and doctrines of devils.

When they have been led to believe that the dead actually return to communicate with them, Satan causes those to appear who went into the grave unprepared. They claim to be happy in Heaven, and even to occupy exalted positions there; and thus the error is widely taught, that no difference is made between the righteous and the wicked. The pretended visitants from the world of spirits sometimes utter cautions and warnings which prove to be correct. Then, as confidence is gained, they present doctrines which directly undermine faith in the Scriptures. With an appearance of deep interest in the well-being of their friends on earth, they insinuate the most dangerous errors. The fact that they state some truths, and are able at times to foretell future events, gives to their statements an appearance of reliability; and their false teachings are accepted by the multitudes as readily, and believed as implicitly, as if they were the most sacred truths of the Bible. The law of God is set aside, the Spirit of grace despised, the blood of the covenant counted an unholy thing. The spirits deny the divinity of Christ, and place even the Creator on a level with themselves. Thus under a new disguise the great rebel still carries forward his warfare against God, begun in Heaven, and for nearly six thousand years continued upon the earth.

Many endeavor to account for spiritual manifestations by attributing them wholly to fraud and sleight of hand on the part of the medium. But while it is true that the results of trickery have often been

206 • The Great Controversy / The Bible Made Plain

palmed off as genuine manifestations, there have been, also, marked exhibitions of supernatural power. The mysterious rapping with which modern Spiritualism began was not the result of human trickery or cunning, but the direct work of evil angels, who thus introduced one of the most successful of soul-destroying delusions. Many will be ensnared through the belief that Spiritualism is a merely human imposture; when brought face to face with manifestations which they cannot but regard as supernatural, they will be deceived, and will be led to accept them as the great power of God.

These persons overlook the testimony of the Scriptures concerning the wonders wrought by Satan and his agents. It was by Satanic aid that Pharaoh's magicians were enabled to counterfeit the work of God. The apostle John, describing the miracle-working power that will be manifested in the last days, declares: "He doeth great wonders, so that he maketh fire come down from heaven on the earth in the sight of men, and deceiveth them that dwell on the earth by the means of those miracles which he had power to do." [REV. 13:13, 14.] No mere impostures are here brought to view. Men are deceived by the miracles which Satan's agents have power to do, not which they pretend to do.

The very name of witchcraft is now held in contempt. The claim that men can hold intercourse with evil spirits is regarded as a fable of the Dark Ages. But Spiritualism, which numbers its converts by hundreds of thousands, yea, by millions, which has made its way into scientific circles, which has invaded churches, and has found favor in legislative bodies, and even in the courts of kings— this mammoth deception is but a revival in a new disguise of the witchcraft condemned and prohibited of old.

Satan beguiles men now, as he beguiled Eve in Eden, by exciting a desire to obtain forbidden knowledge. "Ye shall be as gods," he declares, "knowing good and evil." But the wisdom which Spiritualism imparts is that described by the apostle James, which "descendeth not from above, but is earthly, sensual, devilish." [JAS. 3:15.]

The prince of darkness has a masterly mind, and he skillfully adapts his temptations to men of every variety of condition and culture. He works "with all deceivableness of unrighteousness" to gain control of the children of men; but he can accomplish his object only as they voluntarily yield to his temptations. Those who place themselves in his power by indulging their evil traits of character, little realize where their course will end. The tempter accomplishes their ruin, and then employs them to ruin others.

To those who regard themselves as educated and refined, Satan addresses himself by exciting the imagination to lofty flights in forbidden fields, leading them to take so great pride in their superior wisdom that in their hearts they despise the Eternal One. To this class the great deceiver presents Spiritualism in its more refined and intellectual aspects, and he thus succeeds in drawing many into his snare. He who could appear clothed with the brightness of the heavenly seraphs before Christ in the wilderness of temptation, comes to men in the most attractive manner, as an angel of light. He appeals to the reason by the presentation of elevating themes, he delights the fancy with enrapturing scenes, and he enlists the affections by his eloquent portrayals of love and charity. That mighty being who could take the world's Redeemer to an exceedingly high mountain, and bring before him all the kingdoms of the earth and the glory of them, will present his temptations to men in a manner to pervert the senses of all who are not shielded by divine power.

To the self-indulgent, the pleasure-loving, the sensual, the grosser forms of Spiritualism are adapted; and multitudes eagerly accept teachings that leave them at liberty to follow the inclinations of the carnal heart. Satan studies every indication of the frailty of human nature, he marks the sins which each individual is inclined to commit, and then he takes care that opportunities shall not be wanting to gratify the tendency to evil. He tempts men to excess in that which is in itself lawful, causing them through intemperance to weaken physical, mental, and moral power. He was destroyed and is destroying thousands through the indulgence of the passions, thus brutalizing the entire nature of man. When the people are led to believe that desire is the highest law, that liberty is license, and that man is accountable only to himself, who can wonder that corruption and depravity teem on every hand? The reins of self-control are laid upon the neck of lust, the powers of mind and soul are made subject to the animal propensities, and Satan exultantly sweeps into his net thousands who profess to be followers of Christ.

But none need be deceived by the lying claims of Spiritualism. God has given the world sufficient light to enable them to discover the snare. If there were no other evidence, it should be enough for the Christian that the spirits make no difference between righteousness and sin, between the noblest and purest of the apostles of Christ and the most corrupt of the servants of Satan. By representing the basest of men as in Heaven, and highly exalted there, Satan virtually declares to the world, No matter how wicked you are; no matter whether you believe or disbelieve God and the Bible. Live as you please; Heaven is your home.

Moreover, the apostles, as personated by these lying spirits, are made to contradict what they wrote at the dictation of the Holy Spirit when on earth. They deny the divine origin of the Bible, and thus tear away the foundation of the Christian's hope, and put out the light that reveals the way to Heaven.

Satan is making the world believe that the Bible is a mere fiction, or at least a book suited to the infancy of the race, but now to be lightly regarded, or cast aside as obsolete. And to take the place of the word of God he holds out spiritual manifestations. Here is a channel wholly under his control; by this means he can make the world believe what he will. The book that is to judge him and his followers he puts into the shade, just where he wants it; the Saviour of the world he makes to be no more than a common man. And as the Romish guard that watched the tomb of Jesus spread the lying report which the priests and elders put into their mouths to disprove his resurrection, so do the believers in spiritual manifestations try to make it appear that there is nothing miraculous in the circumstances of our Saviour's life. After thus seeking to put Jesus in the background, they call attention to their own miracles, declaring that these far exceed the works of Christ.

Says the prophet Isaiah: "When they shall say unto you, Seek unto them that have familiar spirits, and unto wizards that peep and that mutter: should not a people seek unto their God? for the living to the dead? To the law and to the testimony. If they speak not according to this word, it is because there is no light in them." [ISA. 8:19, 20.] If men had been willing to receive the truth so plainly stated in the Scriptures, that the dead know not anything, they would see in the claims and manifestations of Spiritualism the working of Satan with power and signs and lying wonders. But rather than yield the liberty so agreeable to the carnal heart, and renounce the sins which they love, the multitudes close their eyes to the light, and walk straight on, regardless of warnings, while Satan weaves his snares about them, and they become his prey. "Because they received not the love of the truth, that they might be saved," therefore "God shall send them strong delusion, that they should believe a lie." [2 THESS. 2:10, 11.]

Those who oppose the teachings of Spiritualism are assailing, not men alone, but Satan and his angels. They have entered upon a contest against principalities and powers and wicked spirits in high places. Satan will not yield one inch of ground except as he is driven back by the power of heavenly messengers. The people of God should be able to meet him, as did our Saviour, with the words, "It is written." Satan can quote Scripture now as in the days of Christ, and he will pervert its teachings to sustain his delusions. But the plain statements of the Bible will furnish weapons powerful in every conflict.

Those who would stand in this time of peril must understand the testimony of the Scriptures concerning the nature of man and the state of the dead; for in the near future many will be confronted by the spirits of devils personating beloved relatives or friends, and declaring the most dangerous heresies. These visitants will appeal to our tenderest sympathies, and will work miracles to sustain their pretensions.

We must be prepared to withstand them with the Bible truth that the dead know not anything, and that they who thus appear are the spirits of devils.

Just before us is the "hour of temptation, which shall come upon all the world, to try them that dwell upon the earth." [REV. 3:10.] All whose faith is not firmly established upon the word of God will be deceived and overcome. But to those who earnestly seek a knowledge of the truth, thus doing what they can to prepare for the conflict, the God of truth will be a sure defense. "Because thou hast kept the word of my patience, I also will keep thee," is the Saviour's promise. He would sooner send every angel out of Heaven to protect his people, than leave one soul that trusts in him to be overcome by Satan.

The prophet Isaiah brings to view the fearful deception which will come upon the wicked, causing them to count themselves secure from the judgments of God: "We have made a covenant with death, and with hell are we at agreement. When the overflowing scourge shall pass through, it shall not come unto us; for we have made lies our refuge, and under falsehood have we hid ourselves." [ISA. 28:15.] In the class here described are included those who in their stubborn impenitence comfort themselves with the assurance that there is to be no punishment for the sinner; that all mankind, it matters not how corrupt, are to be exalted to Heaven to become as the angels of God. But still more emphatically are those making a covenant with death and an agreement with hell, who renounce the truths which Heaven has provided as a defense for the righteous in the day of trouble, and accept the refuge of lies offered by Satan in its stead, — the delusive pretensions of Spiritualism.

Marvelous beyond expression is the blindness of the people of this generation. Thousands reject the word of God as unworthy of belief, and with eager confidence receive the deceptions of Satan. Skeptics and scoffers with great clamor denounce the bigotry of those who contend for the faith of prophets and apostles, and they divert themselves by holding up to ridicule the solemn declarations of the Scriptures concerning Christ and the plan of salvation, and the retribution to be visited upon the rejecters of the truth. They affect great pity for minds so narrow, weak, and superstitious as to acknowledge the claims of God, and obey the requirements of his law. They manifest as much assurance as if, indeed, they had made a covenant with death and an agreement with hell,— as if they had erected an impassable, impenetrable barrier between themselves and the vengeance of God. Nothing can arouse their fears. So fully have they yielded to the tempter, so closely are they united with him, and so thoroughly imbued with his spirit, that they have no power and no inclination to break away from his snare.

Long has Satan been preparing for his final effort to deceive the world. The foundation of his work was laid by the assurance given to Eve in Eden, "Ye shall not surely die." "In the day that ye eat thereof, then your eyes shall be opened, and ye shall be as gods, knowing good and evil." Little by little he has prepared the way for his masterpiece of deception in the development of Spiritualism. He has not yet reached the full accomplishment of his designs; but it will be reached in the last remnant of time, and the world will be swept into the ranks of this delusion. They are fast being lulled into a fatal security, to be awakened only by the outpouring of the wrath of God.

Saith the Lord God: "Judgment also will I lay to the line, and righteousness to the plummet; and the hail shall sweep away the refuge of lies, and the waters shall overflow the hiding-place. And your covenant with death shall be disannulled, and your agreement with hell shall not stand. When the overflowing scourge shall pass through, then ye shall be trodden down by it." [ISA. 28:17, 18.]

Chapter 30

Character and Aims of the Papacy

Romanism is now regarded by Protestants with far greater favor than in former years. There is an increasing indifference concerning the doctrines that separate the reformed churches from the papal hierarchy; the opinion is gaining ground that, after all, we do not differ so widely upon vital points as has been supposed, and that a little concession on our part will bring us into a better understanding with Rome. The time was when Protestants placed a high value upon the liberty of conscience which has been so dearly purchased. They taught their children to abhor Popery, and held that to remain at peace with Rome would be disloyalty to God. But how widely different are the sentiments now expressed.

The defenders of Popery declare that she has been maligned; and the Protestant world is inclined to accept the statement. Many urge that it is unjust to judge the Romish Church of to-day by the abominations and absurdities that marked her reign during the centuries of ignorance and darkness. They excuse her horrible cruelty as the result of the barbarism of the times, and plead that civilization has changed her sentiments.

Have these persons forgotten the claim of infallibility for eight hundred years put forth by this haughty power? So far from relinquishing this claim, the church in the nineteenth century has affirmed it with greater positiveness than ever before. As Rome asserts that she has never erred, and never can err, how can she renounce the principles which governed her course in past ages?

The papal church will never relinquish her claim to infallibility. All that she has done in her persecution of those who reject her dogmas, she holds to be right; and would she not repeat the same acts, should the opportunity be presented? Let the restraints now imposed by secular governments be removed, and Rome be reinstated in her former power, and there would speedily be a revival of her tyranny and persecution.

It is true that there are real Christians in the Roman Catholic communion. Thousands in that church are serving God according to the best light they have. They are not allowed access to his word, and therefore they do not discern the truth. They have never seen the contrast between a living heart-service and a round of mere forms and ceremonies. But God looks with pitying tenderness upon these souls, educated as they are in a faith that is delusive and unsatisfying. He will cause rays of light to penetrate the dense darkness that surrounds them. He will reveal to them the truth as it is in Jesus, and they will yet take their position with his people.

But Romanism as a system is no more in harmony with the gospel of Christ now than at any former period in her history. The Protestant churches are in great darkness, or they would discern the signs of the times. The Roman Church is far-reaching in her plans and modes of operation. She is employing every device to extend her influence and increase her power in preparation for a fierce and determined conflict to regain control of the world, to re-establish persecution, and to undo all that Protestantism has done. Catholicism is gaining ground in our country upon every side. Look at the number of her churches and chapels. Look at her colleges and seminaries, so widely patronized by Protestants. These things should awaken the anxiety of all who prize the pure principles of the gospel.

Protestants have tampered with and patronized Popery; they have made compromises and concessions which Papists themselves are surprised to see, and fail to understand. Men are closing their eyes to the real character of Romanism, and the dangers to be apprehended from her supremacy. The people of our land need to be aroused to resist the advances of this most dangerous foe to civil and religious liberty.

Many suppose that the Catholic religion is unattractive, and that its worship is a dull, stupid round of ceremony. Here they mistake. While Romanism is based upon deception, it is not a coarse and clumsy imposture. The religious service of the Romish Church is a most impressive ceremonial. Its gorgeous display and solemn rites fascinate the senses of the people, and silence the voice of reason and of conscience. The eye is charmed. Magnificent churches, imposing processions, golden altars, jeweled shrines, choice paintings, and exquisite sculpture appeal to the love of beauty. The ear also is captivated. There is nothing to excel the music. The rich notes of the deep-toned organ, blending with the melody of many voices as it swells through the lofty domes and pillared aisles of her grand cathedrals, cannot fail to impress the mind with awe and reverence.

This outward splendor, pomp, and ceremony, that only mocks the longings of the sin-sick soul, is an evidence of inward corruption. The religion of Christ needs not such attractions to recommend it. In the light shining from the cross, true Christianity appears so pure and lovely that external decorations only hide its true worth. It is the beauty of holiness, a meek and quiet spirit, which is of value with God.

Brilliancy of style is not an index of pure, elevated thought. The highest conceptions of art, the most delicate refinement of taste, often spring from minds wholly earthly and sensual. They are often employed by Satan to lead men to forget the necessities of the soul, to lose sight of the future, immortal life, to turn away from their infinite Helper, and to live for this world alone.

A religion of externals is attractive to the unrenewed heart. The pomp and ceremony of the Catholic worship have a seductive, be-witching power by which many are deceived; and they come to look upon the Roman Church as the very gate of Heaven. None are proof against her influence but those who have planted their feet firmly upon the foundation of truth, and whose hearts are renewed by the Spirit of God. Thousands who have not an experimental knowledge of Christ will be swept into this deception. A form of godliness without the power is just what they desire. The Romanist feels at liberty to sin, because the church claims the right to pardon. To him who loves self-indulgence, it is more pleasing to confess to a fellow-mortal than to open the soul to God. It is more palatable to human nature to do penance than to renounce sin. It is easier to mortify the flesh by sackcloth and nettles and galling chains than to crucify fleshly lusts. Heavy is the yoke which the carnal heart is willing to bear rather than bow to the yoke of Christ.

There is a striking similarity between the church of Rome and the Jewish church at the time of Christ's first advent. While the Jews secretly trampled upon every principle of the law of God, they were outwardly rigorous in the observance of its precepts, loading it down with exactions and traditions that made obedience painful and burdensome. As the Jews professed to revere the law, so do Romanists claim to reverence the cross. They exalt the symbol of Christ's sufferings, while in their lives they deny him whom it represents.

Papists place crosses upon their churches, upon their altars, and upon their garments. Everywhere is seen the insignia of the cross. Everywhere it is outwardly honored and exalted. But the teachings of Christ are buried beneath a mass of senseless traditions, false inter-pretations, and rigorous exactions. The Saviour's words concerning the bigoted Jews apply with still greater force to the Romish leaders: "They bind heavy burdens and grievous to be borne, and lay them on men's shoulders; but they themselves will not move them with one of their fingers." [MATT. 23:4.] Conscientious souls are kept in constant terror, fearing the wrath of an offended God, while the dignitaries of the church are living in luxury and sensual pleasure.

Satan instigates the worship of images, the invocation of saints, and the exaltation of the pope, to attract the minds of the people from God and from his Son. To accomplish their ruin, he endeavors to turn their attention from Him through whom alone they can find salvation. He will direct them to any one that can be substituted for the One who has said, "Come unto me, all ye that labor and are heavy laden, and I will give you rest." [MATT. 11:28.]

It is Satan's constant effort to misrepresent the character of God, the nature of sin, and the real issues at stake in the great controversy. By his sophistry he blinds the minds of men, and secures them as his agents to war against God. By perverted conceptions of the divine attributes, heathen nations were led to believe human sacrifices necessary to secure the favor of Deity; and the most horrible cruelties have been perpetrated under the various forms of idolatry. The Romish Church, uniting the forms of paganism and Christianity, and in a similar manner misrepresenting the character of God, has resorted to practices no less cruel and revolting. In the days of Rome's supremacy there were instruments of torture to compel assent to her doctrines. There was the stake for those who would not concede to her claims. There were massacres on a scale that will never be known to mortals. Dignitaries of the church studied, under Satan their master, to invent means to cause the greatest possible torture, and not end the life of their victim. The infernal process was repeated to the utmost limit of human endurance, until nature gave up the struggle, and the sufferer hailed death as a sweet release.

Such was the fate of Rome's opponents. For her adherents she had the discipline of the scourge, of famishing hunger, of bodily austerities in every conceivable, heart-sickening form. To secure the favor of Heaven, penitents violated the laws of God by violating the laws of nature. They were taught to sunder every tie which he has formed to bless and gladden man's earthly sojourn. The churchyard contains millions of victims who spent their lives in vain endeavors to subdue their natural affections, to repress, as offensive to God, every thought and feeling of sympathy with their fellow-creatures.

If we desire to understand the determined cruelty of Satan, manifested for hundreds of years, not among those who never heard of God, but in the very heart and throughout the extent of Christendom, we have only to look at the history of Romanism. And as we see how he succeeds in disguising himself, and accomplishing his work through the leaders of the church, we may better understand why he has so great antipathy to the Bible. If that book is read, the mercy and love of God will be revealed; it will be seen that he lays upon men none of these heavy burdens. All that he asks is a broken and contrite heart, a humble, obedient spirit.

Christ gives no example in his life for men and women to shut themselves in monasteries in order to become fitted for Heaven. He has never taught that love and sympathy must be repressed. The Saviour's heart overflowed with love. The nearer man approaches to moral perfection, the keener are his sensibilities, the more acute is his perception of sin, and the deeper his sympathy for the afflicted. The pope claims to be the vicar of Christ. How does his character bear comparison with that of our Saviour? Was Christ ever known to consign men to the prison or the rack because they did not pay him homage as the King of Heaven? Was his voice heard condemning to death those who did not accept him? When he was slighted by the people of a Samaritan village, the apostle John was filled with indignation, and inquired, "Lord, wilt thou that we command fire to come down from heaven, and consume them, even as Elias did?" Jesus looked with pity upon his disciple, and rebuked his harsh spirit, saying, "The Son of man is not come to destroy men's lives, but to save them. [LUKE 9:54, 56.] How different from the spirit manifested by Christ is that of his professed vicar.

The Romish Church now presents a fair front to the world, covering with apologies her record of horrible cruelties. She has clothed herself in Christlike garments; but she is unchanged. Every principle of Popery that existed in ages past exists to-day. The doctrines devised in the darkest ages are still held. Let none deceive themselves. The Popery that Protestants are now so ready to embrace and honor is the same that ruled the world in the days of the Reformation, when men of God stood up at the peril of their lives to expose her iniquity. She possesses the same pride and arrogant assumption that lorded it over kings and princes, and claimed the prerogatives of God. Her spirit is no less cruel and despotic now than when she crushed out human liberty, and slew the saints of the Most High.

Popery is just what prophecy declared that she would be,— the apostasy of the latter times. It is a part of her policy to assume the character which will best accomplish her purpose; but beneath the variable appearance of the chameleon, she conceals the invariable venom of the serpent. "We are not bound to keep faith and promises to heretics," she declares. Shall this power, whose record for a thousand years is written in the blood of the saints, be now acknowledged as a part of the church of Christ?

It is not without reason that the claim has been put forth that Catholicism is now almost like Protestantism. There has been a change; but the change is in Protestants, not in Romanists. Catholicism indeed resembles the Protestantism that now exists; but it is far removed from Protestantism as it was in the days of Cranmer, Ridley, Knox, and other reformers.

As the Protestant churches have been seeking the favor of the world, false charity has blinded their eyes. They do not see but that it is right to believe good of all evil; and as the inevitable result, they will finally believe evil of all good. Instead of standing in defense of the faith once delivered to the saints, they are now, as it were, apologizing to Rome for their uncharitable opinion of her, begging pardon for their bigotry.

A large class, even of those who look upon Romanism with no favor, apprehend little danger from her power and influence. Many urge that the intellectual and moral darkness prevailing during the Middle Ages favored the spread of her dogmas, superstitions, and oppression, and that the greater intelligence of modern times, the general diffusion of knowledge, and the increasing liberality in matters of religion, forbid a revival of intolerance and tyranny. The very thought that such a state of things will exist in this enlightened age is ridiculed. It is true that great light, intellectual, moral, and religious, is shining upon this generation. In the open pages of God's holy word, light from Heaven has been shed upon the world. But it should be remembered that the greater the light bestowed, the greater the darkness of those who pervert or reject it.

A prayerful study of the Bible would show Protestants the real character of the papacy, and would cause them to abhor and to shun it; but men are so wise in their own conceit that they feel no need of humbly seeking God that they may be led into the truth. Although priding themselves on their enlightenment, they are ignorant both of the Scriptures and of the power of God. They must have some means of quieting their consciences; and they seek that which is least spiritual and humiliating. What they desire is a method of forgetting God which shall pass as a method of remembering him. The papacy is well adapted to meet the wants of all these. It is prepared for two classes of mankind, embracing nearly the whole world,— those who would be saved by their merits, and those who would be saved in their sins. Here is the secret of its power.

A day of great intellectual darkness has been shown to be favorable to the success of Popery. It will yet be demonstrated that a day of great intellectual light is equally favorable for its success. In past ages, when men were without God's word, and without the knowledge of the truth, their eyes were blindfolded, and thousands were ensnared, not seeing the net spread for their feet. In this generation there are many whose eyes become dazzled by the glare of human speculations, "science falsely so called;" they discern not the net, and walk into it as readily as if blindfolded. God designed that man's intellectual powers should be held as a gift from his Maker, and employed in the service of truth and righteousness; but when they are idolized, and laid upon the shrine of Satan to be employed in the service of a false religion, then intelligence can accomplish greater harm than ignorance.

In the movements now in progress in this country to secure for the institutions and usages of the church the support of the State, Protestants are following in the steps of Papists. Nay, more, they are opening the door for Popery to regain in Protestant America the supremacy which she has lost in the Old World. And that which gives greater significance to this movement is the fact that the principal object contemplated is the enforcement of Sunday observance, — a custom which originated with Rome, and which she claims as the sign of her authority.

The spirit of the papacy,— the spirit of conformity to worldly customs, the veneration for human traditions above the commands of

God,— is permeating the Protestant churches, and leading them on to do the same work of Sunday exaltation which the papacy has done before them. Would the reader understand the agencies to be employed in the soon-coming contest? He has but to trace the record of the means which Rome employed for the same object in ages past. Would he know how Papists and Protestants united will deal with those who reject their dogmas? Let him see the spirit which Rome manifested toward the Sabbath and its defenders.

Royal edicts, human councils, and church ordinances sustained by secular power, were the steps by which the pagan festival attained its position of honor in the Christian world. The first public measure enforcing Sunday observance was the law enacted [A.D. 321.] by Constantine, two years before his profession of Christianity. This edict required townspeople to rest on the venerable day of the sun, but permitted countrymen to continue their agricultural pursuits. Though originally a heathen statute, it was enforced by the emperor after his nominal acceptance of the Christian religion.

The royal mandate not proving a sufficient substitute for divine authority, the bishop of Rome soon after conferred upon the Sunday the title of Lord's day. Another bishop, who also sought the favor of princes, and who was the special friend and flatterer of Constantine, advanced the claim that Christ had transferred the Sabbath to Sunday. Not a single testimony of the Scriptures was produced in proof of the new doctrine. The sacred garments in which the spurious Sabbath was arrayed were of man's own manufacture; but they served to embolden men in trampling upon the law of God. All who desired to be honored by the world accepted the popular festival.

As the papacy became firmly established, the work of Sunday exaltation was continued. For a time the people engaged in agricultural labor when not attending church, and the name Sabbath was still attached to the seventh day. But steadily and surely a change was effected. Those in holy office were forbidden to pass judgment in any civil controversy on the Sunday. Soon after, persons of all rank were commanded to refrain from common labor, on pain of a fine for freedmen, and stripes in the case of servants. Later it was decreed that rich men should be punished with the loss of half of their estates; and finally, that if still obstinate they should be made slaves. The lower classes were to suffer perpetual banishment.

Miracles also were called into requisition. Among other wonders it was reported that as a husbandman who was about to plow his field on Sunday, cleaned his plow with an iron, the iron stuck fast in his hand, and for two years he carried it about with him, "to his exceeding great pain and shame."

Later, the pope gave directions that the parish priest should admonish the violators of Sunday, and wish them to go to church and say their prayers, lest they bring some great calamity on themselves and neighbors. An ecclesiastical council brought forward the argument since so widely employed, that because persons had been struck by lightning while laboring on Sunday, it must be the Sabbath. "It is apparent," said the prelates, "how high the displeasure of God was upon their neglect of this day." An appeal was then made that priests and ministers, kings and princes, and all faithful people, "use their utmost endeavors and care that the day be restored to its honor, and, for the credit of Christianity, more devoutly observed for time to come."

The decrees of councils proving insufficient, the secular authorities were besought to issue an edict that would strike terror to the hearts of the people, and force them to refrain from labor on the Sunday. At a synod held in Rome, all previous decisions were reaffirmed with greater force and solemnity. They were also incorporated into the ecclesiastical law, and enforced by the civil authorities throughout nearly all Christendom.

Still the absence of scriptural authority for Sunday-keeping occasioned no little embarrassment. The people questioned the right of their teachers to deny the positive declaration of Jehovah, "The seventh day is the Sabbath of the Lord thy God," in order to honor the day of the sun. To supply the lack of Bible testimony, Satan was ready with expedients. A zealous advocate of Sunday, who about the close of the twelfth century visited the churches of England, was resisted by faithful witnesses for the truth; and so fruitless were his efforts that he departed from the country for a season, and cast about him for some means to enforce his teachings. When he returned, the lack was supplied, and in his after-labors he met with greater success. He brought with him a roll purporting to be from God himself, and containing the needed command for Sunday observance, and awful threats to terrify the disobedient. This precious document— as base a counterfeit as the institution it supported— was said to have fallen from heaven, and to have been found in Jerusalem, upon the altar of St. Simeon, in Golgotha. The pontifical palace at Rome was the source whence it proceeded. Frauds and forgeries to advance the power and prosperity of the church have in all ages been esteemed lawful by the papal hierarchy.

The roll forbade labor from the ninth hour, three o'clock, on Saturday afternoon, till sunrise on Monday; and its authority was declared to be confirmed by many miracles. It was reported that persons laboring beyond the appointed hour were stricken with paralysis. A miller who attempted to grind his corn, saw, instead of flour, a torrent of blood come forth, and the mill-wheel stood still, notwithstanding the strong rush of the water. A woman who placed dough in the oven, found it raw when taken out, though the oven was very hot. Another who had dough prepared for baking at the ninth hour, but determined to set it aside till Monday, found the next day that it had been made into loaves and baked by divine power. A man who baked bread after the ninth hour on Saturday, found, when he broke it the next morning, that blood started therefrom. By such absurd and superstitious fabrications did the advocates of Sunday endeavor to establish its sacredness.

In Scotland, as in England, a greater regard for Sunday was secured by uniting with it a portion of the ancient Sabbath. But the time required to be kept holy varied. A law was passed that Saturday from twelve at noon ought to be accounted holy, and that no man, from that time till Monday morning, should engage in worldly business.

But notwithstanding all the efforts to establish Sunday sacredness, Papists themselves publicly confessed the divine authority of the Sabbath, and the human origin of the institution by which it had been supplanted. In the sixteenth century a papal council plainly declared: "Let all Christians remember that the seventh day was consecrated by God, and hath been received and observed, not only by the Jews, but by all others who pretend to worship God; though we Christians have changed their Sabbath into the Lord's day." Those who were tampering with the divine law were not ignorant of the character of their work. They were deliberately setting themselves above God.

A striking illustration of Rome's policy toward those who honor the Sabbath was given in the long and bloody persecution of the Waldenses. Others suffered in a similar manner for their fidelity to the same truth. Amid the gloom of the Dark Ages, the Christians of Central Africa were lost sight of and forgotten by the world, and for many centuries they enjoyed freedom in the exercise of their faith. But at last Rome learned of their existence, and the emperor of Abyssinia was soon beguiled into an acknowledgment of the pope as the vicar of Christ. Other concessions followed. An edict was issued forbidding the observance of the Sabbath under the severest penalties. But papal tyranny soon became a galling yoke; and the Abyssinians determined to break it from their necks. After a terrible struggle, the Romanists were banished from their dominions, and the ancient faith was restored. The churches rejoiced in their freedom, and they never forgot the lesson they had learned concerning the deception, the fanaticism, and the despotic power of Rome. Within their solitary realm they were content to remain, unknown to the rest of Christendom.

The churches of Africa held the Sabbath as it was held by the papal church before her complete apostasy. While they kept the seventh day in obedience to the commandment of God, they abstained from labor on the Sunday in conformity to the custom of the church.

Upon obtaining supreme power, Rome had trampled upon the Sabbath of God to exalt her own; but the churches of Africa, hidden for nearly a thousand years, did not share in this apostasy. When brought under the sway of Rome, they were forced to set aside the true and exalt the false Sabbath; but no sooner had they regained their independence than they returned to obedience to the fourth commandment.

These records of the past clearly reveal the enmity of Rome toward the true Sabbath and its defenders, and the means which she employs to honor the institution of her creating. The word of God teaches that these scenes are to be repeated as Papists and Protestants shall unite for the exaltation of the Sunday. [REV. 13:11, 12. See Appendix, Note 8] For nearly forty years Sabbath reformers have presented this testimony to the world. In the events now taking place is seen a rapid advance toward the fulfillment of the prediction. There is the same claim of divine authority for Sunday-keeping, and the same lack of scriptural evidence, as in the days of papal supremacy. The assertion that God's judgments are visited upon men for their violation of the Sunday-Sabbath, will be repeated. Already it is beginning to be urged.

Marvelous in her shrewdness and cunning is the Romish Church. She can read what is to be. She bides her time, seeing that the Protestant churches are paying her homage in their acceptance of the false Sabbath, and that they are preparing to employ the very means which she herself employed in bygone days. Those who reject the light of truth will yet seek the aid of this self-styled infallible power to exalt an institution that originated with her. How readily she will come to the help of Protestants in this work, it is not difficult to conjecture. Who understands better than Popery how to deal with those who are disobedient to the church?

The Christian world will learn what Romanism really is, when it is too late to escape the snare. She is silently growing into power. He doctrines are exerting their influence in legislative halls, in the churches, and in the hearts of men. Throughout the land she is piling up her lofty and massive structures, in the secret recesses of which her former persecutions will be repeated. She is stealthily and unsuspectingly strengthening her forces to further her own ends when the time shall come for her to strike. All that she desires is vantage ground, and this is soon to be given her. In the near future we shall see and shall feel what the purpose of the Roman element is. Whoever shall believe and obey the word of God will thereby incur reproach and persecution.

Chapter 31

The Coming Conflict

The greatest and most favored nation upon the earth is the United State.. A gracious Providence has shielded this country, and poured upon her the choicest of Heaven's blessings. Here the persecuted and oppressed have found refuge. Here the Christian faith in its purity has been taught. This people have been the recipients of great light and unrivaled mercies. But these gifts have been repaid by ingratitude and forgetfulness of God. The Infinite One keeps a reckoning with the nations, and their guilt is proportioned to the light rejected. A fearful record now stands in the register of Heaven against our land; but the crime which shall fill up the measure of her iniquity is that of making void the law of God.

Between the laws of men and the precepts of Jehovah will come the last great conflict of the controversy between truth and error. Upon this battle we are now entering,— a battle not between rival churches contending for the supremacy, but between the religion of the Bible and the religion of fable and tradition. The agencies which will unite against truth and righteousness in this contest are now actively at work.

God's holy word, which has been handed down to us at such a cost of suffering and blood, is but little valued. The Bible is within the reach of all, but there are few who really accept it as the guide of life. Infidelity prevails to an alarming extent, not in the world merely, but in the church. Many have come to deny doctrines which are the very pillars of the Christian faith. The great facts of creation as presented by the inspired writers, the fall of man, the atonement, and the perpetuity of the law of God, are practically rejected by a large share of the professedly Christian world. Thousands who pride themselves upon their wisdom and independence regard it an evidence of weakness to place implicit confidence in the Bible, and a proof of superior talent and learning to cavil at the Scriptures, and to spiritualize and explain away their most important truths. Many ministers are teaching their people, and many professors and teachers are instructing their students, that the law of God has been changed or abrogated; and they ridicule those who are so simpleminded as to acknowledge all its claims.

In rejecting the truth, men reject its Author. In trampling upon the law of God, they deny the authority of the Lawgiver. It is as easy to make an idol of false doctrines and theories as to fashion an idol of wood or stone. Satan leads men to conceive of God in a false character, as having attributes which he does not possess. A philosophical idol is enthroned in the place of Jehovah; while the true God, as he is revealed in his word, in Christ, and in the works of creation, is worshiped by but few. Thousands deify nature, while they deny the God of nature. Though in a different form, idolatry exists in the Christian world to-day as verily as it existed among ancient Israel in the days of Elijah. The god of many professedly wise men, of philosophers, poets, politicians, journalists,— the god of polished fashionable circles, of many colleges and universities, even of some theological institutions,— is little better than Baal, the sun-god of Phenicia.

No error accepted by the Christian world strikes more boldly against the authority of Heaven, none is more directly opposed to the dictates of reason, none is more pernicious in its results, than the modern doctrine, so rapidly gaining ground, that God's law is no longer obligatory upon men. Every nation has its laws, which command respect and obedience; and has the Creator of the heavens and the earth no law to govern the beings he has made? Suppose that prominent ministers were publicly to teach that the statutes which govern our nation and protect the rights of its citizens were not obligatory,— that they restricted the liberties of the people, and therefore ought not to be obeyed; how long would such men be tolerated in the pulpit? But is it a graver offense to disregard the laws of States and nations than to trample upon those divine precepts which are the foundation of all government? When the standard or righteousness is set aside, the way is open for the prince of evil to establish his rule in the earth.

It would be far more consistent for nations to abolish their statutes, and permit the people to do as they please, than for the Ruler of the universe to annul his law, and leave the world without a standard to condemn the guilty or justify the obedient. Would we know the result of making void the law of God? The experiment has been tried. Terrible were the scenes enacted in France when atheism became the controlling power. It was then demonstrated to the world that to throw off the restraints which God has imposed is to accept the rule of the cruelest of tyrants.

Wherever the divine precepts are set aside, sin ceases to appear sinful, or righteousness desirable. Those who refuse to submit to the government of God are wholly unfitted to govern themselves. Through their pernicious teachings, the spirit of insubordination is implanted in the hearts of children and youth, who are naturally impatient of control; and a lawless, licentious state of society results. While scoffing at the credulity of those who obey the requirements of God, the multitudes eagerly accept the delusions of Satan. They give the rein to lust, and practice the sins which called down judgments upon the heathen.

Let the restraint imposed by the divine law be wholly removed, and human laws would soon be disregarded. Because God forbids dishonest practices, coveting, lying, and defrauding, men are ready to trample upon his statutes as a hindrance to their worldly prosperity; but the results of banishing these precepts would be such as they do not anticipate. If the law were not binding, why should any fear to transgress? Property would no longer be safe. Men would obtain their neighbor's possessions by violence; and the strongest would become richest. Life itself would not be respected. Those who disregard the commandments of God sow disobedience to reap disobedience. The marriage vow would no longer stand as a sacred bulwark to protect the family. He who had the power, would, if he desired, take his neighbor's wife by violence. The fifth commandment would be set aside with the fourth. Children would not shrink from taking the life of their parents, if by so doing they could obtain the desire of their corrupt hearts. The civilized world would become a horde of robbers and assassins; and peace, rest, and happiness would be banished from the earth.

Already the doctrine that men are released from obedience to God's requirements has weakened the force of moral obligation, and opened the floodgates of iniquity upon the world. Lawlessness, dissipation, and corruption are sweeping in upon us like an overwhelming tide. In the family, Satan is at work. His banner waves, even in professedly Christian households. There is envy, evil surmising, hypocrisy, estrangement, emulation, strife, betrayal of sacred trusts, indulgence of lust. The whole system of religious principles and doctrines, which should form the foundation and frame-work of social life, seems to be a tottering mass, ready to fall to ruin. The vilest of criminals, when thrown into prison for their offenses, are often made the recipients of gifts and attentions, as if they had attained an enviable distinction. The greatest publicity is given to their character and crimes. The press publish the revolting details of vice, thus initiating others into the practice of fraud, robbery, and murder; and Satan exults in the success of his hellish schemes. The infatuation of vice, the wanton taking of life, the terrible increase of intemperance and iniquity of every order and degree, should arouse all who fear God, to inquire what can be done to stay the tide of evil.

Courts of justice are corrupt. Rulers are actuated by desire for gain, and love of sensual pleasure. Intemperance has beclouded the faculties of many, so that Satan has almost complete control of them. Jurists are perverted, bribed, deluded. Drunkenness and revelry, passion, envy, dishonesty of every sort, are represented among those who administer the laws. "Justice standeth afar off; for truth is fallen in the street, and equity cannot enter."

The iniquity and spiritual darkness that prevailed under the supremacy of Rome were the inevitable result of her suppression of the Scriptures; but where is to be found the cause of the wide-spread infidelity, the rejection of the law of God, and the consequent corruption, under the full blaze of gospel light in an age of religious freedom? Now that Satan can no longer keep the world under his control by withholding the Scriptures, he resorts to other means to accomplish the same object. To destroy faith in the Bible serves his purpose as well as to destroy the Bible itself. By introducing the belief that God's law is not binding, he as effectually leads men to transgress as if they were wholly ignorant of its precepts. And now, as in former ages, he has worked through the church to further his designs. As the religious organizations of the day have refused to listen to unpopular truths plainly brought to view in the Scriptures, they have sown broadcast the seeds of skepticism. Clinging to the papal error of natural immortality and man's consciousness in death, they reject the only defense against the delusions of Spiritualism. Nor is this all. As the claims of the fourth commandment are urged upon the people, popular teachers find that the observance of the seventh-day Sabbath is there enjoined; and as the only way to free themselves from a duty which they are unwilling to perform, they declare that the law of God is no longer binding. Thus they cast away the law and the Sabbath together. As the work of Sabbath reform extends, this rejection of the divine law to avoid the claims of the fourth commandment will become well-nigh universal. Upon those religious leaders whose teachings have opened the door to infidelity, to Spiritualism, and to contempt for God's holy law, rests a fearful responsibility for the iniquity that exists in the Christian world.

Yet this very class put forth the claim that the fast-spreading corruption is largely attributable to the desecration of the so-called "Christian Sabbath," and that the enforcement of Sunday observance would greatly improve the morals of society. Combining the temperance reform with the Sunday movement, they represent themselves as laboring to promote the highest interests of society; and those who refuse to unite with them are denounced as the enemies of temperance and reform. But the fact that a movement to establish error is connected with a work which is in itself good, is not an argument in favor of the error. We may disguise poison by mingling it with wholesome food, but we do not thereby change its nature. On the contrary, it is rendered more dangerous, as it is more likely to be taken unawares. It is one of Satan's devices to combine with falsehood just enough truth to give it plausibility. The leaders of the Sunday movement may advocate reforms which the people need, principles which are in harmony with the Bible, yet while there is with these a requirement which is contrary to God's law, his servants cannot unite with them. Nothing can justify them in setting aside the commandments of God for the precepts of men.

Through the two great errors, the immortality of the soul and Sunday sacredness, Satan will bring the people under his deceptions.

While the former lays the foundation of Spiritualism, the latter creates a bond of sympathy with Rome. Protestantism will yet stretch her hand across the gulf to grasp the hand of Spiritualism; she will reach over the abyss to clasp hands with the Roman power; and under the influence of this threefold union, our country will follow in the steps of Rome in trampling on the rights of conscience.

Spiritualism is now changing its form, veiling some of its more objectionable and immoral features, and assuming a Christian guise. Formerly it denounced Christ and the Bible; now it professes to accept both. The Bible is interpreted in a manner that is attractive to the unrenewed heart, while its solemn and vital truths are made of no effect. A God of love is presented; but his justice, his denunciations of sin, the requirements of his holy law, are all kept out of sight. Pleasing, bewitching fables captivate the senses of those who do not make God's word the foundation of their faith. Christ is as verily rejected as before; but Satan has so blinded the eyes of the people that the deception is not discerned.

As Spiritualism assimilates more closely to the nominal Christianity of the day, it has greater power to deceive and ensnare. Satan himself is converted, after the modern order of things. He will appear in the character of an angel of light. Through the agency of Spiritualism, miracles will be wrought, the sick will be healed, and many undeniable wonders will be performed. And as the spirits will profess faith in the Bible, and express regard for Sunday, their work will be accepted as a manifestation of divine power.

The line of distinction between professing Christians and the ungodly is now hardly distinguishable. Church-members love what the world loves, and are ready to join with them; and Satan determines to unite them in one body and thus strengthen his cause by sweeping all into the ranks of Spiritualism. Papists who boast of miracles as a certain mark of the true church, will be readily deceived by this wonder-working power; and Protestants, having cast away the shield of truth, will also be deluded. Papists, Protestants, and worldlings will alike accept the form of godliness without the power, and they will see in this union a grand movement for the conversion of the world, and the ushering in of the long-expected millennium.

Through Spiritualism, Satan appears as a benefactor of the race, healing the diseases of the people, and professing to present a new and more exalted system of religious faith; but at the same time he works as a destroyer. His temptations are leading multitudes to ruin. Intemperance dethrones reason; sensual indulgence, strife, and bloodshed follow. Satan delights in war; for it excites the worst passions of the soul, and then sweeps into eternity its victims steeped in vice and blood. It is his object to incite the nations to war against one another; for he can thus divert the minds of the people from the work of preparation to stand in the day of God.

Satan works through the elements also to garner his harvest of unprepared souls. He has studied the secrets of the laboratories of nature, and he uses all his power to control the elements as far as God allows. When he was suffered to afflict Job, how quickly flocks and herds, servants, houses, children, were swept away, one trouble succeeding another as in a moment. It is God that shields his creatures, and hedges them in from the power of the destroyer. But the Christian world has shown contempt for the law of Jehovah; and the Lord does just what he has declared that he would do, he withdraws his blessings from the earth, and removes his protecting care from those who are rebelling against his law, and teaching and forcing others to do the same. Satan has control of all whom God does not especially guard. He will favor and prosper some in order to further his own designs, and he will bring trouble upon others, and lead men to believe that it is God who is afflicting them.

While appearing to the children of men as a great physician who can heal all their maladies, he will bring disease and disaster until populous cities are reduced to ruin and desolation. Even now he is at work. In accidents and calamities by sea and by land, in great conflagrations, in fierce tornadoes and terrific hailstorms, in tempests, floods, cyclones, tidal waves, and earthquakes, in every place and in a thousand forms, is Satan exercising his power. He sweeps away the ripening harvest, and famine and distress follow. He imparts to the air a deadly taint, and thousands perish by the pestilence. These visitations are to become more and more frequent and disastrous. Destruction will be upon the inhabitants of the world. The beasts of the field will groan, and the earth will languish.

And then the great deceiver will persuade men that those who serve God are causing these evils. The class that have provoked the displeasure of Heaven will charge all their troubles upon the faithful few whom the Lord has sent to them with messages of warning and reproof. It will be declared that the nation is offending God by the violation of the Sunday-Sabbath, that this sin has brought calamities which will not cease until Sunday observance shall be strictly enforced, and that those who present the claims of the fourth commandment, thus destroying reverence for Sunday, are troublers of the nation, preventing its restoration to divine favor and temporal prosperity. Thus the accusation urged of old against the servant of God will be repeated, and upon grounds equally well established. "And it came to pass when Ahab saw Elijah, that Ahab said unto him, Art thou he that troubleth Israel? And he answered, I have not troubled Israel, but thou and thy father's house, in that ye have forsaken the commandments of the Lord, and thou hast followed Baalim." [1 KINGS 18:17,18.] As the wrath of the people shall be excited by false charges, they will pursue a course toward God's ambassadors very similar to that which apostate Israel pursued toward Elijah

The miracle-working power manifested through Spiritualism will exert its influence against those who choose to obey God rather than men. Messages will come from the spirits declaring that God has sent them to inform the rejecters of Sunday that they are in error, and that the laws of the land should be obeyed as the law of God. They will lament the great wickedness in the world, and second the testimony of religious teachers, that the degraded state of morals is caused by the desecration of Sunday. Great will be the indignation excited against all who refuse to accept their testimony.

Those who honor the Bible Sabbath will be denounced as enemies of law and order, as breaking down the moral restraints of society, causing anarchy and corruption, and calling down the judgments of God upon the earth. Their conscientious scruples will be pronounced obstinacy, stubbornness, and contempt of authority. They will be accused of disaffection toward the government. Ministers who deny the obligation of the divine law will present from the pulpit the duty of yielding obedience to the civil authorities as ordained of God. In legislative halls and courts of justice, commandment-keepers will be censured and misrepresented. A false coloring will be given to their words; the worst possible construction will be put upon their motives.

The Protestant churches have rejected the clear, scriptural arguments in defense of God's law, and they long to stop the mouths of those whose faith they cannot overthrow by the Bible. Though they blind their own eyes to the fact, they are now adopting a course which will lead to the persecution of those who conscientiously refuse to do what the rest of the Christian world are doing, and acknowledge the claims of the papal Sabbath.

The dignitaries of Church and State will unite to bribe, persuade, or compel all classes to honor the Sunday. The lack of divine authority will be supplied by oppressive enactments. Political corruption is destroying love of justice and regard for truth, and in order to secure public favor, legislators will yield to the popular demand for a law enforcing Sunday observance. Liberty of conscience, which has cost this nation so great a sacrifice, will no longer be respected. In the soon-coming conflict we shall see exemplified the prophet's words: "And the dragon was wroth with the woman, and went to make war with the remnant of her seed, which keep the commandments of God, and have the testimony of Jesus Christ." [REV. 12:17.]

Our land is in jeopardy. The time is drawing on when its legislators shall so abjure the principles of Protestantism as to give countenance to Romish apostasy. The people for whom God has so marvelously wrought, strengthening them to throw off the galling yoke of Popery, will by a national act give vigor to the corrupt faith of Rome, and thus arouse the tyranny which only waits for a touch to start again into cruelty and despotism. With rapid steps are we already approaching this period. When Protestant churches shall seek the support of the secular power, thus following the example of that apostate church, for opposing which their ancestors endured the fiercest persecution, then will there be a national apostasy which will end only in national ruin.

Chapter 32

The Scriptures...A Safeguard

"To the law and to the testimony. If they speak not according to this word, it is because there is no light in them." [ISA. 8:20.] The people of God are directed to the Scriptures as their safeguard against the influence of false teachers and the delusive power of spirits of darkness. Satan employs every possible device to prevent men from obtaining a knowledge of the Bible; for its plain utterances reveal his deceptions. At every revival of God's work, the prince of evil is aroused to more intense activity; he is now putting forth his utmost efforts for a final, despairing struggle against Christ and his followers. The last great delusion is soon to open before us. Antichrist is to perform his marvelous works in our sight. So closely will the counterfeit resemble the true, that it will be impossible to distinguish between them except by the Holy Scriptures. By their testimony every statement and every miracle must be tested.

Those who endeavor to obey all the commandments of God will be opposed and derided; their way will be made very hard. They can stand only in God. In order to endure the trial before them, they must understand the will of God as revealed in his word; they can honor him only as they have a right conception of his character, government, and purposes, and act in accordance with them. None but those who have trained the intellect to grasp the truths of the Bible will stand through the last great conflict. To every soul will come the searching test, Shall I obey God rather than men? The decisive hour is even now at hand. Are our feet planted on the rock of God's immutable word? Are we prepared to stand firm in defense of the commandments of God and the faith of Jesus?

Before his crucifixion the Saviour explained to his disciples that he was to be put to death, and to rise again from the tomb; and angels were present to impress his words on minds and hearts. But the disciples were looking for temporal deliverance from the Roman yoke, and they could not tolerate the thought that He in whom all their hopes centered should suffer an ignominious death. The words which they needed to remember were banished from their minds; and when the time of trial came, it found them unprepared. The death of Jesus as fully destroyed their hopes as if he had not forewarned them. So in the prophecies the future is opened before us as plainly as it was opened to the disciples by the words of Christ. The events connected with the close of probation and the work of preparation for the time of trouble, are clearly brought to view. But multitudes have no more understanding of these important truths than if they had never been revealed. Satan watches to catch away every impression that would make them wise unto salvation, and the time of trouble will find them unready.

When God sends to men warnings so important that they are represented as proclaimed by holy angels flying in the midst of heaven, he requires every person endowed with reasoning powers to heed the message. The fearful judgments denounced against the worship of the beast and his image, [REV. 14:9-12.] should lead all to a diligent study of the prophecies to learn what the mark of the beast is, and how they are to avoid receiving it. But the masses of the people turn away their ears from hearing the truth, and are turned unto fables. The apostle Paul declared, looking down to the last days, "The time will come when they will not endure sound doctrine." [2 TIM. 4:3.] That time has fully come. The multitudes do not want Bible truth, because it interferes with the desires of the sinful, world-loving heart; and Satan supplies the deceptions which they love.

But God will have a people upon the earth to maintain the Bible, and the Bible only, as the standard of all doctrines and the basis of all reforms. The opinions of learned men, the deductions of science, the creeds or decisions of ecclesiastical councils, as numerous and discordant as are the churches which they represent, the voice of the majority,— not one or all of these should be regarded as evidence for or against any point of religious faith. Before accepting any doctrine or precept, we should demand a plain "Thus saith the Lord" in its support.

Satan is constantly endeavoring to attract attention to man in the place of God. He leads the people to look to bishops, to pastors, to professors of theology, as their guides, instead of searching the Scriptures to learn their duty for themselves. Then by controlling the minds of these leaders he can influence the multitudes according to his will.

When Christ came to speak the words of life, the common people heard him gladly; and many, even of the priests and rulers, believed on him. But the chief of the priesthood and the leading men of the nation were determined to condemn and repudiate his teachings. Though they were baffled in all their efforts to find accusations against him, though they could not but feel the influence of the divine power and wisdom attending his words, yet they encased themselves in prejudice; they rejected the clearest evidence of his Messiahship, lest they should be forced to become his disciples. These opponents of Jesus were men whom the people had been taught from infancy to reverence, to whose authority they had been accustomed implicitly to bow. "How is it," they asked, "that our rulers and learned scribes do not believe on Jesus? Would not these pious men receive him if he were the Christ?" It was the influence of such teachers that led the Jewish nation to reject their Redeemer.

The spirit which actuated those priests and rulers is still manifested by many who make a high profession of piety. They refuse to examine the testimony of the Scriptures concerning the special truths for this time. They point to their own numbers, wealth, and popularity, and look with contempt upon the advocates of truth as few, poor, and unpopular, having a faith that separates them from the world.

Christ foresaw that the undue assumption of authority practiced by the scribes and Pharisees would not cease with the dispersion of the Jews. He had a prophetic view of the work of exalting human authority to rule the conscience, which has been so terrible a curse to the church in all ages. And his fearful denunciations of the scribes and Pharisees, and his warnings to the people not to follow these blind leaders, were placed on record as an admonition to future generations.

With the many warnings against false teachers, why are the people so ready to commit the keeping of their souls to the clergy? There are to-day thousands of professors of religion who can give no other reason for points of faith which they hold than that they were so instructed by their religious leaders. They pass by the Saviour's teachings almost unnoticed, and place implicit confidence in the words of the ministers. But are ministers infallible? How can we trust our souls to their guidance unless we know from God's word that they are light-bearers? A lack of moral courage to step aside from the beaten track of the world, leads many to follow in the steps of learned men; and by their reluctance to investigate for themselves, they are becoming hopelessly fastened in the chains of error. They see that the truth for this time is plainly brought to view in the Bible, and they feel the power of the Holy Spirit attending its proclamation; yet they allow the opposition of the clergy to turn them from the light. Though reason and conscience are convinced, these deluded souls dare not think differently from the minister; and their individual judgment, their eternal interests, are sacrificed to the unbelief, the pride and prejudice, of another.

Many are the forms of human influence through which Satan works to bind his captives. He secures multitudes to himself by attaching them by the silken cords of affection to those who are enemies of the cross of Christ. Whatever this attachment may be, parental, filial, conjugal, or social, the effect is the same; the opposers of truth rule with despotic power, and the souls held under their sway have not sufficient courage or independence to obey their own convictions of duty.

The truth and the glory of God are inseparable; it is impossible for us, with the Bible within our reach, to honor God by erroneous opinions. It is the first and highest duty of every rational being to learn from the Scriptures what is truth, and then to walk in the light, and encourage others to follow his example. Ignorance of God's word is sin, when every provision has been made that we may become wise.

We should day by day study the Bible diligently, weighing every thought, and comparing scripture with scripture. With divine help, we are to form our opinions for ourselves, as we are to answer for ourselves before God.

The truths most plainly revealed in the Bible have been involved in doubt and darkness by learned men, who, with a pretense of great wisdom, teach that the Scriptures have a mystical, a secret, spiritual meaning not apparent in the language employed. These men are false teachers. It was to such a class that Jesus declared, "Ye know not the Scriptures, neither the power of God." [MARK 12:24.] The language of the Bible should be explained according to its obvious meaning unless a symbol or figure is employed. Christ has given the promise, "If any man will do His will, he shall know of the doctrine." [JOHN 7:17.] If men would but take the Bible as it reads, if there were no false teachers to mislead and confuse their minds, a work would be accomplished that would make angels glad, and that would bring into the fold of Christ thousands upon thousands who are now wandering in error.

We should exert all the powers of the mind in the study of the Scriptures, and should task the understanding to comprehend, as far as mortals can, the deep things of God; yet we must not forget that the docility and submission of a child is the true spirit of the learner. Scriptural difficulties can never be mastered by the same methods that are employed in grappling with philosophical problems. We should not engage in the study of the Bible with that self-reliance with which so many enter the domains of science, but with a prayerful depend- ence upon God, and a sincere desire to learn his will. We must come with a humble and teachable spirit to obtain knowledge from the great I AM. Otherwise, evil angels will so blind our minds and harden our hearts that we shall not be impressed by the truth.

Many a portion of Scripture which learned men pronounce a mystery, or pass over as unimportant, is full of comfort and instruction to him who has been taught in the school of Christ. One reason why many theologians have no clearer understanding of God's word is, they close their eyes to truths which they do not wish to practice. An understanding of Bible truth depends not so much on the power of intellect brought to the search as on the singleness of purpose, the earnest longing after righteousness.

Never should the Bible be studied without prayer. The Holy Spirit alone can cause us to feel the importance of those things easy to be understood, or prevent us from wresting truths difficult of comprehension. It is the office of heavenly angels to prepare the heart to so comprehend God's word that we shall be charmed with its beauty, admonished by its warnings, or animated and strengthened by its promises. We should make the psalmist's petition our own: "Open thou mine eyes, that I may behold wondrous things out of thy law."

[PS. 119:18.] Temptations often appear irresistible because through neglect of prayer and the study of the Bible the tempted one cannot readily remember God's promises and meet Satan with the Scripture weapons. But angels are round about those who are willing to be taught in divine things, and in the time of great necessity, they will bring to their remembrance the very truths which are needed. Thus when the enemy comes in like a flood, the Spirit of the Lord will lift up a standard against him.

All who value their eternal interests should be on their guard against the inroads of skepticism. The very pillars of truth will be assailed. It is impossible to keep beyond the reach of the sarcasms and sophisms, the insidious and pestilent teachings, of modern infidelity. Satan adapts his temptations to all classes. He assails the illiterate with a jest or sneer, while he meets the educated with scientific objections and philosophical reasoning, alike calculated to excite distrust or contempt of the Scriptures. Even youth of little experience presume to insinuate doubts concerning the fundamental principles of Christianity. And this youthful infidelity, shallow as it is, has its influence. Many are thus led to jest at the faith of their fathers, and to do despite to the Spirit of grace. Many a life that promised to be an honor to God and a blessing to the world, has been blighted by the foul breath of infidelity. All who trust to the boastful decisions of human reason, and imagine that they can explain divine mysteries, and arrive at truth unaided by the wisdom of God, are entangled in the snare of Satan.

We are living in the most solemn period of this world's history. The destiny of earth's teeming multitudes is about to be decided. Our own future well-being and also the salvation of other souls depends upon the course which we now pursue. We need to be guided by the Spirit of truth. Every follower of Christ should earnestly inquire, "Lord, what wilt thou have me to do?" We need to humble ourselves before the Lord, with fasting and prayer, and to meditate much upon his word, especially upon the scenes of the Judgment. We should now seek a deep and living experience in the things of God. We have not a moment to lose. Events of vital importance are transpiring around us; we are on Satan's enchanted ground. Sleep not, sentinels of God; the foe is lurking near, ready at any moment, should you become lax and drowsy, to spring upon you and make you his prey.

Many are deceived as to their true condition before God. They congratulate themselves upon the wrong acts which they do not commit, and forget to enumerate the good and noble deeds which God requires of them, but which they have neglected to perform. It is not enough that they are trees in the garden of God. They are to answer his expectation by bearing fruit. He holds them accountable for their failure to accomplish all the good which they could have done, through his grace strengthening them. In the books of Heaven they are registered as cumberers of the ground.

When the testing time shall come, those who have made God's word their rule of life will be revealed. In summer there is no noticeable difference between evergreens and other trees; but when the blasts of winter come, the evergreens remain unchanged, while other trees are stripped of their foliage. So the falsehearted professor may not now be distinguished from the real Christian, but the time is just upon us when the difference will be apparent. Let opposition arise, let the voice of the dragon be heard, let persecution be kindled, and the halfhearted and hypocritical will waver and yield the faith; but the true Christian will stand firm as a rock, his faith stronger, his hope brighter, than in days of prosperity.

"Blessed is the man that walketh not in the counsel of the ungodly, nor standeth in the way of sinners, nor sitteth in the seat of the scornful. But his delight is in the law of the Lord; and in his law doth he meditate day and night. And he shall be like a tree planted by the rivers of water, that bringeth forth his fruit in his season; his leaf also shall not wither; and whatsoever he doeth shall prosper." [PS. 1:1-3.]

Chapter 33

The Loud Cry

"I saw another angel come down from Heaven, having great power; and the earth was lightened with his glory. And he cried mightily with a strong voice, saying, Babylon the great is fallen, is fallen, and is become the habitation of devils, and the hold of every foul spirit, and a cage of every unclean and hateful bird." "And I heard another voice from Heaven, saying, Come out of her, my people, that ye be not partakers of her sins, and that ye receive not of her plagues." [REV. 18:1, 2, 4.]

In this scripture the announcement of the fall of Babylon, as made by the second angel, [REV. 14:8.] is repeated, with the additional mention of the corruptions which have been entering the churches since 1844. A terrible condition of the religious world is here described. With every rejection of truth, the minds of the people have become darker, their hearts more stubborn, until they are entrenched in an infidel hardihood. In defiance of the warnings which God has given, they continue to trample upon one of the precepts of the Decalogue, and they persecute those who hold it sacred. Christ is set at naught in the contempt placed upon his word and his people. As the teachings of Spiritualism are accepted by the churches, no real restraint is imposed upon the carnal heart, and the profession of religion becomes a cloak to conceal the basest iniquity. A belief in spiritual manifestations opens the door to seducing spirits and doctrines of devils. The influence of evil angels is felt in the churches throughout the land.

Of Babylon at this time it is declared, "Her sins have reached unto heaven, and God hath remembered her iniquities." [REV. 18:5.] She has filled up the measure of her guilt, and destruction is about to fall upon her. But God still has a people in Babylon; and before the visitation of his judgments, these faithful ones must be called out, that they "partake not of her sins, and receive not of her plagues." Hence the movement symbolized by the angel coming down from Heaven, lightening the earth with his glory, and crying mightily with a strong voice, announcing the sins of Babylon. In connection with his message the call is heard, "Come out of her, my people." As these warnings join the third angel's message, it swells to a loud cry.

Fearful is the issue to which the world is to be brought. The powers of earth, uniting to war against the commandments of God, will decree that no man may buy or sell, save he that has the mark of the beast, and, finally, that whoever refuses to receive the mark shall be put to death. [REV. 13:15, 17.] The word of God declares: "If any man worship the beast and his image, and receive his mark in his

236 • The Great Controversy / The Bible Made Plain

forehead, or in his hand, the same shall drink of the wine of the wrath of God, which is poured out without mixture into the cup of his indignation." [REV. 14:9, 10.] But not one is made to feel the wrath of God until the truth has been brought in contact with his mind and conscience, and has been rejected. There are many in the churches of our country who have never, even in this land of light and knowledge, had an opportunity to hear the special truths for this time. The obligation of the fourth commandment has never been set before them in its true light. Jesus reads every heart, and tries every motive. The decree is not to be urged upon the people blindly. Every one is to have sufficient light to make his decision intelligently. The Sabbath will be the great test of loyalty; for it is the point of truth especially controverted.

Heretofore those who presented the truths of the third message have often been regarded as mere alarmists. The prediction that Church and State would unite to persecute those who keep the commandments of God has been pronounced groundless and absurd. It has been confidently declared that this land could never become other than what it has been, the defender of religious freedom. But as the question of enforcing Sunday observance is widely agitated, the event so long doubted and disbelieved is seen to be approaching, and the third message produces an effect which it could not have had before.

In every generation God has sent his servants to rebuke sin, both in the world and in the church. But the people desire smooth things spoken to them, and the pure, unvarnished truth is not acceptable. Many reformers, in entering upon their work, determined to exercise great prudence in attacking the sins of the church and the nation. They hoped, by the example of a pure Christian life, to lead the people back to the doctrines of the Bible. But the Spirit of God came upon them as it came upon Elijah, and they could not refrain from preaching the plain utterances of the Bible,— doctrines which they had been reluctant to present. They were impelled to zealously declare the truth, and the danger which threatened souls. The words which the Lord gave them they uttered, fearless of consequences, and the people were compelled to hear the warning.

Thus will the message of the third angel be proclaimed. As the time comes for the loud cry to be given, the Lord will work through humble instruments, leading the minds of those who consecrate themselves to his service. The laborers will be qualified rather by the unction of his Spirit than by the training of literary institutions. Men of faith and prayer will be constrained to go forth with holy zeal, declaring the words which God gives them. The sins of Babylon will be laid open. The fearful results of a union of Church and State, the inroads of Spiritualism, the stealthy but rapid progress of the papal power,— all will be unmasked. By these solemn warnings the people will be stirred. Thousands upon thousands have never listened to words like these. In amazement they hear the testimony that Babylon is the church, fallen because of her errors and sins, because of her rejection of the truth sent to her from Heaven. The people go to their former teachers with the eager inquiry, Are these things so? The ministers present fables, prophesy smooth things, to soothe their fears, and quiet the awakened conscience. But many refuse to be satisfied with the mere authority of men, and demand a plain "Thus saith the Lord." The popular ministry, like the Pharisees of old, are filled with anger as their authority is questioned; they denounce the message as of Satan, and stir up the sin-loving multitudes to revile and persecute those who proclaim it.

As the controversy extends into new fields, and the minds of the people are called to God's downtrodden law, Satan is astir. The power attending the message only maddens those who oppose it. The clergy put forth almost superhuman efforts to shut away the light, lest it should shine upon their flocks. By every means at their command they endeavor to suppress the discussion of these vital questions. The church appeals to the strong arm of civil power, and in this work, Papists are solicited to come to the help of Protestants. The movement for Sunday enforcement becomes more bold and decided. The law is invoked against commandment-keepers. They are threatened with fines and imprisonment, and some are offered positions of influence, and other rewards and advantages, as inducements to renounce their faith. But their steadfast answer is, "Show us from the word of God our error,"— the same plea that was made by Luther under similar circumstances. Those who are arraigned before the courts make a strong vindication of the truth, and some who hear them are led to take their stand to keep all the commandments of God. Thus light is brought before thousands who otherwise would know nothing of these truths.

Conscientious obedience to the word of God will be treated as rebellion. Blinded by Satan, the parent will exercise harshness and severity toward the believing child; the master or mistress will oppress the commandment-keeping servant. Affection will be alienated; children will be disinherited, and driven from home. The words of Paul will be literally fulfilled, "All that will live godly in Christ Jesus shall suffer persecution." [2 TIM. 3:12.] As the defenders of truth refuse to honor the Sunday-Sabbath, some of them will be thrust into prison, some will be exiled, some will be treated as slaves. To human wisdom, all this now seems impossible; but as the restraining Spirit of God shall be withdrawn from men, and they shall be under the control of Satan, who hates the divine precepts, there will be strange developments. The heart can be very cruel when God's fear and love are removed.

238 • The Great Controversy / The Bible Made Plain

As the storm approaches, a large class who have professed faith in the third message, but have not been sanctified through it, abandon their position, and take refuge under the banner of the powers of darkness. By uniting with the world and partaking of its spirit, they come to view matters in nearly the same light; and when the test is brought, they are prepared to choose the easy, popular side. Men of talent and pleasing address, who once rejoiced in the truth, employ their powers to deceive and mislead souls. They become the most bitter enemies of their former brethren. When Sabbath-keepers are brought before the courts to answer for their faith, these apostates are the most efficient agents of Satan to misrepresent and accuse them, and by false reports and insinuations to stir up the rulers against them.

The Lord's servants have faithfully given the warning, looking to God and to his word alone. They have not coolly calculated the consequences to themselves. They have not consulted their temporal interests, or sought to preserve their reputation or their lives. Yet when the storm of opposition and reproach bursts upon them, they are overwhelmed with consternation; and some are ready to exclaim, "Had we foreseen the consequences of our words, we would have held our peace." They are hedged in with difficulties. Satan assails them with fierce temptations. The work which they have undertaken seems far beyond their ability to accomplish. They are threatened with destruction. The enthusiasm which animated them is gone; yet they cannot turn back. Then, feeling their utter helplessness, they flee to the Mighty One for strength. They remember that the words which they have spoken were not theirs, but His who bade them give the warning. God put the truth into their hearts, and they could not forbear to proclaim it.

The same trials were experienced by men of God in ages past. Wycliffe, Huss, Luther, Tyndale, Baxter, Wesley, urged that all doctrines be brought to the test of the Bible, and declared that they would renounce everything which it condemned. Against these men, persecution raged with relentless fury; yet they ceased not to declare the truth. Different periods in the history of the church have each been marked by the development of some special truth, adapted to the necessities of the people of God at that time. Every new truth has made its way against hatred and opposition; those who were blessed with its light were tempted and tried. The Lord gives a special truth for the people in an emergency. Who dare refuse to publish it? He commands his servants to present the last invitation of mercy to the world. They cannot remain silent, except at the peril of their souls. Christ's ambassadors have nothing to do with consequences. They must perform their duty, and leave results with God.

As the opposition rises to a fiercer height, the servants of God are again perplexed; for it seems to them that they have brought the crisis. But conscience and the word of God assure them that their course is right; and although the trials continue, they are strengthened to bear them. The contest grows closer and sharper, but their faith and courage rise with the emergency. Their testimony is, "We dare not tamper with God's word, dividing his holy law, calling one portion essential and another nonessential to gain the favor of the world. The Lord whom we serve is able to deliver us. Christ has conquered the powers of earth; and shall we be afraid of a world already conquered?"

Persecution in its varied forms is the development of a principle which will exist as long as Satan exists, and Christianity has vital power. No man can serve God without enlisting against himself the opposition of the hosts of darkness. Evil angels will assail him, alarmed that his influence is taking the prey from their hands. Evil men, rebuked by his example, will unite with them in seeking to separate him from God by alluring temptations. When these do not succeed, then a compelling power is employed to force the conscience.

But as long as Jesus remains man's intercessor in the sanctuary above, the restraining influence of the Holy Spirit is felt by rulers and people. It still controls, to some extent, the laws of the land. Were it not for these laws, the condition of the world would be much worse than it now is. While many of our rulers are active agents of Satan, God also has his agents among the leading men of the nation. The enemy moves upon his servants to propose measures that would greatly impede the work of God; but statesmen who fear the Lord are influenced by holy angels to oppose such propositions with unanswerable arguments. Thus a few men will hold in check a powerful current of evil. The opposition of the enemies of truth will be restrained that the third message may do its work. When the loud cry shall be given, it will arrest the attention of these leading men through whom the Lord is now working, and some of them will accept it, and will stand with the people of God through the time of trouble.

The angel who unites in the proclamation of the third message is to lighten the whole earth with his glory. A work of world-wide extent and unwonted power is here brought to view. The Advent movement of 1840-1844 was a glorious manifestation of the power of God; the first message was carried to every missionary station in the world, and in this country there was the greatest religious interest which has been witnessed in any land since the Reformation of the sixteenth century; but these are to be far exceeded by the mighty movement under the loud cry of the third message. The work will be similar to that of the day of Pentecost. Servants of God, with their faces lighted up and shining with holy consecration, hasten from place to place to proclaim the warning from Heaven. By thousands of voices, all over the earth, the message will be given. Miracles are wrought, the sick are healed, and signs and wonders follow the believers. Satan also works with lying wonders, even bringing down fire from heaven in the sight of men. Thus the inhabitants of the earth are brought to take their stand.

The message will be carried, as was the midnight cry of 1844, not so much by argument as by the deep conviction of the Spirit of God. The arguments have been presented. The seed has been sown, and now it will spring up and bear fruit. The publications distributed by missionary workers have exerted their influence; yet many whose minds have been impressed have been prevented from fully comprehending the truth or from yielding obedience. Now the rays of light penetrate everywhere, the truth is seen in its clearness, and the honest children of God sever the bands which have held them. Family connections, church relations, are powerless to stay them now. Truth is more precious than all besides. Notwithstanding the agencies combined against the truth, a large number take their stand upon the Lord's side.

Chapter 34

The Time of Trouble

"At that time shall Michael stand up, the great prince which standeth for the children of thy people: and there shall be a time of trouble, such as never was since there was a nation even to that same time; and at that time thy people shall be delivered, every one that shall be found written in the book." [DAN. 12:1.]

When the third message closes, mercy no longer pleads for the guilty inhabitants of the earth. The people of God have accomplished their work; they have received the latter rain, or the refreshing from the presence of the Lord, and they are prepared for the trying hour before them. Angels are hurrying to and fro in Heaven. An angel returning from the earth announces that his work is done, that the seal of God [See Appendix, Note 9] has been placed upon his people. Then Jesus ceases his intercession in the sanctuary above. He lifts his hands, and with a loud voice says, "It is done;" and all the angelic host lay off their crowns as he makes the solemn announcement: "He that is unjust, let him be unjust still; and he which is filthy, let him be filthy still; and he that is righteous, let him be righteous still; and he that is holy, let him be holy still." [REV. 22:11] Every case has been decided for life or death. Christ has made the atonement for his people, and blotted out their sins. The number of his subjects is made up; "the kingdom and dominion and the greatness of the kingdom under the whole heaven," is about to be given to the heirs of salvation, and Jesus is to reign as King of kings and Lord of lords.

When he leaves the sanctuary, darkness covers the inhabitants of the earth. In that fearful time the righteous must live in the sight of a holy God without an intercessor. The restraint which has been upon the wicked is removed, and Satan has entire control of the finally impenitent. The power attending the last warning has enraged them, and their anger is kindled against all who have received the message. The people of God are then plunged into those scenes of affliction and distress described by the prophet as the time of Jacob's trouble:—"Thus saith the Lord: We have heard a voice of trembling, of fear, and not of peace." "All faces are turned into paleness. Alas! for that day is great, so that none is like it: it is even the time of Jacob's trouble; but he shall be saved out of it." [JER. 30:5-7.]

Jacob's night of anguish, when he wrestled in prayer for deliverance from the hand of Esau, [GEN. 32:24-30.] represents the experience of God's people in the time of trouble. Because of the deception practiced to secure his father's blessing, intended for Esau, Jacob had fled for his life, alarmed by his brother's deadly threats. After remaining for many years an exile, he had set out, at God's command, to return with his wives and children, his flocks and herds, to his native country. On reaching the borders of the land, he was filled with terror by the tidings of Esau's approach at the head of a band of warriors, doubtless bent upon revenge. Jacob's company, unarmed and defenseless, seemed about to fall helpless victims of violence and slaughter. And to the burden of anxiety and fear was added the crushing weight of self-reproach; for it was his own sin that had brought this danger. His only hope was in the mercy of God; his only defense must be prayer. Yet he leaves nothing undone on his own part to atone for the wrong to his brother, and to avert the threatened danger. So should the followers of Christ, as they approach the time of trouble, make every exertion to place themselves in a proper light before the people, to disarm prejudice, and to avert the danger which threatens liberty of conscience.

Having sent his family away, that they may not witness his distress, Jacob remains alone to intercede with God. He confesses his sin, and gratefully acknowledges the mercy of God toward him, while with deep humiliation he pleads the covenant made with his fathers, and the promises to himself in the night vision at Bethel and in the land of his exile. The crisis in his life has come; everything is at stake. In the darkness and solitude he continues praying and humbling himself before God. Suddenly a hand is laid upon his shoulder. He thinks that an enemy is seeking his life, and with all the energy of despair he wrestles with his assailant. As the day begins to break, the stranger puts forth his superhuman power; at his touch the strong man seems paralyzed, and he falls, a helpless, weeping suppliant, upon the neck of his mysterious antagonist. Jacob knows now that it is the Angel of the covenant with whom he has been in conflict. Though disabled, and suffering the keenest pain, he does not relinquish his purpose. Long has he endured perplexity, remorse, and trouble for his sin; now he must have the assurance that it is pardoned. The divine visitant seems about to depart; but Jacob clings to him, pleading for a blessing. The Angel urges, "Let me go; for the day breaketh;" but the patriarch exclaims, "I will not let thee go, except thou bless me." What confidence, what firmness and perseverance, are here displayed! Had this been a boastful, presumptuous claim, Jacob would have been instantly destroyed; but his was the assurance of one who confesses his weakness and unworthiness, yet trusts the mercy of a covenant-keeping God.

"He had power over the Angel, and prevailed." [HOS. 12:4.] Through humiliation, repentance, and self-surrender, this sinful, erring mortal prevailed with the Majesty of Heaven. He had fastened his trembling grasp upon the promises of God, and the heart of Infinite Love could not turn away the sinner's plea. As an evidence of his triumph, and an encouragement to others to imitate his example, his name was changed from one which was a reminder of his sin, to one that commemorated his victory. And the fact that Jacob had prevailed with God was an assurance that he would prevail with men. He no longer feared to encounter his brother's anger; for the Lord was his defense.

Satan had accused Jacob before the angels of God, claiming the right to destroy him because of his sin; he had moved upon Esau to march against him; and during the patriarch's long night of wrestling, Satan endeavored to force upon him a sense of his guilt, in order to discourage him, and break his hold upon God. Jacob was driven almost to despair; but he knew that without help from Heaven he must perish. He had sincerely repented of his great sin, and he appealed to the mercy of God. He would not be turned from his purpose, but held fast the Angel, and urged his petition with earnest, agonizing cries, until he prevailed. Heavenly messengers were sent to move upon Esau's heart, and his purpose of hatred and revenge was changed to fraternal affection.

As Satan influenced Esau to march against Jacob, so he will stir up the wicked to destroy God's people in the time of trouble. And as he accused Jacob, he will urge his accusations against the people of God. He numbers the world as his subjects; but the little company who keep the commandments of God are resisting his supremacy. If he could blot them from the earth, his triumph would be complete. He sees that holy angels are guarding them, and he infers that their sins have been pardoned; but he does not know that their cases have been decided in the sanctuary above. He has an accurate knowledge of the sins which he has tempted them to commit, and he presents these before God in the most exaggerated light, representing this people to be just as deserving as himself of exclusion from the favor of God. He declares that the Lord cannot in justice forgive their sins, and yet destroy him and his angels. He claims them as his prey, and demands that they be given into his hands to destroy.

As Satan accuses the people of God on account of their sins, the Lord permits him to try them to the uttermost. Their confidence in God, their faith and firmness, will be severely tested. As they review the past, their hopes sink; for in their whole lives they can see little good. They are fully conscious of their weakness and unworthiness. Satan endeavors to terrify them with the thought that their cases are hopeless, that the stain of their defilement will never be washed away. He hopes to so destroy their faith that they will yield to his temptations, and turn from their allegiance to God.

Though God's people will be surrounded by enemies who are bent upon their destruction, yet the anguish which they suffer is not a dread of persecution for the truth's sake; they fear that every sin has not been repented of, and that through some fault in themselves they shall fail to realize the fulfillment of the Saviour's promise, "I will keep thee from the hour of temptation which shall come upon all the world." If they could have the assurance of pardon, they would not shrink from torture or death; but should they prove unworthy, and lose their lives because of their own defects of character, then God's holy name would be reproached.

On every hand they hear the plottings of treason, and see the active working of rebellion; and there is aroused within them an intense desire, an earnest yearning of soul, that this great apostasy may be terminated, and the wickedness of the wicked may come to an end. But while they plead with God to stay the work of rebellion, there is a throb of self-reproach that they themselves have no more power to resist and urge back the mighty tide of evil. They feel that had they always employed all their ability in the service of Christ, going forward from strength to strength, Satan's forces would have less power to prevail against them.

They afflict their souls before God, pointing to their past repentance of their many sins, and pleading the Saviour's promise, "Let him take hold of my strength, that he may make peace with me, and he shall make peace with me." [ISA. 27:5.] Their faith does not fail because their prayers are not immediately answered. Though suffering the keenest anxiety, terror, and distress, they do not cease their intercessions. They lay hold of the strength of God as Jacob laid hold of the Angel; and the language of their souls is, "I will not let thee go, except thou bless me."

Had not Jacob previously repented of his sin in obtaining the birthright by fraud, God would not have heard his prayer and mercifully preserved his life. So in the time of trouble, if the people of God had unconfessed sins to appear before them while tortured with fear and anguish, they would be overwhelmed; despair would cut off their faith, and they could not have confidence to plead with God for deliverance. But while they have a deep sense of their unworthiness, they have no concealed wrongs to reveal. Their sins have gone beforehand to Judgment, and have been blotted out; and they cannot bring them to remembrance.

Satan leads many to believe that God will overlook their unfaithfulness in the minor affairs of life; but the Lord shows in his dealings with Jacob that he will in no wise sanction or tolerate evil. All who endeavor to excuse or conceal their sins, and permit them to remain upon the books of Heaven, unconfessed and unforgiven, will be overcome by Satan. The more exalted their profession, and the more honorable the position which they hold, the more grievous is their course in the sight of God, and the more sure the triumph of their great adversary. Those who delay a preparation for the day of God cannot obtain it in the time of trouble or at any subsequent time. The case of all such is hopeless. Those professed Christians who come up to that last fearful conflict unprepared, will, in their despair, confess their sins in words of burning anguish, while the wicked exult over their distress.

Yet Jacob's history is an assurance that God will not cast off those who have been deceived and tempted and betrayed into sin, but who have returned unto him with true repentance. While Satan seeks to destroy this class, God will send his angels to comfort and protect them in the time of peril. The assaults of Satan are fierce and determined, his delusions are terrible; but the Lord's eye is upon his people, and his ear listens to their cries. Their affliction is great, the flames of the furnace seem about to consume them; but the Refiner will bring them forth as gold tried in the fire. God's love for his children during the period of their severest trial is as strong and tender as in the days of their sunniest prosperity; but it is needful for them to be placed in the furnace fire; their earthliness must be removed that the image of Christ may be perfectly reflected.

The season of distress and anguish before us will require a faith that can endure weariness, delay, and hunger,— a faith that will not faint, though severely tried. The period of probation is granted to all to prepare for that time. Jacob prevailed because he was persevering and determined. His victory is an evidence of the power of importunate prayer. All who will lay hold of God's promises as he did, and be as earnest and persevering as he was, will succeed as he succeeded. Those who are unwilling to deny self, to agonize before God, to pray long and earnestly for his blessing, will not obtain it. Wrestling with God— how few know what it is! How few have ever had their souls drawn out after God with intensity of desire until every power is on the stretch. When waves of despair which no language can express sweep over the suppliant, how few cling with unyielding faith to the promises of God.

Those who exercise but little faith now, are in the greatest danger of falling under the power of Satanic delusions and the decree to compel the conscience. And even if they endure the test, they will be plunged into deeper distress and anguish in the time of trouble, because they have never made it a habit to trust in God. The lessons of faith which they have neglected, they will be forced to learn under a terrible pressure of discouragement.

We should now acquaint ourselves with God by proving his promises. Angels record every prayer that is earnest and sincere. We should rather dispense with selfish gratifications than neglect communion with God. The deepest poverty, the greatest self-denial, with his approval, is better than riches, honors, ease, and friendship without it. We must take time to pray. If we allow our minds to be absorbed by worldly interests, the Lord may give us time by removing from us our idols of gold, of houses, or of fertile lands.

The young would not be seduced into sin if they would refuse to enter any path, save that upon which they could ask God's blessing. If the messengers who bear the last solemn warning to the world would pray for the blessing of God, not in a cold, listless, lazy manner, but fervently and in faith, as did Jacob, they would find many places where they could say, "I have seen God face to face, and my life is preserved." They would be accounted of Heaven as princes, having power to prevail with God and with men.

The time of trouble such as never was, is soon to open upon us; and we shall need an experience which we do not now possess, and which many are too indolent to obtain. It is often the case that trouble is greater in anticipation than in reality; but this is not true of the crisis before us. The most vivid presentation cannot reach the magnitude of the ordeal. And now, while the precious Saviour is making an atonement for us, we should seek to become perfect in Christ. God's providence is the school in which we are to learn the meekness and lowliness of Jesus. The Lord is ever setting before us, not the way we would choose, which is easier and pleasanter to us, but the true aims of life. None can neglect or defer this work but at the most fearful peril to their souls.

The apostle John in vision heard a loud voice in Heaven exclaiming, "Woe to the inhabiters of the earth and of the sea! for the devil is come down unto you, having great wrath, because he knoweth that he hath but a short time." [REV. 12:12.] Fearful are the scenes which call forth this exclamation from the heavenly voice. The wrath of Satan increases as his time grows short, and his work of deceit and destruction reaches its culmination in the time of trouble. God's long-suffering has ended. The world has rejected his mercy, despised his love, and trampled upon his law. The wicked have passed the boundary of their probation, and the Lord withdraws his protection, and leaves them to the mercy of the leader they have chosen. Satan will have power over those who have yielded themselves to his control, and he will plunge the inhabitants of the earth into one great, final trouble. As the angels of God cease to hold in check the fierce winds of human passion, all the elements of strife will be let loose. The whole world will be involved in ruin more terrible than that which came upon Jerusalem of old.

A single angel destroyed all the firstborn of the Egyptians, and filled the land with mourning. When David offended against God by numbering the people, one angel caused that terrible destruction by which his sin was punished. The same destructive power exercised by holy angels when God commands, will be exercised by evil angels when he allows. There are forces now ready, and only waiting the divine permission, to spread desolation everywhere.

Fearful sights of a supernatural character will soon be revealed in the heavens, in token of the power of miracle-working demons. The spirits of devils will go forth to the kings of the earth and to the whole world. Rulers and subjects will be alike deceived. Persons will arise pretending to be Christ, and claiming the title and the worship which belong to the world's Redeemer. They will perform wonderful miracles of healing, and will profess to have revelations from Heaven contradicting the testimony of the Scriptures.

As the crowning act in the great drama of deception, Satan himself will attempt to personate Christ. The church has long professed to look to the Saviour's advent as the consummation of her hopes. Now the great deceiver will make it appear that Christ has come. In different parts of the earth, Satan will manifest himself among men as a majestic being of dazzling brightness, resembling the description of the Son of God given by John in the Revelation. [REV. 1:13-15.] The glory that surrounds him is unsurpassed by anything that mortal eyes have yet beheld. The shout of triumph rings out upon the air, "Christ has come! Christ has come!" The people prostrate themselves in adoration before him, while he lifts up his hands, and pronounces a blessing upon them, as Christ blessed his disciples when he was personally upon the earth. His voice is soft and subdued, yet full of melody. In gentle, compassionate tones he presents some of the same gracious, heavenly truths which the Saviour uttered; he heals the diseases of the people, and then, in his assumed character of Christ, he claims to have changed the Sabbath to Sunday, and commands all to hallow the day which he has blessed. He declares that those who persist in keeping holy the seventh day are blaspheming his name by refusing to listen to his angels sent to them with light and truth. This is the strong, almost overmastering delusion. Like the Samaritans who were deceived by Simon Magus, the multitudes, from the least to the greatest, give heed to these sorceries, saying, This is "the great power of God."

But the people of God will not be misled. The teachings of this false Christ are not in accordance with the Scriptures. His blessing is pronounced upon the worshipers of the beast and his image,— the very class upon whom the Bible declares that God's unmingled wrath shall be poured out. And, furthermore, Satan is not permitted to counterfeit the manner of Christ's advent. The Scriptures teach that "as the lightning cometh out of the east, and shineth even unto the west; so shall also the coming of the Son of man be;" [MATT. 24:27.] that he "cometh with clouds; and every eye shall see him;" [REV. 1:7.] that he will "descend from Heaven with a shout, with the voice of the archangel, and with the trump of God;" [1 THESS. 4:16.] that he will "come in his glory, and all the holy angels with him," [MATT. 25:31.] and will "send his angels with a great sound of a trumpet, and they shall gather together his elect." [MATT. 24:31.] Those who have received the love of the truth will be shielded from the powerful delusion that takes the world captive. By the testimony of the Scriptures they will detect the deceiver in his disguise.

To all, the testing time will come. By the sifting of temptation, the genuine Christian will be revealed. Are the people of God now so firmly established upon his word that they would not yield to the evidence of their senses? Would they, in such a crisis, cling to the Bible, and the Bible only? Satan will, if possible, prevent them from obtaining a preparation to stand in that day. He will so arrange affairs as to hedge up their way, entangle them with earthly treasures, cause them to carry a heavy, wearisome burden, that their hearts may be overcharged with the cares of this life, and the day of trial may come upon them as a thief.

Satan will continue to act a double part. Appearing to be the dispenser of great blessings and divine truths, he will, by his lying wonders, hold the world under his control; and at the same time he will indulge his malignity by causing distress and destruction, and will accuse God's people as the cause of the fearful convulsions of nature and the strife and bloodshed among men which are desolating the earth. Thus he will excite to greater intensity the spirit of hatred and persecution against them. God never forces the will or the conscience; but Satan will employ the most cruel measures to control the consciences of men, and to secure worship to himself. And this work of compulsion is always in favor of human creeds and laws, and in defiance of God's holy law.

In the last conflict the Sabbath will be the special point of controversy throughout all Christendom. Secular rulers and religious leaders will unite to enforce the observance of the Sunday; and as milder measures fail, the most oppressive laws will be enacted. It will be urged that the few who stand in opposition to an institution of the church and a law of the land ought not to be tolerated, and a decree will finally be issued denouncing them as deserving of the severest punishment, and giving the people liberty, after a certain time, to put them to death. Romanism in the Old World, and apostate Protestantism in the New, will pursue a similar course toward those who honor the divine precepts.

The people of God will then flee from the cities and villages, and associate together in companies, dwelling in the most desolate and solitary places. Many will find refuge in the strongholds of the mountains. Like the Christians of the Piedmont valleys, they will make the high places of the earth their sanctuaries, and will thank God for the "munitions of rocks." But many of all nations and all classes, high and low, rich and poor, black and white, will be cast into the most unjust and cruel bondage. The beloved of God pass weary days, bound in chains, shut in by prison bars, sentenced to be slain, some apparently left to die of starvation in dark and loathsome dungeons. No human ear is open to hear their moans; no human hand is ready to lend them help.

Will the Lord forget his people in this trying hour? Did he forget faithful Noah when judgments were visited upon the antediluvian world? Did he forget Lot when the fire came down from heaven to consume the cities of the plain? Did he forget Joseph surrounded by idolaters in Egypt? Did he forget Elijah when the oath of Jezebel threatened him with the fate of the Baal prophets? Did he forget Jeremiah in the dark and dismal pit of his prison-house? Did he forget the three worthies in the fiery furnace? or Daniel in the den of lions? Christ cannot forsake those who are as the apple of his eye, the purchase of his precious blood.

Though the people of God endure privation, and even suffer for want of food, they are not left to perish. While God's judgments are visited upon the earth, and the wicked are dying from hunger and thirst, angels provide the righteous with food and water. Said Jesus, in his lessons of faith to his disciples: "Consider the ravens; for they neither sow nor reap; which neither have storehouse nor barn; and God feedeth them; how much more are ye better than the fowls?" [LUKE 12:24.] "Are not two sparrows sold for a farthing? and one of them shall not fall on the ground without your Father. But the very hairs of your head are all numbered. Fear ye not therefore, ye are of more value than many sparrows." [MATT. 10:29-31.]

Yet to human sight it will appear that the people of God must soon seal their testimony with their blood, as did the martyrs before them. They themselves begin to fear that the Lord has left them to fall by the hand of their enemies. It is a time of fearful agony. Day and night they cry unto God for deliverance. The wicked exult, and the jeering cry is heard, "Where now is your faith? Why does not God deliver you out of our hands if you are indeed his people?" But the waiting ones remember Jesus dying upon Calvary's cross, and the chief priests and rulers shouting in mockery, "He saved others; himself he cannot save. If he be the King of Israel, let him now come down from the cross, and we will believe him." [MATT. 27:42.] Like Jacob, all are wrestling with God. Their countenances express their internal struggle. Paleness sits upon every face. Yet they cease not their earnest intercession.

Could men see with heavenly vision, they would behold companies of angels that excel in strength stationed about those who have kept the word of Christ's patience. With sympathizing tenderness, angels have witnessed their distress, and have heard their prayers. They are waiting the word of their Commander to snatch them from their peril. But they must wait yet a little longer. The people of God must drink of the cup, and be baptized with the baptism. The very delay, so painful to them, is the best answer to their petitions. As they endeavor to wait trustingly for the Lord to work, they are led to exercise faith, hope, and patience, which have been too little exercised during their religious experience. Yet for the elect's sake, the time of trouble will be shortened. The end will come more quickly than men expect. The wheat will be gathered and bound in sheaves for the garner of God; the tares will be bound as fagots for the fires of destruction.

The heavenly sentinels, faithful to their trust, continue their watch. In some cases, before the time specified in the decree, enemies will rush upon the waiting ones to put them to death. But none can pass the mighty guardians stationed about every faithful soul. Some are assailed in their flight from the cities and villages; but the swords raised against them break and fall as powerless as a straw. Others are defended by angels in the form of men of war.

In all ages God has wrought through holy angels for the succor and deliverance of his people. Celestial beings have taken an active part in the affairs of men. They have appeared clothed in garments that shone as the lightning; they have come as men, in the garb of wayfarers. Angels have appeared in human form to men of God. They have rested, as if weary, under the oaks at noon. They have accepted the hospitalities of human homes. They have acted as guides to benighted travelers. They have, with their own hands, kindled the fires of the altar. They have opened prison doors, and set free the servants of the Lord. Clothed with the panoply of Heaven, they came to roll away the stone from the Saviour's tomb.

In the form of men, angels are often in the assemblies of the righteous, and they visit the assemblies of the wicked, as they went to Sodom, to make a record of their deeds, to determine whether they have passed the boundary of God's forbearance. The Lord delights in mercy; and for the sake of a few who really serve him, he restrains calamities, and prolongs the tranquillity of multitudes. Little do sinners against God realize that they are indebted for their own lives to the faithful few whom they delight to ridicule and oppress.

Though the rulers of this world know it not, yet often in their councils angels have been spokesmen. Human eyes have looked upon them; human ears have listened to their appeals; human lips have opposed their suggestions and ridiculed their counsels; human hands have met them with insult and abuse. In the council hall and the court of justice, these heavenly messengers have shown an intimate acquaintance with human history; they have proved themselves better able to plead the cause of the oppressed than their ablest and most eloquent defenders. They have defeated purposes and arrested evils that would have greatly retarded the work of God, and would have caused great suffering to his people. In the hour of peril and distress let it never be forgotten that "the angel of the Lord encampeth round about them that fear him, and delivereth them." [PS. 34:7]

With earnest longing, God's people await the tokens of their coming King. As the watchmen are accosted, "What of the night?" the answer is given unfalteringly, "'The morning cometh, and also the night.' Light is gleaming upon the clouds above the mountain tops. Soon will there be a revealing of His glory. The Sun of Righteousness is about to shine forth. The morning and the night come hand in hand,— the opening of endless day to the righteous, the settling down of eternal night to the wicked."

As the wrestling ones urge their petitions before God, the veil separating them from the unseen seems almost withdrawn. The heavens glow with the dawning of eternal day, and, like the melody of angel songs, the words fall upon the ear, "Stand fast to your allegiance. Help is coming." Christ, the almighty victor, holds out to his weary soldiers a crown of immortal glory; and his voice comes from the gates ajar: "Lo, I am with you. Be not afraid. I am acquainted with all your sorrows; I have borne your griefs. You are not warring against untried enemies. I have fought the battle in your behalf, and in my name you are more than conquerors."

The precious Saviour will send help just when we need it. The way to Heaven is consecrated by his footprints. Every thorn that wounds our feet has wounded his. Every cross that we are called to bear, he has borne before us. The Lord permits conflicts, to prepare the soul for peace. If we had no storms, no shadows, we could not appreciate the sunshine. The time of trouble is a fearful ordeal for God's people; but it is the time for every true believer to look up, and by faith he may see the bow of promise encircling him.

"The redeemed of the Lord shall return, and come with singing unto Zion; and everlasting joy shall be upon their head; they shall obtain gladness and joy; and sorrow and mourning shall flee away. I, even I, am he that comforteth you; who art thou, that thou shouldst be afraid of a man that shall die, and of the son of man which shall be made as grass; and forgettest the Lord thy Maker; ... and hast feared continually every day because of the fury of the oppressor, as if he were ready to destroy? and where is the fury of the oppressor? The captive exile hasteneth that he may be loosed, and that he should not die in the pit, nor that his bread should fail. But I am the Lord thy God, that divided the sea, whose waves roared. The Lord of hosts is his name. And I have put my words in thy mouth, and I have covered thee in the shadow of mine hand."

"Therefore hear now this, thou afflicted and drunken, but not with wine: Thus saith thy Lord the Lord, and thy God that pleadeth the cause of his people, Behold, I have taken out of thine hand the cup of trembling, even the dregs of the cup of my fury; thou shalt no more drink it again. But I will put it into the hand of them that afflict thee; which have said to thy soul, Bow down, that we may go over: and thou hast laid thy body as the ground, and as the street, to them that went over." [ISA. 51:11-16, 21-23.]

The eye of God, looking down the ages, was fixed upon the crisis which his people are to meet, when earthly powers shall be arrayed against them. Like the captive exile, they will be in fear of death by starvation or by violence. But the Holy One who divided the Red Sea before Israel, will manifest his mighty power and turn their captivity. "They shall be mine, saith the Lord of hosts, in that day when I make up my jewels; and I will spare them, as a man spareth his own son that serveth him." [MAL. 3:17.] If the blood of Christ's faithful witnesses were shed at this time, it would not, like the blood of the martyrs, be as seed sown to yield a harvest for God. Their fidelity would not be a testimony to convince others of the truth; for the obdurate heart has beaten back the waves of mercy until they return no more. If the righteous were now left to fall a prey to their enemies, it would be a triumph for the prince of darkness. But Christ has spoken: "Come, my people, enter thou into thy chambers, and shut thy doors about thee; hide thyself as it were for a little moment, until the indignation be overpast. For, behold, the Lord cometh out of his place to punish the inhabitants of the earth for their iniquity." [ISA. 26:20, 21.] Glorious will be the deliverance of those who have patiently waited for him, and whose names are written in the book of life.

Chapter 35

God's People Delivered

As the time appointed in the decree against God's people comes, the inhabitants of the earth unite to destroy the disturbers of their peace. In one night they determine to strike the decisive blow that shall forever silence the voice of the reprover. The waiting ones, in their solitary retreats, are still pleading for divine protection. In every quarter, companies of armed men, urged on by hosts of evil angels, are preparing for the work of death. With shouts of triumph, with jeers and imprecations, they are about to rush upon their prey.

But lo, a dense blackness, deeper than the darkness of the night, falls upon the earth. Then a rainbow, shining with the glory from the throne of God, spans the heavens, and seems to encircle each praying company. The angry multitudes are suddenly arrested. Their mocking cries die away. The objects of their murderous rage are forgotten. With fearful forebodings they gaze upon the symbol of God's covenant, and long to be shielded from its overpowering brightness.

By the people of God a voice, clear and melodious, is heard, saying, "Look up," and, lifting their eyes to the heavens, they behold the bow of promise. The black, angry clouds that covered the firmament are parted, and like Stephen they look up steadfastly into Heaven, and see the glory of God, and the Son of man seated upon his throne. In his divine form they discern the marks of his humiliation; and from his lips they hear the request, presented before his Father and the holy angels, "I will that they also, whom thou hast given me, be with me where I am," Again a voice, musical and triumphant, is heard, saying, "They come! they come! holy, harmless, and undefiled. They have kept the word of my patience; they shall walk among the angels;" and the pale, quivering lips of those who have held fast their faith, utter a shout of victory.

It is at midnight that God manifests his power for the deliverance of his people. The sun appears shining in its strength. Startling signs and wonders follow in quick succession. The wicked look with terror and amazement upon the scene, while the righteous behold with solemn joy the tokens of their deliverance. Everything in nature seems turned out of its course. The streams cease to flow. Dark, heavy clouds come up, and clash against each other. In the midst of the angry heavens is one clear space of indescribable glory, whence comes the voice of God like the sound of many waters, saying, "It is done."

That voice shakes the heavens and the earth. There is a mighty earthquake. The firmament appears to open and shut. The glory from the throne of God seems flashing through. The mountains shake like a reed in the wind, and ragged rocks are scattered on every side. There is a roar as of a coming tempest. The sea is lashed into fury. There is heard the shriek of the hurricane, like the voice of demons upon a mission of destruction. The whole earth heaves and swells like the waves of the sea. Its surface is breaking up. Its very foundations seem to be giving way. Mountain chains are sinking. Inhabited islands disappear with their living freight. The seaports that have become like Sodom for wickedness are swallowed up by the angry waters. Great hailstones, every one "about the weight of a talent," [REV. 16:21.] are doing their work of destruction. The proudest cities of the earth are laid low. The costly palaces, upon which the world's great men have lavished their wealth in order to glorify themselves, are crumbling to ruin before their eyes. Prison walls are rent asunder, and God's people, who have been held in bondage for their faith, are set free.

Graves are opened, and "many of them that sleep in the dust of the earth" "awake, some to everlasting life, and some to shame and everlasting contempt." [DAN. 12:2.] All who have died in faith under the third angel's message come forth from the tomb glorified, to hear God's covenant of peace with those who have kept his law. "They also which pierced Him," those that mocked and derided Christ's dying agonies, and the most violent opposers of his truth and his people, are raised to behold him in his glory, and to see the honor placed upon the loyal and obedient.

Thick clouds still cover the sky; yet the sun now and then breaks through, appearing like the avenging eye of Jehovah. Fierce lightnings leap from the heavens, enveloping the earth in a sheet of flame. Above the terrific roar of thunder, voices, mysterious and awful, declare the doom of the wicked. The words spoken are not comprehended by all; but they are distinctly understood by the false watchmen. Those who a little before were so reckless, so boastful and defiant, so exultant in their cruelty to God's commandment-keeping people, are now overwhelmed with consternation, and shuddering in fear. Their wails are heard above the sound of the elements. Demons acknowledge the divinity of Christ, and tremble before his power, while men are supplicating for mercy, and groveling in abject terror.

Said the prophets of old as they beheld in holy vision the day of God: "Blow ye the trumpet in Zion, and sound an alarm in my holy mountain: let all the inhabitants of the land tremble; for the day of the Lord cometh, for it is nigh at hand." "And the Lord shall utter his voice before his army; for his camp is very great; for he is strong that executeth his word; for the day of the Lord is great and very terrible; and who can abide it?" [JOEL 2:1, 11.] "Howl ye; for the day of the Lord is at hand; it shall come as a destruction from the Almighty." [ISA. 13:6.] "Enter into the rock, and hide thee in the dust, for fear of the Lord, and for the glory of his majesty. The lofty looks of man shall be humbled, and the haughtiness of men shall be bowed down, and the Lord alone shall be exalted in that day. For the day of the Lord of hosts shall be upon every one that is proud and lofty, and upon every one that is lifted up; and he shall be brought low." [ISA. 2:10-12.] "In that day a man shall cast his idols of silver, and his idols of gold, which they made each one for himself to worship, to the moles and to the bats; to go into the clefts of the rocks, and into the tops of the ragged rocks, for fear of the Lord, and for the glory of his majesty, when he ariseth to shake terribly the earth." [ISA. 2:20, 21.]

Through a rift in the clouds, there beams a star whose brilliancy is increased fourfold in contrast with the darkness. It speaks hope and joy to the faithful, but severity and wrath to the transgressors of God's law. Those who have sacrificed all for Christ are now secure, hidden as in the secret of the Lord's pavilion. They have been tested, and before the world and the despisers of truth they have evinced their fidelity to Him who died for them. A marvelous change has come over those who have held fast their integrity in the very face of death. They have been suddenly delivered from the dark and terrible tyranny of men transformed to demons. Their faces, so lately pale, anxious, and haggard, are now aglow with wonder, faith, and love. Their voices rise in triumphant song: "God is our refuge and strength, a very present help in trouble. Therefore will not we fear, though the earth be removed, and though the mountains be carried into the midst of the sea; though the waters thereof roar and the troubled, though the mountains shake with the swelling thereof." [PS. 46:1-3.]

While these words of holy trust ascend to God, the clouds sweep back, and the starry heavens are seen, unspeakably glorious in contrast with the black and angry firmament on either side. The glory of Heaven is beaming from the gates ajar. Then there appears against the sky a hand holding two tables of stone folded together. The hand opens the tables, and there are revealed the precepts of the Decalogue, traced as with a pen of fire. The words are so plain that all can read them. Memory is aroused, the darkness of superstition and heresy is swept from every mind, and God's ten words, brief, comprehensive, and authoritative, are presented to the view of all the inhabitants of earth. Wonderful code! wonderful occasion!

It is impossible to describe the horror and despair of those who have trampled upon God's holy requirements. The Lord gave them his law; they might have compared their characters with it, and learned their defects while yet there was opportunity for repentance and reform; but in order to secure the favor of the world, they set aside its precepts and taught others to transgress. They have endeavored to compel God's people to profane his Sabbath. Now they are condemned by that law which they have despised. With awful distinctness they see that they are without excuse. They chose whom they would serve and worship. "Then shall ye return, and discern between the righteous and the wicked, between him that serveth God and him that serveth him not." [MAL. 3:18.]

The enemies of God's law, from the ministers down to the least among them, have a new conception of truth and duty. Too late they see that the Sabbath of the fourth commandment is the seal of the living God. Too late they see the true nature of their spurious Sabbath, and the sandy foundation upon which they have been building. They find that they have been fighting against God. Religious teachers have led souls to perdition while professing to guide them to the gates of Paradise. Not until the day of final accounts will it be known how great is the responsibility of men in holy office, and how terrible are the results of their unfaithfulness. Only in eternity can we rightly estimate the loss of a single soul. Fearful will be the doom of him to whom God shall say, Depart, thou wicked servant.

The voice of God is heard from Heaven declaring the day and hour of Jesus' coming, and delivering the everlasting covenant to his people. Like peals of loudest thunder, his words roll through the earth. The Israel of God stand listening, with their eyes fixed upward. Their countenances are lighted up with his glory, and shine as did the face of Moses when he came down from Sinai. The wicked cannot look upon them. And when the blessing is pronounced on those who have honored God by keeping his Sabbath holy, there is a mighty shout of victory.

Soon there appears in the east a small black cloud, about half the size of a man's hand. It is the cloud which surrounds the Saviour, and which seems in the distance to be shrouded in darkness. The people of God know this to be the sign of the Son of man. In solemn silence they gaze upon it as it draws nearer the earth, becoming lighter and more glorious, until it is a great white cloud, its base a glory like consuming fire, and above it the rainbow of the covenant. Jesus rides forth as a mighty conqueror, and the armies of Heaven follow him. With songs of triumph, a vast retinue of holy angels escort him on his way. The firmament seems filled with shining forms, ten thousand times ten thousand, and thousands of thousands. No pen can picture, no human mind conceive, the glory of the scene. As the living cloud comes still nearer, Jesus can be clearly seen. He does not wear a crown of thorns, but a crown of glory rests upon his holy brow. His countenance shines as the noonday sun. Upon his vesture and thigh is a name written, "King of kings, and Lord of lords."

Before him every face turns pale, and upon those whom God has rejected, falls the blackness of despair. The righteous cry with trembling, "Who shall be able to stand?" The song of the angels ceases, and there is a period of awful silence. Then the voice of Jesus is heard, saying, "My grace is sufficient for you." The faces of the righteous are lighted up, and joy fills every heart. And the angels strike a note higher, and sing again, as they draw still nearer to the earth.

The King of kings descends upon the cloud, wrapped in flaming fire. The earth trembles before him, the heavens are rolled together as a scroll, and every mountain and every island is moved out of its place. Says the psalmist: "Our God shall come, and shall not keep silence; a fire shall devour before him, and it shall be very tempestuous round about him. He shall call to the heavens from above, and to the earth, that he may judge his people. Gather my saints together unto me; those that have made a covenant with me by sacrifice. And the heavens shall declare his righteousness; for God is judge himself." [PS. 50:3-6.]

"And the kings of the earth, and the great men, and the rich men, and the chief captains, and the mighty men, and every bondman, and every freedman, hid themselves in the dens and in the rocks of the mountains, and said to the mountains and rocks, Fall on us, and hide us from the face of Him that sitteth on the throne, and from the wrath of the Lamb; for the great day of his wrath is come, and who shall be able to stand?" [REV. 6:15-17.]

The derisive jests have ceased. Lying lips are hushed into silence. The clash of arms, the tumult of battle, "with confused noise, and garments rolled in blood," [ISA. 9:5.] is stilled. Naught now is heard but the voice of prayer and the sound of weeping and lamentation. The cry bursts forth from lips so lately scoffing, "The great day of His wrath is come; and who shall be able to stand?" The wicked pray to be covered by the rocks of the mountains, rather than meet the face of Him whom they have despised and rejected.

Those who mocked Christ in his humiliation are in that throng. With thrilling power come to their minds the Sufferer's words, when, adjured by the high priest, he solemnly declared, "Hereafter shall ye see the Son of man sitting on the right hand of power, and coming in the clouds of heaven." [MATT. 26:64.] Now they behold Christ in his glory, and they are yet to see him sitting on the right hand of power.

That voice which penetrates the ear of the dead, they know. How often have its plaintive, tender tones called them to repentance. How often has it been heard in the touching entreaties of a friend, a brother, a Redeemer. To the rejecters of his grace, no other could be so full of condemnation, so burdened with denunciation, as that voice which has so long pleaded, "Turn ye, turn ye; for why will ye die?" Oh that it were to them the voice of a stranger! Says Jesus, "I have called, and ye refused; I have stretched out my hand, and no man regarded. But ye have set at naught all my counsel, and would none of my reproof." [PROV. 1:24, 25.] That voice awakens memories which they would fain blot out,— warnings despised, invitations refused, privileges slighted.

Those who derided his claim to be the Son of God are speechless now. There is the haughty Herod who jeered at his royal title, and bade the mocking soldiers crown him king. There are the very men who with impious hands placed upon his form the purple robe, upon his sacred brow the thorny crown, and in his unresisting hand the mimic scepter, and bowed before him in blasphemous mockery. The men who smote and spit upon the Prince of life, now turn from his piercing gaze, and seek to flee from the overpowering glory of his presence. Those who drove the nails through his hands and feet, the soldier who pierced his side, behold these marks with terror and remorse.

With awful distinctness do priests and rulers recall the events of Calvary. With shuddering horror they remember how, wagging their heads in Satanic exultation, they exclaimed, "He saved others; himself he cannot save. If he be the King of Israel, let him now come down from the cross, and we will believe him. He trusted in God; let him deliver him now, if he will have him." [MATT. 27:42, 43.]

Vividly they recall the Saviour's parable of the husbandmen who refused to render to their lord the fruit of the vineyard, who abused his servants and slew his son. They remember, too, the sentence which they themselves pronounced: The lord of the vineyard will miserably destroy those wicked men. In the sin and punishment of those unfaithful men, the priests and elders see their own course and their own just doom. And now there rises a cry of mortal agony. Louder than the shout, "Crucify him! crucify him!" which rang through the streets of Jerusalem, swells the awful, despairing wail, "He is the Son of God! He is the true Messiah!" They seek to flee from the presence of the King of kings. In the deep caverns of the earth, rent asunder by the warring of the elements, they vainly attempt to hide.

In the lives of all who reject truth, there are moments when conscience awakens, when memory presents the torturing recollection of a life of hypocrisy, and the soul is harassed with vain regrets. But what are these compared with the remorse of that day when "fear cometh as desolation," when "destruction cometh as a whirlwind!" [PROV. 1:27.] Those who would have destroyed Christ and his faithful people, now witness the glory which rests upon them. In the midst of their terror they hear the voices of the saints in joyful strains exclaiming, "Lo, this is our God, we have waited for him, and he will save us." [ISA. 25:9.]

Amid the reeling of the earth, the flashing of lightning, and the roaring of thunder, the voice of the Son of God calls forth the sleeping saints. He looks upon the graves of the righteous, then raising his hands to heaven he cries, "Awake, awake, awake, ye that sleep in the dust, and arise!" Throughout the length and breadth of the earth, the dead shall hear that voice, and they that hear shall live. And the whole earth shall ring with the tread of the exceeding great army of every nation, kindred, tongue, and people. From the prison-house of death they come, clothed with immortal glory, crying, "O death, where is thy sting? O grave, where is thy victory?" [1 COR. 15:55.] And the living righteous and the risen saints unite their voices in a long, glad shout of victory.

All come forth from their graves the same in stature as when they entered the tomb. Adam, who stands among the risen throng, is of lofty height and majestic form, in stature but little below the Son of God. He presents a marked contrast to the people of later generations; in this one respect is shown the great degeneracy of the race. But all arise from their last deep slumber with the freshness and vigor of eternal youth. In the beginning, man was created in the likeness of God, not only in character, but in form and feature. Sin defaced and almost obliterated the divine image; but Christ came to restore that which had been lost. He will change our vile bodies, and fashion them like unto his glorious body. The mortal, corruptible form, devoid of comeliness, once polluted with sin, becomes perfect, beautiful, and immortal. All blemishes and deformities are left in the grave. The redeemed bear the image of their Lord. Oh, wonderful redemption! long talked of, long hoped for, contemplated with eager anticipation, but never fully understood.

The living righteous are changed in a moment, in the twinkling of an eye. At the voice of God they were glorified; now they are made immortal, and with the risen saints are caught up to meet their Lord in the air. Friends long separated by death are united, never more to part. Little children are borne by holy angels to their mothers' arms, and together, with songs of gladness, they ascend to the city of God.

On each side of the cloudy chariot are wings, and beneath it are living wheels; and as the chariot rolls upward, the wheels cry, "Holy," and the wings, as they move, cry, "Holy," and the retinue of angels cry, "Holy, holy, holy, Lord God Almighty." And the people of God shout "Alleluia!" as the chariot moves onward toward the New Jerusalem.

Before entering the city, the saints are arranged in a hollow square, with Jesus in the midst. In height he surpasses both the saints and the angels. His majestic form and lovely countenance can be seen by all in the square. Upon the heads of the overcomers the Saviour, with his own right hand, places the crowns of glory. For every saint there is a crown, bearing his new name, and the inscription, "Holiness to the Lord." In every hand is placed the victor's palm and the shining harp. The commanding angels strike the note, and every voice is raised in grateful praise, every hand sweeps the harp-strings with skillful touch, awaking sweet music in rich, melodious strains.

Before the ransomed throng is the holy city. Jesus opens wide the pearly gates, and the nations that have kept the truth enter in. There they behold the Paradise of God, the home of Adam in his innocency. Then that voice, richer than any music that ever fell on mortal ear, is heard, saying, "Your conflict is ended." The Saviour's countenance beams with unutterable love as he welcomes the redeemed to the joy of their Lord.

Suddenly there rings out upon the air an exultant cry of adoration. The two Adams are about to meet. The Son of God is standing with outstretched arms to receive the father of our race,— the being whom he created, who sinned against his Maker, and for whose sin the marks of the crucifixion are borne upon the Saviour's form. As Adam discerns the prints of the cruel nails, he does not fall upon the bosom of his Lord, but in humiliation casts himself at his feet, crying, "Worthy, worthy is the Lamb that was slain!" Tenderly the Saviour lifts him up, and directs his attention to the Eden home from which he has so long been exiled.

After his expulsion from Eden, Adam's life on earth was filled with sorrow. Every dying leaf, every victim of sacrifice, every blight upon the fair face of nature, every stain upon man's purity, was a fresh reminder of his sin. Terrible was the agony of remorse as he beheld iniquity abounding, and, in answer to his reproofs, met the reproaches cast upon himself as the cause of sin. With patient humility he bore, for nearly a thousand years, the penalty of transgression. Faithfully did he repent of his sin, and trust in the merits of the promised Saviour, and he died in the hope of a resurrection. The Son of God redeemed man's failure and fall, and now, through the work of the atonement, Adam is reinstated in his first dominion.

Transported with joy, he beholds the trees that were once his delight,— the very trees from which he plucked fruit when he rejoiced in the perfection of innocence and holiness. He sees the vines that his own hands have trained, the very flowers that he once loved to care for. His mind grasps the reality of the scene; he comprehends that this is indeed Eden restored, far more beautiful now than when he was banished from it. The Saviour leads him to the tree of life, and plucks the glorious fruit, and bids him eat. He looks about him, and beholds a multitude of his family redeemed, standing in the Paradise of God. Then he casts his glittering crown at the feet of Jesus, and, falling upon his breast, embraces the Redeemer. He touches the golden harp, and the vaults of Heaven echo the triumphant song, "Worthy, worthy, worthy is the Lamb that was slain, and lives again!" The family of Adam take up the strain, and cast their crowns at the Saviour's feet as they bow before him in adoration.

This reunion is witnessed by the angels who wept at the fall of Adam, and rejoiced when Jesus, after his resurrection, ascended to

Heaven, having opened the grave for all who should believe on his name. Now they behold the work of redemption accomplished, and they unite their voices in the song of praise.

The Saviour's chosen have been educated and disciplined in the school of trial. They walked in narrow paths on earth; they were purified in the furnace of affliction. For Jesus' sake they endured opposition, hatred, calumny. They followed him through conflicts sore; they endured self-denial and experienced bitter disappointments. By their own painful experience they learned the evil of sin, its power, its guilt, its woe; and they look upon it with abhorrence. A sense of the infinite sacrifice made for its cure, humbles them in their own sight, and fills their hearts with gratitude and praise which those who have never fallen cannot appreciate. They love much, because they have been forgiven much. Having been partakers of Christ's sufferings, they are fitted to be partakers with him of his glory.

The heirs of God have come from garrets, from hovels, from dungeons, from scaffolds, from mountains, from deserts, from the caves of the earth, from the caverns of the sea. But they are no longer feeble, afflicted, scattered, and oppressed. Henceforth they are to be ever with the Lord. They stand before the throne clad in richer robes than the most honored of the earth have ever worn. They are crowned with diadems more glorious than were ever placed upon the brow of earthly monarchs. The days of pain and weeping are forever ended. The King of glory has wiped the tears from all faces; every cause of grief has been removed. Amid the waving of palm-branches they pour forth a song of praise, clear, sweet, and harmonious; every voice takes up the strain, until the anthem swells through the vaults of Heaven, "Salvation to our God which sitteth upon the throne, and unto the Lamb." And all the inhabitants of Heaven respond in the ascription, "Amen; blessing, and glory, and wisdom, and thanksgiving, and honor, and power, and might, be unto our God forever and ever." [REV. 7:10, 12.]

The theme of redemption has but just begun to be understood. With our finite comprehension we may consider most earnestly the shame and the glory, the life and the death, the justice and the mercy, that meet in the cross; yet with the utmost stretch of our mental powers we fail to grasp its full significance. The length and the breadth, the depth and the height of redeeming love are but dimly comprehended. The plan of redemption will not be fully understood, even when the ransomed see as they are seen and know as they are known; but through the eternal ages, new truth will continually unfold to the wondering and delighted mind. Though the griefs and pains and temptations of earth are ended, and the cause removed, the people of God will ever have a distinct, intelligent knowledge of what their salvation has cost.

The cross of Christ will be the science and the song of the redeemed through all eternity. In Christ glorified they will behold Christ crucified. Never will it be forgotten that He who could command all the powers of nature, who by a word could summon mighty angels to do his will and execute vengeance upon his enemies,— the beloved of God, the Majesty of Heaven,— submitted to insult, torture, and death, that sinners might be redeemed. That the Maker of all worlds, the Arbiter of all destinies, should lay aside his glory, and humiliate himself from love to man, will ever excite the wonder and admiration of the universe. As the nations of the saved look upon their Redeemer, and behold the eternal glory of the Father shining in his countenance; as they behold his throne, which is from everlasting to everlasting, and know that his kingdom is to have no end, they break forth in rapturous song, "Worthy, worthy is the Lamb that was slain, and hath redeemed us to God by his own most precious blood!"

The mystery of the cross explains all other mysteries. In the light that streams from Calvary, the attributes of God which had filled us with fear and awe appear beautiful and attractive. Mercy, tenderness, and parental love are seen to blend with holiness, justice, and power. While we behold the majesty of his throne, high and lifted up, we see his character in its gracious manifestations, and comprehend, as never before, the significance of that endearing title, our Father.

It will be seen that He who is infinite in wisdom could devise no plan for our salvation except the sacrifice of his Son. The compensation for this sacrifice is the joy of peopling the earth with ransomed beings, holy, happy, and immortal. The result of the Saviour's conflict with the powers of darkness is joy to the redeemed, redounding to the glory of God, throughout eternity. And such is the value of the soul that the Father is satisfied with the price paid; and Christ himself, beholding the fruits of his great sacrifice, is satisfied.

Chapter 36

Desolation of the Earth

"Therefore shall her plagues come in one day, death, and mourning, and famine; and she shall be utterly burned with fire; for strong is the Lord God who judgeth her. And the kings of the earth, who have committed fornication and lived deliciously with her, shall bewail her, and lament for her, when they shall see the smoke of her burning, standing afar off for the fear of her torment, saying, Alas, alas, that great city Babylon, that mighty city! for in one hour is thy judgment come. And the merchants of the earth shall weep and mourn over her; for no man buyeth their merchandise any more." [REV. 18:8-11.] Such are the judgments that fall upon Babylon in the day of the visitation of God's wrath. She has filled up the measure of her iniquity; her time has come; she is ripe for destruction.

When the voice of God turns the captivity of his people, there is a terrible awakening of those who have lost all in the great game of life. While probation continued, they were blinded by Satan's deceptions, and they justified their course of sin. The rich prided themselves upon their superiority to those who were less favored; but they had obtained their riches by violation of the law of God. They had neglected to feed the hungry, to clothe the naked, to deal justly, and to love mercy. They had sought to exalt themselves, and to obtain the homage of their fellow-creatures. Now they are stripped of all that made them great, and are left destitute and defenseless. They look upon the destruction of the idols which they preferred before their Maker. They sold their souls for earthly riches and enjoyments, and did not seek to become rich toward God. The result is, their lives are a failure; their pleasures are now turned to gall, their treasures to corruption. The gain of a lifetime is swept away in a moment. The rich bemoan the destruction of their grand houses, the scattering of their gold and silver. But their lamentations are silenced by the fear that they themselves are to perish with their idols.

The wicked are filled with regret, not because of their sinful neglect of God and their fellow-men, but because God has conquered. They lament that the result is what it is; but they do not repent of their wickedness. They would leave no means untried to conquer if they could.

The world see the very class whom they have mocked and derided, and desired to exterminate, pass unharmed through tempest and earthquake and pestilence. He who is to the transgressors of his law a devouring fire, is to his people a safe pavilion.

The minister who has sacrificed truth to gain the favor of men, now discerns the character and influence of his teachings. It is apparent that an omniscient eye was following him as he stood in the desk, as he walked the streets, as he mingled with men in the various scenes of life. Every emotion of the soul, every line written, every word uttered, every act that led men to rest in a refuge of falsehood, has been scattering seed; and now, in the wretched, lost souls around him, he beholds the harvest.

Ministers and people see that they have not sustained the right relation to God. They see that they have rebelled against the Author of all just and righteous law. The setting aside of the divine precepts gave rise to thousands of springs of evil, discord, hatred, iniquity, until the earth became one vast field of strife, one sink of corruption. This is the view that now appears to those who rejected truth and chose to cherish error. No language can express the longing which the disobedient and disloyal feel for that which they have lost forever,— eternal life. Men whom the world has worshiped for their talents and eloquence now see these things in their true light. They realize what they have forfeited by transgression, and they fall at the feet of those whose fidelity they have despised and derided, and confess that God has loved them.

The people see that they have been deluded. They eagerly accuse one another of having led them to destruction; but all unite in heaping their bitterest condemnation upon the ministers. Unfaithful pastors have prophesied smooth things; they have led their hearers to make void the law of God and to persecute those who would keep it holy. Now, in their despair, these teachers confess before the world their work of deception. The multitudes are filled with fury. "We are lost!" they cry, "and you are the cause of our ruin;" and they turn upon the false watchmen. The very ones that once admired them most, will pronounce the most dreadful curses upon them. The very hands that once crowned them with laurels will be raised for their destruction. The swords which were to slay God's people are now employed to destroy their enemies. Everywhere there is strife and bloodshed.

The mark of deliverance has been set upon those "that sigh and that cry for all the abominations that be done." Now the angel of death goes forth, represented in Ezekiel's vision by the men with the slaughtering weapons, to whom the command is given: "Slay utterly old and young, both maids, and little children, and women; but come not near any man upon whom is the mark; and begin at my sanctuary." Says the prophet, "They began at the ancient men which were before the house." [EZE. 9:6.] The work of destruction begins among those who profess to be the spiritual guardians of the people. The false shepherds are the first to fall. There are none to pity or to spare. Men, women, maidens, and little children perish together.

"The Lord cometh out of his place to punish the inhabitants of the earth for their iniquity; the earth also shall disclose her blood, and shall no more cover her slain." [ISA. 26:21.] "And this shall be the plague wherewith the Lord will smite all the people that fought against Jerusalem: Their flesh shall consume away while they stand upon their feet, and their eyes shall consume away in their holes, and their tongue shall consume away in their mouth. And it shall come to pass in that day that a great tumult from the Lord shall be among them; and they shall lay hold every one on the hand of his neighbor, and his hand shall rise up against the hand of his neighbor." [ZECH. 14:12, 13.] In the mad strife of their own fierce passions, and by the awful outpouring of God's unmingled wrath, fall the wicked inhabitants of the earth,— priests, rulers, and people, rich and poor, high and low. "And the slain of the Lord shall be at that day from one end of the earth even unto the other end of the earth; they shall not be lamented, neither gathered, nor buried." [JER. 25:33.]

At the coming of Christ the wicked are blotted from the face of the whole earth,— consumed with the spirit of his mouth, and destroyed by the brightness of his glory. Christ takes his people to the city of God, and the earth is emptied of its inhabitants. "Behold, the Lord maketh the earth empty, and maketh it waste, and turneth it upside down, and scattereth abroad the inhabitants thereof. The land shall be utterly emptied, and utterly spoiled; for the Lord hath spoken this word." "Because they have transgressed the laws, changed the ordinance, broken the everlasting covenant. Therefore hath the curse devoured the earth, and they that dwell therein are desolate; therefore the inhabitants of the earth are burned." [ISA. 24:1, 3, 5, 6.]

The whole earth appears like a desolate wilderness. The ruins of cities and villages destroyed by the earthquake, uprooted trees, ragged rocks thrown out by the sea or torn out of the earth itself, are scattered over its surface, while vast caverns mark the spot where the mountains have been rent from their foundations. Here is to be the home of Satan with his evil angels for a thousand years. Here he will be confined, to wander up and down over the broken surface of the earth, and see the effects of his rebellion against the law of God. For a thousand years he can enjoy the fruit of the curse which he has caused. Limited alone to the earth, he will not have the privilege of ranging to other planets, to tempt and annoy those who have not fallen. During this time, Satan suffers extremely. Since his fall his life of intense activity has banished reflection; but he is now deprived of his power, and left to contemplate the part which he has acted since first he rebelled against the government of Heaven, and to look forward with trembling and terror to the dreadful future, when he must suffer for all the evil that he has done, and be punished for the sins that he has caused to be committed.

Shouts of triumph ascend from the angels and the redeemed saints, that they are to be no more annoyed and tempted by Satan, and that the inhabitants of other worlds are delivered from his presence and temptations.

During the thousand years between the first and the second resurrection, the Judgment of the wicked dead takes place. The righteous reign as kings and priests unto God; and in union with Christ they judge the wicked, comparing their acts with the statute book, the Bible, and deciding every case according to the deeds done in the body. Then the portion which the wicked must suffer is meted out, according to their works; and it is written against their names in the book of death. Satan also and evil angels are judged by Christ and his people.

Chapter 37

The Controversy Ended

At the close of the thousand years, Christ again returns to the earth. He is accompanied by the host of the redeemed, and attended by a retinue of angels. As he descends in terrific majesty, he bids the wicked dead arise to receive their doom. They come forth, a mighty host, numberless as the sands of the sea. What a contrast to those who were raised at the first resurrection! The righteous were clothed with immortal youth and beauty. The wicked bear the traces of disease and death.

Every eye in that vast multitude is turned to behold the glory of the Son of God. With one voice the wicked hosts exclaim, "Blessed is He that cometh in the name of the Lord!" It is not love to Jesus that inspires this utterance. The force of truth urges the words from unwilling lips. As the wicked went into their graves, so they come forth, with the same enmity to Christ and the same spirit of rebellion. They are to have no new probation, in which to remedy the defects of their past lives. Nothing would be gained by this. A lifetime of transgression has not softened their hearts. A second probation, were it given them, would be occupied as was the first, in evading the requirements of God and exciting rebellion against him.

Christ descends upon the Mount of Olives, and as his feet touch the mountain, it parts asunder, and becomes a vast plain. Then the New Jerusalem, in its dazzling splendor, comes down out of Heaven. As it rests upon the place purified and made ready to receive it, Christ, with his people and the angels, enters the holy city.

Now Satan prepares for a last mighty struggle for the supremacy. While deprived of his power, and cut off from his work of deception, the prince of evil was miserable and dejected; but as the wicked dead are raised, and he sees the vast multitudes upon his side, his hopes revive, and he determines not to yield the great controversy. He will marshal all the armies of the lost under his banner, and through them endeavor to execute his plans. The wicked are Satan's captives. In rejecting Christ they have accepted the rule of the rebel leader. They are ready to receive his suggestions and to do his bidding. Yet, true to his early cunning, he does not acknowledge himself to be Satan. He claims to be the Prince who is the rightful owner of the world, and whose inheritance has been unlawfully wrested from him. He represents himself to his deluded subjects as a redeemer, assuring them that his power has brought them forth from their graves, and that he is about to rescue them from the most cruel tyranny. The presence of Christ having been removed, Satan works wonders to support his claims. He makes the weak strong, and inspires all with his own spirit and energy. He proposes to lead them against the camp of the saints, and to take possession of the city of God. With fiendish exultation he points to the unnumbered millions who have been raised from the dead, and declares that as their leader he is well able to overthrow the city, and regain his throne and his kingdom.

In that vast throng are multitudes of the long-lived race that existed before the flood; men of lofty stature and giant intellect, who, yielding to the control of fallen angels, devoted all their skill and knowledge to the exaltation of themselves; men whose wonderful works of art led the world to idolize their genius, but whose cruelty and evil inventions, defiling the earth and defacing the image of God, caused him to blot them from the face of his creation. There are kings and generals who conquered nations, valiant men who never lost a battle, proud, ambitious warriors whose approach made kingdoms tremble. In death these experienced no change. As they come up from the grave, they resume the current of their thoughts just where it ceased. They are actuated by the same desire to conquer that ruled them when they fell.

Satan consults with his angels, and then with these kings and conquerors and mighty men. They look upon the strength and numbers upon their side, and declare that the army within the city is small in comparison with theirs, and that it can be overcome. They lay their plans to take possession of the riches and glory of the New Jerusalem. All immediately begin to prepare for battle. Skillful artisans construct implements of war. Military leaders, famed for their success, marshal the throngs of warlike men into companies and divisions.

At last the order to advance is given, and the countless host moves on,— an army such as was never summoned by earthly conquerors, such as the combined forces of all ages since war began could never equal. Satan, the mightiest of warriors, leads the van, and his angels join their forces for this final struggle. Kings and warriors are in his train, and the multitudes follow in vast companies, each army under its appointed leader. With military precision, the serried ranks advance over the earth's broken and uneven surface to the city of God. By the command of Jesus, the gates of the New Jerusalem are closed, and the armies of Satan surround the city, and make ready for the onset.

Now Christ again appears to the view of his enemies. Far above the city, upon a foundation of burnished gold, is a throne, high and lifted up. Upon this throne sits the Son of God, and around him are the subjects of his kingdom. The power and majesty of Christ no language can describe, no pen portray. The glory of the Eternal Father is enshrouding his Son. The brightness of his presence fills the city of God, and flows out beyond the gates, flooding the whole earth with its radiance.

Nearest the throne are those who were once zealous in the cause of Satan, but who, plucked as brands from the burning, have followed their Saviour with deep, intense devotion. Next are those who perfected Christian characters in the midst of falsehood and infidelity, those who honored the law of God when the Christian world declared it void, and the millions, of all ages, who were martyred for their faith. And beyond is the "great multitude which no man could number, of all nations and kindreds and people and tongues," "before the throne and before the Lamb, clothed with white robes, and palms in their hands." Their warfare is ended, their victory won. They have run the race and reached the prize. The palm branch in their hands is a symbol of their triumph, the white robe an emblem of the spotless righteousness of Christ which now is theirs.

The redeemed raise a song of praise that echoes and re-echoes through the vaults of Heaven, "Salvation to our God which sitteth upon the throne, and unto the Lamb." And angel and seraph unite their voices in adoration. As the redeemed have beheld the power and malignity of Satan, they have seen, as never before, that no power by that of Christ could have made them conquerors. In all that shining throng there are none to ascribe salvation to themselves, as if they had prevailed by their own power and goodness. Nothing is said of what they have done or suffered; but the burden of every song, the keynote of every anthem, is, Salvation to our God and unto the Lamb.

In the presence of the assembled inhabitants of earth and Heaven takes place the final coronation of the Son of God. And now, invested with supreme majesty and power, the King of kings pronounces sentence upon the rebels against his government, and executes justice upon those who have transgressed his law and oppressed his people. Says the prophet of God: "I saw a great white throne, and Him that sat on it, from whose face the earth and the heaven fled away; and there was found no place for them. And I saw the dead, small and great, stand before God; and the books were opened; and another book was opened, which is the book of life; and the dead were judged out of those things which were written in the books, according to their works." [REV. 20:11, 12.]

As soon as the books of record are opened, and the eye of Jesus looks upon the wicked, they are conscious of every sin which they have ever committed. They see just where their feet diverged from the path of purity and holiness, just how far pride and rebellion have carried them in the violation of the law of God. The seductive temptations which they encouraged by indulgence in sin, the blessings perverted, the messengers of God despised, the warnings rejected, the waves of mercy beaten back by the stubborn, unrepentant heart,— all appear as if written in letters of fire.

Above the throne is revealed the cross; and like a panoramic view appear the scenes of Adam's temptation and fall, and the successive steps in the great plan of redemption. The Saviour's lowly birth; his early life of simplicity and obedience; his baptism in Jordan; the fast and temptation in the wilderness; his public ministry, unfolding to men Heaven's most precious blessings; the days crowded with deeds of love and mercy, the nights of prayer and watching in the solitude of the mountains; the plottings of envy, hate, and malice which repaid his benefits; the awful, mysterious agony in Gethsemane, beneath the crushing weight of the sins of the whole world; his betrayal into the hands of the murderous mob; the fearful events of that night of horror,— the unresisting prisoner, forsaken by his best-loved disciples, rudely hurried through the streets of Jerusalem; the Son of God exultantly displayed before Annas, arraigned in the high priest's palace, in the judgment hall of Pilate, before the cowardly and cruel Herod, mocked, insulted, tortured, and condemned to die,— all are vividly portrayed.

And now before the swaying multitude are revealed the final scenes,— the patient Sufferer treading the path to Calvary; the Prince of Heaven hanging upon the cross; the haughty priests and the jeering rabble deriding his expiring agony; the supernatural darkness; the heaving earth, the rent rocks, the open graves, marking the moment when the world's Redeemer yielded up his life.

The awful spectacle appears just as it was. Satan, his angels, and his subjects have no power to turn from the picture of their own work. Each actor recalls the part which he performed. Herod, who slew the innocent children of Bethlehem that he might destroy the King of Israel; the base Herodias, upon whose guilty soul rests the blood of John the Baptist; the weak, timeserving Pilate; the mocking soldiers; the priests and rulers and the maddened throng who cried, "His blood be on us, and our children!" — all behold the enormity of their guilt. They vainly seek to hide from the divine majesty of His countenance, outshining the glory of the sun, while the redeemed cast their crowns at the Saviour's feet, exclaiming, "He died for me!"

Amid the ransomed throng are the apostles of Christ, the heroic Paul, the ardent Peter, the loved and loving John, and their true-hearted brethren, and with them the vast host of martyrs; while outside the walls, with every vile and abominable thing, are those by whom they were persecuted, imprisoned, and slain. There is Nero, that monster of cruelty and vice, beholding the joy and exaltation of those whom he once tortured, and in whose extremest anguish he found Satanic delight. His mother is there to witness the result of her own work; to see how the evil stamp of character transmitted to her son, the passions encouraged and developed by her influence and example, have borne fruit in crimes that caused the world to shudder.

There are papist priests and prelates, who claimed to be Christ's ambassadors, yet employed the rack, the dungeon, and the stake to control the consciences of his people. There are the proud pontiffs who exalted themselves above God, and presumed to change the law of the Most High. Those pretended fathers of the church have an account to render to God from which they would fain be excused. Too late they are made to see that the Omniscient One is jealous of his law, and that he will in no wise clear the guilty. They learn now that Christ identifies his interest with that of his suffering people; and they feel the force of his own words, "Inasmuch as ye have done it unto one of the least of these my brethren, ye have done it unto me."

The whole wicked world stand arraigned at the bar of God, on the charge of high treason against the government of Heaven. They have none to plead their cause; they are without excuse; and the sentence of eternal death is pronounced against them.

It is now evident to all that the wages of sin is not noble independence and eternal life, but slavery, ruin, and death. The wicked see what they have forfeited by their life of rebellion. The far more exceeding and eternal weight of glory was despised when offered them; but how desirable it now appears. "All this," cries the lost soul, "I might have had; but I chose to put these things far from me. Oh, strange infatuation! I have exchanged peace, happiness, and honor, for wretchedness, infamy, and despair." All see that their exclusion from Heaven is just. In their lives they declared, We will not have this Jesus to reign over us.

As if entranced, the wicked have looked upon the coronation of the Son of God. They see in his hands the tables of the divine law, the statutes which they have despised and transgressed. They witness the outburst of wonder, rapture, and adoration from the saved; and as the wave of melody sweeps over the multitudes without the city, all with one voice exclaim, "Marvelous are thy works, Lord God Almighty; just and true are thy ways, thou King of saints;" and falling prostrate, they worship the Prince of life.

Satan seems paralyzed as he beholds the glory and majesty of Christ. He who was once a covering cherub remembers whence he has fallen. A shining seraph, "son of the morning;" how changed, how degraded! From the council where once he was honored, he is forever excluded. He sees another now standing near to the Father, veiling his glory. He has seen the crown placed upon the head of Christ by an angel of lofty stature and majestic presence, and he knows that this office might have been his.

Memory recalls the home of his innocence and purity, the peace and content that were his until he indulged in murmuring against God, and envy of Christ. His accusations, his rebellion, his deceptions to gain the sympathy and support of the angels, his stubborn persistence in making no effort for self-recovery when God would have granted him forgiveness,— all come vividly before him. He reviews his work among men and its results,— the enmity of man toward his fellow-man, the terrible destruction of life, the rise and fall of kingdoms, the overturning of thrones, the long succession of tumults, conflicts, and revolutions. He recalls his constant efforts to oppose the work of Christ and to sink man lower and lower. He sees that his hellish plots have been powerless to destroy those who have put their trust in Jesus. As Satan looks upon his kingdom, the fruit of his toil, he sees only failure and ruin. He has led the multitudes to believe that the city of God would be an easy prey; but he knows that this is false. Again and again in the progress of the great controversy has he been defeated and compelled to yield. He knows too well the power and majesty of the Eternal.

The aim of the great rebel has ever been to justify himself, and to prove the divine government responsible for the rebellion. To this end he has bent all the power of his giant intellect. He has worked deliberately and systematically, and with marvelous success, leading vast multitudes to accept his version of the great controversy which has been so long in progress. For thousands of years this chief of conspiracy has palmed off falsehood for truth. But the time has now come when the rebellion is to be finally defeated, and the history and character of Satan disclosed. In his last great effort to dethrone Christ, destroy his people, and take possession of the city of God, the arch-deceiver has been fully unmasked. Those who have united with him see the total failure of his cause. Christ's followers and the loyal angels behold the full extent of his machinations against the government of God. He is the object of universal abhorrence.

Satan sees that his voluntary rebellion has unfitted him for Heaven. He has trained his powers to war against God; the purity, peace, and harmony of Heaven would be to him supreme torture. His accusations against the mercy and justice of God are now silenced. The reproach which he has endeavored to cast upon Jehovah rests wholly upon himself. And now Satan bows down, and confesses the justice of his sentence.

Every question of truth and error in the long-standing controversy is made plain. God's justice stands fully vindicated. Before the whole world is clearly presented the great sacrifice made by the Father and the Son in man's behalf. The hour has come when Christ occupies his rightful position, and is glorified above principalities and powers and every name that is named.

It was for the joy that was set before him,— that he might bring many sons unto glory,— that he endured the cross and despised the shame. And inconceivably great as was the sorrow and the shame, so great is the joy and the glory. He looks upon the redeemed, renewed in his own image, every face reflecting the likeness of their King. In their perfect purity and surpassing joy he beholds the result of the travail of his soul, and he is satisfied. Then, in a voice that reaches the assembled multitudes of the righteous and the wicked, he declares, "Behold the purchase of my blood! For these I suffered; for these I died; that they might dwell in my presence throughout eternal ages." And the song of praise ascends from the white-robed ones about the throne, "Worthy is the Lamb that was slain to receive power, and riches, and wisdom, and strength, and honor, and glory, and blessing."

Notwithstanding Satan has been constrained to acknowledge God's justice, and to bow to the supremacy of Christ, his character remains unchanged. The spirit of rebellion, like a mighty torrent, again bursts forth. Filled with frenzy, he determines not to yield the great controversy. The time has come for a last desperate struggle against the King of Heaven. He rushes into the midst of his subjects, and endeavors to inspire them with his own fury, and arouse them to instant battle. But of all the countless millions whom he has allured into rebellion, there are none now to acknowledge his supremacy. His power is at an end. The wicked are filled with the same hatred of God that inspires Satan; but they see that their case is hopeless, that they cannot prevail against Jehovah. Their rage is kindled against Satan and those who have been his agents in deception. With the fury of demons they turn upon them, and there follows a scene of universal strife.

Then are fulfilled the words of the prophet: "The indignation of the Lord is upon all nations, and his fury upon all their armies: he hath utterly destroyed them, he hath delivered them to the slaughter." [ISA. 34:2.] "Upon the wicked he shall rain quick burning coals, fire and brimstone, and an horrible tempest: this shall be the portion of their cup." [PS. 11:6. MARGIN.] Fire comes down from God out of heaven. The earth is broken up. The weapons concealed in its depths are drawn forth. Devouring flames burst from every yawning chasm. The very rocks are on fire. The day has come that shall burn as an oven. [MAL. 4:1.] The elements melt with fervent heat, the earth also, and the works that are therein are burned up. [2 PETER 3:10.] The fire of Tophet is "prepared for the king," the chief of rebellion; the pile thereof is deep and large, and "the breath of the Lord, like a stream of brimstone, doth kindle it." [ISA. 30:33.] The earth's surface seems one molten mass,— a vast, seething lake of fire. It is the time of the judgment and perdition of ungodly men, — "the day of the Lord's vengeance, and the year of recompenses for the controversy of Zion." [ISA. 34:8.]

The wicked receive their recompense in the earth. They "shall be stubble; and the day that cometh shall burn them up, saith the Lord of hosts." Some are destroyed as in a moment, while others suffer many days. All are punished according to their deeds. The sins of the righteous have been transferred to Satan, the originator of evil, who must bear their penalty. Thus he is made to suffer not only for his own rebellion, but for all the sins which he has caused God's people to commit. His punishment is to be far greater than that of those whom he has deceived. After all have perished who fell by his deceptions, he is still to live and suffer on. In the cleansing flames the wicked are at last destroyed, root and branch,— Satan the root, his followers the branches. The justice of God is satisfied, and the saints and all the angelic host say with a loud voice, Amen.

While the earth is wrapped in the fire of God's vengeance, the righteous abide safely in the holy city. Upon those that had part in the first resurrection, the second death has no power. [REV. 20:6.] While God is to the wicked a consuming fire, he is to his people both a sun and a shield. [PS. 84:11.]

"And I saw a new heaven and a new earth; for the first heaven and the first earth were passed away." [REV. 21:1.] The fire that consumes the wicked purifies the earth. Every trace of the curse is swept away. No eternally burning hell will keep before the ransomed the fearful consequences of sin. One reminder alone remains: our Redeemer will ever bear the marks of his crucifixion. Upon his wounded head, his hands and feet, are the only traces of the cruel work that sin has wrought.

"O Tower of the flock, the stronghold of the daughter of Zion, to thee shall it come, even the first dominion." [MICAH 4:8.] The kingdom forfeited by sin, Christ has regained, and the redeemed are to possess it with him. "The righteous shall inherit the land, and dwell therein forever." [PS. 37:29.] A fear of making the saints' inheritance seem too material has led many to spiritualize away the very truths which lead us to look upon the new earth as our home. Christ assured his disciples that he went to prepare mansions for them. Those who accept the teachings of God's word will not be wholly ignorant concerning the heavenly abode. And yet the apostle Paul declares: "Eye hath not seen, nor ear heard, neither have entered into the heart of man, the things which God hath prepared for them that love him." [1 COR. 2:9.] Human language is inadequate to describe the reward of the righteous. It will be known only to those who behold it. No finite mind can comprehend the glory of the Paradise of God.

In the Bible the inheritance of the saved is called a country. [HEB. 11:14-16.] There the great Shepherd leads his flock to fountains of living waters. The tree of life yields its fruit every month, and the leaves of the tree are for the service of the nations. There are everflowing streams, clear as crystal, and beside them waving trees cast their shadows upon the paths prepared for the ransomed of the Lord. There the wide-spreading plains swell into hills of beauty, and the mountains of God rear their lofty summits. On those peaceful plains, beside those living streams, God's people, so long pilgrims and wanderers, shall find a home.

There is the New Jerusalem, "having the glory of God," her light "like unto a stone most precious, even like a jasper stone, clear as crystal." [REV. 21:11.] Saith the Lord, "I will rejoice in Jerusalem, and joy in my people." [ISA. 65:19.] "The tabernacle of God is with men, and he will dwell with them, and they shall be his people, and God himself shall be with them, and be their God, And God shall wipe away all tears from their eyes; and there shall be no more death, neither sorrow nor crying, neither shall there be any more pain; for the former things are passed away." [REV. 21:3, 4.]

In the city of God "there shall be no night." None will need or desire repose. There will be no weariness in doing the will of God and offering praise to his name. We shall ever feel the freshness of the morning, and shall ever be far from its close. "And they need no candle, neither light of the sun; for the Lord God giveth them light." [REV. 22:5.] The light of the sun will be superseded by a radiance which is not painfully dazzling, yet which immeasurably surpasses the brightness of our noontide. The glory of God and the Lamb floods the holy city with unfading light. The redeemed walk in the sunless glory of perpetual day.

"I saw no temple therein; for the Lord God Almighty and the Lamb are the temple of it." [REV. 21:22.] The people of God are privileged to hold open communion with the Father and the Son. Now we "see through a glass, darkly." [1 COR. 13:12.] We behold the image of God reflected, as in a mirror, in the works of nature and in his dealings with men; but then we shall see him face to face, without a dimming veil between. We shall stand in his presence, and gaze upon the glory of his countenance.

There, immortal minds will study with never-failing delight the wonders of creative power, the mysteries of redeeming love. There is no cruel, deceiving foe to tempt to forgetfulness of God. Every faculty will be developed, every capacity increased. The acquirement of knowledge will not weary the mind or exhaust the energies. There the grandest enterprises may be carried forward, the loftiest aspirations reached, the highest ambitions realized; and still there will arise new heights to surmount, new wonders to admire, new truths to comprehend, fresh objects to call forth the powers of mind and soul and body.

And as the years of eternity roll, they will bring richer and more glorious revelations of God and of Christ. As knowledge is progressive, so will love, reverence, and happiness increase. The more men learn of God, the greater will be their admiration of his character. As Jesus opens before them the riches of redemption, and the amazing achievements in the great controversy with Satan, the hearts of the ransomed beat with a stronger devotion, and they sweep the harps of gold with a firmer hand; and ten thousand times ten thousand and thousands of thousands of voices unite to swell the mighty chorus of praise.

"And every creature which is in Heaven, and on the earth, and under the earth, and such as are in the sea, and all that are in them, heard I saying, Blessing, and honor, and glory, and power, be unto Him that sitteth upon the throne and unto the Lamb forever and ever."

Sin and sinners are no more; God's entire universe is clean; and the great controversy is forever ended.

Appendix

Note 1: page 110— William Miller's views as to the exact time of the second advent were based on the prophecy of DAN. 8:14: "unto two thousand and three hundred days; then shall the sanctuary be cleansed." That a day in symbolic prophecy represents a year, see NUM. 14:34; EZE. 4:6. As the period of 2300 prophetic days, or literal years, extended far beyond the close of the Jewish dispensation, it could not refer to the sanctuary of that dispensation. Mr. Miller held the generally received view that in the Christian age the *earth* is the sanctuary, and hence concluded that the cleansing of the sanctuary brought to view in DAN. 8:14 represented the purification of the earth by fire at the second coming of Christ. The point from which to reckon the 2300 days is found in DAN. 9:24-27, which is an explanation of the vision of chapter 8. It is stated that 70 weeks, or 490 years, are determined, literally, cut off, as specially pertaining to the Jews. The only period from which the 70 weeks could be cut off is the 2300 days, that being the only period of time mentioned in the vision of chapter 8. The 70 weeks must therefore be a part of the 2300 days, and the two periods must begin together. The 70 weeks are declared by the angel to date from the going forth of the commandment to restore and build Jerusalem. If, then, we can correctly locate this commandment, we have the starting-point for the great period of the 2300 days. The Bible furnishes us with four tests by which we may determine when the true date is found:—

1. From the time the commandment was given, 49 years were to witness the completion of the street and wall of Jerusalem. DAN. 9:25.

2. Threescore and two weeks from this time, or, in all, 69 weeks, 483 years, were to extend to Messiah the Prince, or to the anointing of Christ by the Holy Spirit at His baptism, the word Messiah signifying anointed.

3. Sixty-nine and a half weeks were to extend to the crucifixion,— the cessation of sacrifice and oblation in the midst of the week. Verse 27.

4. The full period of 70 weeks was to witness the complete confirmation of the covenant with Daniel's people. At the termination of this period, the Jews having ceased to be God's chosen people, the gospel would be preached to the gentiles.

In the seventh of Ezra we find the decree which we seek. It was issued by Artaxerxes, king of Persia, B.C. 457. In EZRA 6:14 the house of the Lord at Jerusalem is said to have been built

"according to the commandment [margin, decree] of Cyrus, and Darius, and Artaxerxes king of Persia." The three kings did the one work; it was begun by Cyrus, carried forward by Darius, and completed by Artaxerxes. the scripture counts this action *one decree*. That the later decrees were a continuation or completion of that of Cyrus, see EZRA 6:1-14. Taking B.C. 457 as the date of the commandment, every specification of the prophecy concerning the 70 weeks is fulfilled. That the reader may see the reasonableness of Mr. Miller's position on the prophetic periods, we copy the following, which was published in the *Advent Herald*, Boston, in March, 1850, in answer to a correspondent:—

"It is by the canon of Ptolemy that the great prophetical period of the seventy weeks is fixed. This canon places the seventh year of Artaxerxes in the year B.C. 457; and the accuracy of the canon is demonstrated by the concurrent agreement of more than twenty eclipses. The seventy weeks date from the going forth of a decree respecting the restoration of Jerusalem. There were no decrees between the seventh and twentieth years of Artaxerxes. Four hundred and ninety years, beginning with the seventh, must commence in B.C. 457, and end in A.D. 34 commencing in the twentieth, they must commence in B.C. 444, and end in A.D. 47. As no event occurred in A.D. 47 to mark their termination, we cannot reckon from the twentieth; we must therefore look to the seventh of Artaxerxes. This date we cannot change from B.C. 457 without first demonstrating the inaccuracy of Ptolemy's canon. To do this, it would be necessary to show that the large number of eclipses by which its accuracy has been repeatedly demonstrated, have not been correctly computed; and such a result would unsettle every chronological date, and leave the settlement of epochs and the adjustment of eras entirely at the mercy of every dreamer, so that chronology would be of no more value than mere guesswork. As the seventy weeks must terminate in A.D. 34, unless the seventh of Artaxerxes is wrongly fixed, and as that cannot be changed without some evidence to that effect, we inquire, what evidence marked that termination? The time when the apostles turned to the gentiles harmonizes with that date better than any other which has been named. And the crucifixion, in A.D. 31, in the midst of the last week, is sustained by a mass of testimony which cannot be easily invalidated."

As the 70 weeks and the 2300 days have a common starting-point, the calculation of Mr. Miller is verified at a glance by subtracting the 457 years B.C. from the 2300 thus:—

$$2300$$
$$\underline{-457}$$
$$1843 \text{ A.D.}$$

but it requires 457 full years before Christ, and 1843 full years after Christ, to make the 2300. Now the decree of Artaxerxes did not go into effect at the beginning of the year 457 B.C., but in the autumn of that year; it follows that the 2300 days would not terminate in 1843, but would extend to the autumn of 1844. This is plainly seen by the following simple diagram:—

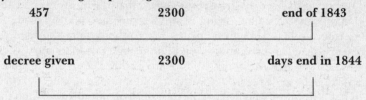

| 457 | 2300 | end of 1843 |

| decree given | 2300 | days end in 1844 |

This fact not being at first perceived by Mr. Miller and his associates, they looked for the coming of Christ in 1843; hence the first disappointment and the seeming delay. It was the discovery of the correct time, in connection with other scripture testimony, that led to the movement known as the midnight cry of 1844. And to this day the computation of the prophetic periods placing the close of the 2300 days in the autumn of 1844, stands without impeachment.

Then the question arises, if Wm. Miller's calculation of time was correct, whence his disappointment? This was due to his mistake as to the *event*. The prophecy says, "unto two thousand and three hundred days; then shall the sanctuary be cleansed." Mr. Miller and his associates failed to understand the subject of the sanctuary and its cleansing. Here was the secret of their disappointment. For a brief explanation of this important point, showing what is the sanctuary, and how its cleansing— beginning at the termination of the 2300 days in 1844— fulfills the prophecy of DAN. 8:14, see chapter 18, entitled "The Sanctuary."

Another question then arises: "if he was mistaken in the event, was not his whole work an error?" That does not follow. The disciples of Christ were utterly mistaken when he rode into Jerusalem, and they hailed him as a king with tokens of victory. They thought he was then to be crowned a king on David's throne. But it was not an error in them to act according to their belief; in so doing they fulfilled the prophecy of ZECH. 9:9, which they would not have done if they had realized that he was going to judgment and to death. But that scripture must be fulfilled, if it were necessary to make the stones cry out: LUKE 19:37-40. In like manner it appears that Mr. Miller and his associates fulfilled prophecy, and gave a proclamation (see REV. 14:6, 7) which they would not have given had they understood that yet other proclamations were to be made before the Lord should come. REV. 14:8-14.

Note 2: page 121—that a wrong use is often made of the text (MATT. 24:36), is evident from the context. One question of the disciples was concerning the sign of Christ's coming and of the end of the world. This question Jesus answered. In verse 29 he gave signs, and said, "When ye shall see all these things, *know* that it is near, even at the doors." Verse 33. One saying of the Saviour must not be made to destroy another. Though no man knoweth the *day* nor the *hour,* we are instructed and required (for it is in the imperative) to know when it is near, even at the doors. And we are further taught that it will be as fatal to us to disregard his warning, and refuse or neglect to know, as it was for those who lived in the days of Noah not to know when the flood was coming. Verses 37-39 and verses 44-51 show in what light Christ, when he comes, will regard and reward those whom he finds watching and teaching His coming, and those denying it. "Blessed are those servants, whom the Lord when he cometh shall find watching." LUKE 12:37.

Note 3: page 123— the story that the adventists made robes with which to ascend "to meet the Lord in the air," was invented by those who wished to reproach the cause. It was circulated so industriously that many believed it; but careful inquiry proved its falsity. For many years a large reward has been offered for proof that one such instance ever occurred; but the proof has not been produced. None who loved the appearing of the Saviour were so ignorant of the teachings of the scriptures as to suppose that robes which they could make would be necessary for that occasion. The only robe which the saints will need to meet the Lord will be that of the righteousness of Christ. see REV. 19:8.

Note 4: page 130— the year 1843, during which adventists at first expected the coming of Christ, was regarded as extending to the spring of 1844. The reason for this, briefly stated, is as follows: anciently the year did not commence in midwinter, as now, but at the first new moon after the vernal equinox. therefore, as the period of 2300 days was begun in a year reckoned by the ancient method, it was considered necessary to conform to that method to its close. Hence, 1843 was counted as ending in the spring, and not in the winter.

Note 5: page 141— that the earth is the sanctuary was inferred from those scriptures which teach that the earth will be purified and fitted up for the eternal dwelling-place of the saints, according to the original design of the creator. Adventists understood this just as it was taught by Wesley and others. And their minds did not rest on any other dwelling-place or any other thing which needed cleansing. The only scriptures which we ever knew to be offered in favor of the earth or any dwelling-place of man being called the sanctuary, fairly disprove the position. They are only three in number, as follows:—

EX. 15:17: "Thou shalt bring them [the people] in, and plant them in the mountain of Thine inheritance, in the place, O Lord, which Thou hast made for Thee to dwell in, the sanctuary, O Lord, which Thy hands have established."

Without taking time or space to give an exposition of the text, it is sufficient for the present purpose to remark that it disproves the idea of *the earth* being the sanctuary. Whatever construction may be placed upon the text, it teaches that the people were not then in the sanctuary; but they were in the earth. Then it is claimed that it referred to that part of the earth into which they were to be brought, namely, Palestine. This is disproved by the second text.

JOSH. 24:26: "And Joshua wrote these words in the book of the law of God, and took a great stone, and set it up there under an oak, that was by the sanctuary of the Lord."

The stone and the oak were in Palestine, but they were by the sanctuary of the Lord— not in it. And the other text is more restrictive still, and equally conclusive against the inference to which reference is herein made.

PS. 78:54: "And he brought them [his people] to the border of his sanctuary, even to this mountain, which his right hand had purchased."

The mountain was Mount Moriah, on which the temple of Solomon was built; yet being brought unto it is called being brought "to the border of his sanctuary." Thus these texts do not prove that the earth is the sanctuary, but rather the reverse.

Jehoshaphat's prayer gives the true idea of the relation of that land to the sanctuary: "art not Thou our God, who didst drive out the inhabitants of this land before Thy people Israel, and gavest it to the seed of Abraham Thy friend forever? And they dwelt therein, and have built Thee a sanctuary therein for Thy name" 2 CHRON. 20:7, 8. This corresponds to the order in EX. 25:8: "and let them make me a sanctuary; that I may dwell among them." In this same book is given a minute description of the sanctuary, its erection, and approval by the Lord. The process of cleansing the sanctuary is described in LEV. 16. When the children of Israel possessed Canaan, Solomon built a temple, in which was a holy and a most holy place, and the vessels of the movable sanctuary, which was made in the desert of Arabia, were transferred to the temple. This was then the sanctuary,— the dwelling place of god's glory upon the earth. Even a partial knowledge of the teachings of the scriptures on this subject will justify all that the author has said in reference to it in pages 141-4.

Note 6: page 146— almost all adventists, including Mr. Miller, did, for a short time after their disappointment in 1844, believe that the world had received its last warning. They could hardly think otherwise, with their faith in the message which they had given,— "the hour of his judgment is come." REV. 14:6, 7. They naturally thought that this proclamation must close the dispensation. They were as unable to find their bearings at once as were the disciples when their Lord, whom they had hailed as their king coming to his throne, was crucified and buried. In both cases they were unable to comprehend their terrible disappointment.

But the idea that the work of the gospel was finished was soon renounced, except by some fanatical ones who would neither be counseled nor receive instruction. But most of those who renounced it, and yet retained their faith in the work, continued to believe that they who clearly saw the light of the heaven-sent warning and persistently rejected it, were rejected of the Lord. There is no more fanaticism in that than there is in the common belief that those obdurate Jews who continued to reject the light of the advanced truth sent to that generation, were rejected of God.

There was one class who soon renounced the idea that "the door of mercy was shut," because they discovered that *other messages* were to be proclaimed after that declaring, the hour of judgment is come; and that that of the third angel, the last one, was to go to "many peoples, and nations, and tongues, and kings." They learned that the judgment sits in heaven before the coming of the Lord; that the judgment of the righteous is fully accomplished while Jesus is yet their advocate before the Father's throne; that eternal life is instantly given to the saints when their Saviour comes, which is proof that they have been judged and acquitted. As the hopes of the disciples revived, and they were "glad when they saw the Lord," and declared his messiahship with yet greater confidence, so did these rejoice when they discovered the truth of the third angel's message, which, to them, was like life from the dead. With renewed zeal and strengthened confidence they began again to proclaim the soon coming of the Lord.

With the light on the third message they also received light on the sanctuary and its cleansing, by which they understood that the antitypical work of the day of atonement, which was accomplished in the most holy place, was that which was pointed out by the message which they had given. They saw that there were two veils or doors in the temple of God; HEB. 9:3; and that at that time one was shut and the other was opened. With earnest zeal and new hope they preached these truths, and urged their fellowmen to seek an entrance by faith into the most holy place within the second veil, where our great high priest is gone to blot out the sins of all his faithful ones, from Abel to the present time. Their faith was in an open door which no man can shut until the work therein is fully done. In the work of inviting sinners to come to this open door, they continue until the present time; and this will be their work until Jesus Himself shall proclaim, "He that is unjust, let him be unjust still;" REV. 22:11; that is, until probation is closed and the ministry of the gospel is ended.

Among the first who taught the third message and the open door, was the author of this book. By her untiring zeal, her earnest appeals, and the clear light of the testimony which she bore, she did much to advance the cause, to correct the errors of fanaticism, to renew the hopes of the desponding, and to cheer the hearts of the "little flock" who loved the appearing of their soon-coming Saviour.

Note 7: page 150— for a brief examination of important points in the third angel's message of REV. 14:9-12, see note 8. This message contains the last warning that men on probation will ever receive, as it is followed by the coming of the Son of Man to reap the harvest of the earth,— to "gather the wheat into his garner," and to cast the clusters of the vine of the earth into the winepress of the wrath of God. See verses 14-20. It is for this reason that it is given in such strong, such terrible language of threatening. The wrath which it denounces upon the worshipers of the beast and his image is contained in "the seven last plagues; for in them is filled up the wrath of God." REV. 15:1. Compare chap. 16:1, 2. That wrath "is poured out without mixture;" for then judgment falls upon the incorrigible without mercy, because our Saviour will then have finished his priestly work, and he will come, not to offer salvation, but to take vengeance on them that know not God, and that obey not the gospel. 2 THESS. 1:6-9.

But the throne of God will be clear, and sinners will be without excuse; for the warnings of the scriptures are given in no uncertain language. To the impious the Lord says: "Because I have called, and ye refused; I have stretched out my hand, and no man regarded; but ye have set at naught all my counsel, and would none of my reproof: I also will laugh at your calamity; I will mock when your fear cometh; when your fear cometh as desolation, and your destruction cometh as a whirlwind; when distress and anguish cometh upon you. Then shall they call upon me, but I will not answer; they shall seek me early, but they shall not find me." PROV. 1:24-28. and the warning of the last message is going to all the world. It also is clear and decisive in its utterance. "the commandments of God," which it enforces, are not obscure or hard to be understood. The fourth says, "the seventh day is the sabbath of the Lord thy God." This was the Lord's day— His holy day— from the creation of the world. He claims no other as his; He sanctified no other; He never commanded any other to be observed. They who turn away from a truth so plain, who reject a warning so solemn, will have no answer to make when the Lord commands them to depart.

But terrible as these words of threatening are, the message is given in mercy. It is a last effort on the part of the Lord to arouse men to a sense of their danger; to induce them to turn from their evil ways— from their transgressions of His holy law — that they may have eternal life. The Lord has no pleasure in the death of the wicked; but that the wicked turn from his way and live. EZE. 33:11. But if they will not come unto him that they may have life; if they choose to follow the multitude to do evil, rather than to walk in the way of God's commandments, then they must bear their iniquity. Their blood will be upon their own heads. God gives them the power to choose, and warns them against the evil which lies before them. Against all his entreaties, they do despite to the spirit of grace, and trample on the precious blood of Christ which was shed for their redemption.

Note 8: page 220— these words are based upon the prophecy of REV. 13 and 14. The people with whom the author stands connected have taught for years that all classes except "the little flock" will unite to exalt the Sunday and enforce it upon all by stringent laws. It may assist the reader in understanding the points in the latter part of chapter 30 to notice the facts of the prophecy on which this idea is based.

1. The beast of REV. 13:1-10 is understood to refer to the papal power. This *has been* the general opinion of Protestants.

2. "The sea" out of which this beast arose is the same as "the waters" of REV. 17:15, explained to be "peoples, and multi-

tudes, and nations, and tongues." The papacy was upheld by many nations.

3. This beast has the characteristics of the four beasts of DAN. 7, which represent the four empires of Babylon, Persia, Greece, and Rome. It is the inheritor of the power held by these four empires successively.

4. The beast with two horns, REV. 13:11-17, is in a different locality, "coming up out of the earth;" not by the conquest of nations and peoples, but growing as a plant, out of the earth. This represents the United States, a locality outside of the dominion of "all the world," as known to the ancients.

5. This beast has two horns, the civil and the ecclesiastical. That a church is represented by a horn is proved in Dan. 7, the "little horn" representing the Roman Church, even before it was possessed of civil power. So also in REV. 13. The dragon (pagan Rome) gave the beast (the church) his power (civil power), and seat (city of Rome), and great authority.

6. The two-horned beast appears in two phases,— with the gentleness of a lamb and the fierceness of the dragon. This has, to some extent, already been shown, in the inconsistency of sending forth to the world the doctrine of the equality of all men in respect to natural rights,— the right of life, liberty, and the pursuit of happiness,— and upholding by law all the evils of American slavery. Also, by professing to grant the privilege to all to worship God according to the dictates of their own consciences, and then persecuting the Baptists and Quakers for following their conscientious convictions. But this will be shown more fully in the future, when Congress shall be called upon to make laws concerning religion.

7. The identity of the "two-horned beast" is further shown by its wonder working; by its deceiving "them that dwell on the earth by those miracles which he had power to do in the sight of the beast." REV. 13:14. Spiritualism arose in the United States, and has gone to all the world by means of American mediums.

8. This beast causes *both* "the earth and them which dwell therein to worship the first beast." This can be easily referred to laws compelling the observance of the Sunday instead of the Sabbath of the Lord,— the seventh day. The Sunday-Sabbath institution is traced directly to the Romish church, which, indeed, claims the honor of originating it; and no one has been able to dispute this claim. The Sabbath of Jehovah commemorates the creation of the heavens and the earth, and the commandment for its observance was given that the earth and its inhabitants might glorify the creator. The

law which compels the observance of the Sunday-Sabbath annuls the commandment of God, and the earth and them that dwell therein are caused to do homage to the power which originated it, by resting thereon. Protestants have ascribed various institutions to the papacy, and applied this prophecy to them; but in none is the earth, in distinction from those who dwell upon the earth, caused to worship that power, except in the Sunday rest enforced upon all the land.

9. And this sufficiently shows that it is no mere assumption to say that Catholics and Protestants will unite in enforcing the Sunday. Catholics honor it as the evidence of their authority to "institute festivals of precept, and to command them under sin," and Protestants are making most strenuous efforts for its universal enforcement. It is a well-known fact that most of the Protestant denominations are greatly modifying their opposition to the Catholic Church, and united action of the two bodies in favor of the Sunday is by no means improbable. But a few years ago this view was taught on the strength of the prophecy alone. Now we *see* in passing events strong indications of its fulfillment. The special object of the "National Reform Association" is to procure a religious amendment to the national constitution that the Sunday may be rescued from desecration and universally enforced.

10. This beast not only compels the earth and its inhabitants to worship the first beast, as above noted, but it causes them that dwell upon the earth to make an image to the first beast. This can be done only by a union of church and state, or by so subordinating the civil to the ecclesiastical power that the state will be compelled to enforce the tenants and requirements of the church. A religious amendment to the constitution of the United States would speedily insure this result.

11. This exposition of the prophecy is confirmed by the message from the Lord found in REV. 14:9-12, which is based altogether on the facts of REV. 13:11-17, and which condemns in the very strongest terms the action of this beast and the worship which it enforces; it also calls to keeping the commandments of God and the faith of Jesus, and one of these commandments enforces the Sabbath of the Lord,— the seventh day. Therefore the contrast in the facts and in the message which refers to the facts, is between the Sabbath of the Lord and an opposing Sabbath, namely, the Sunday.

This is a very brief statement of the facts which justify the expressions of the author on pages 220,221.

Note 9: page 241— the word 'seal' is used in the scriptures in various senses, even as in common life. The definition given by Webster, the most comprehensive, is as follows: "that which confirms, ratifies, or makes stable; assurance; that which authenticates; that which secures, makes reliable, or stable." The terms "mark" and "sign," also given by him, are used in the scriptures as synonymous with seal, as in ROM. 4:11.

In the covenant with Noah it is used in the sense of assurance, or evidence of stability. The bow in the cloud was given as a sign or token that God would not again destroy the earth by a flood. GEN. 9:13. In the covenant with Abraham, circumcision was the token or sign. This ratified, or made sure; for they who had not this token were cut off. GEN. 17:11,14. This sign or token was an institution, a rite. Gesenius gives "a memorial" as one definition of the word found in the original of these texts. But a memorial, in the sense of a reminder, or a remembrancer, is a token or sign.

In EXE. 31:17 and EZE. 20:12,20, the Sabbath of the Lord is called a sign. It is a memorial of the Creator's work, and so a sign of His power and Godhead. ROM. 1:20. This is also *an institution* as was circumcision; but there was this distinction: circumcision was a sign *in the flesh,* while the Sabbath was a sign *in the mind.* "Hallow my Sabbaths; and they shall be a sign between me and you, *that ye may know* that I am the Lord your God" EXE. 20:20.

In EXE. 9:4 the word used in the original is translated mark. Gesenius says, "*a mark, sign.*" The *septuagint* gives the same word in this text that is given in the Greek of ROM. 4:11, rendered "sign." Thus the words token, sign, mark, and seal are applied to the same things, or used as of like signification, in the scriptures.

In EXE. 9:4 and REV. 7:2,3, the mark or sign is said to be placed *in the foreheads* of the servants of God. Both these scriptures refer to a time when utter destruction is coming on the ungodly. The seal is placed upon God's people as a safeguard to preserve them from the evil impending. But "the forehead" is evidently used as a figure, to denote the intellect or mind, as "the heart" is used to denote the disposition or affections. To mark or seal in the forehead is the same as to "write in the mind." HEB. 10:16.

The Sabbath is the sign of God; it is the seal of his law. ISA. 8:16. It is the token of his authority and power. It is a sign whereby *we may know* that he is God, and therefore it is appropriately said to be placed *in the forehead.* The worshipers of the beast (REV. 13) are said to receive his mark in their foreheads or in their hands. As the forehead represents the intellect, the hand represents power, as PS. 89:48, "shall He deliver his soul from the hand of the grave?" Compulsory worship is not acceptable to God; his servants are sealed only in their foreheads. But it is acceptable to wicked powers; it has always been craved by the Romish hierarchy. See note 8 for proof on the nature of this mark. The sign or seal of God is His Sabbath, and the seal or mark of the beast is in direct opposition to it; it is a counterfeit Sabbath on the "day of the sun." In the message of the third angel (REV. 14:9-12) they who do not receive the mark of the beast keep the commandments of God, and the Sabbath is in the fourth precept; they keep the Sabbath of the Lord; they have His sign or seal. The importance of this sign is shown in this, that the fourth commandment is the only one in the law which distinguishes the creator from false gods. Compare JER. 10:10-12; ACTS 17:23,24; REV. 14;6,7; etc. and it is that part of His law for keeping which His people will suffer persecution. But when the wrath of God comes upon the persecutors who are found enforcing the sign or mark of the beast, then they will realize the importance of the Sabbath,— the seal of the living God. They who turn away from that which the Lord spoke when His voice shook the earth, will confess their fatal error when His voice shall shake the heavens and the earth. HEB. 12:25,26: JOEL 3:9-16, and others. See also page 256 of this book.

The Bible
Made Plain

**A Series of Short Bible Studies
for Personal, Family and Group
Study Based on the Fundamental
Truths of the Word of God.**

The Bible Made Plain

Contents

Chapter 1

The Inspiration of The Bible

1. How were the Scriptures given?

"All Scripture is given *by inspiration of God.*" 2 Tim. 3:16.

2. By whom were the men directed who thus spoke for God?

"For prophecy came not in old time by the will of man: but holy men of God spake as they were moved *by the Holy Ghost.*" 2 Peter 1:21.

3. Who therefore did the speaking through these men?

"*God…* at sundry times and in divers manners spake in time past unto the fathers by the prophets." Heb. 1:1.

4. For what purpose were the Scriptures written?

"Whatsoever things were written aforetime were written *for our learning,* that we through patience and comfort of the Scriptures might have hope." Rom. 15:4.

5. For what is all Scripture profitable?

"All Scripture is given by inspiration of God, and is profitable *for doctrine, for reproof, for correction, for instruction in righteousness.*" 2 Tim. 3:16.

6. What was God's design in thus giving the Scriptures?

"*That the man of God may be perfect, thoroughly furnished unto all good works.*" Verse 17.

7. What is the character of God's word?

"Sanctify them through Thy truth: *Thy word is truth.*" John 17:17.

8. What test should therefore be applied to every professed teacher of truth?

"*To the law and to the testimony*: if they speak not according to this word, it is because there is no light in them." Isa. 8:20.

9. What does God design that His word shall be to us in this world of darkness, sin, and death?

"Thy word is *a lamp* unto my feet, and *a light* unto my path." Ps. 119:105.

10. How long will the word of God endure?

"*The word of our God shall stand forever.*" Isa. 40:8. See Matt. 24:35.

11. Of whom did Christ say the Scriptures testify?

"Search the Scriptures; for in them ye think ye have eternal life: and *they are they which testify of Me.*" John 5:39.

12. What is the nature of the word of God?

"The word of God is *quick, and powerful,* and *sharper than any two-edged sword,* ...and is *a discerner of the thoughts and intents of the heart.*" Heb. 4:12.

13. What did Christ declare His words to be?

"The words that I speak unto you, they are *spirit,* and they are *life.*" John 6:63.

14. What name is applied to Jesus as the revelation in the flesh of the thought of God?

"In the beginning was *the Word,* and the Word was with God, and the Word was God." "The Word was made flesh, and dwelt among us." John 1:1, 14.

15. What was in the Word?

"In Him was *life.*" John 1:4.

Chapter 2

The Origin of Evil

1. What is the character of God?

"Art Thou not from everlasting, O Lord my God, mine Holy One?… *Thou art of purer eyes than to behold evil, and canst not look on iniquity.*" Hab. 1:12, 13.

2. With what kind of moral nature did God endow man when He created him?

"*So God created man in His own image*, in the image of God created He him." Gen. 1:27. "*God hath made man upright.*" Eccl. 7:29.

3. What are we told that God saw when He looked upon His finished work, including man?

"*God saw everything that He had made, and, behold, it was very good.*" Gen. 1:31.

4. What did God create besides the earth and man upon it?

"By Him were *all things* created, that are in heaven, and that are in earth, visible and invisible… all things were created by Him, and for Him." Col. 1:16.

5. How did man, when created, compare with the angels?

"*Thou hast made him a little lower than the angels.*" Ps. 8:5.

6. Do we now find the human race upon the same moral plane upon which the Creator originally placed it?

"*All have sinned*, and come short of the glory of God." "*There is none that doeth good, no, not one.*" Rom. 3:23, 12.

7. What is said of some of the angels in regard to sin?

"*God spared not the angels that sinned.*" 2 Peter 2:4.

"The angels which kept not their first estate, but left their own habitation, He hath reserved in everlasting chains under darkness unto the judgment of the great day." Jude 6.

8. What is sin?

"*Sin is the transgression of the law.*" 1 John 3:4.

9. As briefly stated by the Saviour, what does the divine law require?

"Jesus' said unto him, Thou shalt *love the Lord* thy God with all thy heart, and with all thy soul, and with all thy mind. This is the first and great commandment. And the second is like unto it, Thou shalt *love thy neighbor as thyself.*" Matt. 22:37–39.

10. What prohibition was laid upon man in the Garden of Eden?

"Of every tree of the garden thou mayest freely eat: but of *the tree of the knowledge of good and evil, thou shalt not eat of it*: for in the day that thou eatest thereof thou shalt surely die." Gen. 2:16, 17.

11. Since man was created upright in the beginning, how was he led into sin?

"Now the serpent was more subtle than any beast of the field which the Lord God had made... and *the serpent said unto the woman, Ye shall not surely die:* for God doth know that in the day ye eat thereof, then your eyes shall be opened, and ye shall be as gods, knowing good and evil. And when the woman saw that the tree was good for food, and that it was pleasant to the eyes, and a tree to be desired to make one wise, she took of the fruit thereof, and did eat, and gave also, unto her husband with her; and he did eat." Gen. 3:1, 4–6.

12. Who was the real serpent who tempted our first parents?

"The dragon, that old serpent, which is the Devil, and Satan." Rev. 20:2.

13. With whom and under what circumstances did sin originate?

"How art thou fallen from heaven, *O Lucifer*, son of the morning!... For thou hast said in thine heart, I will ascend into, heaven, I will exalt my throne above the stars of God:... I will be like the Most High." Isa. 14:12–14.

NOTE— Lucifer was the angel name of the great leader in rebellion in heaven. After his fall, he was called Satan, a name which Cruden's Concordance says "signifies an adversary, an enemy, an accuser."

14. What do the Scriptures say of Satan before his fall? What was the cause of his fall?

"Thou art the *anointed cherub that covereth;* and I have set thee so... Thou wast perfect in thy ways from the day that thou wast created, till iniquity was found in thee... *Thine heart was lifted up because of thy beauty.*" Eze. 28:14–17.

NOTE— Pride, envy, and covetousness filled Satan's heart before he committed any outward, overt act of rebellion, and these were sins. "All unrighteousness is sin," the apostle says. 1 John 5:17.

15. To what did Satan's rebellion lead?

"There was *war in heaven*... And the great dragon was cast out...into the earth, and his angels were cast out with him." Rev. 12:7–9.

16. What kind of service only is acceptable to God?

"Choose you this day whom ye will serve." Joshua 24:15. See John 3:16.

NOTE— God desires and accepts only willing service, service inspired by love. There is not and never could be any moral responsibility without freedom of the will. This being true, it follows that God is not responsible either for Lucifer's rebellion in heaven or for man's sin upon earth. "I the Lord speak righteousness, I declare things that are right." Isa. 45:19.

Chapter 3

The Plan of Salvation

1. What provision did infinite love and foreknowledge make for man's redemption, even before the fall?

"Behold the Lamb of God," "the Lamb *slain from the foundation of the world.*" John 1:29; Rev. 13:8.

"I will put enmity between thee and the woman, and between thy seed and her seed; it shall bruise thy head, and thou shalt bruise His heel." Gen. 3:15.

NOTE— We learn from Isaiah 45:18 that the divine purpose in creating this world was that it might be inhabited by a race of beings loyal to their Creator. This plan involved everything necessary to its success. Therefore we might know, even if we had not been told, that when, — in the council between the Father and the Son (Gen. 1:26), it was decided to create man, the great propitiatory offering was provided, the sacrifice necessary for his redemption was made.

2. What moved the Father to make this sacrifice in behalf of fallen humanity?

"God so loved the world, that He gave His only-begotten Son, that whosoever believeth in Him should not perish, but have everlasting life." John 3:16.

3. What was the Son's attitude toward the plan for man's redemption?

"There is one God, and one Mediator between God and men, the man Christ Jesus; *who gave Himself a ransom for all,* to be testified in due time." 1 Tim. 2:5, 6.

4. How do we know that the Father and the Son were associated in the creation of man?

"God said, Let *us* make man in *our* image, after *our* likeness." Gen. 1:26. "Whereof I was made a minister, ...to make all men see what is the fellowship of the mystery, which from the beginning of the world hath been hid in God, who *created all things by Jesus Christ.*" Eph. 3:7–9.

5. What beautiful prophetic scripture shows that the Father and the Son are just as closely associated in the work of redemption as in that of creation?

"Behold the man whose name is The BRANCH; and He shall grow up out of His place, and He shall build the temple of the Lord:....and shall sit and rule upon His [the Lord's] throne; and He shall be a priest upon His throne: and *the counsel of peace shall be between them both.*" Zech. 6:12, 13.

6. What is the purpose of the plan of redemption?,

"She shall bring forth a Son, and thou shalt call His name JESUS: for *He shall save His people from their sins.*" Matt. 1:21.

7. What does it mean to be saved from sin?

"If we walk in the light, as He is in the light, we have fellowship one with another, and the blood of Jesus Christ His Son cleanseth us from all sin." "If we confess our sins, He is faithful and just to forgive us our sins, and to cleanse us from all unrighteousness." 1 John 1:7, 9.

8. What besides present salvation from the dominion of sin is included in redemption?

"This is the will of Him that sent Me, that everyone which seeth the Son, and believeth on Him, may have everlasting life: *and I will raise him up at the last day.*" John 6:40. See John 14:3.

9. Was this promise made to the Jews alone?

"Ye have heard of the dispensation of the grace of God which is given me to you-ward:…that the Gentiles should be fellow heirs, and of the same body, and *partakers of His promise in Christ by the gospel.*" Eph.3:2, 6.

10. What further assurance is given that believing Gentiles will share in the Abrahamic promise?

"Now to Abraham and his seed were the promises made. He saith not, And to seeds, as of many; but as of one, And to thy seed, which is Christ." "And if ye be Christ's, *then are ye Abraham's seed,* and heirs according to the promise." Gal. 3:16, 29.

11. To whom does our Saviour Himself say this inheritance will be given?

"*Blessed are the meek: for they shall inherit the earth.*" Matt. 5:5.

Chapter 4

Conversion and Baptism

1. How did Jesus emphasize the necessity of conversion?

"Verily I say unto you, *Except ye be converted,* and become as little children, *ye shall not enter into the kingdom of heaven.*" Matt. 18:3.

2. In what other statement did He teach the same truth?

"Verily, verily, I say unto thee, *Except a man be born again,* he cannot see the kingdom of God." John 3:3.

3. How did He further explain the new birth?

"Jesus answered, Verily, verily, I say unto thee, *Except a man be born of water and of the Spirit,* he cannot enter into the kingdom of God." Verse 5.

4. With what comparison did He illustrate the subject?

"The *wind* bloweth where it listeth, and thou hearest the sound thereof, but canst not tell whence it cometh, and whither it goeth: *so is, everyone that is born of the Spirit.*" Verse 8.

5. To whom are sinners brought by conversion?

"Create in me a clean heart, O God; and renew a right spirit within me." "Then will I teach transgressors Thy ways; and sinners shall be *converted unto Thee.*" Ps. 51: 10, 13.

6. What takes place when one is converted to Christ?

"Therefore if any man be in Christ, he is a new creature: the old things are passed away; behold, all things are become new." 2 Cor. 5:17. See Acts 9:1–22; 22:1–21; 26:1–23.

7. Through what was the original creation wrought?

"*By the word of the Lord* were the heavens made; and all the host of them by the breath of His mouth." Ps. 33:6.

8. Through what instrumentality is conversion wrought?

"Being born again, not of corruptible seed, but of incorruptible, *by the word of God,* which liveth and abideth forever." 1 Peter 1:23.

9. What change is wrought by beholding Jesus?

"We all, with open face beholding as in a glass the glory of the Lord, are *changed into the same image* from glory to glory, even as by the Spirit of the Lord." 2 Cor. 3:18.

10. What are the evidences that one has been born of God?

"If ye know that He is righteous, ye know that *everyone that doeth righteousness is born of Him.*" "Beloved, let us love one another: for love is of God; and *everyone that loveth is born of God,* and knoweth God." 1 John 2:29; 4:7.

11. What is true of everyone who believes in Jesus?

"Whosoever believeth that Jesus is the Christ is *born of God.*" 1 John 5:1.

12. What do those born of God not do?

"We know that *whosoever is born of God sinneth not;* but he that is begotten of God keepeth himself, and that wicked one toucheth him not." Verse 18.

13. What indwelling power keeps such from sinning?

"Whosoever is born of God doth not commit sin; for *His seed remaineth in him:* and he cannot sin, because he is born of God." 1 John 3:9. See 1 John 5:4; Gen. 39:9.

14. What will be the experience of those born of the Spirit?

"There is therefore — now *no condemnation* to them which are in Christ Jesus, who walk not after the flesh, but after the Spirit." Rom. 8:1.

15. In his sermon on the day of Pentecost, what did Peter say should follow repentance?

"*Repent, and be baptized* every one of you in the name of Jesus Christ for the remission of sins, and ye shall receive the gift of the Holy Ghost." Acts 2:38.

16. Into what particular experience of Christ's do we especially enter through true baptism?

"Know ye not, that so many of us as were baptized into Jesus Christ were *baptized into His death?*" Rom. 6:3.

NOTE— Baptism is not only a gospel ordinance commemorating the death, burial, and resurrection of Christ, but it is a profession of a complete change of life, a surrender or abandonment of the old life of sin, and the acceptance of a new life in and through Christ, to be lived by Him in the believer as expressed by the apostle in Galatians 2:20: "I am crucified with Christ: nevertheless I live; yet not I, but Christ liveth in me: and the life which I now live in the flesh I live by the faith of the Son of God, who loved me and gave Himself for me."

17. How is gospel baptism described?

"Therefore we are buried with Him by baptism into death: that like as Christ was raised up from the dead by the glory of the Father, even so we also should walk in newness of life." Rom. 6:4.

18. What would we understand from Romans 6:4, 5 to be the meaning of "baptize" as used in the Sacred Scriptures?

To immerse.

NOTE— It is plain that the apostle had in mind only immersion of the whole body in water. Indeed, that is just what the Greek word baptizo means. That is the reason the King James Version does not translate the word at all, but simply gives it an English form. Homer, writing eight hundred years before

Christ, tells how the smiths would bapto red-hot steel in water to temper it. Herodotus, nearly five centuries before Christ, tells us that the dyer would bapto fabrics in the dye to color them, and that potters were wont to bapto earthern vessels in a liquid preparation for the purpose of glazing them. If the word had ever meant to sprinkle or pour, would not the translators of the Authorized, or common version of our English Scriptures, have so rendered it, instead of bringing the original word over into the English untranslated? They certainly would.

19. Who alone are fit subjects for baptism?

"He that believeth and is baptized shall be saved." Mark 16:16.

Chapter 5

The Great Image of Daniel 2

1. What occurred in the second year of the reign of Nebuchadnezzar, king of Babylon?

"In the second year of the reign of Nebuchadnezzar *Nebuchadnezzar dreamed dreams,* wherewith his spirit was troubled,and his sleep brake from him." Dan.2:1.

2. What did he say to his wise men?

"The king said unto them, *I have dreamed a dream, and my spirit was troubled to know the dream."* Dan. 2:3.

3. After the wise men had confessed their inability to do what the king required, who offered to interpret the dream?

"Then *Daniel* went in, and desired of the king that he would give him time, and that he would show the king the interpretation." Verse 16.

4. After Daniel and his fellows had sought God earnestly, how were the dream and its interpretation revealed to Daniel?

"Then was the secret revealed unto Daniel *in a night vision.* Then Daniel blessed the God of heaven." Verse 19.

5. When brought before the king, what did Daniel say ?

"Daniel answered in the presence of the king, and said, The secret which the king hath demanded cannot the wise men, the astrologers, the magicians, the soothsayers, shew unto the king; but *there is a God in heaven that revealeth secrets,* and maketh known to the king Nebuchadnezzar what shall be in the latter days." Verses 27, 28.

6. What did Daniel say the king had seen in his dream?

"Thy dream, and the visions of thy head upon thy bed, are these:... Thou, O king, sawest, and behold *a great image.* This great image, whose brightness was excellent, stood before thee; and the form thereof was terrible." Verses 28, 31.

7. Of what were the different parts of the image composed?

"This image's head was of fine *gold,* his breast and his arms of *silver,* his belly and his thighs of *brass,* his legs of *iron,* his feet *part of iron and part of clay."* Verses 32, 33.

8. What became of the image?

"Thou sawest till that *a stone was* cut out without hands, which smote the image upon his feet that were of iron and clay, and brake them to pieces. Then was the iron, the clay, the brass, the silver, and the gold, broken to pieces together, and *became like the chaff of the summer threshing floors; and the wind carried them away,* that no place was found for them: and the stone that smote the image became a great mountain, and filled the whole earth." Verses 34, 35.

9. With what words did Daniel begin the interpretation of the dream?

"Thou, O king, art a king of kings: for the God of heaven hath given thee a kingdom, power, and strength, and glory. And whereso-ever the children of men dwell, the beasts of the field and the fowls of the heaven hath He given into thine hand, and hath made thee ruler over them all. *Thou art this head of gold." Verses 37, 38.*

10. What was to be the nature of the next kingdom after Babylon?

"After thee shall arise another kingdom *inferior to thee."* Verse 39, first part.

11. Who was the last Babylonian king?

"In that night was *Belshazzar* the king of the Chaldeans slain. And Darius the Median took the kingdom, being about threescore and two years old." Dan. 5:30,31. See also verses 1, 2.

12. To whom was Belshazzar's kingdom given?

"Thy kingdom is divided, and given to the *Medes and Persians."* Dan. 5:28.

13. By what was the Medo-Persian Empire represented in the great image?

By the breast and arms of silver. Dan. 2:32.

14. By what was Grecia, the kingdom succeeding Medo-Persia, represented in the image?

"His belly and his thighs of *brass."* "Another *third kingdom of brass,* which shall bear rule over all the earth." Verses 32, 39.

15. What was said of the fourth kingdom?

"The fourth kingdom *shall be strong as iron:* forasmuch as iron breaketh in pieces and subdueth all things: and as iron that breaketh all these, *shall it break in pieces and bruise."* Verse 40.

16. What were the four kingdoms?

Babylon, Medo-Persia, Grecia, and Rome.

17. What was indicated by the mixture of clay and iron in the feet and toes of the image?

"Whereas thou sawest the feet and toes, part of potters' clay, and part of iron, *the kingdom shall be divided."* Verse 41.

18. In what prophetic language was the varying strength of the ten kingdoms of the divided empire indicated

"As the toes of the feet were *part of iron, and part of clay,* so the kingdom shall be *partly strong, and partly broken* [margin, "brittle"]." Verse 42.

19. Were any efforts to be made to reunite the parts of the divided Roman Empire?

"Whereas thou sawest iron mixed with miry clay, *they shall mingle themselves with the seed of men:* but they shall not cleave one to another, even as iron is not mixed with clay." Verse 43.

NOTE— Charlemagne, Charles V, Louis XIV, Napoleon, and others have tried to reunite the broken fragments of the Roman Empire, but failed. By marriage and intermarriage, ties have been formed with a view to strengthening and cementing together the parts of the divided kingdom; but none have succeeded.

20. What is to take place in the days of these kingdoms of divided Rome?

"In the days of these kings shall *the God of heaven set up a kingdom, which shall never be destroyed:* ...but it shall break in pieces and consume all these kingdoms, and it shall stand for ever." Verse 44.

NOTE— This verse foretells the establishment of another universal kingdom, the kingdom of God. This kingdom is to overthrow and supplant all existing earthly kingdoms, and is to stand forever. The time for the setting up of this kingdom was to be "in the days of these kings." This cannot refer to the four preceding empires, or kingdoms, for they were not contemporaneous, but successive; neither can it refer to an establishment of the kingdom at Christ's first advent, for the ten kingdoms which arose out of the ruins of the Roman Empire were not then in existence. The establishment of the kingdom of God could not, therefore, have occurred before 476 A.D.; and as it has not been set up since that time, it must be still in the future.

21. For what have we been taught to pray?

"*Thy kingdom come.* Thy will be done in earth, as it is in heaven." Matt. 6:10.

22. What event is closely associated with the establishment of God's everlasting kingdom?

"I charge thee therefore before God, and the Lord Jesus Christ, who shall judge the quick and the dead at *His appearing* and His kingdom." 2 Tim. 4:1.

23. With what prayer do the Scriptures close?

"He which testifieth these things saith, Surely I come quickly. Amen. *Even so, come, Lord Jesus.*" Rev. 22:20.

Chapter 6

The Four Beasts of Daniel 7

1. What experience came to the prophet Daniel in the first year of Belshazzar?

"Daniel had *a dream and visions* of his head upon his bed: then he wrote the dream, and told the sum of the matters." Dan. 7:1.

2. What did the prophet see in this vision?

"Behold, *the four winds of the heaven strove upon the great sea.*" Verse 2.

3. What was the result of this strife?

"*Four great beasts came up from the sea,* diverse one from another." Verse 3.

4. What did these four beasts represent?

"These great beasts, which are four, are *four kings, which shall arise out of the earth.*" Verse 17.

NOTE— The word "kings" here, as in Daniel 2:44, denotes kingdoms, as explained in verses 23 and 24 of the seventh chapter, the two words being used interchangeably in this prophecy.

5. What did Daniel ask of one of the heavenly attendants who stood by him in his dream?

"I came near unto one of them that stood by, *and asked him the truth of all this.* So he told me, and made me know the interpretation of the things." Verse 16.

6. In prophecy, what is represented by winds?

Strife, war, commotion. See Jer. 25:31–33; 49:36, 37.

NOTE— That winds denote strife and war is evident from the vision itself. As a result of the striving of the winds, kingdoms rise and fall.

7. What, in prophecy, is symbolized by waters?

"The waters...are *peoples,* and *multitudes,* and *nations,* and *tongues.*" Rev. 17:15

8. What was the first beast like?

"*The first was like a lion,* and had eagle's wings: I beheld till the wings thereof were plucked, and it was lifted up from the earth, and made stand upon the feet as a man, and a man's heart was given to it." Dan. 7:4.

NOTE— The lion represented Babylon. The eagle's wings doubtless denote the rapidity with which Babylon extended its conquests, under Nebuchadnezzar, who reigned from 604 to 561 B.C.

9. By what was the second kingdom symbolized?

"Behold another beast, *a second, like to a bear,* and it raised up itself on one side, and it had three ribs in the mouth of it between the teeth of it: and they said thus unto it, Arise, devour much flesh." Verse 5.

NOTE— "This was the *Medo-Persian Empire,*" the successor of Babylon. "The Medes and Persians are compared to a bear on account of their *cruelty* and *thirst after blood,* a bear being a most voracious and cruel animal."—*Adam Clarke, on Daniel 7:5.*

10. By what was the third universal empire symbolized?

"After this I beheld, and lo another, *like a leopard,* which had upon the back of it four wings of a fowl; the beast had also four heads; and dominion was given to it." Verse 6.

NOTE— If the wings of an eagle on the back of a lion denoted rapidity of movement in the Babylonian, or Assyrian, Empire (see Hab. 1:6–8), four wings on the leopard must denote unparalleled speed of movement in the Grecian Empire, which followed the Medo-Persian Kingdom. This we find to be historically true. "The beast also had four heads." The Grecian Empire maintained its unity but a short time after the death of Alexander, which occurred in 323 B.C. Within twenty-two years after the close of his brilliant career, or by 301 B.C., the. empire was divided among his four leading generals. Cassander took Macedonia and Greece in the west; Lysimachus had Thrace and the parts of Asia on the Hellespont and Bosporus in the north; Ptolemy received Egypt, Lydia, Arabia, Palestine, and Coele-Syria in the south; and Seleucus had all the rest of Alexander's dominions in the east.

11. How was the fourth kingdom represented?

"After this I saw in the night visions, and behold *a fourth beast, dreadful and terrible, and strong exceedingly; and it had great iron teeth:* it devoured and brake in pieces, and stamped the residue with the feet of it: and it was diverse from all the beasts that were before it; *and it had ten horns."* Verse 7.

NOTE— "This is allowed on all hands to be the Roman Empire. It was *dreadful, terrible, and exceeding strong…* and became in effect, what the Roman writers delight to call it, the *empire of the whole world."*—*Adam Clarke on Daniel 7:7.*

The final overthrow of the Greeks by the Romans was at the battle of Pydna, in 168 B.C.

12. What was the fourth beast declared to be?

"Thus he said, *The fourth beast shall be the fourth kingdom upon earth,* which shall be diverse from all kingdoms, and shall devour the whole earth, and shall tread it down, and break it in pieces." Verse 23.

13. What was denoted by the ten horns on the head of the fourth beast?

"The ten horns out of this kingdom are *ten kings that shall arise."* Verse 24.

NOTE— The Roman Empire was broken up into ten kingdoms between the years 351 and 476 A.D.

"The historian Machiavelli, without the slightest reference to this prophecy, gives the following list of the nations which occupied the territory of the Western Empire at the time of the fall of Romulus Augustulus [476 A.D.], the last emperor of Rome: The Lombards, the Franks, the Burgundians, the Ostrogoths, the Visigoths, the Vandals, the, Heruli, the Sueves, the Huns, and the Saxons— ten in all."— *"The Divine Program of the World's History," H. Grattan Guinness, p. 318.*

"Amid unceasing and almost countless fluctuations, the kingdoms of modern Europe, have from their birth to the present day averaged ten in number. They have never since the breakup of old Rome been united into one single empire; they have never formed *one whole* even like the, United States. No scheme of proud ambition seeking to reunite the broken fragments has ever succeeded; when such have arisen, they have been invariably dashed to pieces."— *Id., pp. 220, 221.*

14. What change took place in these horns?

"I considered the horns, and, behold, *there came up among them another little horn, before whom there were three of the first horns plucked up by the roots:* and, behold, in this horn were eyes like the eyes of man, and a mouth speaking great things." Verse 8.

15. What inquiry on the part of Daniel shows that the fourth beast, and especially the little horn, constitutes the leading feature of this vision?

"Then *I would know the truth of the fourth beast,* which was diverse from all the others, exceeding dreadful, whose teeth were of iron, and his nails of brass; which devoured, brake in pieces, and stamped the residue with his feet; *and of the ten horns* that were in his head, *and of the other which came up, and before whom three fell;* even of that horn that had eyes, and a mouth that spake very great things, whose look was more stout than his fellows." Verses 19, 20.

16. When was the little horn to arise?

"And another shall rise *after them.*" Verse 24.

NOTE— The ten horns, as already shown, arose when Rome, the fourth kingdom, was divided into ten kingdoms. This division was completed in 476 A.D. The little horn power was to arise "after them."

17. What was to be the character of the little horn?

"He shall be *diverse* from the first, and he shall *subdue three kings.*" Verse 24, last part.

NOTE— The power that arose in the Roman Empire after the fall of Rome in 476 A.D., that was entirely different from all the ten kingdoms into which Rome was divided (for it demanded and exercised spiritual power over the other kingdoms), and before whom three of the other kings fell, was the Papacy.

18. What attitude was the Papacy, represented by the little horn, to assume toward the Most High?

"He shall *speak great words against the Most High.*" Verse 25.

19. How does Paul, speaking of the "man of sin," describe this same power?

He "opposeth and exalteth himself above all that is called God, or that is worshiped; so that he as God sitteth in the temple of God, shewing himself that he is God." 2 Thess. 2:4.

NOTE— The following extracts from authoritative works, most of them by Roman Catholic writers, will indicate to what extent the Papacy has done this:

"All the names which in the Scriptures are attributed to Christ, by virtue of which it is established that He is over the church, all the same names are applied to the Pope."— *Bellarmine, "On the Authority of Councils," book 2, chap. 17, ed. 1619.*

"Thou art the shepherd, thou art the physician, thou art the director, thou art the husbandman; finally, thou art another God on earth."— *From the Oration of Christopher Marcellus, in the fourth session of the Fifth Lateran Council, 1512; quoted in Labbe and Cossart's, "History of the Councils," Vol. XIV, cot. 109, ed. 1672.*

"The Pope is the supreme judge of the law of the land. He is the vicegerent of Christ, who is not only a priest forever, but also King of kings and Lord of lords.'— *From the Civilta Cattolica, March 18, 1871; quoted in "Vatican Council," Leonard Woolsey Bacon, American Tract Society edition, p. 220.*

"Hence the Pope is crowned with a triple crown, as king of heaven, and of earth, and of the lower regions."— *"Prompta. Bibliotheca," Ferraris, Vol. VI, p. 26, art. "Papa?" (the Pope).*

20. How was the little horn to treat God's people?

He "shall *wear out the saints* of the Most High." Dan. 7:25.

NOTE— "The church has persecuted. Only a tyro in church history will deny that,... We have always defended the persecution of the Huguenots, and the Spanish Inquisition. When she thinks it good to use physical force, she will use it. ...But will the Catholic Church give bond that she will not persecute at all? Will she guarantee absolute freedom and equality of all churches and all faiths? The Catholic Church gives no bonds for her good behavior."—*Editorial in Western Watchman (Catholic), of St. Louis, Mo., Dec. 24, 1908.*

21. What else does the prophecy say the little horn would do?

"He shall *think to change the times and the law.*" Dan. 7:25, A. R. V.

NOTE— Although the ten commandments, the law of God, are found in the Roman Catholic copies of the Scriptures as they were originally given, yet the "faithful" are instructed from the catechisms of the church, and not directly from the Bible.

The second commandment, which forbids the making of and bowing down to images, is omitted in the Catholic catechisms in general use, and the tenth, which forbids coveting, is divided into two, while the fourth is made to apply to Sunday.

22. Until what time were the saints, times, and the law of the Most High to be given into the hands of the little horn?

"They shall be given into his hand *until a time and times and the dividing of time.*" Dan. 7:25, last clause.

23. In what other prophecy is this period mentioned?

"To the woman were given two wings of a great eagle, that she might fly into the wilderness, into her place, where she is nourished for *a time, and times, and half a time,* from the face of the serpent." Rev. 12:14. "And there was given unto him a mouth speaking great things and blasphemies; and power was given unto him to continue [margin, "to make war,"] *forty and two months.*" Rev. 13:5. See Rev. 11:2. "And the woman fled into the wilderness, where she hath a place prepared of God, that they should feed her there *a thousand two hundred and threescore days.*" Rev. 12:6.

24. In symbolic prophecy what length of time is represented by a day ?

"After the number of the days in which ye searched the land, even forty days, *each day for a year,* shall ye bear your iniquities, even forty years." Num. 14:34. See Eze. 4:6.

NOTE— A time in prophecy being the same as a year (Dan. 11:13, margin), three and one half times would be three and one half years, or forty-two months, or twelve hundred sixty days, since the calendar year of 360 days, or twelve months of thirty days each, is used in prophetic chronology. As each day represents a year, the period, the end of which was to mark the time limit of the supremacy of the little horn, or the Papacy, over the saints, times, and law, would be twelve hundred sixty years.

In 533 A.D. the emperor Justinian issued a decree styling the Bishop or Pope of Rome head over all the churches, to which he added, a few months later but the same year, the title, corrector of heretics. But it was not until the power of the Ostrogoths was broken, five years later, that these decrees became effective. It is therefore from 538 A.D. that we reckon the twelve hundred and sixty years of papal domination. This supremacy ended, then, in 1798, with the temporary overthrow of the papal government by the French under

General Berthier, who declared the Papacy abolished and carried the Pope a prisoner to France.

25. What will finally be done with the dominion exercised by the little horn?

"The judgment shall sit, and they shall *take away his dominion, to consume and to destroy it unto the end.*" Dan. 7:26.

26. To whom will the dominion finally be given?

"The kingdom and dominion, and the greatness of the kingdom under the whole heaven, shall be given *to the people of the saints of the Most High,* whose kingdom is *an everlasting kingdom,* and *all dominions* shall serve and obey Him." Verse 27.

Chapter 7

The 2300 Days of Daniel 8 and 9

1. What symbols were shown to Daniel the prophet, in vision, as described by him in Daniel 8:3, 5?

A ram with two horns, and a he-goat.

2. How did the prophet learn what these symbols represented ?

"I heard a man's voice between the banks of Ulai, which called, and said, *Gabriel, make this man to understand the vision.*" Dan. 8:16.

3. What did the angel Gabriel say was represented by the ram?

"The ram which thou sawest having two horns are the kings [or kingdoms] of *Media and Persia.*" Dan. 8:20.

4. What was represented by the rough goat?

"The rough goat is the king of *Grecia:* and the great horn that is between his eyes is *the first king.* Now that being broken, whereas four stood up for it, *four kingdoms shall stand up out of the nation,* but not in his power." Dan. 8:21, 22.

5. What did the little horn represent?

"In the latter time of their kingdom, when the transgressors are come to the full, *a king of fierce countenance, and understanding dark sentences,* shall stand up. And his power shall be mighty, but not by his own power: and he shall destroy wonderfully, and shall prosper, and practise, and shall destroy the mighty and the holy people. And through his policy also he shall cause craft to prosper in his hand; and he shall magnify himself in his heart, and by peace shall destroy many: he shall also stand up against the Prince of princes; but he shall be broken without hand." Dan. 8:23–25.

NOTE— Rome in both its pagan and papal forms here comes to view in the figure of the little horn, just as it is represented in chapter 2 by the legs of iron, and in chapter 7 by the fourth beast.

6. Did the angel at this time complete his explanation of the vision?

"*I Daniel fainted,* and was sick certain days; afterward I rose up, and did the king's business; and I was astonished at the vision, but none understood it." Dan. 8:27.

7. What portion of the vision remained unexplained?

"I heard one saint speaking, and another saint said unto that certain saint which spake, How long shall be the vision concerning the daily sacrifice, and the transgression of desolation, to give both the sanctuary and the host to be trodden under foot? And he said unto me, Unto two thousand and three hundred days; then shall the sanctuary be cleansed." Dan. 8:13, 14.

"UNTO 2300 DAYS"

THEN SHALL THE SANCTUARY BE CLEANSED." Dan. 8:14.

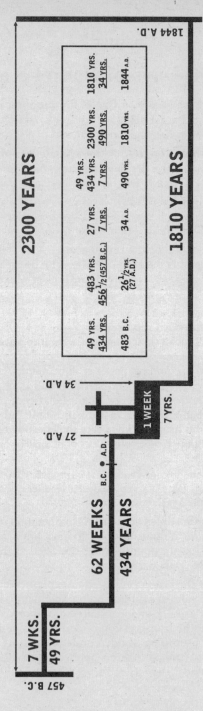

	49 YRS.	483 YRS.	27 YRS.	49 YRS. 434 YRS.	2300 YRS.	1810 YRS.
	49 YRS. 434 YRS.	456½ (457 B.C.)	7 YRS.	7 YRS.	490 YRS.	34 YRS.
	483 B.C.	26½ YRS. (27 A.D.)	34 A.D.	490 YRS.	1810 YRS.	1844 A.D.

2300 YEARS

1810 YEARS

7 WKS. 49 YRS. — 457 B.C.

62 WEEKS 434 YEARS — 27 A.D. — 34 A.D. — 1 WEEK 7 YRS.

1844 A.D.

The decree to restore and rebuild Jerusalem, following the Babylonian captivity, marked the beginning of the 2300-year period. That decree was given 457 B.C. Ezra 7:11–26; Dan. 9:25. The work of restoration continued for 49 years. This period was part of the 69 weeks (483 years) which were to reach to the Messiah, the Anointed One.

Christ was anointed with the Holy spirit in 27 A.D., at the time of His baptism. Matt. 3:13–17; Acts 10:38. In the midst of the seventieth week, in 31 A.D., Christ was crucified. Dan. 9:26, 27. Three and one-half years later, in 34 A.D., Stephen was stoned, and the disciples went everywhere preaching the word. Acts 7:59; 8:4. This closed the 70 weeks (490 years) allotted to the Jews.

The 70 weeks were cut off from the 2300 days. Since the 70 weeks reached to 34 A.D., the remaining 1810 years of the 2300-year period must reach to 1844, when the cleansing of the heavenly sanctuary, the hour of God's judgment, was to begin. Rev. 14:6, 7.

8. At a later time, while Daniel was praying, who came and talked with him?

"Yea, whiles I was speaking in prayer, even the man *Gabriel,* whom I had seen in the vision at the beginning, being caused to fly swiftly, touched me about the time of the evening oblation (religious offering)." Dan. 9:21.

9. What was the angel's mission?

"He informed me, and talked with me, and said, O Daniel, *I am now come forth to give thee skill and understanding.*" Dan. 9:22.

10. What did he tell Daniel to do?

"At the beginning of thy supplications the commandment came forth, and I am come to shew thee; for thou art greatly beloved: therefore *understand the matter, and consider the vision.*" Dan. 9:23.

NOTE— It was formerly supposed that the Belshazzar of the eighth of Daniel was the same as Nabonidus, known from secular history to have been the last king of Babylon. The work of archaeologists during the last half century has made it clear that he, was the son of Nabonidus, with whom he reigned jointly for more than two years. Therefore it was probably only a few months between the vision of the third year of Belshazzar (Dan. 8:1) and that of the first year of Darius. When the angel returned to complete his explanation, the prophet's mind would at once revert to the vision, the symbols of which had been explained, but not the time.

11. What part of the 2300 days did Gabriel say had been apportioned to the Jews?

"*Seventy weeks* are determined upon thy people and upon thy holy city, to finish the transgression, and to make an end of sins, and to make reconciliation for iniquity and to bring in everlasting righteousness, and to seal up the vision and prophecy, and to anoint the most Holy." Dan. 9:24.

NOTE— The original Hebrew word here translated "determined" means "cut off." Gesenius, in his Hebrew Lexicon, thus defines it: "Properly, to cut off; topically to divide; and so to determine or decree." Whiting's translation very properly renders the text: "Seventy weeks have been cut off upon thy people and upon thy holy city."

12. In symbolic prophecy what is represented by a day?

"After the number of the days in which ye searched the land, even forty days, *each day for a year,* shall ye bear your iniquities, even forty years." Num. 14:34.

13. How long a period is thus covered by the seventy weeks?

Four hundred ninety years.

NOTE— Seventy weeks are equal to 490 symbolic days. Counting each day for a year would give 490 literal years. Likewise, using a day for a year, 2300 days would be 2300 literal years.

14. When did the long period of 2300 years begin?

"Know therefore and understand, that from *the going forth of the commandment to restore and to build Jerusalem* unto the Messiah the Prince shall be seven weeks, and threescore and two weeks: the street shall be built again, and the wall, even in troublous times." Dan. 9:25.

15. When was the commandment given to restore and to build Jerusalem?

In 457 B.C. See Ezra 7:11–26.

NOTE— As the angel predicted, the city was built in troublous times, for the nearby nations were bent upon hindering the restoration of the city. As a result the Jews were compelled to work and fight by turns. See Josephus.

16. How are the seventy weeks divided?

"Know therefore and understand, that from the going forth of the commandment to restore and to build Jerusalem unto the Messiah the Prince shall be *seven weeks*, and *threescore and two weeks*." Dan. 9:25.

17. How long a time was consumed in restoring Jerusalem?

Exactly *forty-nine years,* or seven prophetic weeks.

18. How long a time would be measured from the decree for the restoring and rebuilding of Jerusalem to Messiah the Prince?

Exactly 483 years. See verse 25.

NOTE— Seven weeks added to sixty-two weeks give sixty-nine prophetic weeks, or 483 literal years.

19. What is the meaning of the word "Messiah"?

"We have found the Messiah, which is, being interpreted, *the Christ* [margin, "the Anointed"]." John 1:41.

NOTE— "Messiah" in Hebrew and "Christ" in Greek have the same meaning, namely, "The Anointed." The original Hebrew word is so rendered in the Revised Version.

20. With what was Christ anointed?

"*God anointed Jesus of Nazareth with the Holy Ghost and with power:* who went about doing good, and healing all that were oppressed of the devil; for God was with Him." Acts 10:38.

21. Where was He anointed?

"It came to pass in those days, that Jesus came from Nazareth of Galilee, and *was baptized of John in Jordan.*" Mark 1:9.

"When all the people were baptized, it came to pass, that Jesus also being baptized, and praying, the heaven was opened, and *the Holy Ghost descended in a bodily shape like a dove upon Him,* and a voice came from heaven, which said, Thou art My beloved Son; in Thee I am well pleased." Luke 3:21, 22.

22. In what year was this?

In 27 A.D. See International Standard Bible Encyclopedia, Vol. III, art. "Jesus Christ, Date of Baptism," p. 1628.

NOTE— Exactly 483 full years intervened between the seventh month of the year 457 B.C. and the seventh month of the year 27 A.D.

23. In what words did Jesus Himself call attention to the termination of this time period?

"After that John was put in prison, Jesus came into Galilee, preaching the gospel of the kingdom of God, and saying, The time is fulfilled, and the kingdom of God is at hand: repent ye, and believe the gospel." Mark 1:14, 15.

NOTE— It was impossible that these words of Jesus should have applied to another time period than this, for none other came to an end at that time.

24. What did the angel tell Daniel would take place in the midst of the seventieth week?

"He shall confirm the covenant with many for one week: and in the midst of the week He shall cause the sacrifice and the oblation to cease." Dan. 9:27.

25. What did all the sacrifices and offerings of the ancient Levitical system typify?

"Behold *the Lamb of God,* which taketh away the sin of the world." John 1:29.

26. After the sixty-nine weeks bad passed, what did the angel say would happen to Jesus the Messiah?

"After threescore and two weeks shall Messiah be *cut off,* but not for Himself." Dan. 9:26.

27. How long after His baptism was Jesus crucified?

Three and one-half years.

NOTE— That the time of Jesus' ministry was about one half of a prophetic week, or three and one-half years, is shown by the record of the Gospels that He attended only four Passovers. It should be remembered in this connection that, as is now known, Jesus was born four years before the beginning of our era. He was therefore thirty years of age at His baptism, as stated in Luke 3:23.

28. What significant event occurred in connection with the crucifixion of Christ, indicating that the sanctuary, where sacrifices and oblations were offered, was no longer holy?

"Behold, the veil of the temple was rent in twain from the top to the bottom; and the earth did quake, and the rocks rent." Matt. 27:51.

NOTE— This rending by unseen hands of the beautiful temple veil which separated the holy from the most holy place of the sanctuary, exposed the sacred apartment to the view of all, and showed that type had met antitype, that the true Lamb of God had died, thereby paying forever the penalty for the sins of mankind.

29. How did the Messiah confirm the covenant with many for one week?

"How shall we escape, if we neglect so great salvation; which at the first began to be spoken by the Lord, and was confirmed unto us by them that heard Him?" Heb. 2:3.

NOTE— By His own ministry for three and a half years, by His death upon the cross "in the midst of the week," and by the testimony of His disciples to the Jews for three and a half years more before turning to the Gentiles with the gospel, Christ the Messiah confirmed the covenant, or promise, to the Jews, according to the prophecy of Daniel 9:24, 27.

30. In 34 A.D., when the 490 years ended, what events took place indicating that God's special work for the Jews as a nation had ceased?

The stoning of Stephen, the rejection of the gospel by the Sanhedrin, and the conversion of Paul, the apostle to the Gentiles. See Acts 7 and 9:1–21.

31. Subtracting 490 years from 2300 leaves how much time?

Exactly 1810 years.

32. Since the 490 years bring us to 34 A.D., when do the 2300 years end?

In 1844.

33. What did the angel say would occur at the end of the 2300 years?

"He said unto me, Unto two thousand and three hundred days; then shall the sanctuary be cleansed." Dan. 8:14.

Chapter 8

The Sanctuary and Its Cleansing

1. What was the purpose of God in commanding Moses to make the earthly sanctuary?

"Let them make Me a sanctuary; *that I may dwell among them.*" Ex. 25:8.

2. How did Moses know exactly what was required?

"According to all that I shew thee, after the pattern of the tabernacle, and the pattern of all the instruments thereof, even so shall ye make it." *"Look that thou make them after their pattern, which was shewed thee in the mount."* Ex. 25:9, 40.

3. What sanctuary has now taken the place of the earthly tabernacle?

"Every high priest is ordained to offer gifts and sacrifices: wherefore it is of necessity that this Man have somewhat also to offer:....*who serve unto the example and shadow of heavenly things,* as Moses was admonished of God when he was about to make the tabernacle: for, See, saith He, that thou make all things according to the pattern shewed to thee in the mount." Heb. 8:3, 5.

4. Who ministers in the heavenly sanctuary?

"Now of the things which we have spoken this is the sum: *We have such an High Priest, who is set on the right hand of the throne of the Majesty in the heavens; a minister of the sanctuary, and of the true tabernacle, which the Lord pitched, and not man.*" Heb. 8:1, 2.

5. How many apartments had the earthly sanctuary?

Two. "Into the *second* went the high priest alone once every year, not without blood, which he offered for himself, and for the errors of the people." Heb. 9:7.

6. How many apartments, or "holy places," has the heavenly sanctuary?

"Christ is not entered into the *holy places* made with hands,...but into heaven itself, now to appear in the presence of God for us." Heb. 9:24.

7. How were these apartments divided?

"After the *second veil,* the tabernacle which is called the Holiest of all." Heb. 9:3.

8. What was contained in the first apartment of the earthly sanctuary?

"There was a tabernacle made; the first [apartment], wherein was the *candlestick,* and the *table,* and the *shewbread;* which is called the sanctuary ["holy," margin]." Heb. 9:2.

9. What was contained in the second apartment?

"After the second veil, the tabernacle which is called the Holiest of all; which had *the golden censer,* and *the ark of the covenant* overlaid round about with gold, wherein was *the golden pot that had manna,* and *Aaron's rod that budded,* and *the tables of the covenant;* and over it *the cherubims of glory shadowing the mercyseat;* of which we cannot now speak particularly." Heb. 9:3–5.

10. What did Moses place in the ark?

"At that time the Lord said unto me, Hew thee two tables of stone like unto the first, and come up unto Me into the mount, and make thee an ark of wood. And I will write on the tables the words that were in the first tables which thou brakest, and thou shalt put them in the ark. And I made an ark of shittim wood, and hewed two tables of stone like unto the first, and went up into the mount, having the two tables in mine hand. And He wrote on the tables, according to the first writing, the ten commandments, which the Lord spake unto you in the mount out of the midst of the fire in the day of the assembly: and the Lord gave them unto me. And I turned myself and came down from the mount, and *put the tables in the ark which I had made;* and there they be, as the Lord commanded me." Deut. 10:1–5.

11. When given a vision of the heavenly sanctuary, did the apostle John see the seven lamps of fire and the altar of incense?

"There were *seven lamps of fire* burning before the throne, which are the seven Spirits of God." "Another angel came and stood at *the altar,* having a golden censer; and there was given unto him much incense, that he should offer it with the prayers of all saints upon the golden altar which was before the throne." Rev. 4:5; 8:3.

12. What did the apostle see in the second apartment?

"The temple of God was opened in heaven, and there was seen in His temple *the ark of His testament.*" Rev. 11:19.

13. Since the earthly and heavenly sanctuaries are patterned alike, what must be contained in the ark in the heavenly sanctuary?

The ten commandments.

14. What was the service in the first, or outer, apartment of the sanctuary, and what portion of the year did it occupy?

The service whereby sins were confessed over the heads of animals; and these beasts in type bore the penalty of the sin by surrendering their lives. A portion of the blood was conveyed into the first apartment, the sins being lodged there, in figure, until the day of atonement, or cleansing, which ceremony took place *once each year.* See Leviticus 4 and parallel scriptures.

15. How often did the priest minister in the most holy place, or the second apartment?

"Into the second went the high priest alone *once every year,* not without blood, which he offered for himself, and for the errors of the people." Heb. 9:7. See also Lev. 16:2, 34.

16. Upon what day of the year was this service performed?

"This shall be a statute forever unto you: that *in the seventh month, on the tenth day of the month,* ye shall afflict your souls, and do no work at all, whether it be one of your own country, or a stranger that sojourning among you: for on that day shall the priest make an atonement for you, to cleanse you, that ye may be clean from all your sins before the Lord." Lev. 16:29, 30.

17. What did the priest do before entering the most holy place?

"He shall take of the congregation of the children of Israel two kids of the goats for a sin offering, and one ram for a burnt offering. And Aaron shall offer his bullock of the sin offering, which is for himself, and make an atonement for himself, and for his house.

"And he shall take the two goats, and present them before the Lord at the door of the tabernacle of the congregation. And Aaron shall cast lots upon the two goats; one lot for the Lord, and the other lot for the scapegoat. And Aaron shall bring the goat upon which the Lord's lot fell, and offer him for a sin offering. But the goat, on which the lot fell to be the scapegoat, shall be presented alive before the Lord, to make an atonement with him, and to let him go for a scapegoat into the wilderness.

"And Aaron shall bring the bullock of the sin offering, which is for himself, and shall make an atonement for himself, and for his house, and shall kill the bullock of the sin offering which is for himself : and he shall take a censer full of burning coals of fire from off the altar before the Lord, and his hands full of sweet incense beaten small, and bring it within the veil: and he shall put the incense upon the fire before the Lord, that the cloud of the incense may cover the mercy seat that is upon the testimony, that he die not: and he shall take of the blood of the bullock, and sprinkle it with his finger upon the mercy seat eastward; and before the mercy seat shall he sprinkle of the blood with his finger seven times.

"Then shall he kill the goat of the sin offering, that is for the people, and bring his blood within the veil, and do with that blood as he did with the blood of the bullock, and sprinkle it upon the mercy seat, and before the mercy seat: and he shall make an atonement for the holy place, because of the uncleanness of the children of Israel, and because of their transgressions in all their sins: and so shall he do for the tabernacle of the congregation, that remaineth among them in the midst of their uncleanness." Lev. 16:5–16.

18. When the service within the sanctuary was completed, what did the priest do with the live goat, the scapegoat?

"When he hath made an end of reconciling the holy place, and the tabernacle of the congregation, and the altar, he shall bring the live goat: and Aaron shall lay both his hands upon the head of the live goat, and *confess over him all the iniquities of the children of Israel,* and all their transgressions in all their sins, putting them upon the head of the goat, *and shall send him away by the hand of a fit man into the wilderness."* Lev. 16:20, 21.

19. What did the scapegoat bear?

"The goat shall bear upon him all their iniquities unto a land not inhabited: and he shall let go the goat in the wilderness." Lev. 16:22.

20. Whom did the Lord's goat represent?

"Behold the Lamb of God, which taketh away the sin of the world." John 1:29.

21. Whom did the scapegoat represent?

Satan.

NOTE— See margin of Leviticus 16:8. Azazel is to the Hebrews a proper name; they understand it to mean Satan. To say that the scapegoat represented Satan is not to make the fallen angel a sin bearer for man. As the author of sin and the tempter of mankind, Satan is man's partner in every sin. He bears the guilt of these sins, not as a saviour, but as *particeps criminis* [a participant in crime].

22. What was the object of the service in the second apartment?

To cleanse the sanctuary of all sin. "He shall make an atonement for the holy place, because of the uncleanness of the children of Israel, and because of their transgressions in all their sins." Lev. 16:16.

23. What does the apostle Paul say concerning this service of cleansing in the heavenly sanctuary?

"It was therefore necessary that the patterns of things in the heavens should be purified with these; but *the heavenly things themselves with better sacrifices than these."* Heb. 9:23.

24. From what is the heavenly sanctuary to be cleansed ?

From sin transferred from the repentant sinner to Christ, the Lamb of God "slain from the foundation of the world." Rev. 13:8.

Chapter 9

The Judgment and the Judgment Hour Message

1. How do we know that there will be a judgment?

"God...hath appointed a day, in the which He will judge the world." Acts 17:30, 31.

2. Was the judgment still future in Paul's day?

"As he reasoned of righteousness, temperance, and *judgment to come*, Felix trembled." Acts 24:25.

3. How many must meet the test of the judgment?

"*We must all* appear before the judgment seat of Christ." 2 Cor. 5:10. Compare Eccl. 3:17.

4. How comprehensive will be the judgment?

"*God shall bring every work into judgment,* with every secret thing, whether it be good, or whether it be evil." Eccl. 12:14.

5. What view of the judgment scene was given Daniel?

"I beheld till the thrones were cast down ["placed," A.R.V.], and the Ancient of days did sit, whose garment was white as snow, and the hair of His head like the pure wool: His throne was like the fiery flame, and His wheels as burning fire. A fiery stream issued and came forth from before Him: thousand thousands [of angels] ministered unto Him, and ten thousand times ten thousand stood before Him: the judgment was set, and the books were opened." Dan. 7:9, 10.

6. Out of what will all be judged?

"*The books were opened:* and another book was opened, which is the book of life: and *the dead were judged out of those things which were written in the books,* according to their works." Rev. 20:12.

7. What does Christ, as the advocate of His people, confess before the Father and His angels?

"He that overcometh, the same shall be clothed in white raiment; and I will not blot out his name out of the book of life, *but I will confess his name before My Father, and before His angels.*" Rev. 3:5. See Matt. 10:32, 33; Mark 8:38.

8. Who is brought before the Father at this time?

"I saw in the night visions, and, behold, *one like the Son of man* came with the clouds of heaven, and came to the Ancient of days, and they brought Him near before Him." Dan. 7:13.

9. After it has been determined in the investigative judgment who shall be the subjects of the kingdom, what is given to Christ?

"There was given Him *dominion*, and *glory*, and a *kingdom*, that all people, nations, and languages, should serve Him." Dan. 7:14.

10. What important event will then take place?

"The Lord Himself shall descend from heaven with a shout, with the voice of the Archangel, and with the trump of God." 1 Thess. 4:16.

11. When will rewards be given?

"The Son of man shall come in the glory of His Father with His angels; and *then He shall reward every man according to his works.*" Matt. 16:27. See also Rev. 22:12.

12. What will be the standard in the judgment?

"For whosoever shall keep the whole law, and yet offend in one point, he is guilty of all. For He that said, Do not commit adultery said also, Do not kill. Now if thou commit no adultery, yet if thou kill , thou art become a transgressor of the law. So speak ye, and so do, as they that shall be judged *by the law of liberty.*" James 2:10-12.

13. Who will execute the decisions of the judgment?

"As the Father hath life in Himself; so hath He given to the Son to have life in Himself; and hath given Him authority to execute judgment also, *because He is the Son of man.*" John 5:26, 27.

14. How will the decisions of the judgment be executed ?

"Out of His [Christ's] mouth goeth a sharp sword, that with it He should smite the nations: and He shall rule them with a rod of iron: and He treadeth the wine press of the fierceness and wrath of Almighty God." Rev. 19:15.

15. What message announces the judgment-hour come?

"And I saw another angel fly in the midst of heaven, having everlasting gospel to preach unto them that dwell on the earth, and to every nation, and kindred, and tongue, and people, saying with a loud voice, Fear God, and give glory to Him: for *the hour of His judgement is come:* and worship Him that made heaven, and earth, and the sea, and the fountains of waters." Rev. 14:6, 7.

16. In view of the judgment-hour, what is proclaimed anew?

"The everlasting gospel." Verse 6, first part.

17. How extensively is this message to be proclaimed?

"To *every nation,* and *kindred,* and *tongue,* and *people.*" Verse 6, first part.

18. What is the whole world called upon to do?

"Fear God, and give glory to Him" Verse 7.

19. What special reason is given for this?

"For *the hour of His judgment is come.*" Same Verse.

20. Whom are all called upon to worship?

"*Him that made heaven, and earth.*" Same verse.

21. What prophetic period extends to the time of the cleansing of the sanctuary, or the judgment hour come?

"And he said unto me, Unto *two thousand and three hundred days*; then shall the sanctuary be cleansed." Dan. 8:14

22. When did this long period expire?

In A.D. 1844. See study on page 329.

23. How is the true God distinguished from all false gods?

"Thus shall ye say unto them, *The gods that have not made the heavens and the earth, even they shall perish from the earth. ... He [the true God] hath made the earth by His power, He hath established the world by His wisdom, and hath stretched out the heavens by His discretion.*" Jer. 10:11, 12.

24. For what reason is worship justly due to God?

"For the Lord is a great God, and a great King above all gods. *...The sea is His, and He made it: and His hands formed the dry land.* O come, let us worship and bow down: let us kneel before the Lord our *Maker*." Ps. 95:3-6.

25. Why do the inhabitants of heaven worship God?

"The four and twenty elders fall down before Him, ...saying, Thou art worthy, O Lord, to receive glory and honor and power: f*or Thou hast created all things,* and for Thy pleasure they are and were created." Rev. 4:10, 11.

26. What memorial did God establish of His creative power?

"Remember the sabbath day, to keep it holy. ...For in six days the Lord made heaven and earth, the sea, and all that in them is, and rested the seventh day: wherefore the Lord blessed the Sabbath day, and hallowed it." Ex.20:12.

27. What place has the Sabbath in the work of salvation?

"Moreover also I gave them My Sabbaths, to be a *sign* between Me and them, that they might know that I am the Lord that *sanctify* them." Eze. 20:12.

28. In view of the judgment, what exhortation is given?

Let us hear the conclusion of the whole matter: *Fear God, and keep His commandments*: for this is the whole duty of man. For God shall bring every work into judgment, with every secret thing, whether it be good, or whether it be evil." Eccl. 12:13, 14.

Chapter 10

The Law and the Gospel

1. Where are the ten commandments recorded?
In Exodus 20:2–17.

2. How comprehensive are these commandments?
"Fear God, and keep His commandments: for *this is the whole duty of man.*" Eccl. 12:13.

3. How do those with renewed hearts and minds regard the commandments of God?
"This is the love of God, that we keep His commandments: and *His commandments are not grievous.*" I John 5:3. See also Matt. 19:17.

4. What is said of one who professes to know the Lord but does not keep His commandments?
"He that saith, I know Him, and keepeth not His commandments, is a liar, and *the truth is not in him.*" 1 John 2:4. See also Matt. 7:21; James 2:10, 11.

5. What promise is made to the willing and obedient?
"If ye be willing and obedient, *ye shall eat the good of the land.*" Isa. 1:19.

6. What is said of the stability of God's character?
"I am the Lord, *I change not.*" Mal. 3:6.

7. How enduring are His commandments?
"The works of His hands are verity and judgment; *all His commandments are sure. They stand fast forever and ever.*" Ps. 111:7, 8.

8. Did Christ come to abolish or destroy the law?
"Think not that I am come to destroy the law, or the prophets: *I am not come to destroy, but to fulfill.*" Matt. 5:17.

9. When used with reference to prophecy, what does the word *fulfill* mean?
To fill up; to accomplish; to bring to pass; as, "that it might be *fulfilled* which was spoken by Esaias the prophet." Matt. 4:14.

10. What does it mean when used with reference to law?
To perform, to keep, or to act in accordance with; as, "Bear ye one another's burdens, and so *fulfill* the law of Christ." Gal. 6:2. See Matt. 3:15; James 2:8, 9.

11. How did Christ treat His Father's commandments?
"I have *kept* My Father's commandments, and abide in His love." John 15:10.

12. Does faith in God make void the law?

"Do we then make void the law through faith? *God forbid: yea, we establish the law.*" Rom. 3:31.

13. What, more than all else, proves the perpetuity and immutability of the law of God?

"*God so loved the world, that He gave His only be-gotten Son,* that whosoever believeth in Him should not perish, but have everlasting life." John 3:16. "Christ died for our sins." 1 Cor. 15:3.

NOTE— Could the law have been abolished and sin disposed of in this way, Christ need not have come and died for our sins. The gift of Christ, therefore, more than all else, proves the immutability of the law of God. Christ must come and die, and satisfy the claims of the law, or the world must perish. The law could not give way. Says Spurgeon in his sermon on "The Perpetuity of the Law of God," "Our Lord Jesus Christ gave a greater vindication of the law by dying because it had been broken, than all the lost can ever give by their miseries." The fact that the law is to be the standard in the judgment is another proof of its enduring nature. See Eccl. 12:13, 14; James 2:8–12.

14. What relation does a justified person sustain to the law?

"Not the hearers of the law are just before God, but the *doers of the law shall be justified.*" Rom. 2:13.

15. How may we know we have been born again?

"We know that we have passed from death unto life, *because we love the brethren.*" I John 3:14.

16. How may we know that we love the brethren?

"By this we know that we love the children of God, *when we love God, and keep His commandments.*" 1 John 5:2.

17. What is the love of God?

"This is the love of God, *that we keep His commandments.*" Verse 3.

18. How are those described who will be prepared for the coming of Christ?

"Here is the patience of the saints: here are they that *keep the commandments of God, and the faith of Jesus.*" Rev. 14:12.

19. By whom was the ten commandment law proclaimed?

"*The Lord spake unto you out of the midst of the fire:* ye heard the voice of the words, but saw no similitude; only ye heard a voice. And *He declared unto you His covenant, which He commanded you to perform, even ten commandments;* and *He wrote them upon two tables of stone.*" Deut. 4:12, 13.

20. Were the ten commandments a distinct and complete law by themselves?

"*These words the Lord spake* unto all your assembly in the mount out of the midst of the fire, of the cloud, and of the thick darkness, with a great voice: *and He added no more.* And He wrote them in two tables of stone, and delivered them unto me." Deut. 5:22. "And the

Lord said unto Moses, Come up to Me into the mount, and be there: and I will give thee *tables of stone,* and *a law,* and *commandments* which I have written." Ex. 24:12.

21. How was the ceremonial law made known?

"The Lord called unto Moses,…saying, *Speak unto the children of Israel, and say unto them, If any man of you bring an offering…*" Lev.1:1,2. *"This is the law of the burnt offering, of the meat offering, and of the sin offering, and of the trespass offering, and of the consecrations, and of the sacrifice of the peace offerings*; which the Lord commanded Moses in Mt. Sinai, in the day that He commanded the children of Israel to offer their oblations unto the Lord, in the wilderness of Sinai." Lev. 7:37, 38.

22. Was the ceremonial law a complete law in itself?

"The law of commandments *contained in ordinances."* Eph. 2:15.

23. On what did God write the ten commandments?

"He wrote them *upon two tables of stone."* Deut. 4:13.

24. In what were the laws, or commandments, respecting sacrifices and burnt offerings written?

"They removed the burnt offerings, that they might give according to the divisions of the families of the people, to offer unto the Lord, as it is written in the *book of Moses."* 2 Chron. 35:12.

25. Where were the ten commandments placed?

"He took and put the testimony *into the ark,*…and put the mercy seat above upon the ark." Ex. 40:20.

26. Where did Moses command the Levites to put the book of the law which he had written?

"Moses commanded the Levites, which bare the ark of the covenant of the Lord, saying, Take this book of the law, and *put it in the side* ["by the side," A. R. V.] *of the ark* of the covenant of the Lord your God." Deut. 31: 25, 26.

27. What is the nature of the moral law?

"The law of the Lord is *perfect,* converting the soul." Ps. 19:7. "We know that the law is *spiritual."* Rom. 7:14.

28. Could the offerings commanded by the ceremonial law satisfy the conscience or make a man perfect?

"Which was a figure for the time then present, in which were offered both gifts and sacrifices, *that could not make him that did the service perfect, as pertaining to the conscience."* Heb. 9:9.

29. How did Christ's death affect the ceremonial law?

"Blotting out the handwriting of ordinances that was against us, which was contrary to us, and took it out of the way, nailing it to His cross." Col. 2:14. "Having abolished in His flesh the enmity, even *the law of commandments contained in ordinances."* Eph. 2:15.

30. Why was the ceremonial law taken away?

"There is a disannulling of a foregoing commandment because of its weakness and unprofitableness (for the law made nothing perfect), and a bringing in thereupon of a better hope, through which we draw nigh unto God." Heb. 7:18, 19, A.R.V.

31. What miraculous event occurred at the death of Christ, signifying that the sacrificial system was forever at an end?

"Jesus, when He had cried again with a loud voice, yielded up the ghost. And, behold, *the veil of the temple was rent in twain* from the top to the bottom." Matt. 27:50, 51.

32. In what words had the prophet Daniel foretold this ?

"He shall confirm the covenant with many for one week: and in the midst of the week He shall cause the sacrifice and the oblation to cease." Dan. 9:27.

33. How enduring is the moral law?

"Concerning Thy testimonies, I have known of old that *Thou hast founded them forever.*" Ps. 119:152.

34. What is one of the uses of the law?

"Therefore by the deeds of the law there shall no flesh be justified in His sight: *for by the law is the knowledge of sin.*" Rom. 3:20.

35. In thus making known sin, and the consequent need of a Saviour, what part does the law act?

"Wherefore the *law was our schoolmaster to bring us unto Christ,* that we might be justified by faith." Gal. 3:24.

36. What is the gospel declared to be?

"It is *the power of God unto salvation* to everyone that believeth." Rom. 1:16.

37. What is the significance of the name bestowed by the angel upon the Saviour before His birth?

"She shall bring forth a Son, and thou shalt call His name *Jesus:* for *He shall save His people from their sins.*" Matt. 1:21.

38. What was foretold concerning Christ's attitude toward the law of God?

"Then said I, Lo, I come: in the volume of the book it is written of Me, *I delight to do Thy will, O My God: yea, Thy law is within My heart.*" Ps. 40:7, 8.

39. Does the faith which brings righteousness abolish the law?

"Do we then make void the law through faith? God forbid: yea, *we establish the law.*" Rom. 3:31.

NOTE— The law reveals the perfection of character required and so gives a knowledge of sin, but it is powerless to confer the character demanded. In the gospel, the law, first written in the heart of Christ, becomes "the law of the Spirit of life in Christ Jesus," and is thus transferred to the heart of the believer, in whose heart Christ dwells by faith. Thus the new covenant promise that the law shall be written in the heart is fulfilled. This is the genuine experience of righteousness by faith, a righteousness which is witnessed by the law and revealed in the life in harmony with the law. The gospel is thus seen to be the provision for restoring the law to its place in the heart and life of the one who believes on Christ and accepts His mediatorial work. Such faith, instead of making void the law, establishes it in the heart of the believer. The gospel is not against the law, therefore, but upholds, maintains, and presents the law to us in Christ.

40. What did Christ take away when He died upon the cross?

"The next day John seeth Jesus coming unto him, and saith, Behold the Lamb of God, which taketh away *the sin of the world.*" John 1:29.

41. What did Christ abolish by His death and resurrection ?

"Jesus Christ, who hath *abolished death,* and hath brought life and immortality to light through the gospel." 2 Tim. 1:10.

42. What scripture shows that God's remnant people will have a right conception of the proper relation between the law of God and the gospel of Jesus Christ?

"Here is the patience of the saints: *here are they that keep the commandments of God, and the faith of Jesus.*" Rev. 14:12.

Chapter 11

The Bible Sabbath

1. When and by whom was the Sabbath made?

"Thus the heavens and the earth were finished, and all the host of them. And *on the seventh day God ended His work* which He had made; and *He rested on the seventh day* from all His work which He had made." Gen. 2:1, 2.

2. After resting on the seventh day, what did God do?

"God *blessed the seventh day, and sanctified it:* because that in it He had rested from all His work which God created and made." Verse 3.

3. By what distinct acts, then, was the Sabbath made?

God *rested* on it; He *blessed* it; He *sanctified* it. Sanctify: "To make sacred or holy; to set apart to a holy or religious use."— Webster.

4. Did Christ have anything to do with creation and the making of the Sabbath?

"*All things were made by Him; and without Him was not anything made that was made.*" John 1:3. See also Eph. 3:9; Col. 1:16; Heb. 1:2.

NOTE— Christ, being the active agent in creation, must have rested on the seventh day with the Father. It is therefore His rest day as well as the Father's.

5. For whom does Christ say the Sabbath was made?

"He said unto them, *The Sabbath was made for man,* and not man for the Sabbath." Mark 2:27.

NOTE— It was not made for the Jews alone, for it was made more than two thousand years before there was a Jew.

6. What does the Sabbath commandment require?

"*Remember the Sabbath day, to keep it holy. Six days shalt thou labor, and do all thy work: but the seventh day i*s the Sabbath of the Lord thy God: *in it thou shalt not do any work,* thou, nor thy son, nor thy daughter, thy manservant, nor thy maidservant, nor thy cattle, nor thy stranger that is within thy gates." Ex. 20:8–10.

7. What reason is given in the commandment for keeping the Sabbath day holy?

"*For in six days the Lord made heaven and earth, the sea, and all that in them is, and rested the seventh day:* wherefore the Lord blessed the Sabbath day, and hallowed it." Verse 11.

NOTE— The Sabbath is the memorial of creation and the sign of God's creative power. Through the keeping of it God designed that man should forever remember Him as the true and living God, the Creator of all things.

8. How did God prove Israel in the wilderness?

"Then said the Lord unto Moses, Behold, *I will rain bread from heaven for you;* and the people shall go out and gather a certain rate every day, *that I may prove them, whether they will walk in My law, or no.*" Ex. 16:4.

9. On which day was a double portion of manna gathered?

"It came to pass, that *on the sixth day they gathered twice as much bread,* two omers for one man; and all the rulers of the congregation came and told Moses." Verse 22.

10. What reply did Moses make to the rulers?

"He said unto them, *This is that which the Lord hath said, Tomorrow is the rest of the holy Sabbath* unto the Lord." Verse 23.

NOTE— This was a full month and more before they came to Sinai.

11. What did some of the people do on the seventh day?

"It came to pass, that *there went out some of the people on the seventh day for to gather,* and they found none." Ex. 16:27.

12. How did God reprove their disobedience?

"The Lord said unto Moses, *How long refuse ye to keep My commandments and My laws?*" Verse 28.

13. How, then, did the Lord prove the people (verse 4) whether they would keep His law or not?

Over the keeping of the Sabbath.

NOTE— Thus we see that the Sabbath commandment was a part of God's law before this law was spoken from Sinai; for this incident occurred in the wilderness of Sin, before the children of Israel came to Sinai, where the law was given. Both the Sabbath and the law existed from creation.

14. What does God command men to observe in memory of the work of creation?

"Remember the Sabbath day, to keep it holy." Ex. 20:8.

15. How long does God design that His great work of creating the heavens and the earth shall be remembered ?

"The works of the Lord are great, sought out of all them that have pleasure therein. His work is honorable and glorious: and His righteousness endureth forever. *He hath made His wonderful works to be remembered.*" Ps. 111:2–4. See also text and note following Question 18.

16. In addition to being a memorial of creation, of what is the Sabbath a sign?

"Hallow My Sabbaths; and they shall be a sign between Me and you, *that ye may know that I am the Lord your God.*" Eze. 20:20.

17. How long was the Sabbath to be a sign of the true God?

"*It is a sign between Me and the children of Israel forever:* for in six days the Lord made heaven and earth, and on the seventh day He rested, and was refreshed." Ex. 31:17.

NOTE— It is manifest that if the object of the Sabbath was to keep God in mind as the Creator, and it had been faithfully kept from the first, there would not now be a heathen or an idolater on the face of the earth.

18. How often will the redeemed congregate to worship the Lord?

"As the new heavens and the new earth, which I will make, shall remain before Me, saith the Lord, so shall your seed and your name remain. And it shall come to pass, that *from one new moon to another,* and *from one Sabbath to another,* shall all flesh come to worship before Me, saith the Lord." Isa. 66:22, 23.

NOTE— The Sabbath, which is the memorial of God's creative power, will never cease to exist.

19. Of what did Christ say of the Son of man?

"The Son of man is Lord even *of the Sabbath day.*" Matt. 12:8. See also Mark 2:28.

20. Did Christ, while on earth, keep the Sabbath?

"*As His custom was, He went into the synagogue on the Sabbath* day, and stood up for to read." Luke 4:16.

21. Although Lord, maker, and an observer of the Sabbath, how was *Jesus* spied upon by the scribes and Pharisees on this day?

"'The scribes and Pharisees watched Him, *whether He would heal on the Sabbath day;* that they might find an accusation against Him." Luke 6:7.

22. With what question did Christ meet their false ideas and reasonings regarding Sabbath keeping?

"Then said Jesus unto them, I will ask you one thing: *Is it lawful on the Sabbath days to do good, or to do evil? to save life, or to destroy it?*" Verse 9.

23. According to Isaiah, what was Christ to do with the law?

"He will *magnify* the law, and make it *honorable*." Isa. 42:21.

NOTE— In nothing, perhaps, was this more strikingly fulfilled than in the matter of Sabbath observance. By their traditions, numerous regulations, and senseless restrictions, the Jews had made the Sabbath a burden and anything but a delight. Christ removed all these and by His life and teachings put the Sabbath back in its proper place and setting, as a day of worship and beneficence, a day for doing acts of charity and mercy, as well as engaging in contemplation of God and in acts of devotion. Thus He magnified it and made it honorable.

24. According to the New Testament, what day immediately precedes the first day of the week?

"When the Sabbath was past,…very early in the morning the first day of the week, they came unto the sepulcher at the rising of the sun." Mark 16:1, 2.

NOTE— Observe that the day which Inspiration here calls the Sabbath was the day just before the first day of the week.

25. After the crucifixion, what day was kept by the women who followed Jesus?

"They returned, and prepared spices and ointments; and *rested the Sabbath day according to the commandment.*" Luke 23:56.

26. What day is the Sabbath, "according to the commandment"?

"The *seventh day is the Sabbath* of the Lord thy God." Ex. 20:10.

27. What was Christ's custom concerning the Sabbath?

"He came to Nazareth, where He had been brought up: and, as His custom was, *He went into the synagogue on the Sabbath day, and stood up for to read.*" Luke 4:16.

28. In what instruction to His disciples did Christ recognize the existence of the Sabbath long after His ascension ?

"Pray ye that your flight be not in the winter, *neither on the Sabbath day.*" Matt. 24:20.

NOTE— The context of this instruction was given in foresight of their need to flee from Jerusalem before its destruction. The destruction of Jerusalem under Titus occurred in 70 A.D.

29. On what day did the Jews meet for worship?

"Moses of old time hath in every city them that preach him, being read in the synagogues every *Sabbath day.*" Acts 15:21.

30. On what day did Paul and Barnabas preach at Antioch?

"They came to Antioch in Pisidia, and went into the synagogue on *the Sabbath day.*" Acts 13:14.

31. When did the Gentiles request that Paul should repeat the sermon he had preached at Antioch on the Sabbath?

"When the Jews were gone out of the synagogue, the Gentiles besought that these words might be preached to them *the next Sabbath.*" Verse 42.

32. On what day did Paul and his companions preach to the devout women at Philippi?

"*On the Sabbath* we went out of the city by a river side, where prayer was wont to be made; and we sat down, and spake unto the women which resorted thither." Acts 16:13.

33. What was Paul's custom on the Sabbath?

"They came to Thessalonica, where was a synagogue of the Jews: and Paul, *as his manner was, went in unto them, and three Sabbath days reasoned with them out of the Scriptures."* Acts 17:1, 2.

NOTE— It was Paul's manner, as it was Christ's custom (Luke 4:16), to attend religious services on the Sabbath.

34. How did the apostle spend the working days of the week when at Corinth?

"After these things Paul departed from Athens, and came to Corinth; and found a certain Jew named Aquila, born in Pontus, lately come from Italy, with his wife Priscilla;...and because he was of the same craft, he abode with them, and *wrought:* for by their occupation they were *tent makers."* Acts 18:1–3.

35. What did he do on the Sabbath days?

"He reasoned in the synagogue every Sabbath, and persuaded the Jews and the Greeks." Acts 18:4.

36. On what day of the week was John in the Spirit?

"I was in the Spirit *on the Lord's day."* Rev. 1:10.

37. Who is Lord of the Sabbath?

"The Son of man is Lord also of the Sabbath." Mark 2:28.

Chapter 12

Who Changed The Sabbath?

1. Of what is the Sabbath commandment a part?

It is a part of the law of God. See Ex. 20:8–11.

2. What, according to prophecy, was to be Christ's attitude toward the law?

"The Lord is well pleased for His righteousness' sake; *He will magnify the law, and make it honorable.*" Isa. 42:21.

3. In His first recorded discourse, what did Christ say of the law?

"Think not that I am come to destroy the law, or the prophets: I am not come to destroy, but to fulfill." Matt. 5:17.

4. How enduring did He say the law is?

"Verily I say unto you, Till heaven and earth pass, one jot or one tittle shall in no wise pass from the law, till all be fulfilled." Verse 18.

5. What did He say of those who should break one of the least of God's commandments, and teach men so to do?

"Whosoever therefore shall break one of these least commandments, and shall teach men so, *he shall be called the least in the kingdom of heaven.*" Verse 19.

NOTE— From this it is evident that the entire code of the ten commandments is binding in the Christian dispensation, and that Christ had no thought of changing any of them. One of these commands the observance of the seventh day as the Sabbath. But the practice of most Christians is different; they keep the first day of the week instead, many of them believing that Christ changed the Sabbath. But from His own words we see that He came for no such purpose. This change was made by man, not by God.

6. What did God, through the prophet Daniel, say the power represented by the "little horn" would think to do?

"He shall speak words against the Most High, and shall wear out the saints of the Most High: and *he shall think to change the times and the law.*" Dan. 7:25, A. R. V.

7. What did the apostle Paul say the "man of sin" would do?

"That day shall not come, except there come a falling away first, and that man of sin be revealed, the son of perdition; *who opposeth and exalteth himself above all that is called God, or that is worshipped.*" 2 Thess. 2:3, 4.

NOTE— There is only one way by which any power could exalt itself above God, and that is by assuming to change the law of God, and to require obedience to its own law instead of to God's law.

8. What power has claimed authority to change the law of God?

The Papacy.

9. What part of the law of God, especially, has the Papacy thought to change?

The fourth commandment.

NOTE— "They [the Catholics] allege the changing of the Sabbath into the Lord's day, contrary, as it seemeth, to the Decalogue; and they have no example more in their mouths than the change of the Sabbath. They will needs have the power to be very great, because it hath done away with a precept of the Decalogue."— *Augsburg Confession, Art. VII, par. 12; quoted in "The Library of Original Sources," Vol. V, pp. 173, 1711.*

10. Why did God command Israel to hallow the Sabbath?

"Hallow My Sabbaths; and they shall be a sign between Me and you, *that ye may know that I am the Lord your God.*" Eze. 20:20.

11. Does the Papacy acknowledge that it has changed the Sabbath?

It does.

NOTE— "*Question*— How prove you that the church hath power to command feasts and holy days?"

"*Answer*— By the very act of changing the Sabbath into Sunday, which Protestants allow of; and therefore they fondly contradict themselves by keeping Sunday strictly, and breaking most other feasts commanded by the same church."

"*Ques.*— How prove you that?"

"*Ans.*— Because by keeping Sunday, they acknowledge the church's power to ordain feasts, and to command them under sin; and by not keeping the rest [of the feasts] by her commanded, they again deny, in fact the same power"— "*An Abridgment of the Christian Doctrine," composed in 1649 by Rev, Henry Tuberville, D. D., of the English College of Douay, France, p. 58.*

"The Catholic Church...by virtue of her divine mission, changed the day from Saturday to Sunday." *Catholic Mirror, official organ of Cardinal Gibbons, Baltimore, Sept. 23, 1893.*

12. Do Catholic authorities acknowledge that there is no command in the Bible for the sanctification of Sunday?

They do.

NOTE— "You may read the Bible from Genesis to Revelation, and you will not find a single line authorizing the sanctification of Sunday. The Scriptures enforce the religious observance of Saturday, a day which we never sanctify."—"*The Faith of Our Fathers," Cardinal Gibbons, edition 1893, p. 111.*

13. Do Protestant writers acknowledge the same?

They do.

NOTES— "The Scriptures nowhere call the first day of the week the Sabbath...There is no Scriptural authority for so doing, nor of course any Scriptural obligation."— *The Watchman (Baptist).*

"The observance of the first instead of the seventh day rests on the testimony of the church, and the church *alone.*"— *Hobart Church News (Episcopalian), July 2, 1894.*

Papal claims and Protestant admissions show, therefore, who changed the Sabbath.

14. Did this change in observance of days come about suddenly or gradually?

Gradually.

NOTE— "The Christian church made no formal, but a gradual and almost unconscious, transference of the one day to the other."— *"The Voice from Sinai," Archdeacon F. W. Farrar, p. 167.*

15. For how long a time was the seventh-day Sabbath observed generally in the Christian church?

For many centuries; in fact, its observance has never wholly ceased.

NOTE— The historian Socrates, who wrote about the middle of the fifth century, says: "Almost all churches throughout the world celebrate the sacred mysteries on the Sabbath of every week, yet the Christians of Alexandria and at Rome, on account of some ancient tradition, refuse to do this."— *"Ecclesiastical History," book 5, chap. 22.*

Sozomen, another historian of the same period, writes: "The people of Constantinople, and of several other cities, assemble together on the Sabbath, as well as on the next day; which custom is never observed at Rome, or at Alexandria."— *Id., book 7, chap. 19.*

16. What striking testimony is borne by Neander, the noted church historian, regarding the origin of Sunday observance?

The Sunday festival, he says, "was always only a human ordinance." (See following note.)

NOTE— "Opposition to Judaism introduced the particular festival of Sunday very early, indeed, into the place of the Sabbath...The festival of Sunday, like all other festivals, was always only a human ordinance; and it was far from the intentions of the apostles to establish a divine command in this respect, far from them, and from the early apostolic church, to transfer the laws of the Sabbath to Sunday. Perhaps at the end of the second century a false application of this kind had begun to take place; for men appear by that time to have considered laboring on Sunday as a sin." — *Neander's "Church History," Rose's translation, p. 186.*

17. Who first enjoined Sunday keeping by law?

Constantine the Great.

NOTE— "The earliest recognition of the observance of Sunday as a legal duty is a constitution of Constantine in A.D. 321."— *Encyclopedia Britannica, ninth edition, art. "Sunday."*

18. What did Constantine's law require?

"Let all the judges and town people, and the occupation of all trades rest on the venerable day of the sun; but let those who are situated in the country freely and at full liberty attend to the business of agriculture; because it often happens that no other day is so fit for sowing corn and planting vines; lest, the critical moment being let slip, men should lose the commodities granted by heaven."— *Edict of March 7; A.D. 321; Corpus Juris Civilis Codicis, lib. 3, tit. 12, 3.*

19. What testimony does Eusebius (270–338), a noted bishop of the church, a flatterer of Constantine, and known as the father of ecclesiastical history, bear upon this subject?

"All things whatsoever that it was duty to do on the Sabbath [Jewish seventh day], these *we* have transferred to the Lord's day."— *"Commentary on the Psalms" in Migne, "Patralogia Græca," Vol. XXIII, Col. 1171.*

NOTE— The change of the Sabbath was the result of the combined efforts of church and state, and centuries passed before it was fully accomplished.

20. When and by what church council was the observance of the seventh day forbidden, and Sunday observance enjoined?

"The seventh-day Sabbath was...solemnized by Christ, the apostles, and primitive Christians, till *the Laodicean Council* did in a manner quite abolish the observation of it... The Council of Laodicea [364 A.D.]...first settled the observation of the Lord's day."— *Prynne's "Dissertation on the Lord's Day Sabbath," P. 44.*

21. What did this council, in its twenty-ninth canon, decree concerning the Sabbath, and concerning the Christians who continued to observe it.

"Christians ought not to Judaize, and to rest in the Sabbath, but to *work* in that day... Wherefore if they shall be found to Judaize, *let them be accursed from Christ.*"— Id., pp. 33, 34.

NOTE— Some of the further steps taken by church and state authorities in bringing about this change may be noted as follows:

"In 386, under Gratian, Valentinian, and Theodosius, it was decreed that all litigation and business should cease [on Sunday]....

"Among the doctrines laid down in a letter of Pope Innocent I, written in the last year of his papacy (416), is that Saturday should be observed as a fast day. [p. 265] ...

"In 425, under Theodosius the Younger, abstinence from theatricals and the circus [on Sunday] was enjoined. [p. 266] ...

"In 538, at a council at Orleans ... it was ordained that everything previously permitted on Sunday should still be lawful; but that work at the plow, or in the vineyard, and cutting, reaping, threshing, tilling, and hedging should be abstained from, that people might more conveniently attend church. [pp. 266, 267] ...

"About 590, Pope Gregory, in a letter to the Roman people, denounced as the prophets of antichrist those who maintained that work ought not to be done on the seventh day" [P. 267].— *"Law of Sunday," James P. Ringgold, pp. 265–267.*

The last paragraph of the foregoing quotation indicates that even as late as 590 A.D. there were those in the church who observed and taught the observance of the seventh day, the Bible Sabbath.

22. What determines whose servants we are?

"Know ye not, that to whom ye yield yourselves servants to obey, *his servants ye are to whom ye obey?" Rom. 6:16.*

23. When tempted to bow down and worship Satan, what reply did Christ make?

"Get thee hence, Satan: for it is written, Thou shalt worship the Lord thy God, and *Him only shalt thou serve."* Matt. 4:10.

24. What do Catholics say of the observance of Sunday by Protestants?

"It was the Catholic Church which, by the authority of Jesus Christ, has transferred this rest to the Sunday in remembrance of the resurrection of our Lord. Thus *the observance of Sunday by the Protestants is an homage they pay, in spite of themselves, to the authority of the [Catholic] church."— "Plain Talk About the Protestantism of Today," Monsignor Segur, p. 213.*

25. What kind of worship does the Saviour call that which is not according to God's commandments?

"In vain they do worship Me, teaching for doctrines *the commandments of men."* Matt 15:9.

ENGRAVED IN THE ROCK

"When God confirmed His law to men
Through Israel's waiting flock,
He spake aloud His precepts ten,
And graved them in the rock."

"Within the tent's most holy place
That sacred law was brought,
Nor can the hand of man efface
What great Jehovah wrought."

Chapter 13

The Seal of God and the Mark of Apostasy

1. What does the Bible present as the object of a sign, or seal?

"Now, O king, *establish* the decree, and s*ign the writing, that it be not changed.*" Dan. 6:8.

NOTE— That is, affix the royal signature that the decree may have the proper authority, and thus be of force. Anciently it was customary for kings to use for this purpose a ring containing their name, initials, or monogram. Jezebel, the wife of Ahab, "wrote letters in Ahab's *name*, and sealed them with his *seal*." 1 Kings 21:8. Of the decree issued under Ahasuerus for the slaying of all the Jews throughout the Persian Empire, it is said that "in the *name* of King Ahasuerus was it written, and sealed with the king's *ring*." Esther 3:12.

2. What are the essentials of a seal?

A seal must not only authenticate that to which it is attached or upon which it is impressed, but it must show the authority of the author of the law, decree, proclamation, or other writing upon which it appears.

3. With what is God's seal connected?

"Bind up the testimony, *seal* THE LAW *among My disciples.*" Isa. 8:16.

4. Does the first commandment identify the Author of the law as Creator of the world?

No.

NOTE— That Jehovah, who spake these words, is the Creator, the commandment itself does not state. Such a prohibition might come from any source.

"Thou shalt have no other gods before *Me*." Ex. 20:3.

5. Does the second, third, fifth, sixth, seventh, eighth, ninth, or tenth commandment indicate that the Creator is the author of the Decalogue?

No; none of them.

NOTE— The second commandment forbids the making of and bowing down to images, but does not in itself reveal the true God, the Creator. The third commandment says, "Thou shalt not take the name of the Lord thy God in vain," but it likewise fails to reveal the Creator of the world as the Giver of the law. So of the other commandments here referred to.

6. Which commandment alone of the Decalogue reveals the Creator as the Author of the law?

The fourth, which reads, "Remember the Sabbath day, to keep it holy. Six days shalt thou labor, and do all thy work: but the seventh day is the Sabbath of the Lord thy God: in it thou shalt not do any work, thou, nor thy son, nor thy daughter, thy manservant, nor thy maidservant, nor thy cattle, nor thy stranger that is within thy gates: for in six days *the Lord made heaven and earth, the sea, and all that in them is,* and rested the seventh day: wherefore the Lord blessed the Sabbath day, and hallowed it." Ex. 20:8–11.

NOTE— The fourth commandment alone reveals at once the *name*, *authority*, and *dominion* of the Author of this law. In six days (1) the *Lord* (name); (2) *made* (office, Creator); (3) *heaven and earth* (dominion). This commandment alone, therefore, contains "the *seal* of the living God." By what is revealed in this commandment is shown what God is referred to in the other commandments. By the great truth revealed here all other gods are shown to be false. The Sabbath commandment, therefore, contains the seal of God; and the Sabbath itself, the observance of which is enjoined by the commandment, is inseparably connected with this seal; it is to be kept in memory of the fact that the Author of the law is the Creator of all things; and it is itself called a "sign" of the knowledge of this great truth. (Ex. 31:17; Eze. 20:20.)

7. What reason does God give for making the Sabbath an everlasting sign between Him and His people?

"It is a *sign* between Me and the children of Israel forever: *for in six days the Lord made heaven and earth, and on the seventh day He rested, and was refreshed.*" Ex. 31:17.

NOTE— The Sabbath is the sign, or mark, or seal, of the true God, the Creator.

8. Of what does God say the keeping or hallowing of the Sabbath is a sign?

"Hallow My Sabbaths; and they shall be a *sign* between Me and you, *that ye may know that I am the Lord your God,*" Eze. 20:20.

9. Of what besides a knowledge of God as Creator, is the Sabbath a sign?

"Verily My Sabbaths ye shall keep: for it is *a sign* between Me and you throughout your generations; *that ye may know that I am the Lord that doth* SANCTIFY *you.*" Ex. 31:13.

NOTE— The Sabbath is the great sign of God's creative power wherever and however manifested, whether in creation or redemption; for redemption is creation— *re*-creation. It requires the same power to *redeem* that it does to *create*. "*Create* in me a clean heart." Ps. 51:10. "We are His workmanship, *created* in Christ Jesus unto good works." Eph. 2:10. At each recurrence of the Sabbath, God designs that it shall call Him to mind as the one who created us, and whose grace and sanctifying power are working in us to fit us for His eternal kingdom.

10. What scripture shows that a special sealing work is to be done just before the letting loose of the winds of destruction upon the earth?

"After these things I saw four angels standing on the four corners of the earth, holding the four winds of the earth, that the wind should not blow on the earth, nor on the sea, nor on any tree. And I saw another angel ascending from the east, *having the seal of the living God*: and he cried with a loud voice to the four angels, to whom it was given to hurt the earth and the sea, saying, *Hurt not the earth, neither the sea, nor the, trees, till we have sealed the servants of our God in their foreheads.* And I heard the number of them which were sealed: and there were sealed a hundred and forty and four thousand of all the tribes of the children of Israel." Rev. 7:1–4. See Eze. 9:1–6.

11. Where did the apostle see this same company a little later, and what did they have in their foreheads?

"I looked, and, lo, a Lamb stood *on the Mount Sion*; and with Him an hundred forty and four thousand, *having His Father's name written in their foreheads.*" Rev. 14:1.

NOTE— The *seal of God* and the Father's *name* must refer to the same thing. The seal is the sign, or stamp, of perfection, and God's name stands for His character, which is perfect. And the Sabbath of God, kept as God ordained it to be kept, holy and in holiness, is *a sign* of this same thing— perfection of character. When this seal is finally placed upon God's people, it will be an evidence that His grace and His sanctifying power have done their work and fitted them for heaven. In the world to come, all will keep the Sabbath and will therefore have this seal, or mark, of sanctification, holiness, and perfection of character. (Isa. 66:22, 23.)

12. What is said of the character of these sealed ones?

"In their mouth was found no guile: *for they are without fault before the throne of God.*" Rev. 14:5.

13. How is the remnant church described?

"Here is the *patience* of the saints: here are they that *keep the commandments of God, and the faith of Jesus.*" Verse 12.

14. Against what three things does the third angel of Revelation 14 warn men?

"The third angel followed them, saying with a loud voice, If any man *worship the beast and his image, and receive his mark in his forehead, or in his hand*, the same shall drink of the wine of the wrath of God." Verses 9, 10.

NOTE— The beast represents the Papacy; the image to the beast represents another ecclesiastical system dominating the civil power. And over against the seal of God stands the mark of the beast, the mark of apostasy. Against this false and idolatrous worship and the reception of this mark, God sends this solemn warning.

15. What power mentioned in the thirteenth chapter of Revelation is to enforce this mark?

"He [the lamblike beast with two horns] causeth all, both small and great, rich and poor, free and bond, to receive *a mark* in their right hand, or in their foreheads." Rev. 13:16.

NOTE— The lamblike beast is understood to represent a religio-political power arising in and dominating the United States of America. As a powerful combination of religious forces compels this nation to repudiate her principles of religious liberty, and thus become a persecuting power, other nations will follow her example in oppressing those who refuse to renounce, in effect, their allegiance to God.

16. What does the Papacy set forth as the mark, or sign, of its power and authority?

The act of changing the Sabbath to Sunday.

NOTE— In a letter written in November, 1895, Mr. H. F. Thomas, chancellor to Cardinal Gibbons, replying to an inquiry as to whether the Catholic Church claims to have changed the Sabbath, said: "Of course the Catholic Church claims that the change was her act,...and the act is *a mark* of her ecclesiastical authority."

The true Sabbath being a sign of loyalty to the true God, it is but natural that the false Sabbath should stand forth as a sign of allegiance to apostasy. And such we find to be the case.

17. What will be Satan's attitude toward the remnant people who keep the commandments of God?

"The dragon [the devil, or Satan. See Rev. 12:9]— *was wroth with the woman [God's church.* See 2 Cor. 11:2], *and went to make war with the remnant of her seed,* which keep the commandments of God, and have the testimony of Jesus Christ." Rev. 12:17.

18. How strongly will this false worship and the enforcement of this mark be urged?

"That the image of the beast should both speak, and cause [decree] that as many as would not worship the image of the beast *should be killed.* And he causeth all, both small and great, rich and poor, free and bond, to receive *a mark* in their right hand, or in their foreheads: and *that no man might buy or sell, save he that had the mark."* Rev. 13:15–17.

19. Over what do the people of God finally gain the victory?

"I saw as it were a sea of glass mingled with fire: and them that had gotten the victory *over the beast* [the Papacy], and *over his image* [a similar worldwide persecuting power], *and over his mark, and over the number of his name,* stand on the sea of glass, having the harps of God." Rev. 15:2.

Chapter 14

The Condition of Man in Death

1. Where do the dead sleep?

"Many of them that *sleep in the dust of the earth shall awake.*" Dan. 12:2. See also Eccl. 3:20; 9:10.

2. How long will they sleep there?

"Man lieth down, and riseth not: *till the heavens be no more,* they shall not awake, nor be raised out of their sleep." Job 14:12.

3. For what did Job say he would wait after death?

"If a man die, shall he live again? all the days of my appointed time will I wait, *till my change come.*" Verse 14.

4. Where did he say he would wait?

"*If I wait, the grave is mine house:* I have made my bed in the darkness." Job 17:13.

5. While in this condition, how much does one know about those he has left behind?

"His sons come to honor, and *he knoweth it not;* and they are brought low, but *he perceiveth it not of them.*" Job 14:21.

6. What becomes of man's thoughts at death?

"His breath goeth forth, he returneth to his earth; in that very day his thoughts perish." Ps. 146:4.

7. Do the dead know anything?

"The living know that they shall die: but the dead know not anything, neither have they any more a reward; for the memory of them is forgotten." Eccl. 9:5.

8. Do they take any part in earthly things?

"Also their *love,* and their *hatred,* and their *envy,* is now *perished; neither have they any more a portion forever in anything that is done under the sun.*" Verse 6.

9. Since the dead know not anything, what are the manifestations seen in spiritualist séances?

"*They are the spirits of devils, working miracles.*" Rev. 16:14.

10. In sacrificing to demigods [deceased heroes] and to ancestors, to whom do the heathen do homage?

"The things which the Gentiles sacrifice, *they sacrifice to devils.*" 1 Cor. 10:20.

11. What commandment was given the children of Israel concerning all the various forms of spiritualistic mediumship in their day?

"There shall not be found among you anyone...that useth divination, or an observer of times, or an enchanter, or a witch, or a charmer, or a consulter with familiar spirits, or a wizard, or a necromancer. For all that do these things are an abomination unto the Lord." Deut. 18:10–12.

12. Touching this same matter, what positive counsel is given to God's people through the prophet Isaiah?

"When they shall say unto you, Seek unto them that have familiar spirits, and unto wizards that peep, and that mutter: should not a people seek unto their God? [*"on behalf of the living should they seek unto the dead?"* A. R. V.] *To the law and to the testimony: if they speak not according to this word, it is because there is no light in them."* Isa. 8:19, 20.

13. How much does one, when dead, know of God?

"In death *there is no remembrance of Thee.*" Ps. 6:5.

NOTE— There is not even a remembrance of God. As already seen, the Bible everywhere represents the dead as being *asleep.* If they were in heaven or hell, would it be fitting to represent them thus? Was Lazarus, whom Jesus loved, in heaven when the Saviour said, "Our friend Lazarus *sleepeth*"? John 11:11. If so, calling him to life was really robbing him of the bliss of heaven that rightly belonged to him. The parable of the rich man and Lazarus, recorded in Luke 16, was given to teach, not consciousness in death, but that in the judgment riches will avail nothing unless rightly and beneficently used, and that poverty will not keep one out of heaven.

14. Were there to be no resurrection of the dead, what would be the condition of those fallen asleep in Christ?

"If the dead rise not, then is not Christ raised: and if Christ be not raised, your faith is vain; ye are yet in your sins. *Then they also which are fallen asleep in Christ are perished.*" 1 Cor. 15:16–18.

15. When is the resurrection of the righteous to take place?

"The Lord Himself shall descend from heaven with a shout, with the voice of the Archangel, and with the trump of God: *and the dead in Christ shall rise."* 1 Thess. 4:16.

NOTE— If, as stated in Ecclesiastes 9:5, the dead know not anything, then they have no knowledge of the lapse of time. "Six thousand years in the grave to a dead man is no more than a wink of the eye to the living." To them, consciousness, our only means of measuring time, is gone; and it will seem to them when they awake that absolutely no time has elapsed.

16. Who only possesses inherent immortality?

"The King of kings, and Lord of lords; who only hath immortality." 1 Tim. 6:15, 16.

17. When will the faithful be changed to immortality?

"Behold, I shew you a mystery; We shall not all sleep, but *we shall all be changed, in a moment, in the twinkling of an eye, at the last trump:* for the trumpet shall sound, and the dead shall be raised incorruptible, and we shall be changed." 1 Cor. 15:51, 52.

18. What is then to be swallowed up?

"So when this corruptible shall have put on incorruption, and this mortal shall have put on immortality, then shall be brought to pass the saying that is written, *Death is swallowed up in victory.*" Verse 54. See verse 57.

Chapter 15

Christ's Second Coming

1. During those sad hours just before His trial and crucifixion, what precious promise did Christ make to His disciples?

"Let not your heart be troubled: ye believe in God, believe also in Me. In My Father's house are many mansions: if it were not so, I would have told you. I go to prepare a place for you. And if I go and prepare a place for you, *I will come again,* and receive you unto Myself; that where I am, there ye may be also." John 14:1–3.

2. How visible is His coming to be?

"As the lightning cometh out of the east, and shineth even unto the west; so shall also the coming of the Son of man be." Matt. 24:27. See Acts 1:9–11.

3. How many will see Him when He comes?

"Behold, He cometh with clouds; and *every eye shall see Him,* and they also which pierced Him." Rev. 1:7.

NOTE— Christ's second coming will be as real as was His first, and as visible as His ascension, and far more glorious. To spiritualize our Lord's return is to pervert the obvious meaning of His promise, "I will come again," and nullify the whole plan of redemption; for the reward of the faithful of all ages is to be given in connection with this most glorious of all events.

4. What warning has Christ given concerning false views of the manner of His coming?

"If any man shall say unto you, *Lo, here is Christ, or there; believe it not.* For there shall arise false Christs, and false prophets, and shall shew great signs and wonders; insomuch that, if it were possible, they shall deceive the very elect. Behold, I have told you before. Wherefore if they shall say unto you, Behold, He is in the *desert; go not forth*: behold, He is in the *secret chambers; believe it not.*" Matt. 24:23–26.

5. What will take place at the Lord's coming?

"The Lord Himself shall descend from heaven *with a shout, with the voice of the Archangel, and with the trump of God.*" 1 Thess. 4:16.

6. What part will the angels have in this event?

"He shall send His angels with a great sound of a trumpet, and *they shall gather together His elect* from the four winds, from one end of heaven to the other." Matt. 24:31.

7. What takes place at the sounding of the trumpet?

"The Lord Himself shall descend from heaven...with the trump of God: and *the dead in Christ shall rise first.*" 1 Thess. 4:16.

8. What will be done with the righteous living?

"Then we which are alive and remain shall be *caught up together with them in the clouds* to meet the Lord in the air: and so shall we ever be with the Lord." Verse 17.

9. What change will then take place in both the living and the sleeping saints?

"We shall not all sleep, *but we shall all be changed,* in a moment, in the twinkling of an eye, at the last trump: for the trumpet shall sound, and the dead shall be raised *incorruptible*, and we shall be changed. For this corruptible must put on *incorruption*, and this mortal must put on *immortality*." I Cor. 15:51-53.

10. What saying is then brought to pass?

"So when this corruptible shall have put on incorruption, and this mortal shall have put on immortality, then shall be brought to pass the saying that is written, Death is swallowed up in victory. *O death, where is thy sting? O grave, where is thy victory?*" Verses 54, 55.

11. What immediately follows the resurrection of those who sleep in Jesus, and the change to immortality of the living saints?

"The Lord Himself shall descend from heaven with a shout, with the voice of the Archangel, and with the trump of God: and the dead in Christ shall rise first: then *we which are alive and remain shall be caught up together with them in the clouds to meet the Lord in the air: and so shall we ever be with the Lord*." 1 Thess. 4:16, 17.

NOTE— "To my mind this precious doctrine— for such I must call it of the return of the Lord to this earth is taught in the New Testament as clearly as any other doctrine in it; yet I was in the church for fifteen or sixteen years before I ever heard a sermon on it. The devil does not want us to see this truth; for nothing would wake up the church so much. The moment a man takes hold of the truth that Jesus Christ is coming back again to receive His followers to Himself, this world loses its hold on him."— *"The Second Coming of Christ," D. L. Moody, pp. 6, 7.*

"Considering the solemn emphasis thus laid upon this doctrine, and considering the great prominence given to it throughout the teaching of our Lord and of His apostles, how was it that for the first five years of my pastoral life it had absolutely no place in my preaching? Undoubtedly, the reason lay in the lack of early instruction. Of all the sermons heard from childhood on, I do not remember listening to a single one upon this subject."— *"How Christ Came to Church," A. J. Gordon, D. D., pp. 44, 45.*

12. How many will receive a reward when Christ comes?

"The Son of man shall come in the glory of His Father with His angels; and then He shall reward *every man* according to his works." Matt. 16:27. See Rev. 22:12; Luke 14:14.

13. Have the worthies of old gone to their reward?

"These all, having obtained a good report through faith, *received not the promise*: God having provided some better thing for us, *that they without us should not be made perfect*." Heb. 11:39, 40.

14. When did Paul expect his crown?

"Henceforth there is laid up for me a crown of righteousness, which the Lord, the righteous judge, shall give me *at that day*." 2 Tim. 4:8.

15. What great separation will then take place?

"When the Son of man shall come in His glory, and all the holy angels with Him, then shall He sit upon the throne of His glory: and before Him shall be gathered all nations: and *He shall separate them one from another, as a shepherd divideth his sheep from the goats*." Matt. 25:31, 32.

16. Will the world be prepared to meet Him?

"Then shall appear the sign of the Son of man in heaven: and *then shall all the tribes of the earth mourn*." Matt. 24:30. "Behold, He cometh with clouds; and every eye shall see Him,...*and all kindreds of the earth shall wail because of Him*." Rev. 1:7.

17. Why will many be unprepared for this event?

"But and if that evil servant shall say in his heart, *My lord delayeth his coming*; and shall begin to smite his fellow servants, and to eat and drink with the drunken; the lord of that servant shall come in a day when he looketh not for him, and in an hour that he is not aware of, and shall cut him asunder, and appoint him his portion with the hypocrites: there shall be weeping and gnashing of teeth." Matt. 24:48–51.

18. What will the world be doing when Christ comes?

"As the days of Noah were, so shall also the coming of the Son of man be. For as in the days that were before the flood *they were eating and drinking, marrying and giving in marriage*, until the day that Noah entered into the ark, and knew not until the flood came, and took them all away; so shall also the coming of the Son of man be." Verses 37–39. "Likewise also as it was in the days of Lot; *they did eat, they drank, they bought, they sold, they planted, they builded;* but the same day that Lot went out of Sodom it rained fire and brimstone from heaven, and destroyed them all. Even thus shall it be in the day when the Son of man is revealed." Luke 17:28–30.

NOTE— The idea is not that it is wrong in itself to eat, drink, marry, buy, sell, plant, or build, but that men's minds will be so taken up with these things that they will give little or no thought to the future life, and make no preparation to meet Jesus when He comes.

19. Has the exact time of Christ's coming been revealed ?

"Of that day and hour *knoweth no man*, no, not the angels of heaven, but my Father only." Matt. 24:36.

20. In view of this fact, what does Christ tell us to do?

"*Watch therefore*: for ye know not what hour your Lord doth come." Verse 42.

NOTE— "In the Scriptures, the constant, the continually recurring exhortation, is to be prepared for the Lord's coming."—*Dean Alford.*

21. What warning has Christ given that we might not be taken by surprise by this great event?

"Take heed to yourselves, lest at any time your hearts be overcharged with surfeiting, and drunkenness, and cares of this life, and so that day come upon you unawares. For as a snare shall it come on all them that dwell on the face of the whole earth. Watch ye therefore, and pray always, that ye may be accounted worthy to escape all these things that shall come to pass, and to stand before the Son of man." Luke 21:34–36.

22. What Christian grace are we exhorted to exercise in our expectant longing for this event?

"Be *patient* therefore, brethren, unto the coming of the Lord. Behold, the husbandman waiteth for the precious fruit of the earth, and hath long patience for it, until he receive the early and latter rain. Be ye also *patient*; stablish your hearts: for the coming of the Lord draweth nigh." James 5:7, 8.

Chapter 16

The Signs of the Times

1. What question did the disciples ask Christ concerning omens of His *second* coming?

"As He sat upon the Mount of Olives, the disciples came unto Him privately, saying, Tell us, when shall these things be? and *what shall be the sign of Thy coming, and of the end of the world?*" Matt. 24:3.

2. How, according to Luke, did Christ answer this question ?

"*There shall be signs* in the *sun*, and in the *moon*, and in the *stars;* and upon the earth *distress of nations, with perplexity; the sea and the waves roaring; men's hearts failing them for fear*, and for looking after those things which are coming on the earth." Luke 21:25, 26.

3. What, according to Matthew's account, did Christ say were to be the signs in the sun, moon, and stars indicating the approach of His second advent and the end of the world?

"Immediately after the tribulation of those days shall the sun be *darkened*, and the moon shall *not give her light*, and the stars shall *fall from heaven*." Matt. 24:29.

NOTE— These "days" are the twelve hundred and sixty prophetic days, or literal years, of papal supremacy foretold in Daniel 7:25, during which the law and people of God were to be given into the hands of that apostate power. These days ended with the temporary overthrow of the Papacy by the French in February, 1798. It was "immediately" after general persecution had ceased that the signs foretold by our Lord began to appear, as we shall see.

4. In what language had some of the Old Testament prophets, centuries before Christ, foretold these signs?

"The *sun* and the *moon* shall be *darkened,* and the *stars* shall *withdraw their shining*." Joel 3:15. "*The stars of heaven and the constellations thereof shall not give their light: the sun shall be darkened in his going forth, and the moon shall not cause her light to shine.*" Isa. 13:10.

5. When were the sun and moon darkened?

May 19, 1780.

NOTE— "The nineteenth of May, 1780, was a remarkably dark day. Candles were lighted in many houses. The birds were silent, and disappeared. The fowls retired to roost. It was the general opinion that the day of judgment was at hand."— *President Dwight, in "Historical Collections."*

"In some places, persons could not see to read common print in the open air for several hours together. Birds sang their evening song, disappeared, and became, silent; fowls went to roost; cattle sought the barnyard; and candles were lighted in the houses. The obscuration began about ten o'clock in the morning, and continued till the middle of the next night, but with differences of degree and duration in different places.... The true cause of this remarkable phenomenon is not known."—*Webster's Unabridged Dictionary, article "The Dark Day," edition— 1883.*

Herschel, the great astronomer, says: "The dark day in Northern America was one of those wonderful phenomena of nature which will always be read with interest, but which philosophy is at a loss to explain."

The darkness was not caused by any eclipse of the sun by the moon, for the moon had fulled only the night before, and consequently was on the opposite side of the earth from the sun.

6. When was there a remarkable display of falling stars?
November 13, 1833.

NOTE— The celebrated astronomer and meteorologist, Professor Olmsted, of Yale College, says: "The extent of the shower of 1833 was such as to cover no inconsiderable part of the earth's surface, from the middle of the Atlantic on the east to the Pacific on the west; and from the northern coast of South America to undefined regions among the British possessions on the north, the exhibition was visible, and everywhere presented nearly the same appearance."

Frederick Douglass, in his book, "My Bondage and My Freedom," page 186, says: "I witnessed this gorgeous spectacle, and was awe-struck... It was not without the suggestion at that moment that it might be *the harbinger of the coming of the Son of man*; and in my state of mind I was prepared to hail Him as my friend and deliverer. I had read that the stars should fall from heaven, and they were now falling."

It will be seen that these signs produced the very impression that God evidently intended they should that the day of judgment, Christ's coming, and the end of the world are near at hand.

7. Besides the signs to be seen in sun, moon, and stars, what did Jesus say would appear upon the earth?
"Upon the earth *distress of nations, with perplexity*." Luke 21:25.

8. What did our Lord say would be seen upon the sea, and with what feelings would men behold all these things ?
"*The sea and the waves roaring; men's hearts failing them for fear*, and for looking after those things which are coming on the earth." Luke 21:25, 26.

NOTE— For example, a volcanic eruption at Krakatau, Straits of Sunda (Indonesia), in 1883, caused a tidal wave which drowned more than thirty thousand persons, besides destroying a large amount of property. September 8, 1900, a great tidal wave, raised by a West Indian hurricane, destroyed property in Galveston, Texas, to the value of more than twenty million dollars, and swept to death in the surging waters about six thousand men, women, and children. August 29, 1916, the United States armored cruiser "Memphis," lying at anchor in the harbor of Santo Domingo, W. I., was utterly wrecked by a tidal wave of unknown origin, that picked the vessel up as though it had been only a chip, and with crushing force dashed it upon a reef, where it still lies, a mute witness to the irresistible force of the wave. October 25,

1921, a West Indian hurricane swept a part of the coast of Florida, inflicting a property loss amounting to a million or more dollars at Tampa alone.

9. According to the prophecy of Daniel, what was to characterize the time of the end?

"But thou, O Daniel, shut up the words, and seal the book, even to the time of the end: *many shall run to and fro, and knowledge shall be increased*." Dan. 12:4.

NOTE— "The time of the end" is a comparatively brief period between 1798, the close of the 1260 years of papal supremacy, and the second appearing of our Lord. Within that period men have been "running to and fro" through both the material world and the word of God. The prophecies of Daniel are now themselves understood.

Concerning the increase of knowledge in the material, scientific, and intellectual worlds, it is scarcely necessary to speak. Everyone who thinks realizes that we are living in the most wonderful age of this world. Things undreamed of a century ago are now too common to attract attention.

10. What is predicted of the moral condition of the world in the last days?

"This know also, that in *the last days perilous times shall come*. For men shall be lovers of their own selves, covetous, boasters, proud, blasphemers,... lovers of pleasures more than lovers of God; having a form of godliness, but denying the power thereof." 2 Tim. 3:1–5.

NOTE— The age in which we live is noted for its pleasure loving spirit. The Cumberland *Presbyterian*, Nashville, Tennessee, November 27, 1919, said:

"The world today is politically and socially and industrially in turmoil, because the church of the Son of God has practically ceased evangelizing in the power of its 'first love.' It has cut loose its moorings, and is being 'carried about with every wind of doctrine, by the sleight of men,' who 'lie in wait to deceive' by stealthily substituting social service panaceas for personal salvation from sin. What wonder that 'the whole head is sick, and the whole heart faint'!"

11. What sign closely related to the increase of knowledge did our Saviour give?

"*This gospel of the kingdom shall be preached in all the world* for a witness unto all nations; and *then shall the end come*." Matt. 24:14.

NOTE— Well within the memory of many now living, practically the whole Protestant world has adopted the slogan, "The gospel to the world in this generation." What does it mean?— Clearly the soon coming of the Lord; for when this gospel of the kingdom shall have been preached in all the world for a witness to all nations, the end will come.

12. What other sign is now especially manifest before all the world?
Increase of wealth and labor troubles.

NOTE— Never was the unprecedented wealth in the hands of a comparatively few people greater than now, nor the consequent labor troubles more serious. Read in the New Testament, James 5:1–8, and how faithfully present-day conditions are described. "Be ye also patient; stablish your hearts: for the coming of the Lord draweth nigh."

Chapter 17

The Millennium

1. What text definitely brings the millennium to view?

"I saw thrones, and they sat upon them, and *judgment was given unto them*…and *they lived and reigned with Christ a thousand years*." Rev. 20:4.

2. Whom does Paul say the saints are to judge?

"Dare any of you, having a matter against another, go to law before the unjust, and not before the saints? *Do ye not know that the saints shall judge the world?…Know ye not that we shall judge angels?*" 1 Cor. 6:1–3. See also Dan. 7:21, 22.

NOTE— From the Scriptures it is plain that the saints of all ages are to be engaged with Christ in a work of "judgment" upon the wicked during the millennium, or one thousand years.

3. How many resurrections are there to be?

"Marvel not at this: for the hour is coming, in the which all that are in the graves shall hear His voice, and shall come forth; they that have done good, unto *the resurrection of life*; and they that have done evil, unto *the resurrection of damnation*." John 5:28, 29.

4. What class only have part in the first resurrection?

"*Blessed and holy* is he that hath part in the first resurrection: on such the second death hath no power." Rev. 20:6.

5. What will Christ do with the saints when He comes?

"I will come again, and *receive you unto Myself*; that where I am, there ye may be also." John 14:3. See John 17:24.

NOTE— In other words, Christ will take them to heaven, there to live and reign with Him during the one thousand years.

6. What becomes of the living wicked when Christ comes?

"*As it was in the days of Noah*, so shall it be also in the days of the Son of man. They did eat, they drank, they married wives, they were given in marriage, until the day that Noah entered into the ark, and *the flood came, and destroyed them all. Likewise also as it was in the days of Lot;*…the same day that Lot went out of Sodom it rained fire and brimstone from heaven, and *destroyed them all. Even thus shall it be in the day when the Son of man is revealed*." Luke 17:26–30.

NOTE— When Christ comes, the righteous will be delivered and taken to heaven, and all the living wicked will be suddenly destroyed, as they were at the time of the flood. For further proof see 1 Thess. 5:3; 2 Thess. 1:7–9; Rev. 6:14–17; 19:11–21; Jer. 25:30–33. There will be no general resurrection of the wicked until the end of the one thousand years. This will leave the earth desolate and without inhabitant during this period.

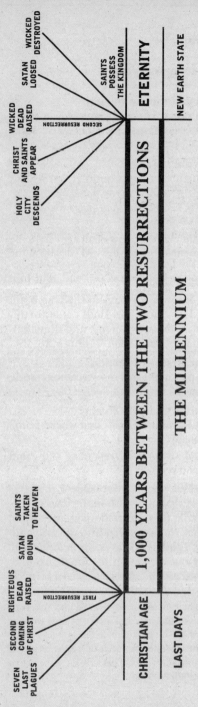

CHRISTIAN AGE	1,000 YEARS BETWEEN THE TWO RESURRECTIONS	ETERNITY
LAST DAYS	THE MILLENNIUM	NEW EARTH STATE

The millennium is the closing period of God's great week of time—a great Sabbath of rest to the earth and to the people of God.

It follows the close of the gospel age, and precedes the setting up the everlasting kingdom of God on earth.

It comprehends what in the scriptures is frequently spoken of as "the day of the Lord."

It is bounded at each end by a resurrection.

Its beginning is marked by the pouring out of the seven last plagues, the second coming of Christ, the resurrection of the righteous dead, the binding of Satan, and the translation of the saints to heaven; and its close, by the descent of the New Jerusalem, with Christ and the saints, from heaven, the resurrection of the wicked dead, the loosing of Satan, and the final destruction of the wicked.

During the one thousand years the earth lies desolate; Satan and his angels are confined here; and the saints, with Christ, sit in judgment on the wicked, preparatory to their final punishment.

The wicked dead are then raised; Satan is loosed for a little season, and he and the host of the wicked encompass the camp of the saints and the Holy City, when fire comes down from God out of heaven and devours them. The earth is cleansed by the same fire that destroys the wicked, and, renewed, becomes the eternal abode of the saints.

The millennium is one of "the ages to come." Its close will mark the beginning of the new earth state.

7. What description does the prophet Jeremiah give of the earth during this time?

"I beheld the earth, and, lo, it was *without form*, and *void*; and the heavens, and they had no light. I beheld the mountains, and, lo, they trembled, and all the hills moved lightly. I beheld, and, lo, *there was no man*, and all the birds of the heavens were fled. I beheld, and, lo, *the fruitful place was a wilderness, and all the cities thereof were broken down* at the presence of the Lord, and by His fierce anger." Jer. 4:23–26.

NOTE— At the coming of Christ the earth is reduced to a chaotic state— to a mass of ruins. The heavens depart as a scroll when it is rolled together, mountains are moved out of their places, and the earth is left a dreary, desolate waste. See Isa. 24:1–3, 21, 22; Rev. 6:14–17.

8. How long is Satan imprisoned on this earth?

"I saw an angel come down from heaven, having the key of the bottomless pit and a great chain in his hand. And he laid hold on the dragon, that old serpent, which is the Devil, and Satan, and *bound him a thousand years*, and cast him into the bottomless pit, and shut him up, and set a seal upon him, that he should deceive the nations no more, till the thousand years should be fulfilled." Rev. 20:1–3.

NOTE— The Scriptures make it clear that the expression "bottomless pit," or, as given in the original, abussos, or abyss, is used in Genesis 1:2 that in the beginning, before life existed upon the earth, it "was without form, and void; and darkness was upon the face of the *deep*." The Greek word *abussos*, translated in Revelation 20:1 "bottomless pit," is the same word that is used in the Septuagint translation of Genesis 1:2, where is rendered "deep" in the King James Version.

9. The righteous dead are raised at Christ's second coming. When will the rest of the dead, the wicked, be raised?

"The rest of the dead lived not again *until the thousand years were finished*." Rev. 20:5.

NOTE— This period is bounded by distinct events. Its beginning is marked by the close of probation, the pouring out of the seven last plagues, the second coming of Christ, and the resurrection of the righteous dead. It closes with the resurrection of the wicked, and their final destruction in the lake of fire.

10. What change is made in Satan's condition at the close of the one thousand years?

"After that *he must be loosed a little season*." Rev. 20:3.

NOTE— At the close of the one thousand years, Christ, accompanied by the saints, comes to the earth again to execute judgment upon the wicked, and to prepare the earth, by a re-creation, for the eternal abode of the righteous. At this time, in answer to the summons of Christ, the wicked dead of all ages awake to life. This is the second resurrection, the "resurrection of damnation" John 5:29. The wicked come forth with the same rebellious spirit which possessed them in this life. By their resurrection, Satan is loosed from his long period of inactivity.

11. As soon as the wicked are raised, what does Satan at once proceed to do?

"When the thousand years are expired, Satan shall be loosed out of his prison, and shall go out to *deceive the nations* which are in the four quarters of the earth, Gog and Magog, *to gather them together to battle:* the number of whom is as the sand of the sea." Rev. 20:7, 8.

12. Against whom do the wicked go to make war, and what is the outcome?

"They went up on the breadth of the earth, and *compassed the camp of the saints about, and the beloved city* [New Jerusalem. See Rev. 21:2]: *and fire came down from God out of heaven, and devoured them.*" Verse 9.

13. After this destruction of the earth and of all sin and sinners with it, for what may the saints look?

"Nevertheless we, according to His promise, look for *new heavens and a new earth*, wherein dwelleth righteousness." 2 Peter 3:13.

14. How does the prophet Isaiah describe this restoration?

"Behold, I create new heavens and a new earth: and the former shall not be remembered, nor come into mind." Isa. 65:17

15. What is the apostle John's testimony concerning the new earth?

"I saw a new heaven and a new earth: for the first heaven and the first earth were passed away; and there was no more sea." Rev. 21:1

16. What reward awaits the righteous?

"The ransomed of the Lord shall return, and come to Zion with songs and everlasting joy upon their heads: they shall obtain joy and gladness, and sorrow and sighing shall flee away." Isa. 35:10

17. What prophecy will then be fulfilled?

"Thou, O tower of the flock, the stronghold of the daughter of Zion, unto Thee shall it come, even the first dominion; the kingdom shall come to the daughter of Jerusalem. " Micah 4:8.

Chapter 18

The End of the Wicked

1. What does the Bible say is the wages of sin?

"The wages of sin is *death*." Rom. 6:23. "The soul that sinneth, it shall *die*." Eze. 18:4.

NOTE— *Die:* "To pass from physical life; to suffer a total and irreparable loss of action of the vital functions; to become dead; to expire; perish."—*Webster.*

2. What will be the character of this death?

"Who shall be punished with *everlasting destruction* from the presence of the Lord, and from the glory of His power." 2 Thess. 1:9.

NOTE— *Destroy:* "To unbuild; to break up the structure and organic existence of; to demolish; to spoil utterly; to bring to naught; to put an end to; to annihilate."— *Webster.*

3. How complete will be the destruction of the wicked?

"Fear Him which is able to *destroy both soul and body in hell*." Matt. 10:28.

4. To what are the wicked compared?

"The wicked shall perish, and the enemies of the Lord shall be *as the fat of lambs: they shall consume; into smoke shall they consume away.*" Ps. 37:20.

NOTE— *Consume*: "To destroy; as by decomposition, dissipation, waste, or fire."— *Webster.*

5. How does John the Baptist describe the destruction of the wicked?

"*He will burn up the chaff with unquenchable fire.*" Matt. 3:12.

6. Will any part of the wicked be left?

"The day that cometh shall *burn them up*, saith the Lord of hosts, that *it shall leave them neither root nor branch*." Mal. 4:1.

7. Where will the place of the wicked then be?

"Yet a little while, and the wicked shall not be; yea, *thou shalt diligently consider his place, and it shall not be.*" Ps. 37:10. See also 2 Peter 3:12, 10.

8. Do the wicked go directly to their punishment at death or wait till the day of judgment?

"The Lord knoweth how to deliver the godly out of temptations, and *to reserve the unjust unto the day of judgment to be punished*." 2 Peter 2:9.

9. Whence will come the fire that will destroy them?

"They went up on the breadth of the earth, and compassed the camp of the saints about, and the beloved city [see Rev. 21:2]: *and fire came down from God out of heaven, and devoured them.*" Rev. 20:9.

NOTE— This is called God's "strange act" and His "strange work"— the work of destruction. (Isa. 28:21.) But by this means God will once and forever cleanse the universe of sin and all its sad results. Death itself will then be at an end— cast into the lake of fire. (Rev. 20:14.)

10. To what will this fire reduce the wicked?

"Ye shall tread down the wicked; *for they shall be ashes under the soles of your feet in the day that I shall do this*, saith the Lord of hosts." Mal. 4:3.

11. What is the final destruction of the wicked called?

"This is *the second death.*" Rev. 20:14.

12. After the burning day, what will appear?

"*New heavens and a new earth*, wherein dwelleth righteousness." 2 Peter 3:13.

Chapter 19

The Home of the Saved

1. For what purpose was the earth created?

"Thus saith the Lord that created the heavens; God Himself that formed the earth and made it; He hath established it, He created it not in vain, *He formed it to be inhabited*." Isa. 45:18

2. To whom has God given the earth?

"The...heavens are the Lord's: but *the earth hath He given to the children of men*." Ps. 115:16.

3. For what purpose was man made?

"Thou madest him *to have dominion over the works of Thy hands*." Ps. 8:6. See Gen. 1:26; Heb. 2:8.

4. How did man lose his dominion?

Through sin. Rom. 3:23; 5:12.

5. When man lost his dominion, to whom did he yield it?

"Of whom a man is overcome, of the same is he brought in bondage." 2 Peter 2:19.

NOTE— Man was overcome by Satan in the Garden of Eden, and there yielded himself and his possessions into the hands of his captor.

6. Through whom is this dominion to be restored?

"Thou, *O tower of the flock*, the stronghold of the daughter of Zion, *unto Thee shall it come, even the first dominion*." Micah 4:8.

NOTE— The "tower of the flock" is Christ, and through Him the dominion will be given to His people, here spoken of as "the daughter of Zion." See Gal. 3:29.

7. Why did Christ say the meek are blessed?

"Blessed are the meek: *for they shall inherit the earth*." Matt. 5:5.

NOTE— This inheritance cannot be realized in this life; for here the truly meek generally have little of earth's good things.

8. Who does David say have most now?

"I was envious at *the foolish*, when I saw the *prosperity of the wicked*... Their eyes stand out with fatness: *they have more than heart could wish*." Ps.73:3–7.

9. Where are the righteous to be recompensed?

"Behold, the righteous shall be recompensed *in the earth*." Prov. 11:31.

10. What will be the difference between the portion of the righteous and that of the wicked?

"Wait on the Lord, and keep His way, and *He shall exalt thee to inherit the land: when the wicked are cut off, thou shalt see it.*" Ps. 37:34.

11. What promise was made to Abraham concerning the land?

"The Lord said unto Abraham…Lift up now thine eyes, and look from the place where thou art:… for *all the land which thou seest, to thee will I give it, and to thy seed forever.*" Gen. 13:14, 15.

12. How much did this promise comprehend?

"*The promise, that he should be the heir of the world,* was not to Abraham, or to his seed, through the law, but through the righteousness of faith." Rom. 4:13.

13. How much of Canaan did Abraham own?

"*He gave him none inheritance in it, no, not so much as to set his foot on.*" Acts 7:5. See HEB. 11:8–13.

14. Who is the seed to whom this promise is made?

"To Abraham and his seed were the promises made. He saith not, And to seeds, as of many; but as of one, *And to thy seed, which is Christ.*" Gal. 3:16.

15. Who are heirs of the promise?

"*If ye be Christ's, then are ye Abraham's seed, and heirs according to the promise.*" Verse 29.

16. Why did not these ancient worthies receive the promise ?

"These all, having obtained a good report through faith, received not the promise: God having provided some better thing for us, *that they without us should not be made perfect.*" HEB. 11:39, 40.

17. What is to become of our earth?

"The day of the Lord will come as a thief in the night; in the which the heavens shall pass away with a great noise, and *the elements shall melt with fervent heat, the earth also and the works that are therein shall be burned up.*" 2 Peter 3:10.

18. What will follow this great conflagration?

"Nevertheless we, according to His promise, *look for new heavens and a new earth*, wherein dwelleth righteousness." Verse 13.

19. To what promise did Peter evidently refer?

"Behold, I create new heavens and a new earth: and the former shall not be remembered, nor come into mind." Isa. 65:17.

20. What was shown the apostle John in vision?

"I saw *a new heaven and a new earth*: for the first heaven and the first earth were passed away." Rev. 21:1.

21. What was one of Christ's parting promises?

"In My Father's house are many mansions: if it were not so, I would have told you. *I go to prepare a place for you.*" John 14:2.

22. What has God prepared for His people?

"Now they desire a better country, that is, a heavenly: wherefore God is not ashamed to be called their God: for *He hath prepared for them a city.*" Heb. 11:16.

23. For what did Abraham look?

"He *looked for a city* which hath foundations, whose builder and maker is God." Heb. 11:10.

24. Where is this city, and what is it called?

"*Jerusalem which is above is free*, which is the mother of us all." Gal. 4:26.

25. What did John see concerning this city?

"*I John saw the holy city, New Jerusalem, coming down from God out of heaven*, prepared as a bride adorned for her husband." Rev. 21:2.

26. What will be excluded from this city?

"There shall in no wise enter into it *anything* that *defileth, neither whatsoever worketh abomination, or maketh a lie.*" Verse 27.

27. Who will be permitted to enter it?

"*Blessed are they that do His commandments*, that they may have right to the tree of life, and may enter in through the gates into the city." Rev. 22:14.

28. When this city becomes the metropolis of the new earth, what will be the condition of God's people?

"God shall wipe away all tears from their eyes; and there shall be no more death, neither sorrow, nor crying, neither shall there be any more pain: for the former things are passed away." Rev. 21:4. "And there shall be no more curse." Rev. 22:3.

29. What will be the condition of all the earth?

"The wolf also shall dwell with the lamb, and the leopard shall lie down with the kid; and the calf and the young lion and the fatling together; and a little child shall lead them. And the cow and the bear shall feed; their young ones shall lie down together: and the lion shall eat straw like the ox. And the sucking child shall play on the hole of the asp, and the weaned child shall put his hand on the cockatrice' den. They shall not hurt nor destroy in all My holy mountain." Isa. 11:6–9.

30. How completely will the pains and sorrows of the former world have passed away?

"Behold, I create new heavens and a new earth: *and the former shall not be remembered, nor come into mind.*" Isa. 65:17.

31. Who will dwell with the redeemed?

"*He* will dwell with them, and they shall be His people, and *God Himself shall be with them*, and be their God." Rev. 21:3.

32. What will it mean to dwell in God's presence?

"In Thy presence is *fullness of joy*; at Thy right hand there are *pleasures forevermore*." Ps. 16:11.

33. How will the ransomed of the Lord return to Zion?

"The ransomed of the Lord shall return, and come to Zion *with songs and everlasting joy upon their heads*: they shall obtain joy and gladness, and sorrow and sighing shall flee away." Isa. 35:10.

34. How long will they possess the future kingdom?

"The saints of the Most High shall take the kingdom, and possess the kingdom *forever*, even *forever and ever*." Dan. 7:18. See Isa. 65:22